Repatriation Reader

Who Owns American Indian Remains?

Edited by Devon A. Mihesuah

University of Nebraska Press
Lincoln and London

Acknowledgments for the use of previously
published material appear on page 325, which
constitutes an extension of the copyright page.
© 2000 by the University of Nebraska Press
Manufactured in the United States of America
⊗
Library of Congress Cataloging-in-Publication Data
Repatriation reader : who owns American Indian
remains? / edited by Devon A. Mihesuah.
p. cm.
Includes bibliographical references and index.
ISBN 0-8032-8264-8 (pbk. : alk. paper)
1. Indians of North America—Material culture—Law
and legislation. 2. Indians of North America—
Antiquities—Law and legislation. 3. Human remains
(Archaeology)—Law and legislation—United States.
4. Cultural property—Repatriation—United States—
Philosophy. 5. Cultural property—Government
policy—United States. 6. Anthropological
ethics—United States. 7. United States. Native
American Graves Protection and Repatriation Act.
I. Mihesuah, Devon A. (Devon Abbott), 1957–
E98.M34 R46 2000
973.04'97—dc21
00–036380
𝒩

To Don Worcester,
Professor Emeritus of History,
Texas Christian University

Contents

Repatriation Reader

Devon A. Mihesuah

Introduction

The issue of repatriation of American Indian skeletal remains and funerary objects is a timely and complicated one. In the past decade scholarly conferences have included sessions that deal with repatriation, and the topic stirs heated debate even before the presentations begin. American Indians have formed organizations to help create legislation to protect burial sites and to acquire skeletal remains and sacred items from museums, university archives, and private collectors and repatriate to tribes.[1] Journals have published special issues that focus on repatriation, and committees composed of American Indians, archaeologists, physical anthropologists, lawyers, museologists, and forest service and military representatives have been formed across the country in an effort to find common ground on this issue.[2] But many anthropologists, museum curators, landowners, and hobbyists—some of whom are, ironically, American Indians—are hesitant to return objects, citing scientific and academic freedom. Nonacademic looters find the monetary reward from ransacking graves too enticing to stop. Indeed, this is not a minor issue. At present there are approximately one million American Indian remains in public and private institutions; this number does not include the myriad collections held by private landowners, nor does it include the remains that have been shipped to Europe, Japan, and other places.

The disturbance of buried human remains is not something recent; it has always taken place all over the world. In Egypt tombs have been pilfered for centuries, and the mummified remains of the dead along with their burial goods have been displayed in museums in dozens of countries. In central Mexico Mayan ruins have been plundered by treasure hunters, and archaeologists still excavate in hopes of finding artifacts. Antiquities continue to disappear throughout Central America and Canada and from temples in Nepal. The disturbance of Indian remains occurs in virtually every part of the United States.[3]

Desecration of Indian remains and sacred objects began with the European invasion of the Western Hemisphere. Pilgrims looted Indian graves after arriving in Cape Cod in 1620, as did subsequent colonists. The inquisitive Thomas Jefferson investigated the contents of several Indian burials and documented his findings. Spanish invaders in the Southwest showed contempt for "heathen idols" when priests and ministers felt obliged, in the name of Christianity, to destroy all traces of native religions. Disregard for symbols of non-Christian religions persists in this country, but today those symbols are collected, not destroyed.[4]

The bodies of Indians also have been and still are collected for "scientific study" and for black-market sale. In chapter 1, "The Representations of Indian Bodies in Nineteenth-Century American Anthropology," historian Robert E. Bieder chronicles the use of Indian remains for "cultural comparison" studies. In the early part of the century race was a popular topic in scientific and political communities. American Indians were seen by scientists, social scientists, and the general public as inferior to the Caucasian race. Utilizing Indian skeletons, funerary objects, and other items, researchers set out to prove this inferiority and began focusing on comparative anatomy and the social aspects of everyday tribal life. The rise of phrenology and craniology in the early nineteenth century resulted in the collection of thousands of Indian remains in museums for study and display. Some archaeologists and anthropologists suspected, however, that collecting religious items might be unethical, mainly because the "living fossils" (the living tribespeople) objected.

Although many scientists reevaluated their collecting procedures, not all stopped amassing religious items or skeletons for comparative anatomy studies. In the mid-1800s, for example, after battles between tribes and the U.S. army (such as the Massacre at Sand Creek, Colorado, where in 1884 Cheyennes were slaughtered by the U.S. cavalry led by a Methodist minister) dead Indians were decapitated by order of the surgeon general of the army, for "Indian Crania Study." In 1900 at least forty-five hundred skulls and bones were transferred from the Army Medical Museum to the Smithsonian Institution.[5] Another example is that of the founder of the Smithsonian's division of physical anthropology, Czechoslovakian Ales Hrdlicka, who led an expedition to Larsen Bay in Alaska around 1900. In front of the anguished villagers, he dug up and left with the remains of eight hundred Konaig natives. In 1919 he removed the remains of a man who had died of influenza, despite protests from the dead man's grandchildren.[6]

Other collectors have been and still are either self-proclaimed "amateur archaeologists" or black-market dealers. By the 1890s antiquities found in the Southwest were recognized as art, and by the 1920s art markets dealing

in them were organized in Santa Fe, New Mexico. Dealers in Indian artifacts soon found a global market—in part because of Wild West literature
and other stereotypes of savage Indians. But it was the Museum of Modern
Art's 1975 exhibit on primitivism that announced to the world that Indian
artifacts were marketable and dealers were willing to pay exorbitant prices
for Indian artworks. These include not only the art made by living Indians
but also the art found under the ground.

Why did Americans dig for Indian remains and relics? Scientific study is
one reason, but historian Curtis M. Hinsley Jr. believes it may have been
related to identity. In chapter 2, "Digging for Identity: Reflections on the
Cultural Background of Collecting," Hinsley suggests that non-Indian
Americans felt compelled to explore ancient sites because "Digging in the
prehistoric dirt and constructing heroic tales on what they found, these
men . . . faced the challenge of replacing a heritage of heroism built on
classical literature with an identity constructed of shards and bones and
preliterate silence. " Hinsley describes nineteenth-century digging, excavation, and collecting as deeply psychological and patriotic. Scholars, politicians, and young men were all contributors in "creating" the new American
nation by imposing their versions of Indian history and cultures onto
American history. They even created their own identities by "absorbing and
domesticating their predecessors . . . into themselves." Today popular Hollywood characters such as the adventurous archaeologist Indiana Jones or
the "skeleton detective" literary hero Gideon Oliver have captured collectors' imaginations. The possibility of uncovering treasure, intrigue, or even
mystical forces may be too much of a lure to stop excavating and collecting.

Indians have always objected to the desecration of their dead and sacred
items, but they were not able to do much about it until the late 1960s,
when numerous national American Indians groups began forming. These
groups, as well as local and state organizations and writers such as Vine
Deloria Jr. (particularly in his 1969 publication, *Custer Died for Your Sins:
An Indian Manifesto,* which included a scathing description of Indians'
perceptions of anthropologists), began educating the public about Indians'
concerns over the appropriation of skeletal remains and sacred objects.

Indian groups have influenced many states to pass laws prohibiting
archaeological digging without a state permit. For example, in 1990 the
Human Remains Protection Act (SB 1412), which prohibits the disturbance of graves on private land, was passed in Arizona, but enforcing the
law has proven to be difficult.[7] In 1990 the Native American Graves Protection and Repatriation Act (NAGPRA) was signed into law by President
Bush in order to protect burials, sacred objects, and funerary objects on
federal and tribal lands.[8] The act also disallows trafficking of Indian skeletal

remains, allows American Indian remains and sacred objects held by museums and federal agencies to be repatriated to tribes, and requires federally funded institutions to release inventories of their human skeletons to tribes.

Indeed, repatriation is a complicated matter and appears to be a multifaceted, twelve-way cross-cultural conflict among:

1. nonacademic grave-robbers who look for remains and funerary objects to sell for personal profit;

2. amateur archaeologists who believe the academic community does not document its findings any better than the hobbyists do and thus continue to improperly excavate sites;

3. the portion of the archaeological community that continues to exhume and hold these items for study and display, with no desire to return items to tribes;

4. some American Indians and sympathizers who want tribal remains and sacred objects repatriated and never studied;

5. some American Indians who are willing to allow the study of remains and certain burial objects but who expect them to be returned to tribes afterward;

6. American Indians who believe remains should be studied for educational purposes and not repatriated;

7. American Indians who object to desecration and scientific study but for religious reasons do not want skeletal remains returned to their tribe;

8. social scientists and scientists who work with tribes to determine what can and cannot be studied;

9. social scientists and scientists who are willing to return remains only after they have been studied;

10. museum directors who will not take skeletal remains and sacred objects off display, much less return them to tribes;

11. museum directors who will remove items from display but still will not return items; and

12. museum directors who attempt to cooperate with tribes and who will return items.

Indians, Archaeologists, and Pothunters

A common problem faced by both Indians and scholars who study remains is caused by nonacademic looters who look for graves on private and public property in order to sell skeletal remains and funerary objects for personal profit (a few professional archaeologists also do this).[9] These "grave-robbers" have no regard for Indians' religious beliefs, nor are they concerned with the destruction they cause. Property owners often see nothing wrong with exploring burials that might be on their land; they believe that everything on and under the ground is theirs.

Since arriving in North America, settlers have felt a need to own the land, to survey it, map it, and fence it off into parcels of private property because, after all, "good fences make good neighbors." The idea prevails today that property belongs to the owner, American Indian skeletal remains and all. Indians have been robbed of their lands since contact with non-Indians, and millions of buried remains existed (and still do) under private, mostly non-Indian property. An example that epitomizes the ideology that the land and everything on and under it belongs to the owner took place in Salina, Kansas, in the 1930s, when a landowner discovered the seven-hundred-year-old burial site of 146 Caddo Indians. He then sold the site to a local grocer, who proceeded to dig up and shellac the bones, construct a metal shed over the area, and charge tourists $3.50 each to view the burial. In 1985 a curious Indian woman saw the site and then notified local Indian leaders. As a result of their intervention, the Treaty of Smoky Hill was signed, guaranteeing sale of the site to the state of Kansas, which in turn gave the remains back to the Caddo tribes for reburial. Another example occurred near Young, Arizona, were there were once five thousand Indian graves on a 520-acre ranch. By 1990 the owner had already removed more than fifteen hundred of them for sale. "What you buy is what you own," he said.[10] In forested east Texas there are hundreds of thousands of Caddo burials on private property, and almost all of them have been desecrated. In 1986 the Texas Historical Commission estimated that within a decade all would be gone, and they almost are.[11]

The collecting of American Indian art in the form of baskets, paintings, pottery, jewelry, beadwork, and rugs, in addition to sacred objects such as pipes, pipe-bags, medicine bundles, rattles, kachinas, fans, fetishes, and drums, has been a hobby and business among non-Indians for decades. Shrines throughout many reservations contain religious offerings that are stolen by hiking tourists; others are taken by those looking for items to sell. Because of the demand for these items, illegally removed Indian remains and sacred tribal items from burial sites are sold through the underground markets, either to people ignorant of the origin of these items or to disreputable collectors fully aware of what they are buying. Looters arrive at sites on reservations, forest lands, and public and private property with their "pokey sticks," backhoes, infrared sensors, and weapons, are very quick about their work, and leave the site in total disarray. Looters are not just non-Indians. Many items are stolen by tribespeople to finance alcohol or drug problems.

The plundering of sites for profit is big business. Caddo pots in Texas, for example, sell for thousands of dollars apiece, and human skulls are sold for several hundred. Despite legislation against looting, protection of many burial sites poses a tremendous challenge for several reasons, including the inaccessibility of the sites combined with the speed and skill of the pilferers. Often an illegal excavator conspires with the private landowner, who gets a portion of the profit from sales.

While NAGPRA might force museums to disclose the contents of their collections, most private collectors do not release details of their inventories, much less the items themselves. Artifact collectors in the United States, Germany, and Japan are buyers on a large scale and do not publicize their items as having come from burials or reservations. This has been especially true since the FBI helped Hopis of Arizona recover three stolen masks that are vital to their ceremonies. One, the black ogre mask, had been sold to a collector in Germany, who was pressured into returning it. Collectors now know that when they buy ceremonial goods they may have to give them up, so they keep their collections secret. On the other hand, what makes this business attractive is that individuals can often deduct the appraised value of some artifacts from their taxes when donating them to museums. There is also contention between professional archaeologists and amateur archaeologists, who believe the academic community does not document its findings any better than the hobbyists do. Many of these amateurs, including Boy Scout troops, continue to improperly excavate sites, rendering them worthless for study.[12] Former Texas State archaeologist Robert J. Mallouf—who has seen hundreds of ransacked burial sites in Texas—discusses the enormity of the problem in chapter 3, "An Unraveling Rope: The Looting of America's Past."

Indians and Social Scientists

Physical anthropologists, bio-archaeologists, human osteologists, and others believe that bone biology (utilizing human remains for study) is vital for our understanding of our past, not just to understand the cultural past but also to understand disease, human variation, demography, diet, tooth decay, and so on. Because methods of study and theories change over time, many of these scholars are reluctant to give up their collections of Indian bones—old and new—for reburial.[13] In chapter 4, "Why Anthropologists Study Human Remains," D. Gentry Steele, a physical anthropologist, and graduate student Patricia M. Landau counter the argument put forth by many Indians that the research of old bones does not yield information that helps humankind (and especially Indians) today. Steele and Landau believe that by studying Indian remains they are attempting to understand all of humankind. Their essay focuses on the importance of studying human remains and the methods and value of human paleobiology and the impact of reburial on the study of prehistoric human biology. American Indians, however, seeing that these studies have not benefited them, question the need for such research.

Another major point of contention between Indians and archaeologists revolves around interpretation of the past. Many Indians maintain that knowledge of their histories is transmitted through oral stories, not solely through excavations of burials. But some anthropologists (like many historians) depend upon tangible evidence—archaeological and written—to reconstruct past cultures, often discounting the Indians' versions as nothing but inaccurate, albeit interesting, "myths."[14]

I have been active in the repatriation issue for over fifteen years and have served on committees composed of individuals with a variety of interests in the issue. I try to delineate the different religious, moral, political, and philosophical opinions about repatriation among American Indians and those who study their remains and grave goods in chapter 5, "American Indians, Anthropologists, Pothunters, and Repatriation: Ethical, Religious, and Political Differences."

Indians and Indians

Who speaks for all tribes, if anyone? The repatriation issue is complicated by the reality that not all Indians have the same opinions about repatriation. Indians are not all alike, and within each tribe are progressive and traditional representatives. Some tribal people adhere to their particular tribe's traditional religions, languages, and social mores, while others do not. Individual Indians do indeed possess a variety of social and cultural values and therefore express an array of viewpoints on this issue. Some Indians are willing to allow the study of remains and certain burial objects but expect items to be returned to tribes afterward. Who determines when the studies are complete? Unless the researcher is sympathetic to the tribes' desires, the materials may remain in a state of indefinite study.

There are a few Indians who believe remains should be studied for educational purposes and not repatriated. James Riding In, a Pawnee historian active in his tribe's efforts to repatriate remains, offers his opinions regarding the primary reasons—religious, philosophical, and ethical—why American Indians object to having remains and funerary objects studied and not returned for reburial in chapter 6, "Repatriation: A Pawnee's Perspective." He refers to the disinterment of Pawnee remains for scientific study as a "spiritual holocaust" and the attitudes of those scholars wishing to study the remains as "imperial archaeology."

Jack F. Trope and Walter R. Echo-Hawk outline the origins, scope, and nature of the repatriation issue in chapter 7, "The Native American Graves Protection and Repatriation Act: Background and Legislative History." They discuss the failure of the legal system to protect native burial sites, the legal theories supporting protection and repatriation of the native dead, and state and federal legislation. Trope and Echo-Hawk explain that NAGPRA is the first legislation "to consider what is sacred from an Indian perspective."

Vine Deloria Jr., in chapter 8, "Secularism, Civil Religion, and the Religious Freedom of American Indians," briefly traces the history of religious freedom and explores the development of "civil religion"—a joining of political and religious beliefs—and how it suppresses American religious freedom. Secularity has an important bearing on repatriation, for the religious beliefs of tribes have been forced to take a backseat to state police powers. Indeed, neither the American Indian Freedom of Religion Act nor the First Amendment to the Constitution protects Indian religious freedom.

Some American Indians and sympathizers want tribal remains and sacred objects repatriated and never studied, but no single Indian or organization speaks for all tribes, making it difficult for museum and archive personnel to understand the motivations behind some requests or to know who has authority to ask for items to be returned. Indeed, some tribal councils—because of the religious beliefs regarding the handling the dead—do not want remains returned and resent those Indians who attempt to "help" them. These crusaders have been christened "URPies" (Universal Reburial Proponents) by Bruce D. Smith, an anthropologist at the Museum of Natural History.[15] Many Indians, however, are quite aggressive in their quest to have tribal items repatriated. Individual tribes determine what they do and do not want repatriated, and many Indians and social scientists agree that repatriation should be considered on a case-by-case basis.

Social Scientists and Social Scientists

Within the anthropological profession there are radically different opinions about repatriation, the role and responsibilities of archaeologists, and the definition of "ethics." Some social scientists and scientists are willing to return remains, but only after they have been studied. Others, however, are amenable to working with tribes to determine what can and cannot be studied.

A large portion of the anthropological community desires to exhume and hold remains and artifacts for study and display, with no intention of returning items to tribes. This attitude is expressed by anthropologist Clement W. Meighan in chapter 10, "Some Scholars' Views on Reburial." Stringently opposed to reburial, Meighan expresses his doubts about Indians' abilities to chronicle their own histories and, concerned about the fate of archaeology, believes that with the demise of classes in ethnology and archaeology there will be "an increasing loss to archaeology, and of course to the Indians whose history is dependent upon it."

A more moderate stance is taken by Lynne Goldstein and Keith Kintigh in chapter 9, "Ethics and the Reburial Controversy." The authors state that archaeologists need to become more sensitive to Indians' needs and concerns, yet they maintain the attitude that archaeologists have a "mandate to preserve and protect the past for the future." The view at the other end of the spectrum is expressed in chapter 11 by archaeologists Shirley Powell and Anthony L. Klesert in "A Perspective on Ethics and the Reburial Controversy." Their idea of "covenantal archaeology" stresses that science is not more important than the people it studies and that the assertions of some anthropologists and archaeologists that they have an obligation to tell the Indians' stories are incorrect. According to Powell and Klesert, archaeologists have "no special proprietary claim on the dead, thus they have no natural right to dig up anything at all." Their argument, reprinted from *American Antiquity,* is especially interesting in that it is the revision deemed acceptable to *American Antiquity*; their first essay submissions were seen as containing pro-repatriation ideas too radical for the anthropological field (the essay was in large part a critique of Goldstein and Kintigh's essay) and therefore unacceptable for publication.[16]

The discovery of a ninety-three-hundred-year-old skeleton along the banks of the Columbia River at Columbia Park in 1996 has resulted in volatile debates between those wanting "Kennewick Man" repatriated and those who want to retain his remains for scientific study. A key question seems to be, Who "owns" Kennewick Man? Is he European, Asian, or indigenous to the United States? The answer to this (and who answers it) will have a strong impact on Native rights and NAGPRA. To illustrate the importance of Kennewick Man, professor of Native American Studies Bruce E. Johansen commented in a 1999 essay that "Assertions that Kennewick Man was from Europe have made him something of a hero to non-Natives who would like to abrogate treaties and limit Native American sovereignty in our time."[17] In chapter 12, "(Re)Constructing Bodies: Semiotic Sovereignty and the Debate over Kennewick Man," Suzanne J. Crawford offers discussion on how "narratives explicating social identity and history are inscribed on the body," in this case, Kennewick Man. Her essay illustrates that the controversy surrounding the discovery goes far beyond political issues; the disposition of Kennewick Man poses religious, ethical, economic, and social dilemmas.

Museums and Indians

The attitude among museum directors is as varied as opinions among anthropologists.[18] Some museum directors will not take skeletal remains and sacred objects off display, much less return items to tribes. Some museum directors will at least remove items from display but still will not return items. In Texas and Oklahoma some social scientists and curators have agreed that remains should be protected and not displayed in museums or sold at auction—yet they still keep objects in their basements.[19] The latter often will attempt to "sensitively handle" the items, although most have no idea what that might mean. ("Isn't storing the remains on a royal purple towel and packed with sage adequate?" I was once asked.) Many museum directors attempt to cooperate with tribes and will return items if proof of descendancy or cultural kinship is given.

Three essays discuss how tribes handle the reality that the academic community still retains power over the people they study and whose artifacts they collect. In chapter 13, "Repatriation at the Pueblo of Zuni: Diverse Solutions to Complex Problems," T. J. Ferguson, Roger Anyon, and Edmund J. Ladd, anthropologists who have worked extensively with Zunis on repatriation issues, chronicle the Zuni tribe's success at reclaiming their sacred War Gods from American museums and from private collectors. The authors discuss the complexity of formulating tribal policies and explain that because of the multifaceted concerns of Zunis over repatriation, the tribe has not accepted all items to be repatriated.

Ira Jacknis explores the efforts of the Kwakiutls of British Columbia to have ceremonial paraphernalia, taken from them in 1922, repatriated to the tribe in chapter 14, "Repatriation as Social Drama: The Kwakiutl Indians of British Columbia, 1922–1980." The Canadian government, which had outlawed their potlatch feasts and dancing, confiscated the material as part of the legal proceedings and deposited it in the National Museum. In the late 1970s the museum agreed to return the artifacts on the condition that the materials would go into a museum that government would build. Two native-run museums opened in 1979 and 1980. Employing the concept of "social drama," the essay explores fundamental and differing notions of artifacts and ownership among the Kwakiutls, the government, and museums.

Kurt E. Dongoske discusses in chapter 15, "NAGPRA: A New Beginning, Not the End, for Osteological Analysis—A Hopi Perspective," the positive benefits of a working relationship between archaeologists and the Hopi tribe. He maintains that NAGPRA need not be the end of anthropological research of Indian remains and cultural objects. Instead, by making their investigations of American Indians' ancestors' remains relevant to the tribe's needs, anthropologists may find more opportunities for osteological research.

Finally, Larry J. Zimmerman, an archaeologist active in the repatriation issue, discusses the direction be believes archaeology must go in order to survive as a discipline in chapter 16, "A New and Different Archaeology? With a Postscript on the Impact of the Kennewick Dispute." An optimistic supporter of "covenantal archaeology," Zimmerman proposes that the syncretic relationship between Indians and archaeologists (that is, using a combination of tribes' oral traditions and archaeological methods) could give both a more complete picture of the past. Zimmerman warns, however, that archaeology will have to alter its ethics, methodology, and dictatorial stance in relation to Indians, because it "has the most to lose" in the repatriation issue if it does not. He emphasizes the importance of the World Archaeological Congress (WAC) code: that Indians have a powerful voice regarding archaeological ethics, and they should not have to submit to archaeologists dictating terms to them. In addition, he supports the adage among Indians that there should be indigenous control over indigenous heritage.

The purpose of this anthology is to introduce readers to the many facets of the repatriation issue, including religion, law, philosophy, ethics, history, museology, race relations, cultural differences, science, and concepts of power and land ownership, as well as what has been interpreted by some as racism and prejudice. I was fortunate to coerce a group of prominent physical and cultural anthropologists, archaeologists, historians, and Indian activists to express their opinions and concerns on the issue. To be sure, not everyone agrees on the matter, but this is how we educate one another.

Because of the varied viewpoints expressed in this special issue, the aim of this project has not been to prove only one thesis, nor to solve the repatriation conflict. My intention has been to compile thoughtful essays to be used as a tool of education for a variety of readers, such as scholars whose careers focus upon the study of American Indian skeletal remains; museologists who display, store, and collect Indian remains and artifacts and who are faced with requests from tribes wanting items returned to them; members of the general public who plunder Indian burials for profit; and those who know little about the issue and who are not aware of the complexity of the problem. Many more essays could have been included, but I hope that these will stimulate more conversation and someday an equitable solution for all concerned will be found.

Notes

1. The most prominent of such organizations are: American Indians Against Desecration, American Indian Science and Engineering Society, Association of American Indian Affairs, the National Congress of American Indians, and the Native American Rights Fund. Numerous individuals have worked extensively on legislation and education, such as Walter Echo-Hawk. See Montgomery Brower and Conan Putnam, "Walter Echo-Hawk Fights for His People's Right to Rest in Peace, Not in Museums," *People,* September 1989, 42–44. Also active in the issue are Suzan Shown Harjo, Roger Echo-Hawk, Thomas King, and James Riding In. See also Jan Hammil, director, American Indians Against Desecration, statement at American Anthropological Association symposium, The Protection of Native American Burials: Cultural Values and Professional Ethics in the Treatment of the Dead, Washington DC, December 5, 1985, unpublished paper.

2. Examples of special issues include: "Special Edition: Repatriation of American Indian Remains," *American Indian Culture and Research Journal* 16 (1992); "Symposium: The Native American Graves Protection and Repatriation Act of 1990 and State Repatriation-Related Legislation," *Arizona State Law Journal* 24 (1992). For more information on such committees, see Frank McLemore and David Alcoze, "Texas American Indians and Colleagues Initiate Action to Protect Skeletal Remains and Sacred Objects," *Texas Association of Museums Quarterly* (spring 1985): 20; Lt. Col. Ronald A. Torgerson, "Warriors," *Air Force Engineering and Services Quarterly* (summer 1995): 14–15; "Peacekeeper Program: United States Air Force and American Indians Against Desecration, Conference on Reburial," University of South Dakota, Brookings, November 1985, transcript by American Indian Research Project.

3. John Dorfman, "Getting Their Hands Dirty? Archaelogists and the Looting Trade," *Lingua Franca* (May/June 1998): 28–36; David M. Pendergast and Elizabeth Graham, "The Battle for the Maya Past: The Effects of International Looting and Collecting in Belize," in *The Ethics of Collecting Cultural Property: Whose Culture? Whose Property?* ed. Phyllis Mauch Messenger (Albuquerque: University of New Mexico Press, 1990), 51–60; David Sassoon, "Considering the Perspective of the Victim: The Antiquities of Nepal," in *Ethics of Collecting,* 61–72; Thomas K. Seligman, "The Murals of Teotihuacan: A Case Study of Negotiated Resolution," in *Ethics of Collecting,* 73–84; Ian Christie Clack, "The Protection of Cultural Property," *Museum* 28 (1986): 182–92; R. J. Lambert, "Aboriginal Remains and the Australian Museum," *Council for Museum Anthropology* 7 (October 1983): 4–5.

4. William Bradford et al., *Homes in the Wilderness: A Pilgrim's Journal of Plymouth Plantation in 1620* (New York: William R. Scott, Inc., 1939), 11, 23–24; Karl Lehman-Hartleben, "Thomas Jefferson, Archaeologist," *American Journal of Archaeology* 47 (1943): 163; Thomas Jefferson, *Notes on the State of Virginia* (New York: W. W. Norton, 1982), 100.

5. Susan Shown Harjo, "Indian Remains Deserve Respect," *San Jose (California) Mercury News*, October 10, 1989; "Battle over Indian Relics Shows Our Basic Ignorance," *Albany (New York) Times-Union*, October 8, 1989; James Riding In, "Six Pawnee Crania: Historical and Contemporary Issues Associated with the Massacre and Decapitation of Pawnee Indians in 1869," *American Indian Culture and Research Journal* 16 (1992): 101–19; Riding In, "Without Ethics and Morality: A Historical Overview of Imperial Archaeology and American Indians," *Arizona State Law Journal* 24 (1992): 11–34; Juti Winchester, "The Collection and Repatriation of Native American Remains" (M.A. thesis, San Diego State University, 1992), 25–44.

6. "Villagers Still Wait for Remains," *Anchorage Daily News*, March 14, 1990.

7. Robert M. Peregoy, "Nebraska's Repatriarion Law: A Study of Cross-Cultural Conflict and Resolution," *American Indian Culture and Research Journal* 16 (1992): 139–95; Peregoy, "The Legal Basis, Legislative History, and Implementation of Nebraska's Landmark Reburial Legislation," *Arizona State Law Journal* 24 (1992): 329–90; Suzan Shown Harjo, "Native Peoples' Cultural and Human Rights: An Unfinished Agenda," *Arizona State Law Journal* 24 (1992): 321–28; Paul Bender, "1990 Arizona Repatriation Legislation," *Arizona State Law Journal* 24 (1992): 391–418; Winchester, "Collection and Repatriation," 45–62.

8. 25 U.S.C.A. 3001–3013 (West Supp. 1991), reprinted in the appendix to this volume. See also essays by Walter R. Echo-Hawk and Jack F. Trope, (chap. 7, this vol.), Sherry Hutt, Ralph W. Johnson and Sharon I. Haensly, Rennard Strickland, Edward Halealoha Ayau, Francis P. McManamon and Larry V. Nordby, Thomas H. Boyd, and Jonathan Haas in *Arizona State Law Journal* 24 (1992).

9. Catherine Elston, "Thieves of Time: The Pillage of American Pre-History," *Wildfire* (winter 1990): 21–25; Deborah L. Nichols, Anthony L. Klesert, and Roger Anyon, "Ancestral Sites, Shrines, and Graves: Native American Perspectives on the Ethics of Collecting Cultural Properties," in *Ethics of Collecting*, 27–38; Ann M. Early, "Profiteers and Public Archaeology: Antiquities Trafficking in Arkansas," in *Ethics of Collecting*, 39–50; Stanley N. Wellborn, "When Greedy Collectors Plunder the Past," *U.S. News and World Report*, March 4, 1985; Ian M. Thompson, "Looters and Losers in the San Juan Country," *Early Man* (summer 1982): 28–34; Grace Lichtenstein, "Taking Back the Past," *Outside* (April 1991): 108–68; "Grave Robbers Plague Indians," *Fort Worth Star Telegram*, February 16, 1986; "Time Bandits: Vandals Destroying Archaeological Sites," *Flagstaff Arizona Daily Sun*, November 12, 1994.

10. "Grave Robbers: Arizona Style," *Phoenix Gazette*, January 31, 1990. The rancher commented, "I think it's sort of ridiculous not to dig up the stuff at all. I enjoy the things we find just for their beauty and historic value—not just their monetary value."

11. "East Texas Heritage Plundered by Relic Hunters," *Tyler (Texas) Courier Times*,

July 1986; *A Legacy in Pieces: Your Land and the Texas Past,* Living with the Texas Past series no. 2 (Austin TX: Office of the State Archaeologist, n.d.)

12. For example, Peter Hester of Arizona makes his living at what he terms "private, avocational archaeology." He owns the Montezuma Hotel in Camp Verde and makes hundreds of thousands of dollars a year selling graves goods through his company, Fourth World Native American Art.

Under article 2 of the Constitution and By-Laws of the Texas Arrow Point and Artifact Society of Hunters, Appraisers, and Collectors (T.A.P.A.-S.H.A.C.), the society endorses artifact collecting: "2. To assist and provide for a means and method of appraising artifacts owned or possessed by the members; and 3. To provide a means of acquiring reasonable rates of insurance for collections owned by the members."

In the column "Antique Q & A" in the *Dallas Morning News,* Saturday, March 15, 1986, a reader inquired where he might buy a skull for "artistic purposes." The answer: collector Michael Justings has four two-hundred-year-old skulls for sale, "along with a variety of other antiques relating to death and burial. . . . Justings says that human skulls can be imported from India, but that they lack the character of the American Indian skulls he has for sale." Write him at 210 W. 78th St. Suite 1-B, New York NY, 10024.

13. Jane E. Buikstra and C. C. Gordon, "The Study and and Restudy of Human Skeletal Series: The Importance of Long Term Curation," *Annals of the New York Academy of Sciences* 376 (1981): 449–66; Buikstra, "Reburial: How We All Lose—An Archaeologist's Opinion," *Society for California Archaeology Newsletter* 17 (February 1983); Douglas W. Owsley, "Human Bones from Archaeological Context: An Important Source of Information," *Council for Museum Anthropology Newsletter* 8 (April 1984): 2–8.

14. For discussion on the controversy over the accuracy of American Indian oral history versus written and tangible documentation, see Angela Cavender Wilson, "Grandmother to Granddaughter: Generations of History in a Dakota Family," in *Natives and Academics: Researching and Writing about American Indians,* ed. Devon A. Mihesuah (Lincoln: University of Nebraska Press, 1998), 27–36.

15. Bruce D. Smith, "URPIE Logic: An Analysis of the Structure of the Supporting Arguments of Universal Reburial Proponents," unpublished essay. His main targets are members and supporters of American Indians Against Desecration. See also Carolyn Shea, "Advocate Group: American Indians Against Desecration," *Indian Studies* (Cornell) 2 (winter 1985–86): 8–9.

16. For other opinions about the need for the two groups to work together, see Michael Tymchuk, "Skeletal Remains: In Defense of Sensitivity and Compromise," *Council for Museum Anthropology* 8 (July 1984): 2–8; Robert L. Reeder, "Reburial: Science versus Religion?" *Missouri Archaeological Society Quarterly* 2 (October–December 1985): 7–16; Duane Anderson, "Reburial: Is It Reasonable?" *Archaeol-*

ogy 38 (September–October 1985): 48–51; Larry Zimmerman, "Desecration and Reburial as an Anthropological Issue: The Tactics of Self-Delusion," paper presented at the Annual Meeting of the American Anthropological Association, Washington DC, 1985.

17. For more information on the Kennewick Man, see Bruce E. Johansen, "Great White Hope? Kennewick Man, the Facts, the Fantasies, and the Stakes," *Native Americas Journal* (spring 1999), web version, *http://nativeamericas.aip.cornell.edu*; Cate Montana, "Unknowns Still Shroud Kennewick Man," *Indian Country Today* (March 29–April 5, 1999), sec. A1, p. 9; Cate Montana, "Kennewick Man Unveiled" and "Kennewick Man: A Lot Ailed Him," *Indian Country Today* (April 5–12, 1999): sec. A1, p. 2; Douglas Preston, "The Lost Man," *New Yorker* (June 16, 1997): 70–81.

18. For discussion on the relationship between Indians and museums, see Charles Baker, "In My Opinion: Indian Artifacts and Museums: A Question of Ownership," *Museum News* 40 (April 1985): 14–16; Walter Echo-Hawk, "Museum Rights vs. Indian Rights: Guidelines for Assessing Competing Legal Interests in Native Cultural Resources," *Review of Law and Social Change* 14 (1986): 437–452; Candace Floyd, "The Repatriation Blues: Museum Professionals and Native Americans Wrestle with Questions of Ownership and Disposition of Tribal Materials," *History News* 40 (April 1985): 6–12; James D. Nason, Kenneth R. Hopkins, and Bea Medicine (individual commentaries), "Finders Keepers?" *Museum News* 51 (March 1973): 20–26; Sara J. Wolfe and Lisa Mibach, "Ethical Considerations in the Conservation of Native American Sacred Objects," *Journal of the American Institute for Conservation* 23 (1983): 1–6; Ellen Ferguson and James Nason, "Human Subject Rights and Museum Research," *Museum News* 58 (1980): 44–47; Nancy Oestreich Lurie, "American Indians and Museums: A Love-Hate Relationship," *The Old Northwest* 2 (May 1976): 235–51; Bowen Blair, "American Indians vs. American Indians: A Matter of Religious Freedom," *American Indian Journal* 5 (May–June 1979): 13–21.

19. Resolution 3, passed June 15, 1985, Committee for the Protection of Human Remains and Sacred Objects, organized by the Texas Historical Commission and the Texas Indian Commission.

Part I

History

1

Robert E. Bieder

The Representations of Indian Bodies in

Nineteenth-Century American Anthropology

By the end of the eighteenth century, the interest in science roused a corresponding interest in the study of man.[1] The great age of exploration had inundated Europe with fauna and flora from around the world, and explorers and travelers returned with tales of people never before seen. The great Swedish botanist, C. Linnaeus, had devised a system of classification that promised to bring order to the biological world; to impose an order on humankind was now thought necessary. Social philosophers erected stages of progress from savagery through barbarism to civilization to better describe their world. Non-European peoples were duly assigned a rank on the scale of progress. This ordering was a political act. Europeans not only negotiated and then defined the borders among non-European peoples but also inscribed their inferiority. Although methodologies for the comparative investigation of cultures largely were absent, this did not prevent Europeans from constructing representations of non-European peoples, searching for their origins, reading[2] their bodies, assigning differences, and determining ranks. The authorial discourse of ethnology was a complex interweaving of multiple narratives that possessed power-laden meanings and resonances for the time.

In America, early ethnology was both a political and an ideological discourse addressing national and international constituencies. In the multiple ethnological narratives written during the nineteenth century, representations of Native Americans articulated different social agendas. Although other races received attention, Native Americans were the privileged object of ethnological scrutiny and knowledge. Because of the repatriation theme of this book, this chapter will explore concepts of the body and power along with how representations of Indians were constructed and what these representations meant in nineteenth-century ethnology and archaeology.

The concept of the body underlies nineteenth-century ethnological theory. If historian Dorinda Outram is correct, eighteenth-century French scholars brought new meaning to representations of the body. Depersonalized and desacralized, the body became data. It was redefined symbolically, politically, and scientifically and was seen more as a specimen for observation than as the temple of the soul. Scientists collected bodies for medical and racial research. As Outram noted, in Paris hospitals of the late eighteenth century, "older ways of seeing the body disappeared. In their place came a penetrating medical gaze that used new techniques of observation to make the deepest recesses of the body transparent to the medical eye," and therefore analyzable.[3] The moment when "human calculable" replaced "human spiritual" was the moment when, according to Michael Foucault, "the sciences of man became possible, the moment when a new technology of power and a new political anatomy of the body was implemented."[4] Medical science embraced the idea that the body was measurable and legible: it could be decoded and encoded. Science inscribed upon the body not only information on internal states but also class, race, potential for civilization or degeneracy, intelligence, and gender roles.[5] The lessons learned in the hospitals of Paris were quickly brought to America. The bodies of Indians became important for the investigations of ethnologists and anthropologists throughout the nineteenth century. Here they found the imprint of the environment, searched for Indian origins, observed effects of disease and customs, and defined the body's limitations and deficiencies.

It was this growing awareness of the body out of which American ethnology was born. In his *Historie naturelle,* published in 1761, the renowned French naturalist, Count Buffon, employed the bodies of Indians as evidence to denigrate the New World environment. He concluded that "some elements" or other "physical causes" made New World animals smaller and weaker than those in the Old World and operated against a full natural development. Buffon applied the same debilitating factors to human populations in the Americas. American Indians were weak and passive; they were incapable of mastering their environment. Physically, they were defective. In an age of expansion and progress, they evinced little ability to (re)produce. Buffon claimed that their "organs of generation are small and feeble." Indians lacked body hair and sexual ardor. Buffon thought that Indian males—lacking the sexual prowess and appeal of the European male, and because of their natural cruelty—controlled women by force and reduced them to slaves and chattel. Indians were hostages to environmental forces. Living in this "state of nature," Indians lacked the social bonds necessary for family, the political state, and the exercise of power.[6] According to Buffon, the dismal environment of the New World shaped Indians into grotesque humans. Here was a case of environmentalism producing degeneration, not progress.

The concept of environmentalism—the influence of the natural and social environments on human mental and physical characteristics—infused most thinking in the eighteenth century. The concept extended to the ancient Greeks, but during the Enlightenment it received renewed attention as a way of explaining physical and intellectual variation among races. This explanation presupposed a single human species with a shared psychic (ability to reason) unity. Despite the criticism by many Enlightenment thinkers of the Christian world view, most held to the Biblical thesis of a single human creation or monogenism. An exalted belief in progress that required psychic unity weighed heavily in constructing that belief. Environmental forces—climate, geography, society, education—became the preferred explanation to account for human variations rather than polygenism that postulated multiple human creations.[7]

Buffon's pejorative views extended to nature. For Buffon, nature was conceived of as "other," a force opposed to civilization and hence something to be conquered. It "could be a ruthless adversary when untamed by human hands."[8] Nature, for many, was understood politically and representationally and was also perceived in gender terms. Historian Ludmiller Jordanova notes that in the eighteenth and nineteenth centuries,

> Nature has been presented . . . as different, as threatening or powerful, and by those very tokens, as an object of intense curiosity. The idea of conquering or mastering nature is a case in point, when the source of otherness implied by the idea is also generally understood in terms of gender, with nature commonly, but by no means universally, being identified with women.[9]

Since Indians were also associated with nature and, for many thinkers—both in Europe and America—personified nature to such a degree, they became a metonymy for what was natural.

Whether Europeans and Americans saw nature as female and passive or female and threatening, it was female nature in need of control by masculine civilization/culture. When Europeans proceeded to link Indians with nature, it was an easy step to consider Indians in gender terms. Indians, seen in feminine terms, were presumed passive and accepting of nature and hence easily influenced by environments. Their credulity and superstitions, their bouts of lethargy, their outbursts of emotion (violence), their lack of hair and ardor produced an effete portrait. Linked to nature and feminized, Indians were represented as "primitive types" and stood in the minds of many as a force opposed to civilization, an adversary to be conquered, subdued, and made productive.

It mattered little to Americans that Buffon's charges, as historian Gilbert Chinnard contends, were merely attempting to defend civilization from the threat of primitivism. Buffon's claims disturbed many Americans who proceeded to construct their own narratives. One of the first to respond was Thomas Jefferson, who, in his *Notes on the State of Virginia,* attempted to refute Buffon.[10] Jefferson's work, written in response to questions from François Barbé-Marbois, secretary to the French legation at Philadelphia, questioned not environmentalism but Buffon's data. In shifting the terms of debate from methodology to data, Jefferson sought to strengthen the American position and better defend the American Indian and hence the American environment.

Jefferson would proceed from the observation of "some thousand" Indians.[11] This act of "witnessing"[12] that Jefferson emphasized in his *Notes* was a shrewd maneuver to discredit Buffon's data.[13] Here was a crucial factor in the drive for scientific validity. Enlightenment science stressed an empirical approach. The act of witnessing, the eliciting of facts through experience, would count more than those derived from texts. By appropriating the role of witness, Americans assumed a position of authority.[14]

In the debate between Jefferson and Buffon, the Indian body proved not only a source of data but also a space for a political and theoretical contest. Jefferson's narrative, while noting Indian "deficiencies," spoke of them in the context of intelligent adjustments to a way of life and stated that, as a people, Indians demonstrated a talent for change and civilization. Other defenders of the American environment also constructed sympathetic narratives of Indians in the 1770s and 1780s in stories that carried a political burden.[15]

Between 1790 and the first two decades of the nineteenth century, these earlier "sympathetic" (re)presentations of Indian cultures—now no longer needed for political rhetoric—gave way to new narratives less enchanted with Indian life. Many shared the assumption that Indians—their language, society, and customs—had degenerated and that this decline was not the fault of cultural contact with Europeans but had indigenous roots. This presumed degeneration assumed more than the spectacle of American Indians' wrenching adjustment to social-cultural change; it also assumed a model of what the Indian ought to be.

This theme was best expressed in the writings of the Philadelphia physician Benjamin Smith Barton. In various papers before the American Philosophical Society and in his *New Views of the Origins of the Tribes and Nations of America* (1797), Barton drew on his study of the Ohio Valley mounds and

Indian languages and pronounced that not only had Indians declined from an ancient civilization to a rude state over a long period of time but also that it was impossible for them to advance toward civilization as Americans defined it without the help of whites.[16]

Many white Americans were doubtful. There was a growing sense that the Indian was incapable of such civilization. Then too, the civilizing idea clashed with the realities of Indian-white contact along a rapidly expanding frontier. As historian Reginald Horsman noted, "the rhetoric of improvability and assimilation did not convince the Georgian or the Tennesseans." They rejected a government civilization policy that threatened to leave Indians on the land. "They wanted to expel Indians not transform them."[17]

By the 1830s these increasingly negative views of Indians produced a new representation[18] of Indians that competed with the older environmental monogenist narratives. Many white Americans sincerely believed that the rapidly changing American environment had not altered Indian life. Why was it that an environment that invigorated the white race caused Indians to decline? Some white Americans were convinced Indians could not change because they were innately unable to do so. It was not their environment but their biology. To such thinkers, Indians were a separate, inferior species. Many of those who subscribed to polygenic beliefs did not miss the discrepancy between the hopes and expectations of some white Americans for the advancement of Indians on the one hand and the evidence of their seeming—as defined in nineteenth-century terms—inability to progress on the other. That they continued to live as their fathers had caused little surprise. The environment proved ineffectual against the force of innate constraints, nor could it influence what many polygenists considered impossible to alter. In their attack on environmentalism as an agent for change polygenists denied change itself.

In 1839 Samuel G. Morton, a Philadelphia physician, published his voluminous *Crania americana.* In this statistical account of cranial differences—primarily a comparison of American Indians with Euroamericans—Morton constructed a new representation of Indians more in line with racial frontier thinking. Born in Philadelphia, Morton studied medicine in Edinburgh and Paris, residing in the latter at a time when the new Paris medicine was reshaping how science looked at the body. He returned a "somatic determinist," believing that through the measurement of the cranium he could assess intelligence, and with an appreciation of phrenology.[19]

Along with many others, Morton sought an empirical means to discover human temperament and intelligence and how these were distributed among racial groups. Phrenologists led the way by proclaiming not only that the brain was the organ of the mind but that the brain was divisible into thirty-seven (the number varied among phrenologists) parts or faculties. Intelligence and traits such as sociability, greed, lust, and frugality could be localized in these faculties, which, in turn, could be mapped on the skull. According to phrenology, individuals manifested a propensity for a particular trait by an enlarged area or bump on the cranium at the place where the faculty for that trait was located.[20]

Although most scientists rejected phrenology by the 1850s, in 1839 Morton expressed a reserved sympathy for the "science." Although a craniologist and more interested in cranial measurement than in personality formation, Morton drew upon phrenological theory—especially the concept that size of brain determines intelligence—in his research.[21]

Both phrenology and craniology inscribed bones with multiple messages and emphasized the medical gaze. The body became divisible and carried political meaning. Culture and society ceased to have relevance in shaping individuals. As one historian noted, "human beings were what they were because of the tilt of their faces and the shape of their skulls." In short, "bodies determined minds." In the new medicine, "real knowledge about individuals could come only through their bodies."[22] Cultural data were irrelevant for any analysis of the capability or potential of a race. The only real evidence for Morton was bones. For Morton and other polygenists of the so-called American School of Anthropology, not only could the cranium articulate information about the individual, it also spoke "truths" about the individual's race.

When Morton first attempted his craniological research, he discovered that few skulls were available. His original goal was a comparative study of the five human types identified by the German craniologist-anthropologist Johann Friedrich Blumenbach. Difficulty in obtaining crania of the five groups, however, led Morton to focus on Indian crania from North and South America. To collect these crania, Morton enlisted the aid of Indian agents, along with civilian and military physicians, in various parts of the country. Grave robbing kept many people busy on the frontier supplying Morton and the growing number of phrenologists. Angry and horrified Indians tried to prevent the desecration of their graves, but such activity often was carried out by military personnel against defeated tribal groups. Epidemics that periodically swept through Indian communities often made the collecting of crania an easy task. Still other crania were unearthed from grave sites long abandoned because of tribal removal and were sent to Morton and to phrenologists building "cranial libraries."[23]

Morton's readings of his data indicated that not only were Indians less intelligent than Caucasians and Mongolians but also that their crania size had not varied in hundreds of years. In these calculations, Morton believed he found evidence of the Indians' inferiority. Although Morton did not reject environmentalism, he relegated it to a minor, if not inconsequential, role in producing change. Morton saw crania as innate and immune to environmental factors. Because, by his calculations, each race possessed crania of a particular size and shape that did not seem to vary over time, Morton reasoned that each race was uniquely constituted. Morton did not claim separate creation for the various races, but such a conclusion was evident. Morton's less timid followers, and eventually even Morton himself, would scoff at the proponents of environmentalism and assert that races were not varieties of humankind but separate inferior species.[24]

Although the classification of crania and ranking of intelligence were political and representational decisions and not biological ones, they passed beyond the realm of speculation to become for many statements of fact. As historian Donna Haraway cautions, "facts are always theory-laden; theories are value-laden, therefore, facts are value-laden."[25] The readings of the osteological data encouraged the construction of stories by those who supported black servitude. The readings produced for Native Americans led to conclusions that were just as bleak. Most of the polygenists believed the Indians would never change because they could not. Indian inferiority— like that of other non-whites and women—was permanently inscribed in their crania. Their biology equipped them to survive only in a world of savagery and dependency. Most polygenists saw education and philanthropic attempts to civilize Indians as doomed to failure and viewed the impending extinction of the Indian as perhaps tragic but inevitable. Stories told by polygenists underwrote the expansive ideology of Manifest Destiny.[26]

Despite these attacks, environmentalism as an explanation for variation in man did not disappear. Nor did most ethnologists rush to embrace polygenism. On the contrary, pressures brought about by deep-seated American values, religious and philosophical assumptions, and developments in science prompted some ethnologists to adjust environmental theory. The result was to make the theory more useful to ethnology as an explanatory device to (re)construct representation of Indians and a more suitable theory upon which both government and philanthropic endeavors could be erected.

From the late 1820s to mid-century, there were still those who followed an older ethnological tradition that saw environment affecting man's external features. As Albert Gallatin, retired from government service, co-founder of the American Ethnological Society, and perhaps the most noted ethnologist of the 1840s, stated in 1845, "but it is well known, that at least color and other subordinate external appearances are modified and altered by climate, localities, and the state of society."[27] Other writers echoed Gallatin.

But as early as the 1830s and '40s, this ethnological tradition with its emphasis on external body features was giving way to psychological features. Phrenology, along with a more inclusive view of progress and new ways of reading the body, led to a preoccupation with psychological or internal traits. The historian-ethnologist-physician James McCulloch marked this shift in a book written in 1829. Although admitting that climate and states of civilization might modify some aspects of physiognomy, physical characteristics were more the result of "moral" causes, or the interplay of mind with environment. As a prime example McCulloch cites the effect of the mind on facial features. Lack of mental stimulation among Indians led them to manifest little facial emotion. According to McCulloch, the Indian's mind "is hardly ever exercised [and] the features assume a fixed, grave, and even stern expression, according to the peculiar temper of the mind."[28]

Other ethnologists followed McCulloch's lead and claimed that the Indian's mind seemed to differ radically from the white man's; that Indians did not seem to possess the ability to reason and think in the abstract. Lacking proper stimulation, the Indian's mind stagnated. So rejecting polygenistic arguments, monogenists sought answers for the Indians' deficiency of ratiocination in their environment.

The ethnologist Henry Rowe Schoolcraft, perhaps the best-known authority on Indians in early-nineteenth-century America, drew heavily upon psychology for his ethnological theories. Although not a phrenologist, he did incorporate elements of phrenology in his thinking. Early in his career he postulated that Indians lacked a moral or philosophical sensibility.[29] As a government Indian agent among the Ojibwas in Michigan from 1822 to 1841, Schoolcraft had ample opportunity to observe Indians and to think about their fate. He relied upon his wife, Jane, her sisters, and her Ojibwa mother for access to Ojibwa language and culture. During his years as agent, Schoolcraft collected the legends and tales of the Ojibwa and the Ottawa Indians, which he reconstructed and published in his valuable work *Algic Researches* (1839).[30] For Schoolcraft, these tales "where men are transformed into animals or winds or stars and are then transformed into men again" offered the "deepest insight into Indian character . . . and the clearest coincidences with Oriental rites and opinions." The tales allowed him to penetrate "the dark cave of the Indian mind."[31] They collapsed the boundaries that whites had erected between humans and nature.

Obviously Schoolcraft was less interested in the legends than in how they could be employed to gain admittance to the "Indian mind." A confirmed monogenist, Schoolcraft firmly believed that the legends (re)presented a decidedly Oriental mentality. Since he believed the Oriental mind rigid and impervious to new ideas, he recognized that those who sought to alter the Indian mind would encounter much resistance. Yet Schoolcraft would not yield in his belief that eventually an improved environment would prevail in reshaping the Indians' mental outlook. The small crania that some craniologists claimed characterized the "Indian race" were due, according to Schoolcraft, more to a lack of opportunistic stimuli than to any innate deficiency.

Accepting that part of phrenology that conceived of the brain as an organ of the mind that could be altered and improved through exercise, Schoolcraft held that Indians could be saved from extinction by being forced to exercise their brains through the experience of education. The change of lifestyle had to be abrupt. Indians had to be wrested from forest life. They were capable of change, of "civilization," but the change could not be gradual, thus exposing them to vices and moral degeneration. The mind had to be altered and ideas forced upon it. Behavioral examples, not theory, were crucial to Indian mental development; only by imitating "civilization" would a benign and lasting effect on the Indians' minds be produced. The burden of the Indians' past had to be lifted and their minds set free so they could progress. Schoolcraft, a staunch Presbyterian, sought through his writings to impress these "ethnological truths" upon the American Board of Commissioners for Foreign Missions. Ethnological discoveries would allow the grand goals of civilizing and converting the Indians to proceed on scientific assumptions.[32] Others held similar views connecting experience with the development of mental faculties.[33]

The ethnological narrative presented by monogenist ethnologists around midcentury reflected changes in American society produced through commercial and industrial forces that required a more predictable (manipulative?) social behavior in the population. Many ethnologists believed Indians could be shaped into productive citizens. Like polygenists, monogenists drew on medical science, phrenology, pathology, and the medical gaze to support their theories. Facial expressions, legends, languages, and customs were viewed as windows into the brain that fostered penetration of the body and the possible reshaping of mental processes. The focus on internal capabilities rather than external characteristics emerged out of a desire to learn how best to stimulate and manipulate the minds of subject populations for contemporary socially defined ends. The new narrative shared with society and polygenists a goal of dominance and control. In the new representation, Indians were no longer "children of nature" but were seen as plastic objects to be acted on.

The end of the Civil War saw changes in ethnology. Phrenology, by 1850, as noted, had fallen into disrepute in most of the scientific community, but certain of its assumptions had passed into anthropology. The writings of Charles Lyell in geology and Charles Darwin in biology initiated a revolution in biology that was more interested in evolutionary theory than in classification. This was a blow to polygenism, more interested in the rigidity of types than in change. Yet some forms of polygenetic thought lingered on into the twentieth century.[34] Ethnology still was rooted in monogenism and a modified environmentalism, although the latter was shorn of the exaggerated claims made by some earlier ethnologists. The end of the war also unleashed demographic change as an advancing population circumscribed the territories of western tribes. Fearful that many of the tribes would soon disappear, anthropologists sensed an urgency in collecting "anthropological data."

If the Civil War proved a pivotal event for American society, it also was one for anthropology. As one historian noted, "the war marks a watershed not so much because its conclusions were new but because nearly all subsequent late nineteenth-century institutionalized attitudes of racial inferiority focused upon war anthropometry as the basis for their beliefs." The founding of the U.S. Sanitary Commission during the war to examine and improve the fighting ability of the northern troops led to extensive measurements of recruits' bodies.[35] Whereas Morton and phrenological research focused on the skull, the new studies included the whole body. Bodies were seen as providing clues to the evolution of race since the ratio of length of forearm to the distance from fingertips to knee was presumed an index to evolutionary distance from anthropoid apes. The short forearm of whites, as compared with those of blacks and Indians, was seen as a mark of evolutionary advancement. Although post–Civil War anthropology concerned itself with the whole body, the cranium and brain still provided important evidence on race, intelligence, and temperament.[36] Indeed one historian described the postwar period as "the Baroque period of craniology," noting that "craniology flourished as never before."[37] The bodies and bones of Indians became condensed stories of evolution, inferiority, and migration.

After the Civil War there was a gradual shift in focus in the study and collection of crania. The search in anthropology for racial origins receded in importance, and the foregrounding of racial differences and their meanings for evolutionary theory, politics, and society took place. Darwin and the discovery of ancient human remains in Europe shattered the old time frame for human habitation that studies in geology already had placed at risk. Evolutionary theory, however, found a mixed reception in America.[38] In anthropology, lack of institutional support (there still was no professional anthropological association) proved an impediment to the rapid diffusion of Darwin's theory.[39] Despite this, evolutionary theory eventually made an impact, especially in archaeology. Archaeologist Robert Braidwood notes, "it appears to me that the prime hallmark of later nineteenth and early twentieth-century prehistory was the notion of unilinear progressive evolution," a concept he attributes to Darwin.[40] This concept of unilinear evolution infused anthropological theory penetrating archaeology, physical anthropology, and ethnology in the last half of the nineteenth century.

In physical anthropology, the furious collecting of Indian skeletal remains was partly fueled by a debate between those who saw the path of human evolution as resulting from the growth of the brain and those who believed progress was achieved by the slow movement toward an upright posture. For those who favored brain size, crania were important for charting the progress (or lack of it) in the American Indian population.

Perhaps as a result of the U.S. Sanitary Commission's work, the Army Medical Museum was founded in 1862. While the museum sought crania of all races, after 1865 it gathered primarily Indian remains. According to the assistant surgeon general, writing in 1868, "The chief purpose had in view in forming this collection is to aid in the progress of anthropological science by obtaining measurements of a large number of skulls of aboriginal races of North America." Exotic or abnormal skulls would not be rejected and could be useful for comparison, but normal crania were most desired, along with any artifacts that would be useful for establishing "ethnic character."[41] Such ethnic characteristics as determined by the collector would become part of the documentation and "inscribed in" the bones.

Other museums also quickly moved to build collections. Even before the founding of the American Museum of Natural History in New York in 1891 and the Chicago Field Museum later in the decade, other museums were on the scene. The Smithsonian Institution, founded in 1846, and Harvard's Museum of Comparative Zoology, founded in 1859, were establishing collections of Indian bones and artifacts. European museums, sensing the urgency to collect Indian artifacts—before Indians disappeared—also entered the field. The furious "mining" of American Indian cemeteries became extremely competitive. But museums were not the only institutions out to portray the early history of human progress. Collecting for world fairs—especially the World's Columbian Exposition of 1893, which sought to document the history of human evolution from savagery to civilization—combined to strip whole Indian villages of artifacts and human remains.[42]

Bodies drawn from Indian and, to a lesser extent, from black populations were interrogated because social, economic, and political policy depended on the "answers" obtained. Indians, as represented in the stories of the researchers, were flawed specimens of evolution. For some, it was clear that Indians were mentally inferior to whites, that they could not compete successfully with whites in nineteenth-century America, and that they were doomed to racial extinction. Others were not convinced. Whether such corporal data would make problematic attempts to ameliorate the lot of tribal peoples was a matter of debate carried out in museums, on reservations, in off-reservation boarding schools, in Congress, in Mohonk conferences, and in ethnology.

Evolutionary theory also infused American ethnology in post–Civil War America. Sometimes thought of as the "father of American anthropology," Lewis Henry Morgan pioneered the study of kinship and erected a theory of social evolution that pervaded the study of Indian ethnology in the last half of the nineteenth century. Morgan, a lawyer in upstate New York, began his ethnological career with the publication of *League of the Ho-de-sau-ne, or Iroquois* in 1851, a book that some describe as the first ethnology of an Indian group. Critical of polygenetic thinking, Morgan set out to prove that Indians were descended from people in Asia. Convinced that the kinship system he discovered among the Iroquois—a system that differed dramatically from the Euroamerica system—was widespread throughout the Americas and could perhaps be traced to Asia, Morgan set out to collect kinship data. On field trips to the West and through posting questionnaires to government Indian agents and to missionaries in Asia, Morgan amassed information for his narrative.

Utilizing models drawn from philology to organize his kinship data, Morgan saw similarities between American Indian kinship systems and those in Asia.[43] These kinship systems were too complex to evolve separately, Morgan thought. Instead, he believed that both systems were products of the same "mind" and concluded that the indigenous people of the Americas were descended from Asians. These kinship systems "are entrusted to every person who speaks the common language, and their channel of transmission is the blood."[44] To further validate his theory of physical and mental kinship between the people of the Western Hemisphere and Asia, Morgan drew attention to similar customs in food, songs, dance, and dress that he discovered in both parts of the world. Rather than seeing these similarities in terms of cultural diffusion as Schoolcraft and others had, Morgan saw them in biological terms as carried in the blood and as the working of the same mentality. Although divided by an ocean, the same mind was at work.

Morgan believed that these similarities of customs, along with social, economic, and political institutions—which he subsumed under the traditional tripartite division of savagery, barbarism, and civilization—did not evolve gradually. Rather, they were derived from divinely embedded mental "germs" carried like seeds in the race and germinating under proper environmental conditions. Subjecting Indians to education would advance the germination of higher institutions, but physically crossing the Indian with the white race would speed up the "civilization" process.

For Morgan, the body represented the space in which progress would take place, and the bodies of Indian women were privileged in determining the racial destiny of the Indian people through the diluting of "Indian blood." Mixed marriages would produce children who "will intermarry respectably with our white people and thus the children will become respectable and, if educated, in the second and third generations [become more white] will become beautiful and attractive. This is to be the end of the Indian absorption of a small portion, which will improve and toughen our race, and residue [will be] run out or forced into the regions of the mountains."[45] But, Morgan cautioned later, change is not to be expected quickly. Indians still had the "skulls and brains of barbarians, and must grow toward civilization as all mankind have done who attained it by progressive experience."[46]

Morgan's germ theory articulated a political narrative that appealed to many of his contemporaries. Although critical of the insensitivity expressed toward Indians by government policies to promote civilization among tribal peoples, Morgan's theory placed the onus of blame for the slow acculturation on Indian biology. Morgan's anthropology was a gendered science. For him the bodies of Indians were more than data. Bodies freighted the burdens of history; they transported the customs and institutions from the past while at the same time carried the germs for future growth. The importance of the body lay in reproduction. In Morgan's preoccupation with the Indian female's ability to experience passion and in his articulation of Euroamericans' duty to advance the Indian race through racial genocide are revealed the sexual side of Morgan's Indian studies. Kinship studies are fundamentally studies of reproduction, the essence of Victorian womanhood. They also are politically gendered studies of naming and drawing sexual lines of power and property distribution, a topic very much privileged in late-nineteenth-century America.

Morgan died in 1881, but his theories were promoted by John Wesley Powell, director of the Bureau of American Ethnology, who made Morgan's *Ancient Study* required reading for bureau employees. Powell saw himself as continuing where Morgan left off. Where Morgan had combined kinship, institutions, family, and government, Powell sought to construct a master narrative where customs, language, and mythology were to be included in one large evolutionary structure. Powell did not employ his data to explicate the cultures and histories of particular tribes but rather to use it selectively to buttress the scaffolding of his grand evolutionary theory.

During the tenure of Powell and W. J. McGee, Powell's assistant at the bureau, institutional science was beginning to change and even the nineteenth-century evolutionary narrative began to weaken. The early decades of the twentieth century saw the old narrative replaced with a new one crafted by Franz Boas, a German immigrant anthropologist who, in redefining anthropology, chipped away at many of the assumptions basic to evolutionary theory.[47]

The interpretation presented in this brief study of nineteenth-century anthropology is one that stresses changing representation of Indian bodies. In the last half of the eighteenth century and through the first decade of the nineteenth century the emphasis in the emerging "science" of ethnology focused on the classification of racial groups based primarily on external physical characteristics of skin color, hair, and physiognomy. Such physical characteristics were seen as the product of the environment. Increasingly after the 1820s the discourse on race switched to internal characteristics of the body and focused on bones, crania, and brain size. Although this shift was most noticeable in the polygenetic writings of Morton and those associated with him, it could also be found in ethnology. The new orientation emerged in the context of the rising interest in phrenology and craniology, new attitudes regarding the body, and the debate over the incorporation of the Indian in American society.

After midcentury physical anthropology still proved important in racial studies, and the collecting of Indian skeletal material along with artifacts assumed a major preoccupation of museums. In ethnology, the body also was privileged in social evolutionary theory as propounded by Morgan and his followers at the Bureau of American Ethnology. Morgan's concern with the evolution and transmission of social institutions established a theoretical link between body and mind; mental germs gave rise to inventions that in turn were transmitted over time in the blood or through the body.

The shift from an emphasis on external characteristics linked to the environment to internal characteristics linked to heredity allowed Americans not only to retain confidence in the American environment as a positive force for change but also to place the fault of Indian deficiency on their biology and heredity. This freed Americans from having to assume responsibility for the condition of tribal peoples and their future. This did not mean that missionaries, educators, and philanthropists gave up trying to rectify the deplorable conditions of reservation life, but it did place the onus of change squarely on the Indian. The destiny of Indians was in their own hands—in correcting their biology—and not in the hands of the dominant culture. Representation of the Indian had shifted from seeing them as part of nature to seeing them controlled by their nature or biology.

Notes

1. F. C. T. Moore in Joseph-Marie, *The Observation of Savage Peoples,* ed. and trans. F. C. T. Moore (Berkeley: University of California Press, 1969), 1–2.

2. I use the word "reading" as currently used in many works in literary criticism and in recent studies on the writing of history. See, for example, Robert F. Berkhofer Jr., "A New Context for a New American Studies?" *American Quarterly* 41:2 (Dec. 1989): 588–613. Here, since I consider "bones" as a kind of text, the term is quite appropriate.

3. Dorinda Outram, *The Body in the French Revolution: Sex, Class and Political Power* (New Haven: Yale University Press, 1989), 45–46.

4. Michel Foucault, *Discipline and Punish: The Birth of the Prison*, trans. Alan Sheridan (New York: Vintage, 1977), 193.

5. Ludmilla Jordanova, *Sexual Visions: Images of Gender in Science and Medicine between the Eighteenth and Twentieth Centuries* (Madison: University of Wisconsin Press, 1989), chaps. 2 and 3; Cynthia Eagle Russett, *Sexual Science: The Victorian Construction of Womanhood* (Cambridge: Harvard University Press, 1989), 24–28.

6. Bernard Sheehan, *Seeds of Extinction: Jeffersonian Philanthropy and the American Indian* (Chapel Hill: University of North Carolina Press, 1973), 68–69.

7. Robert F. Berkhofer Jr., *The White Man's Indian: Images of American Indians from Columbus to the Present* (New York: Vintage, 1968), 38–42; Jordanova, *Sexual Visions,* 25.

8. Sheehan, *Seeds of Extinction, 68.*

9. Jordanova, *Sexual Visions,* 14–15; Donna Haraway, *Primate Visions: Gender, Race, and Nature in the World of Modern Science* (New York: Routledge, 1989), 136; Carolyn Merchant, *The Death of Nature: Women, Ecology and the Scientific Revolution* (New York: Harper and Row, 1980).

10. Thomas Jefferson, *Notes on the State of Virginia* (New York: Harper and Row, 1964).

11. Thomas Jefferson, *The Papers of Thomas Jefferson,* 8th ed., ed. Julian Boyd (Princeton: Princeton University Press, 1953), 184–85.

12. I am using the term "witnessing" in the sense recently introduced into historical discourse by Stephen Greenblatt in *Marvelous Possessions: The Wonder of the New World* (Chicago: University of Chicago Press, 1991). The term, used often in the

Enlightenment period, focuses on actual observation as distinct from learning through the reading of texts.

13. This was also a major validating point for other scholars writing on ethnology at this time. See Samuel Stanhope Smith, *An Essay on the Causes of the Variety of Complexion and Figure in the Human Species,* ed. Winthrop Jordan (Cambridge: Harvard University Press, 1965); Benjamin Smith Barton, *New Views on the Origin of Tribes and Nations of America* (Philadelphia: n.p., 1797); and Robert E. Bieder, "Due gentlemen di Filadelfia e il loro contributo alle origini dell'antropologia americana," *La ricerca folklorica* 32 (1995).

14. Greenblatt, *Marvelous Possessions,* 126.

15. Berkhofer, *White Man's Indian,* 77–80.

16. Barton, *New Views;* Benjamin Smith Barton, "Observations and Conjectures concerning certain Articles which were taken out of an ancient Tumulus, or Grave, at Cincinnati," *Transactions of the American Philosophical Society* 4 (1799): 181–215; Bieder, "Due gentlemen di Filadelfia."

17. Reginald Horsman, *Race and Manifest Destiny* (Cambridge: Harvard University Press, 1981), 114.

18. Again, I use the term *representation* to indicate a construction of "reality" by an individual, class, or culture. In this sense I follow, among others, Edward W. Said in *Orientalism* (New York: Vintage, 1978) and more recently Hayden White in *The Content of the Form: Narrative Discourse and Historical Representation* (Baltimore: Johns Hopkins, 1987).

19. The term is Russett's. See *Sexual Science,* 48; Robert E. Bieder, *Science Encounters the Indian, 1820–1880: The Early Years of American Ethnology* (Norman: University of Oklahoma Press, 1986), 55–80.

20. David De Giustino, *Conquest of Mind: Phrenology and Victorian Social Thought* (London: Croon and Helm Press, 1975); Bieder, *Science Encounters the Indian,* chap. 3.

21. Bieder, *Science Encounters the Indian,* 70–76.

22. Russett, *Sexual Science,* 24, 48.

23. For a more extensive account of bone collecting, see Bieder, *Science Encounters the Indian,* 64–70; Robert E. Bieder, *A Brief Historical Survey of the Expropriation of American Indian Remains* (Boulder: Native American Rights Fund, 1990), 7–17; Robert E. Bieder, "The Return of the Ancestors," *Zeitschrift fur Ethnologie* 118 (1990): 229–40; and Robert E. Bieder, "The Collecting of Bones for Anthropological Narratives," *American Indian Culture and Research Journal* 16:2 (1992): 21–33.

24. Bieder, *Science Encounters the Indian,* 20–103.

25. Haraway, *Primate Visions*, 288. See also Robert M. Young, "Science *Is* Social Relations," *Radical Science Journal* 5 (1977): 229–40.

26. Bieder, *Science Encounters the Indian*, chap. 3; Horsman, *Race*.

27. Albert Gallatin, "Notes on the Semi-civilized Nations of Mexico, Yucatan, and Central America," *Transactions of the American Ethnological Society* 1 (1845): 175.

28. James McCulloch, *Researches, Philosophical and Antiquarian, Concerning the Aboriginal History of America* (Baltimore: Fielding Lucas, 1829), 14–15.

29. Henry R. Schoolcraft, *The Literary Voyager or Muzzenigum,* ed. Philip P. Mason (East Lansing: Michigan State University, 1962), 16.

30. Henry R. Schoolcraft, *Algic Researches, Comprising Inquiries Respecting the Mental Characteristics of the North American Indians,* 2 vols. (New York: Harper and Row, 1839).

31. Schoolcraft quoted in Bieder, *Science Encounters the Indian,* 170.

32. Henry R. Schoolcraft, "Mythology, Superstitions and Languages of the North American Indians," *Literary and Theological Review* 2 (1835): 118; Henry R. Schoolcraft, *Personal Memoirs of a Residence of Thirty Years with the Indian Tribes on the American Frontiers* (Philadelphia: Lippincott and Grambo, 1851), 468–71; John Freeman, "Religion and Personality in the Anthropology of Henry Schoolcraft," *Journal of the History of Behavioral Sciences* 1 (1965): 301–13; Bieder, *Science Encounters the Indian,* 183–93.

33. Gallatin, "Notes," 181, 191; Joseph R. Buchanan, *Outline of Lectures on the Neurological Systems of Anthropology, as discovered, demonstrated and taught in 1841 and 1842* (Cincinnati: Buchanan's Journal of Man, 1854), appendix 4; R. S. H. "Sketches of American Life: Indian Women," *The Literary World* 3 (June 24, 1848): 401–2.

34. George W. Stocking Jr., *Race, Culture and Evolution: Essays in the History of Anthropology* (New York: The Free Press, 1968), chap. 3; John S. Haller, *Outcasts of Evolution: Scientific Attitudes of Racial Inferiority, 1859–1900* (Urbana: University of Illinois Press, 1971), 78–79.

35. Haller, *Outcasts,* 19–20.

36. Ibid., 37–39; Russett, *Sexual Science,* 30–31, 52.

37. Elizabeth Fee quoted in Russett, *Sexual Science,* 31.

38. Edward J. Pfeifer, "United States," in *The Comparative Reception of Darwin,* ed. Thomas F. Glick (Austin: University of Texas Press, 1972), 168–206; R. J. Wilson, *Darwinism and the American Intellectual* (Homewood IL: Dorsey Press, 1967); Richard Hofstadter, *Social Darwinism* (Boston: Beacon Press, 1955); Charles Rosenberg, "Science and American Social Thought," in *Science and Society in the*

United States, ed. David Van Tassel and Michael Hall (Homewood IL: Dorsey Press, 1966), 135–62.

39. T. D. Stewart, "The Effects of Darwin's Theory of Evolution on Physical Anthropology," in *Evolution and Anthropology: A Centennial Approach,* ed. Betty J. Meggers (Washington DC: Anthropological Society of Washington, 1959), 20–21.

40. Robert J. Braidwood, "Archaeology and the Evolutionary Theory," in *Evolution and Anthropology,* 84.

41. Quoted in D. S. Lamb, "A History of the United States Army Medical Museum: 1862–1917," Ms. in National Museum of Health and Medicine (n.d.): 56–56b; Bieder, *Historical Survey,* 35–52.

42. Bieder, *Historical Survey,* 23–52; Douglas Cole, *Captured Heritage: The Scramble for Northwest Coast Artifacts* (Seattle: University of Washington Press, 1985).

43. Thomas R. Trautmann, *Lewis Henry Morgan and the Invention of Kinship* (Berkeley: University of California Press, 1987), 58–83.

44. Quoted in Bieder, *Science Encounters the Indian,* 229.

45. Quoted in ibid., 220.

46. Quoted in ibid., 241–42.

47. Curtis Hinsley, *Savages and Scientists: The Smithsonian Institution and the Development of American Anthropology, 1846–1910* (Washington DC: Smithsonian, 1981), 137–40; Arnold Krupat, *Ethnocriticism: Ethnography, History, Literature* (Berkeley: University of California Press, 1992), 63–66.

2

Curtis M. Hinsley Jr.

Digging for Identity

Reflections on the Cultural Background of Collecting

If they've lost their lands, it's because they could not come up with the proper ancestors.—Ariel Dorfman, "The Lone Ranger's Last Ride"

Telling Stories

Q. Is it true that the valley of the Mississippi shows signs of the passage of a race of men more civilised than those who inhabit it today?

A. Yes. I have often come across fortified works which bear evidence of the existence of a people who had reached a fairly high state of civilisation. Whence did that people come? Whither did it vanish? There is a mystery there. But one cannot doubt that it existed, and nothing indicates that the Indians of our day are the remnants thereof.

Thus Sam Houston responded to the queries of Alexis de Tocqueville on the last day of 1831 (Tocqueville 1971: 254–55). The visiting Frenchman dutifully recorded the answers in what became known to scholars as *Notebook E: Miscellaneous papers which cannot be easily classified. Notes. Reflections. Ideas.* Which category of the miscellaneous Tocqueville had in mind for Houston's opinions of the moundbuilders of America is unknown, and understandably so, for his informant was transmitting widely shared notions that were at once unclassifiable and—allowing for differences of detail—seemingly unquestioned. They were, indeed, cultural reflections: an American self-dialogue performed over several generations, noted and ingrained by the 1830s, and constantly confirmed through the most common activities: digging and collecting, touching and telling. Thus was a democratic archaeology—an archaeology of democracy—formed and practiced early in the Republic; thus was a founding American myth established and rooted.

In its fullness the myth lasted only another half century, until its explosion by the Cyrus Thomas "mounds survey" for the Smithsonian Institution's Bureau of American Ethnology in the 1890s. But the common democratic activities continued:

1900

I hope the Bureau [of American Ethnology] will not give up the archaeological field and if they conclude to continue and want the benefit of my studies this winter, I will carry it on for them. I know where the old Walpi burial ground is and it is full of ancient ware which could be extracted with little expense. (Jesse Walter Fewkes, archaeologist, to Frederick Webb Hodge, Smithsonian Institution, 18 January 1900, Hodge-Cushing Papers, Southwest Museum, Los Angeles)

1924

It was sickening to an archeologist to see the skeletons chopped to pieces with hoes and dragged ruthlessly forth to be crushed underfoot by the vandals—who were interested only in finding something to sell, caring nothing for the history of a vanished people. . . . What could I do? There was no way of stopping the . . . destruction of so much that might have been of value to science—so I made the best of it and bought from the diggers, and from those who had financed them, such of the artifacts as I thought we needed. (Mark Harrington, archeologist, qtd. in Harrington 1991: 26)

1991

I know some boys that make $20,000 in the wintertime digging pots. Ain't but just a very few diggers . . . they're farmers . . . they drive tractors and anything else they can do. They make enough money in the wintertime so they don't do nothin' in the summertime. They sit on their ass until next winter. (Harry Elrod, Arkansas "night digger," qtd. in Harrington 1991: 27)

"Who," Paul Carter asks in *The Road to Botany Bay*, "are more liable to charges of unlawful usurpation and constitutional illegitimacy than the founders of colonies?" (1988: xvi). And who, therefore, more desirous of creating the founding and legitimating myths that secure title to the land? Carter continues, *apropos* of the English naming and settlement of Australia, by asking: "When archaeologists 'push back' the date of first aboriginal settlement, who gains?" And he answers: "the increase of knowledge increases our control. For it is we Europeans who associate antiquity with 'a rich cultural heritage'. In discovering the Aboriginal past, we demonstrate our piety towards the household gods of our own history: the very variousness of Australia's cultural origins suggests an epic potential. The very

elusiveness of any convincing cause-and-effect pattern becomes, paradoxically, evidence of a special destiny" (xviii–xix).

Three hundred years ago the eastern seaboard of North America was, like
the eastern coast of Carter's Australia somewhat later, spotted with a tenta-
tive and insecure array of settler colonies, shallowly rooted and still ambiva-
lently committed to permanence. A century later, in the politically tumul-
tuous first decade of the new nation, Euroamerican settlers began crossing
the Appalachian chain through western New York, Pennsylvania, and Virginia, secured in their intentions by national government ordinances designed for the gridding, mapping, and occupying of the Ohio River Valley.
Linear road to square mile, wagon-train circle to rectilinear community, it
was a massive enterprise of Euclidean ordering. The settlers found mile after
mile of disorder: thick forests, flowing rivers, daunting Indian opposition—
and numerous mysterious, artificial mounds. The ever-curious Thomas
Jefferson, describing the factual and the fabulous of his native land to a
European audience at this time (1784), recorded the excavation of a burial
mound in his northern Virginia locale: he cut a deep and wide trench,
discovered layered bones and stones and estimated a total burial of possibly
one thousand persons over time. He closely examined the skull and jawbone
of a child, commented on the relative states of osteological decay, and mused
upon the relationship of such mounds to the living Indians of the region:
"But on whatever occasion they may have been made, they are of considerable notoriety among the Indians; for a party passing, about thirty years
ago, through the part of the country where this barrow is, went through the
woods directly to it, without any instructions or inquiry, and having staid
about it for some time, with expressions which were construed to be those of
sorrow, they returned to the high road, which they had left about half a
dozen miles to pay this visit, and pursued their journey" (Foner 1944: 118).

Jefferson cited no source for this (in all likelihood) apocryphal account.
Nor did he indicate whether he closed over the mound excavation. But
his musing and his wondering became famous through endless repeating:
"Great question has arisen from whence came those aboriginals of America?"

Whence indeed? Jefferson's questioning voice ran through a century of
digging and trenching. The line of inquiry has been traced in detail (Tax
1973; Silverberg 1968; Deuel 1967; Willey and Sabloff 1980) and requires
only brief summation here: Although Euroamericans first encountered the
human earthworks of the Ohio and Mississippi River valleys in the 1780s,
it was not until after the War of 1812 that Caleb Atwater of Circleville,
Ohio, undertook a systematic local investigation. The American Antiquarian Society published his results in 1820. Atwater saw in the earthworks evidence of occupation by a sedentary, law-abiding people. Concor-

dant with the general tendency to explanation through migration and borrowing in this period of Anglo-American anthropology (Stocking 1973: xciv), Atwater hypothesized a migration from northern Asia at a remote period; a long, fixed abode for the "moundbuilders" in North America; and subsequent movement southward to found the ancient civilizations of Mexico and Peru. He further suggested that a second migration, from southern Asia by ancestors of modern Indians, had superseded the original occupation of North America.

Even more speculative observers followed Atwater. Most attempted to account for the differences between the supposed high civilization of the ancient moundbuilders and the more primitive condition of the historical Indians by positing waves of migration, war, and displacement. James H. McCulloh was both cautious and exceptional in arguing against affinities based on superficial study of artifacts in the mounds, which might be, he said, merely the products of a common human nature. His *Researches Philosophical and Antiquarian Concerning the Aboriginal History of America* (1829), a compilation of the work of others, concluded that ancestors of the present Indians came from the South and built the mounds. In this respect, too, McCulloh remained a distinctly minority voice. Despite disagreement over the identity of the moundbuilders, most investigators agreed that the ancient inhabitants of America had originated elsewhere—probably Asia.

By the 1840s the empirical and theoretical state of North American archaeology could only be described as chaotic (cf. Willey and Sabloff 1980: 23–25). John R. Bartlett expressed a common judgment when he wrote that "the practical [site] investigations made from time to time by various individuals, have not been sufficiently thorough and extensive, nor have they developed sufficient data to warrant or sustain any definite or satisfactory conclusions" (Bartlett 1848: 4). In 1848, however, the Smithsonian Institution published Epraim G. Squier and Edwin H. Davis's *Ancient Monuments of the Mississippi Valley*, the most systematic and closely edited archaeological study to that time. Squier and Davis not only established a new standard of comprehensiveness in their survey, they also began to throw shadow on the notion of a separate moundbuilder race—if only by keeping the question open. A series of local studies followed under Smithsonian and private sponsorship in the 1850s (e.g., Squier 1851; Whittlesey 1852; Lapham 1855). The appearance in 1856 of Samuel F. Haven's *Archaeology in the United States*, also under the aegis of the Smithsonian, marked the end of this phase of mounds enthusiasm. Haven rejected the more outlandish speculations about migrations—Welsh, Greeks, Egyptians, Phoenicians—but allowed the possibility of Asiatic connections. Significantly, he saw no evidence of a "moundbuilder race" distinct from historical Indian peoples. Joseph Henry, secretary of the Smithsonian, lauded Haven as spokesman for a new era of soberly factual, descriptive archaeology. Still, four more decades passed before the publication of Cyrus Thomas's authoritative mounds survey for the Bureau of American Ethnology (1894) consigned the moundbuilders to the status of myth.

Recounting the intellectual rise and fall of moundbuilder theory obscures, however, its persistence and cultural resonance. In fact, by concentrating on exotic ideas and characters, such as the flamboyance of a Constantine Rafinesque or the poetic incantations of Welsh Indians and Phoenician exiles, we may miss a greater significance: the elemental consistency—what Paul Carter calls the "epic potential"—of the moundbuilder presence in early American culture. It seems clear that a metanarrative was under construction. Over nearly a century, the central, ubiquitous trope of the moundbuilder genre was war—specifically, reluctant self-defense and ultimate defeat of the lost moundbuilders in battle—as the Ohio Valley landscape became an imaginative locus and stage for prehistoric romance, valor, and tragedy. Robert Silverberg noted in his classic study of moundbuilder theories that "what delighted the public most keenly was the stirring depiction of a great empire dragged down to destruction by hordes of barbarians" (1968: 82). Josiah Priest, writing in 1833, conjured armies "equal to those of Cyrus, of Alexander the Great, or of Tamerlane the powerful" flourishing their trumpets and marching to battle on the shores of the Ohio River; he envisioned, too, "the remnant of a tribe or nation, acquainted with the arts of excavation and defense, making a last struggle against the invasion of an overwhelming foe; where, it is likely, they were reduced by famine, and perished amid the yells of their enemies" (qtd. in Silverberg 1968: 83–84).[1] In thirty months Priest's best-seller, *American Antiquities and Discoveries in the West*, sold twenty-two thousand copies (Silverberg 1968: 83).

It is understandable that many have viewed such constructions as rather transparent justifications for violent land-grabbing ("after all, it wasn't theirs in the first place"), and the contemporaneity of such myth-making with the tragic removal of eastern tribes certainly underscores the interpretation. As Stephen Williams comments in *Fantastic Archaeology*, "The Myth of the Moundbuilder could grow happily without too many tawdry reminders of the dispossessed" (1991: 43). True enough, but one suspects that there is still more to the matter. For example, consider the authorial positioning in most moundbuilder accounts. The following passage is from a late (1885) version:

However long the war [of expulsion] may have continued it is evident that the final overthrow or expulsion of the Mound Builders was sudden and complete. It was so sudden that the mines of Lake Superior were abandoned in such haste as to cause them to leave their implements behind. On the temple mounds were probably scenes of carnage. They never would submit to give up these places without first offering the most stubborn resistance. Those mounds were covered with multitudes of brave and self-sacrificing men, who shed their blood in defense of their home and religion. The grim visage of war, with its relentless fury, burst upon them, carrying death and destruction in its course. At last this peaceable and quiet people were expelled from the Ohio, and never after returned. (MacLean 1885: 145)

In such passages—dozens of similar tone and construction could be adduced—the observer/narrator stands apart, invariably at a "bird's-eye" vantage, surveying both action and aftermath, an invisible guide painting and narrating history into the landscape, investing it with moral meaning. Stephen Greenblatt has analyzed, in a different context, a complex "fusing" of landscape, artifact, and text in which physical objects such as rocks become partially "transformed": "These objects are natural features in the landscape, but they are features that have been transformed by the momentous events that have occurred on them and still more by the simple physical presence, the literal weight, of certain remarkable persons. . . . [T]he weight of sacred events and persons has a profound effect, an effect related to but distinct from the principle of possession by virtue of physical occupation." Such natural objects (e.g., hills, rocks) "are then further transformed into texts by virtue of their embeddedness in sacred stories" (1991: 38–40).[2]

In the textual transformation of moundbuilder landscapes, both theatrical description and a panoramic eye (Carter 1988: xix–xxi) are at work, combining to create historical diorama and moral drama. The moundbuilder genre bears some resemblance in this respect to Mary Louise Pratt's European "imperial eye" (Pratt 1992: 58–67)—notably in its authorial invisibility—but the claimstaking power of the moundbuilder-destruction narrative lies precisely in the creation of morally charged spaces in the landscape by providing tragic drama, so to speak, on the spot.

One of the critical debates of the early American republic concerned the relationship between historical time and the national landscape. The panoramic historians of the early Republic—George Bancroft, Francis Parkman, William Prescott, John Motley—were concerned above all with the violent, dialectical energies of history operating over space; as Ann Douglas has summarized this complex phenomenon, "their common interest was less in liberty than in 'the course of empire,' the phenomena of discovery, expansion, struggle, conquest and exploitation" (1977: 176). The preoccupation was widely expressed in the cultural productions of the antebellum decades: Fourth of July speeches, Thomas Cole landscapes, Revolutionary War memorials, as well as the many volumes of Bancroft's history, and it reached an apotheosis of sorts with the brilliant sacralizing of space in the Gettysburg Address (Wills 1992). Understandably, then, the particular force of the prehistoric narrative lay in granting primal, deep meaning to place(s), in a timescape prior to the speeches, signings, and other nation-building acts of more recent national memory. Prehistory was deep history, deep knowledge, deep belonging.

The attribution of deep, grounded history enjoyed all the more resonance if the narrator was a contemporary political-military hero, such as William Henry Harrison, governor of Indiana Territory, president of the United States (quite briefly), and author of *Discourse on the Aborigines of the Ohio Valley* (1839). As ethnologist Henry Rowe Schoolcraft exhorted the New League of the Iroquois (a fraternal order of young white males in Rochester, New York) in 1846: "[the Indians'] history is, to some extent, our history," a past full of deeply tragic and poetic events. "The tomb that holds a man derives all its moral interest *from* the man, and would be destitute of it, without him. America is the tomb of the Red man" (Schoolcraft 1846: 29; emphasis in original). Schoolcraft's phrases captured the appeal of this moralizing, nationalizing discourse and the earth-embeddedness of its message: "No people can bear a true nationality, which does not exfoliate, as it were, from its bosom, something that expresses the peculiarities of its own soil and climate. . . . [America must draw] from the broad and deep quarries of its own mountains, foundation stones, and columns and capitals, which bear the impress of an indigenous mental geognosy" (Schoolcraft 1846: 29).

Digging Dirt

> Oh Metz you don't know how I want to be out in the field with you. I am just crazy to get away from here this spring.–(F. W. Putnam in Cambridge to Charles Metz in southern Ohio, 31 March 1883)

> I must see the wonderful things in the mounds. Oh dear if I were only with you instead of having to peg away at so much outside work.–(Putnam to Metz, 10 December 1883)

> Oh I wish I were on the Little Miami [River] now going into the Turner Mound instead of talking fish breeding.–(Putnam to Metz, 7 March 1884)

Frank D. Sanborn, adherent and biographer of Henry David Thoreau, tells the charming story of a summer's day in 1839 when the Thoreau brothers, John and Henry, took a group of schoolboys out for a trip on the Concord River. Henry rowed to a spot on the shore and announced that, if he had a spade, he could possibly uncover there an Indian "rude fireplace." Returning the next week with the boys, he asked them: "Do you see anything here that would be likely to attract Indians to this spot?" He pointed to a protecting hillside and a spring of cool water: "Then, moving inland a little farther, and looking carefully about, he struck in his spade several times, without result. Presently, when the boys began to think their young teacher and guide was mistaken, his spade struck a stone. . . . He soon uncovered the red, fire-marked stones of the long-disused Indian fireplace; thus proving that he had been right in his conjecture. Having settled the point, he carefully covered up his find and replaced the turf,—not wishing to have the domestic altar of the aborigines profaned by mere curiosity" (Sanborn 1917: 205–6).

If the epic potential of American prehistory marked one pole of significance for aboriginal remains in the early republic, the other pole of significance was deeply personal: reenactment through display of "native" intuition, the opportunity to demonstrate possession of that "indigenous mental geognosy" of which Schoolcraft spoke—in short, the chance to "play Indian." The charm of the Thoreau anecdote lies precisely in his boyish ego: he displays his "Indianness," and thus his essential Americanness, by digging beneath the surface of the present to expose the Indian past and show off the result to equally boyish admirers ("proving that he had been right in his conjecture")—including, not incidentally, Sanborn, who preserves and narrates the story to posterity. James Fenimore Cooper's Leatherstocking similarly retraces ancient trails; Daniel Boone intuits his way home, Indian-like, through miles of dense forest; anthropologist Frank Hamilton Cushing, exploring southern Arizona in 1887, claims to be able to sense the remains of ancient dwellings under the earth, instructing his Mexican workers exactly where to dig for architectural outlines; and another century later *American Way Magazine* (November 1989) features Stanford anthropology professor John Rick, an "Achiever" who is pictured sitting "with son Matthew" at Zuñi pueblo, "an important archaeological excavation site," practicing prehistoric stone toolmaking. So it continues: American history and literature have been populated from the start by intermediary figures who undergo wilderness quests and return to enrich and regenerate their settler culture with aboriginal knowledge (Slotkin 1974). The distinctive character of the dig-as-quest lies in its mimetic quality—"thinking like an Indian," knowing where to look, etc.—and most particularly in the presumed knowledge, or reknowing, of place.

It seems to have been, too, largely a male quest: father to son, brother to brother, mentor to student, digging up aboriginal America contributed to (if it did not specifically create) a shared male identity that, one might suggest, went *through* the earth (and its inhabitants). From George Wharton James's *What We Can Learn from the Indians* through the YMCA's father-son Indian Guides program of the 1950s to, perennially, the Boy Scouts of America, the (imagined) Indian of the past has served as resource for more than iconic or metaphorical purposes. As often as not, nineteenth-century backyard archaeology served as a field for male play. While the heroic explorers of classical (Old World) archaeology—Austin Henry Layard, Heinrich Schliemann, Sir William Matthews Flinders Petrie—came across as intrepid, aggressive male force, straining on behalf of empire and civilization (Hinsley 1992), their American counterparts were more likely to appear as hybrids between social misfit and clamdigger. "My uncle tells me you have been pitching into some clam heaps at Salisbury," the young George Peabody wrote to Jeffries Wyman in 1867, referring to the latter's kitchen-midden fieldwork.[3] S. Wier Mitchell, student of Wyman, lovingly recalled such an outing: "I had once a like pleasure in raking over an Indian shell-heap with Wyman. The quiet, amused amazement of the native who plied the spade for us was an odd contrast to Wyman's mood of deep interest and serious occupation. He had a boy's pleasure in the quest, and again displayed for me the most ready learning as to everything involved in the search. Bits of bones were named as I would name the letters of the alphabet: bone needles, fragments of pottery and odds and ends of nameless use went with a laugh or some ingenious comment into his little basket. In truth, a walk with Wyman at Mount Desert [Maine] was something to remember" (Mitchell 1875: 356).

The meaning of such moments between men a century and a half ago is only beginning to be studied today (Rotundo 1993; Carnes and Griffin 1990). Historians Ann Douglas (1977) and Mark Carnes (1989) have suggested, in quite different ways, that in the course of the nineteenth century American males were largely displaced from "official" Protestant church circles by women, contributing to a loss of outlet for spiritual and emotional expression. Carnes argues that the fraternal orders to which millions of middle-class men belonged between 1830 and 1900 provided "an alternative form of religion, of family life and of social organization" for such men (1989: 158). The overwhelmingly male world of fieldwork in such sciences as geology, surveying, and archaeology may have provided a sense of continuity and male lineage as well; certainly, as in fraternal orders, elements of ritual were developed and maintained (as, for example, John Wesley Powell's "Great Basin Lunch Mess" at the U.S. Geological Survey at the end of the century).

But what was so appealing about prehistoric graves? Some scholars have recently examined the enthusiasm for cemeteries—especially rural cemeteries—in the middle third of the nineteenth century (Linden-Ward 1989; Sloane 1991). Gary Wills, in a remarkable analysis of "the culture of death" in the early American republic, has suggested that the cemetery was intended to be a training ground for aesthetic sensibilities, a feminized landscape of reverie and appreciation of the sublime (Wills 1992: 63–89). Perhaps, then, the burying of one's own dead in sacred spaces increasingly gendered as feminine, and the digging up of prehistoric burials in spaces associated with war, under conditions of male tutelage, may have been not only contemporaneous but complementary as well.

What I am suggesting is that, as is obliquely indicated in the anecdote of Thoreau's Indian campfire, the earthly (pre)history of America was inarticulately but intimately associated with the nation's future manhood, with the Indian's earth serving as a medium of lineage. William Henry Harrison began his 1839 *Discourse on the Aborigines of the Valley of the Ohio* by expressing concern over the deleterious effects of fiction on the moral and patriotic fiber of the nation's (male) youth and exhorting the importance of studying the nation's history. He then proceeded to portray the defeat on the banks of the Ohio of the moundbuilders—a brave and advanced agricutural people, "assailed both from their northern and southern frontier," ultimately forced downriver, southward to Mexico, making their last stand at the mouth of the Great Miami River:

> This position . . . , strong by nature, and improved by the expenditure of great labor, directed by no inconsiderable degree of skill, would be the last hold they would occupy and the scene of their last efforts to retain possession of the country they had so long inhabited. The interest which every one feels, who visits this beautiful and commanding spot, would be greatly heightened, if he could persuade himself of the reasonableness of my deductions. . . . That this elevated ridge, from which are now to be seen flourishing villages, and plains of unrivalled fertility, possessed by a people in the full enjoyment of peace and liberty, . . . whose matrons, like those of Sparta, have never seen the smoke of an enemy's fire, once presented a scene of war, and war in its most horrid form, where blood is the object, and the deficiencies of the field made up by the slaughter of innocence and imbecility. That it was here that a feeble band was col-

lected "remnant of mighty battles fought in vain," to make a last effort for the country of their birth, the ashes of their ancestors, and the altars of their gods. (Harrison 1839: 225–26)

Harrison's urgency to establish and inculcate martial valor in the core of nationhood arose from a fear that, in contrast to classical Europe, the very pristineness of the American land—its historical and moral virginity— would deprive its male youth of the vital object lessons that only history could teach. James McCulloh, in his *Researches on America* of 1817, was even more explicit on this point:

> When we contemplate the ruins of Ilium, of Carthage, or of Palmyra, amid all our regret and concern for their fate, yet there are incidents connected with their histories which we reflect on with enthusiasm. Though they have fallen, their fame yet lives. The genius and talents of antiquity still shine with original splendour, and the triumph of time and desolation, over the labors of man, is incomplete. . . .
>
> But with the mounds and fortifications of America, we have no agree-able, no inspiring associations. We see "The bones of men in some forgotten battle slain,"—we see the labours of their hands desolated,— their rude works overgrown by the trees of the forest;—whilst the nation that raised these works, together with her patriots and her heroes, has disappeared, and has not left even a name behind. And the last and only remembrance of them which has reached our time, has been only pre-served by a recollection of their ruin and extermination, and the terrible effusion of their blood. (McCulloh 1817: 209–10)

"Not left even a name behind." Digging in the prehistoric dirt and con-structing heroic tales on what they found, these men of the early American republic faced the challenge of replacing a heritage of heroism built on classical literacy with an identity constructed of shards and bones and preliterate silence. No wonder they kept digging.

Collecting Things

> Six months later they had become archaeologists, and their house looked like a museum.–(Gustave Flaubert, *Bouvard & Pecuchet*)

> I have mounted my entire collection of bone relics from the Ferris ancient cemetery, on Spanish cedar boards faced with heavy plain white paper.–(Charles Metz, Madisonville, Ohio, to F. W. Putnam, Peabody Museum, 1882)

Somewhere on the continuum between epic potential and personal identity one finds local community and private property. Over the nineteenth century the moundbuilders/Indians and their material cultural legacies became objects to collect, curiosities for cabinets and mantelpieces, intellectual and material property to buy and sell—but all the while they also served as icons of belonging, enmeshed and embroiled in the dynamics of community and regional growth. In *The Search for Order, 1877–1920* (1967) Robert Wiebe demonstrated the remarkable strength of local and regional identities in post–Civil War America; a recent study of the 1893 Chicago World's Fair by James Gilbert confirms that most Americans came to the White City self-identified as citizens of a state or inhabitants of a locale: the state pavilions were heavily visited (Gilbert 1994). In other words, throughout the nineteenth century Americans saw themselves locally. Despite the seismic shock and reorientations of the Civil War, even at the turn of the twentieth century national identity was still more veneer than grain.

Tocqueville, it is true, had noticed a curious ambivalence toward place in the young American democracy; he perceived a troubling lack of attachment and a wanderlust, which he attributed to the horizontal leveling of social relations and ease of physical movement. Accordingly he viewed with some skepticism American protestations of love of home—a skepticism shared by subsequent commentators (see, e.g., Somkin 1967) and reinforced by a historiography that has frequently portrayed mobility as inherently upward (it is not) and rootedness as, somehow, failure. Many young men went "west," to be sure, and some moved incessantly; but many others stayed and built.

It is hard to collect on the move. Collecting in Euroamerican cultures "has long been a strategy for the development of a possessive self, culture, and authenticity," as individual identity formation under capitalism features "the individual surrounded by accumulated property and goods" (Clifford 1988: 217–18). The image of Thoreau's farmer sardonically comes to mind: "How many a poor immortal soul have I met well nigh crushed and smothered under its load, creeping down the road of life, pushing before it a barn seventy-five feet by forty, its Augean stables never cleansed, and one hundred acres of land, tillage, mowing, pasture, and wood-lot!" (1962: 108).

According to Susan Stewart, acts of collecting—finding, selecting, ordering, displaying—establish control over environment, objects, and history. The process may be especially prominent, she argues, under conditions of pioneering, exploration, and settlement, when claims to locale, landscape, and property are tenuous, and thus may involve "intentional ignoring of proprieties of native history and topography" (Stewart 1984: 153).

Collecting and the dynamics of settlement were, it seems, intimately entwined. As Euroamericans established themselves in the Ohio and Mississippi Valleys between the Revolution and the Civil War, they formed communities that brought forth and expressed in countless ways a strong sense of competitive loyalty to place. In addition to his theorizing about ancient migrations, Caleb Atwater composed rhapsodic passages celebrating the "wisdom and benevolence of the Creator" in providing the Rocky and Allegheny Mountains as barriers to protect the wide, green valley of mid-America (Atwater 1833: 373–74). Ohio Valley residents became furious over the sale of Edwin H. Davis's collection of Ohio antiquities to England, and they subsequently guarded their personal collections fiercely. Collecting for Harvard's Peabody Museum in 1875, Lorenzo Stratton wrote to Frederick Putnam from Cumberland County, Tennessee, of the immediate situation in the field:

> Heretofore it has been quite easy and at small expense to procure of the country people anything in this line that was found. But last Spring the great freshets brought so much to light that agents for the European Museum were attracted by it and offered higher prices than I had been in the habit of paying. But my living here gives me some advantage after all. I am some how not pleased to have all our curiosities go to London & Vienna & Paris and should your [*sic*] lack anything in this line I think by being on hand after the next Spring freshets that I might make something of a collection. You will please write if anything is wanted.[4]

In the same year Edward Foreman, trying to persuade Cincinnati collectors to loan artifacts to the Smithsonian for the 1876 Centennial, reported his growing frustration: "All the collectors freeze hard to their specimens and are unwilling to let them go out of their sight. . . . They know & feel that Ohio has great claims to consideration on account of her antiquities."[5] Locally, too, competition was fierce: Charles Metz, a Madisonville physician who became F. W. Putnam's valued collaborator, chuckled over the discomfiture of Cincinnati gentlemen at his discoveries and collections (Fort Ancient, Turner): "I am exceedingly pleased that the Turner mounds have proved so rich; how it does make the Cincinnati fellows squirm."[6]

Foreman was experiencing and Metz was expressing a behavioral characteristic of America's unique history of regional growth: prideful claim-staking of the locale through collection and display of local materials—Schoolcraft's "columns and capitals" of national architecture. Men who saw themselves as civic leaders quite literally brought their backyards indoors to the parlor, sorting and assorting their natural and aboriginal neighborhoods into boxes, shelves, and mantelpiece museums. The practice was widespread and highly respected among the aspiring boosters of small-town America—especially among physicians and businessmen, it appears (McKusick 1991; Shapiro 1976). Individual collectors customarily combined to form a local "scientific and literary" society for occasional comparison, display, and discussion of their finds; eventually some men might establish larger horizons with statewide or even national organizations (such as the Smithsonian or Harvard's Peabody Museum). But the general tendency was centripetal, toward local pride and jealousy of outside meddling (see, e.g., McKusick 1991 for a revealing case study in Iowa). Sale of a collection to outsiders, except under severe financial stress (which often occurred, in fact), brought serious ostracism.

Consider Butler County in southern Ohio. In 1885 J. P. MacLean, a local businessman, published *The Mound Builders*, which featured an "investigation into the archaeology" of Butler County. MacLean's volume, heavily illustrated and complete with a township-by-township description of sites and a foldout map of the county, recounted the loss of a local collection sold at auction out of the county, "and perhaps the country." In addition, "traders, hucksters and speculators" had been recently coming through the county picking up artifacts, "barter[ing] trinkets for them, placing fictitious values on their wares." These conditions had spurred, in 1878, the formation of the Butler County Geological and Archaeological Society, whose purposes were "to become better acquainted with the science of geology and archaeology, and to form a cabinet which shall contain representative specimens of all the fossils that may be found within the county, and to preserve all such aboriginal relics as may be obtained" (MacLean 1885: 227). The society undertook a survey of all private archeological collections in the county and published a summary chart of owners and contents (figure 1). The city council of Hamilton, Ohio, appropriated $150 for display cases for the society's collections, which were to be placed in the public library.

The rhetoric and the actions of the good folk of Butler County in the 1880s speak of stability, commitment, and belonging in the face of larger, external forces of disruption, dishonesty, and ignorant greed. Marshall McKusick's careful study of the "Davenport Conspiracy" of the same period indicates similar intentions and fears in that town. It seems, finally, that the formation of American communal and individual identities came to involve digging, collecting, and displaying aboriginal "relics," and that these activities were fully accepted as an index of civic respect and belonging. At the same time, surrounding "moundbuilder landscapes" were appropriated and domesticated as uniquely regional and national (figure 2). Whatever

ARCHÆOLOGICAL CABINETS IN BUTLER COUNTY, OHIO.

TOWNSHIP.	NAME.	Axes.	Hatchets.	Hammers.	Chisels.	Fleshers.	Spades.	Pestles.	Mortars.	Knives.	Rimmers.	Arrow Heads.	Spear Heads.	Pipes.	Polishers.	Shuttles.	Wands.	Crescents.	Tubes.	Gorgets.	Pendants.	Images.	Pottery.	Miscellaneous.
Hamilton	W. P. Cooch	14	9	6	1	1	1	8			6	50	50	1	1		1		1					1
"	W. H. Harr	12	22			9		11				213	213		8		6				1	3	1		4
"	Wm. Huber, Jr.	15	6			7	2	11			9	252	127				8			2	2				5
"	Dr. J. L. Kirkpatrick	39	35	7	5	15	1	12		1	13	236	53			2			1	1					324
"	G. B. McKnight	40	7			9		5		1	12	120	50								12				
"	J. P. MacLean	51	15			47		36		1	13	200	200								1				
"	J. G. Shepherd	20	6			10	2	10				50	127												
"	F. I. Whitehead	8	1			20	1	6		2		12	25	2					2	1					
Lemon	P. W. Clark	9	4	1	1	4		3	1			40	21					1			1	1	1		
"	J. P. Sharkey		3		5		3	5		1		12	13				9								
"	R. T. Shepherd	1	6		1			8		1	1	145	294								10	3			
"	Marion Warner	1	3	2		2		1	1	1		34	33							1	5	1			4
"	F. W. Whittaker	3	8			2		2		1		25	25				3	2		2	4	1	1		
"	Prof. J. A. Clark		4	3	4	3	6	16	1	4	4	275	294	2						1					66
Oxford	J. L. Evans	8	20	1		6	1	2			13	24	25				3		2		4				
"	Minter Morris	9	4					6		1		20	19												
"	John R. Bevis		5	1		6		10		2	3	107	66	1			3						1		
"	Llewellyn G. Bonham	26	1					19			11	238	63				3						1		
"	Samuel Gath, Jr.	14		16	4			10			1	107	82				3								
Morgan	D. A. McCord		20	1	5	6		16		1	11	42	33						1				1		
"	Prof. B. F. Marsh	33	4	1			1	12		1	4	34	25				2					1			3
"	Wm. and Richard Martindale	24	5	1				10				70	9				3								
"	John M. Stern	10	1					19		2		80	64	1										1	
Ross	Harry Wetmore	33	32			6		13				50	50			2							1		5
"	Richard Brown	1					1			1	2	4	66											1	
"	J. and J. Demoret		5					5	4		11	10	61												
"	Col. Griffin Halstead	10	1		4		1	7				80	17				2				1	1		1	
"	Harvy Ross	18	10		5	10	8	16		1		60	30		4						3	5		1	18
"	Mrs. John Ross	20	6	2		13	6	17			4	60	180		1						1	3			2100
St. Clair	W. L. Clark	8	10		1	4	1	6		1	1	30	30	1	1		1			1		5			
"	John T. Waldron	5	2			1		3				12	20												
Union	Mrs. Eliza Walker	8	6			1		2	2			25	2							2	1				5
"	J. K. Aydelott	1	1			1	1	3	1	1	1	20	3				1			1	1	1		2	
"	Judge Z. W. Selby											12													
Wayne	Dr. J. B. Owsley	20	38		1	6	1	23		25		56	44	1		1	3		2	5					6

Figure 1. Archaeological Cabinets in Butler County, Ohio. From J. P. MacLean, *The Mound Builders* (Cincinnati: R. Clarke, 1885)

Figure 2. The Domestication of a Prehistoric Landscape: The Grave Creek Mound in West Virginia. From E. G. Squier and E. H. Davis, *Ancient Monuments of the Mississippi Valley* (New York: Bartlett and Welford; Cincinnati: J.A. and U. P. James, 1848).

we may think of these activities today, more than a century ago, acting out their roles as responsible inheritors of the stewardship of the continent (or their corners of the continent), the settler citizens of Cincinnati, Davenport, and numerous other communities absorbed their predecessors—mysterious moundbuilders, savage Indians—into their own identities and into the civilized future they foresaw for their America.

Notes

1. After the Civil War, as settlement crossed the Mississippi and entered the new southwestern territories, the trope was transferred virtually intact to the new region: here the peaceful "cliffdwellers," presumed ancestors to the sedentary pueblo peoples, served as analogue to the moundbuilders. William Henry Holmes daydreamed while standing in the ruins along the San Juan River in the summer of 1876: "With their fields and flocks and the supply of water within the hands of an enemy . . . [they] must have perished or have crept down the cliffs to fight or yield to the foe. They are gone now indeed and have been for centuries and now like vandals we invade their homes and sack their cities. We . . . carry off their earthen jars and reprimand them for not having left us more gold and jewels." (WHH,4:30).

2. For a historically and currently resonant example of sacralization of a rock, see the discussion of "King Philip's Chair" in Krech 1994, esp. 63, 166.

3. Peabody to Wyman, 27 May 1867, Jeffries Wyman Papers, Countway Library, Harvard University Medical School, Boston.

4. Lorenzo Stratton to F. W. Putnam, 27 December 1875, Peabody Museum Papers, Harvard University Archives, Cambridge MA.

5. Edward Foreman to Spencer F. Baird, November [n.d.] 1875, National Anthropological Archives, Smithsonian Institution, Washington DC.

6. Charles Metz to F. W. Putnam, 29 September 1882, Peabody Museum Papers Harvard University Archives, Cambridge MA.

References

Atwater, Caleb. 1833. *The Writings of Caleb Atwater*. Columbus OH: Author.

Bartlett, John R. 1848. *The Progress of Ethnology. An Account of Recent Archaeological, Philological, and Geographical Researches in Various Parts of the Globe, Tending to Elucidate the Physical History of Man.* Transactions of the American Ethnological Society 2. New York. Appendix.

Carnes, Mark C. 1989. *Secret Ritual and Manhood in Victorian America*. New Haven: Yale University Press.

Carnes, Mark C., and Clyde Griffen, eds. 1990. *Meanings for Manhood: Constructions of Masculinity in Victorian America*. Chicago: University of Chicago Press.

Carter, Paul. 1988. *The Road to Botany Bay: An Exploration of Landscape and History*. New York: Alfred A. Knopf.

Clifford, James. 1988. *The Predicament of Culture: Twentieth-Century Ethnography, Literature and Art*. Cambridge: Harvard University Press.

Deuel, Leo. 1967. *Conquistadores without Swords: Archaeologists in the Americas*. New York: Schocken.

Dorfman, Ariel. 1983. *The Empire's Old Clothes: What the Lone Ranger, Babar, and Other Innocent Heroes Do to Our Minds*. New York: Pantheon.

Douglas, Ann. 1977. *The Feminization of American Culture*. New York: Alfred A. Knopf.

Flaubert, Gustave. 1976. *Bouvard & Péchucet*. Trans. A. J. Krailsheimer. Baltimore: Penguin.

Foner, Philip S., ed. 1944. *Basic Writings of Thomas Jefferson*. Garden City NY: Halcyon House.

Gilbert, James. 1994. On the Two Texts of the Fair. Unpublished Paper.

Greenblatt, Stephen. 1991. *Marvelous Possessions: The Wonder of the New World*. Chicago: University of Chicago Press.

Harrington, Spencer P. M. 1991. The Looting of Arkansas: How One State Copes with the Erosion of Its Cultural Heritage. *Archaeology* 44:3 (May/June): 22–30.

Harrison, William Henry. 1839. *A Discourse on the Aborigines of the Valley of the Ohio*.

Transactions of the Historical and Philosophical Society of Ohio 1, pt. 2. Cincinnati. 217–67.

Haven, Samuel F. 1856. *Archaeology in the United States*. Smithsonian Contributions to Knowledge 8. Washington: GPO.

Hinsley, Curtis M. 1992. Images of the Archaeological Expedition, 1850–1920. In *Alonzo Pond and the 1930 Logan Museum Expedition to North Africa: The 1985 Beloit College Symposium*, ed. Larry B. Breitborde. Beloit WI: Museums of Beloit College. 1–24.

Krech, Shepard, III, ed. 1994. *Passionate Hobby: Rudolf Frederick Haffenreffer and the King Philip Museum*. Providence: Haffenreffer Museum of Brown University.

Lapham, Increase. 1855. *Antiquities of Wisconsin*. Smithsonian Contributions to Knowledge 7. Washington: GPO.

Linden-Ward, Blanche. 1989. *Silent City on a Hill: Landscapes of Memory and Boston's Mount Auburn Cemetery*. Columbus: Ohio State University Press.

MacLean, J. P. 1885. *The Mound Builders: Being an Account of a Remarkable People That Once Inhabited the Valleys of the Ohio and Mississippi, Together with an Investigation into the Archaeology of Butler County, O*. Cincinnati: Robert Clarke & Co.

McCulloh, James H. 1829. *Researches, Philosophical and Antiquarian, Concerning the Aboriginal History of America*. Baltimore: Fielding Lucas, Jr.

—— 1817. *Researches on America; Being an Attempt to Settle Some Points Relative to the Aborigines of America, &c*. Baltimore: Joseph Robinson.

McKusick, Marshall. 1991. *The Davenport Conspiracy Revisited*. Ames: Iowa State University Press.

Mitchell, S. Wier. 1875. The Scientific Life. *Lippincott's Magazine*: 352–56.

Pratt, Mary Louise. 1992. *Imperial Eyes: Travel Writing and Transculturation*. London: Routledge.

Regis, Pamela. 1992. *Describing Early America: Bartram, Jefferson, Crèvecoeur, and the Rhetoric of Natural History*. DeKalb IL: Northern Illinois University Press.

Rotundo, E. Anthony. 1993. *American Manhood: Transformations in Masculinity from the Revolution to the Modern Era*. New York: Basic Books.

Sanborn, Frank B. 1917. *The Life of Henry David Thoreau*. Boston: Houghton Mifflin Company.

Schoolcraft, Henry Rowe. 1846. *An Address, delivered before the Was-Ah-Ho-De-No-Son-Ne, or New Confederacy of the Iroquois, at its Third Annual Council, August 14, 1846*. Rochester NY.

Shapiro, Henry D. 1976. The Western Academy of Natural Sciences of Cincinnati and the Structure of Science in the Ohio Valley, 1810–1850. In *The Pursuit of Knowledge in the Early American Republic: American Scientific and Learned Societies from Colonial Times to the Civil War*, ed. Alexandra Oleson and Sanford C. Brown. Baltimore: Johns Hopkins University Press. 219–47.

Silverberg. Robert. 1968. *Mound Builders of Ancient America: The Archaeology of a Myth*. Greenwich CT: New York Graphic Society Ltd.

Sloane, David Charles. 1991. *The Last Great Necessity: Cemeteries in American History*. Baltimore: Johns Hopkins University Press.

Slotkin, Richard L. 1974. *Regeneration through Violence: The Mythology of the American Frontier, 1600–1860.* Middletown CT: Wesleyan University Press.

Somkin, Fred. 1967. *Unquiet Eagle: Memory and Desire in the Idea of American Freedom, 1815–1860.* Ithaca: Cornell University Press.

Squier, Ephraim G. 1851. *Aboriginal Monuments of New York.* Smithsonian Contributions to Knowledge 2. Washington: GPO.

Squier, Ephraim G., and Edwin H. Davis. 1848. *Ancient Monuments of the Mississippi Valley: Comparing the Results of Extensive Original Surveys and Explorations.* Smithsonian Contributions to Knowledge 1. Washington: GPO.

Stewart, Susan. 1984. *On Longing: Narratives of the Miniature, the Gigantic, the Souvenir, the Collection.* Baltimore: Johns Hopkins Press.

Stocking, George W., ed. 1973. *Researches into the Physical History of Man, by James Cowles Prichard.* Chicago: University of Chicago Press.

Tax, Thomas G. 1973. The Development of American Archeology, 1800–1879. Ph.D. diss., University of Chicago.

Thomas, Cyrus. 1894. *Report on the Mound Explorations of the Bureau of Ethnology.* Bureau of Ethnology Annual Report for 1891. Washington: GPO. 3–370.

Thoreau, Henry David. 1962. *Walden and Other Writings,* ed. Joseph Wood Krutch. New York: Bantam Books.

Tocqueville, Alexis de. 1971. *Journey to America,* ed. J. P. Mayer. Garden City NY: Anchor Books.

WHH. Field Notes of W. H. Holmes in charge of the San Juan Division of the Geological Survey of the Territories. *William Henry Holmes Papers: Random Records of a Lifetime,* vol. 4. Washington DC: Archives of American Art, Smithsonian Institution.

Whittlesey, Charles. 1852. *Ancient Works in Ohio.* Smithsonian Contributions to Knowledge 3. Washington: GPO.

Wiebe, Robert H. 1967. *The Search for Order, 1877–1920.* New York: Hill & Wang.

Willey, Gordon R., and Jeremy A. Sabloff. 1980. *A History of American Archaeology.* 2nd ed. San Francisco: W. H. Freeman and Company.

Williams, Stephen. 1991. *Fantastic Archaeology: The Wild Side of North American Prehistory.* Philadelphia: University of Pennsylvania Press.

Wills, Gary. 1992. *Lincoln at Gettysburg: The Words That Remade America.* New York: Touchstone.

Part 2

The Current Debate

3

Robert J. Mallouf

An Unraveling Rope

The Looting of America's Past

The place was north-central Texas, on a high, windy terrace overlooking the muddy Colorado River in 1961. The boy sat on a wind-sculpted slab of sandstone, letting the early rays of sunshine chase away the chill of a late autumn morning. The teenager had been to this spot many times before. It was a magical place—a place littered with the memories of past peoples. The ground here was scattered with flint that glinted in the early morning sunlight. There were remnants of ancient stone hearths and burned rock ovens in seeming disarray across the terrace surface. The boy sat spellbound—lost in thought about what this Indian campsite and its inhabitants must have looked like so long ago. Like so many other youngsters, he had little in the way of education to draw on in his mental reconstruction of the camp. The concept of "prehistory" was essentially unknown to him. His small-town schooling in history began with the arrival of Columbus in the New World, and his concepts of Native Americans were based more on Western movies of the 1950s than anything else. Unbeknownst to him at the time, the boy's craving for knowledge would eventually lead him to a university and ultimately into a career in archaeology. Many years later he would anxiously return to the ancient campsite, only to find it devastated by looting and construction.

Like the boy on the river, most people have an inherent curiosity about the past, but in varying degrees of intensity. The romanticism and mystery of the past lead some people to seek higher levels of understanding through reading and other educational outlets. For the vast majority of people, however, this same curiosity—undirected and unchanneled—evolves into an entangling web of unwitting and even purposeful destruction. Were it not for a fortuitous set of circumstances, the boy on the river might well have become a collector of antiquities. He easily could have ended up channeling his intense interest into digging archaeological sites as a hobby or even as a commercial enterprise. The site-looting phenomenon, which is so rampant in Texas and other states, should be of particular interest and concern to archaeologists, conservationists, and Native Americans and other minorities, for it is clearly the single most destructive force to our nation's historical legacy.

The Looting Plague

The mindless looting of archaeological sites is not unique to Texas. It is, in fact, a worldwide phenomenon with roots in antiquity. The temples, mounds, cemeteries, villages, and campsites of all past human populations—from the Orient to the ancient Near East, from Europe to Mesoamerica—have been subjected to looters since time immemorial. In addition to being the principal targets of treasure hunters, archaeological sites also have provided convenient sources of stone, lime, fill, and other building materials for local residents. Many ancient temples have ended up as stone linings for irrigation ditches and wells or as walls for houses. Many of the world's greatest archaeological treasures continue to be attritioned away in this manner.

In the United States today, much of the destruction of archaeological resources is attributable to site looters and commercial relic hunters. In Texas archaeologists usually apply the term "looter" or "pothunter" to people who carry out unregulated and unscientific "digs" of archaeological deposits to obtain artifacts for their personal collections or for sale. While construction projects such as pipelines, reservoirs, and highways take a heavy toll on archaeological resources, looters are particularly ruinous because they carry out selective destruction, targeting the best-preserved and scientifically most important sites for digging. Literally thousands of archaeological sites—primarily of prehistoric Native American populations— are subjected to varying degrees of damage by hobbyists and looters each year in Texas alone. This appalling situation continues to worsen as the state's population grows, particularly in areas within easy reach of urban centers.

Who are these people and why do they destroy the irreplaceable historical legacy of Texas and other states with seemingly callous abandon? After years of educational and legislative efforts, why have we been unable to stem the tide of destruction of our past, and what are our prospects for the future? In order to address these and other questions, we might first make a brief examination of the emotional underpinnings of the collecting mentality. We must return momentarily to the boy on the river.

The *Querencia*

> Under normal conditions, the average coyote ranges habitually within
> certain boundaries. This is his querencia—his haunt.—J. Frank Dobie,
> *The Voice of the Coyote*

A *querencia* is a favorite place or area that one frequents as often as possible—
for any of a variety of reasons. It is a place that is remembered fondly—even
longingly—during necessary separations. A *querencia* may be a favorite fishing spot, a special meadow in the woods, or even a particular tree or a
comfortable boulder in a river. Most people have a *querencia,* the memory of
which conjures up almost mystical feelings, even if it now exists only in
their mind's eye. Walden Pond was Henry David Thoreau's *querencia.* The
boy's *querencia* was an Indian campsite on the bank of the Colorado River in
Texas. It is here, at one's *querencia,* that critical development of a person's
attitudes toward archaeological and other resources commonly takes place.

Artifact collectors frequently begin their hobby as a result of their feelings for a haunt they have come to love. It may be the place where they
found their first arrowhead, and it can be just as captivating to an adult as to
a child, regardless of gender or race. Initially collectors return over and over
again to the same sites where they began their hobby, thus establishing
strong emotional bonds to their find spots. With some people the *querencia*
becomes an end in itself, and they may focus their collecting on only a
single site or a few sites for years, or even a lifetime. In the best of scenarios
the collector may come to the realization that the site, if left undisturbed,
has the potential for yielding important scientific information about the
past, and he or she may become a self-appointed guardian of the site.
Unfortunately, this is the exception rather than the rule.

More typically, the hobbyist continues to build his or her artifact collection within an informational vacuum of his or her own creation—until the
act of collecting begins to override both curiosity and concern for the site.
As the acquisition of artifacts gains in importance, the hobbyist tends to
broaden his or her search to other sites and eventually to other areas. A
growing obsession with artifacts then leads to interaction with other collectors with similar interests. Friendly competitions to see who can find the
most or best artifacts are frequently the result, as the act of collecting
becomes more of a communal than an individual activity. As more sites are
included, the feeling of *querencia* may be obscured.

As his or her artifact orientation continues to grow, and is promoted by
associates, the hobbyist may begin to enter the realm of the true "pothunter," or looter. This significant and often irreversible step occurs when
the hobbyist turns to digging—as well as surface collecting—archaeological

deposits. Hobbyists are frequently led into excavation by pothunting associates or by their discovery of a feature such as a burial or cache that simply cannot be ignored. After an initial taste of digging, some will turn back to surface collecting as a hobby but many will not. Those who elect to continue the digging of sites become ever more deeply entrenched, as what began as a hobby evolves into a truly destructive obsession. Their sphere of associates may expand once again to include "hard-core" pothunters and even commercial looters. Having reached this advanced stage, the hobbyist turned looter becomes hardened to most educational and preservation efforts. He or she may actively seek out professional archaeologists to "authenticate" artifacts in order to increase their monetary value, and he or she may become actively involved in the buying and selling of specimens at artifact shows. The looter has become a machine of destruction.

Bookburning as a Satisfying Hobby

The level of destruction wrought on archaeological resources by looters cannot be overstated. Archaeologists often refer to archaeological sites as being "pages of our history book." Each site destroyed is a page torn out of that book. The uncontrolled digging of sites destroys most of the scientific information therein, because artifacts, features, soils, pollens, and other diagnostic materials must be found and recorded in their original context in the ground in order to be meaningful. In tearing through an archaeological deposit, the looter disrupts and mixes the contents of the deposit, thus effectively destroying the site (figure 1). The result of the looter's quest is a pile of objects having little or no meaning, often stored in cigar boxes in a garage or carefully mounted in geometric patterns and hung on a living-room wall. Because archaeological sites are our only sources of information for more than twelve thousand years of human history in the New World, their unnecessary destruction by people intent on personal gain is both deplorable and heartrending. The appalling rate at which our most significant archaeological sites are being destroyed puts archaeologists—who are focused on the tedious and time-consuming task of reconstructing the past—in a futile race against time.

The principal targets of looters in Texas are cemeteries and mounds of the late prehistoric Caddo Indians in northeast Texas, deep stratified midden sites and rock shelters of central Texas, late prehistoric Antelope Creek–phase villages of the Texas Panhandle, and rock shelter and sinkhole sites of southwest and trans-Pecos Texas (figure 2). Caddo Indian cemeteries, many dating as early as the ninth and tenth centuries A.D., are among the hardest hit, particularly by commercial looters who sell the burial

Figure 1. A looter at work in a deeply stratified prehistoric campsite near a major urban area in central Texas. The massive destruction to this privately owned site was carried out over a few weeks. Photo by Bob Parvin.

artifacts (primarily pottery vessels, pipes, arrow points, and skulls) through outlets in Arkansas and other states. In the sandy soils of northeastern Texas and adjoining areas of Oklahoma, Arkansas, and Louisiana, looters locate the cemeteries through the use of "pokey rods"—long metal probes that are pushed into the sandy soil to "feel" for bone and objects.

Having located a cemetery, small groups of looters will arrange a transaction with the landowner to allow them to dig, or they may lease the site for the purpose of digging the burials. In some cases bulldozers are used to strip off the overlying archaeological deposits in order to quickly locate burial pits, which are then dug up swiftly by hand. Skeletal material is crushed and thrown out of the burials during the frantic search for artifacts. In cases where a landowner refuses access, it is relatively common for looters to trespass on the property at night and to dig burials by lantern light— often working under tarps to avoid detection. Landowners typically have little or no idea as to the quantity, significance, or monetary value of artifacts removed from their property. What once was an ancient Caddo Indian cemetery or Plains Indian village is left with the appearance of an artillery battlefield, artifacts are sold, and the looters move on to their next target. The effect of looting activities on archaeologists—who understand

Figure 2. One of many looted prehistoric rock-shelters in the Lower Pecos region of southwest Texas. Dry rock-shelters containing perishable artifacts such as basketry, matting, and human burials are a major target of looters throughout the southwestern United States. Photo by Bob Parvin.

the full scientific significance of the loss—is debilitating. The resulting loss of information for researchers, and ultimately the public at large, is staggering and irretrievable. The cultural and aesthetic loss to Native Americans and other victimized ethnic groups is beyond comprehension.

The Looters' Holy Writ

Site looters have a variety of procedures and imagined justifications. They often attempt to achieve legitimacy by grouping together in loose organizations or by obtaining membership under false pretenses in bona fide archeological societies. Looters use the terms "archaeology" and "archaeologist" loosely, often misrepresenting themselves as avocational or professional archaeologists to landowners and others. Some carry false business cards that imply an affiliation with a university, the state, or a professional archaeological organization. They subscribe to artifact magazines that pretend to decry the destruction of sites on the one hand while promoting looting and the sale of artifacts on the other. Looters sometimes write pseudoscientific articles for pseudoscientific collectors' journals and artifact magazines in order to convince others of their concocted archaeological qualifications.

They justify their sale of artifacts—often from looted human burials—as being healthy "free enterprise" and loudly label as socialists or communists those who would question the appropriateness of applying the concept of free enterprise to a market in human remains and burial goods. They may sell the artifacts directly to wealthy collectors or to art galleries that cater to wealthy and sometimes politically influential collectors. Most transactions are conducted in cash in order to avoid paying taxes.

Looters brand professional archaeologists as greedy antiquarians who want to monopolize archeological sites for their own personal gain, and they often do so with little or no knowledge of what the science of archaeology is all about. At times they join forces with dealers of antiquities and influential artifact collectors to fight legislation intended to protect archaeological sites and cemeteries. Rarely are looters able to see beyond their own lifetime to a world in need of the archaeological sites that they are in the process of destroying. Only rarely would they care.

If this summation seems overly harsh, one should consider the long-range consequences of humanity's losses to looters. Much of what we know about ancient Egypt today comes from the discovery by archaeologists of just a few tombs—such as that of Tutankhamen—that were fortuitously overlooked by looters through the ages. Commercial looters have wreaked havoc for generations on the ancient population centers of Mesoamerica and South America, even to the extent that armed guards are necessary to protect sites during ongoing scientific investigations.

Closer to home, most of the more significant Puebloan sites of the southwestern United States have at one time or another suffered massive destruction at the hands of looters. Even the waters of time cannot conceal important archaeological sites from looters, as attested by the many devastated historical shipwrecks in our coastal zones. When viewed over the long term, the cumulative effects of selective looting are almost beyond comprehension. Clearly archaeologists today are left with only a fraction of the data base needed to adequately reconstruct past human lifeways. As this sentence is being written, literally hundreds of archaeological sites are being surface collected and dug by hobbyists and looters across Texas alone.

Milquetoast Advocacy

Archaeologists in Texas and other states have been publishing ominous warnings about the long-term consequences of site looting since at least the early 1930s. Witness Victor J. Smith's early observation that: "It is important that complete [records] be secured before the damage or entire loss of materials make investigations impossible. For example, pictographs in certain localities are being rapidly obliterated by vandals, and treasure hunters are digging into much valuable scientific material with no thought of the havoc being wrought to anthropological research" (1931: 60–61). Or Cyrus N. Ray's lament that: "Many of the Indian burial sites in this section have been destroyed either by readers of current treasure hunting fiction books who take their stories seriously or by arrowhead collectors who imagine that every aboriginal grave must be full or arrowheads. . . . it is very unfortunate that people who care nothing for the preservation of the bones of these curious human types for scientific study continue to excitedly dig into every rock pile found" (1932:63).

Although archaeologists have long been aware of the magnitude of site destruction, they have been ineffectual at combating the problem. This circumstance is in part the result of a double standard long practiced by archaeologists in their dealings with artifact collectors and site looters. In effect, the archaeological community has advanced a kind of contradictory "milquetoast advocacy" in dealing with hard-core looters—on the one hand using only gentle persuasion to discourage their activities, while on the other hand soliciting whatever tidbits of information the looters are willing to part with concerning their "finds."

In Texas archaeologists have for years attempted to validate this approach with polemic debate over whether confrontation would result in the looters going underground with their finds and their booty, thus ruling out any possibility of an information flow. As archaeologists have waffled in typical fashion over this issue, hard-core looters have happily plied their trade, confident in the knowledge that the archaeological community was divided, manageable, and loath to interfere. A secondary outgrowth of this deplorable situation has been the ever-increasing sophistication with which looters manipulate and beguile archaeologists and preservationists.

In reality the archaeologists' continued fears about the potential loss of information that might occur if hard-core looters were to go underground with their discoveries are, at best, unfounded. While it is true that many significant archaeological discoveries have been made by persons other than archaeologists, such finds have typically been reported to professional archaeologists by hobbyists, avocational archaeologists, or the general public—and not by hard-core looters and pothunters. The amount of truly substantive archaeological data contributed through the years by looters—who are identifiable by their shovels and picks, not their pencils and notebooks—would hardly fill a thimble. The decades-long reluctance of archaeologists to remove their gloves to confront looting head-on has only served to fuel the fires of site destruction. This is particularly true of states like

Texas, where more than 95 percent of the land is privately owned and not subject to federal or state antiquities laws.

The small size of the archaeological community also has been a major factor limiting site preservation efforts. There are untold thousands of artifact collectors for each archaeologist in the United States, thus necessitating the use of television and the printed word to spread the preservation message. The development of educational messages and programs for television are expensive and time-consuming, and relatively few archaeologists are willing to take time away from pressing research and contractual deadlines to devote to fundraising and preservation issues. In those cases where strong, effective media messages have been successfully developed, their use has been restricted almost exclusively to educational television channels that are either unavailable to, or unlikely to be watched by, the majority of collectors and looters. Devising ways of bringing the preservation message to expensive prime-time television is a major challenge that has yet to be faced by the archaeological and preservationist communities.

Under Not-So-Friendly Fire

The rise of Native American repatriation issues during the past twenty years has served to further exacerbate the site-looting problem. As archaeologists have become more preoccupied with the pressing issues of reburial and have come increasingly under attack by Native American and other proponents of repatriation, pothunters and antiquities dealers have enjoyed unprecedented periods of worry-free looting and commercial trade.

In their quest to win the emotionally and politically heated issue of repatriation, Native Americans have ignored the much larger, insidious problem of site looting. The remarkable apathy characteristically shown by Native Americans toward looters and pothunters has long perplexed archaeologists—particularly those who have dedicated the better part of their careers to preserving Native American sites, including cemeteries. Attempts by archaeologists to promote anti-looting activism among Native Americans have failed. Ironically, those archaeologists who have alone carried out the brunt of the battle against looting through the decades suddenly found themselves targeted as "looters" by Native Americans during the 1980s. During long-running repatriation debates, archaeologists ultimately squared off against each other, and Native Americans broke down into a multitude of pan-Indian and tribal factions.

The eventual passage of the Native American Graves Protection and Repatriation Act at the federal level was viewed as a major victory by

Native Americans, but it is a hollow victory at best. While Native Americans busy themselves seeing that major universities and museums turn over our nation's only scientifically derived collections of skeletal remains, burial artifacts, and ceremonial objects for reburial, enterprising looters are diligently churning through the last remaining Native American cemeteries for objects to collect and sell. The invaluable and irreplaceable scientific collections contained in our university repositories and museums are miniscule in comparison to those in the hands of collectors and looters nationwide. For each human burial scientifically excavated by archaeologists, untold numbers have been ripped out of the ground by looters. While preoccupied with a tree, Native Americans and archaeologists are losing what remains of the forest.

Archaeologists should learn from their experiences with legislators and with the media during the repatriation debate. Archaeologists have been variously portrayed by Native American activists as callous, self-serving, greedy, ruthless, and racist. Activists have effectively exploited the emotional appeal of their cause to the general public with the aid and abetment of the media. Archaeologists, on the other hand, have typically found themselves backed into defensive positions, often having to explain the basic tenants of archaeological inquiry as well as the differences between professional archaeologists, avocational archaeologists, museum curators, hobbyists, collectors, looters, pothunters, and antiquities dealers to legislators and journalists—all usually in five minutes or less. Archaeologists generally have not fared well in these situations—much to the delight of the activists. In fact, the explanatory difficulties faced by archaeologists clearly point out weaknesses in the way the discipline has interacted—or more appropriately, not interacted—with the public through the years.

Large segments of the general public still do not recognize the difference between nineteenth-century antiquarianism and modern archaeology. In their efforts to provide simple and succinct fare for the public, journalists have further blurred the distinction between artifact collectors and professional archaeologists. The failure of archaeologists to effectively make their case understood should be a major point of concern, particularly when one considers that, having won the first battle, Native American activists can now be expected to pursue additional legislative efforts aimed at further restricting the freedoms of legitimate archaeological practitioners. If nothing else, archaeologists should now be more cognizant of the need for professionalization of the discipline.

A very positive outcome of the repatriation debacle, however, has been the passage in numerous states of new laws to protect unmarked human burials and burial objects on both public and private lands—while at the same time allowing for legitimate scientific inquiry. Passage of such legislation has proven more difficult in some states than in others, for a variety of reasons. In Texas hard-fought attempts beginning in 1987 to pass unmarked burial legislation were thwarted first by antiquities dealers and influential artifact collectors and most recently (1993) by pan-Indian organizations narrowly focused on repatriation of scientific collections rather than in-ground protection for burials. During an attempt at passage in Texas in 1993, state officials were wrongly accused by pan-Indian groups of trying to circumvent the federal Native American Graves Protection and Repatriation Act, and professional archaeologists and museum officials were—as expected—portrayed as being collectors and looters during public testimonies by pan-Indian representatives. Through it all, looters have proceeded with their destruction of Native American sites and burials on private property, particularly in the prehistoric Caddo Indian area of northeastern Texas.

States that have successfully passed new legislation to protect unmarked burials, of course, now are faced with the task of how to effectively enforce the law. Looters, like poachers, are difficult to catch, particularly when they are focusing their activities on private property, with or without landowner permission. Once apprehended, vigorous prosecution of looters must be pursued by local law enforcement officials if the law is to be truly effective. Since many looters make large profits from the sale of artifacts from burials (figure 3), it is the prospect of incarceration, rather than fines, that should be emphasized. At any rate, the acid test for these new state laws will be in courts across the country, and both scientific and Native American communities should strive to provide cooperative support of law enforcement efforts.

Entering the Twenty-First Century

Archaeologists and Native Americans alike could profit from a period of self-analysis and reflection as we enter the twenty-first century. The Native American community, which, as a result of the repatriation issue, is again entangled in the question of who does or does not qualify as "Indian," should attempt an objective analysis of what it expects to gain through past and projected future confrontations with scientists and preservationists. Having once targeted the archaeological community as the "enemy" and easily won, Native Americans perhaps should now ask if archaeologists are not, in fact, their most natural and consistent ally in their battle to gain respect and equality in American society.

Do Native Americans really believe—as they have so often expressed dur-

Figure 3. Commercial looters sell much of their booty to antiquities dealers, who in turn exhibit and sell the items in artifact shows like this one in west-central Texas. Photo by Bob Parvin.

ing heated debate—that scientific findings concerning their cultures are meaningless in light of their cultures' oral traditions? Do they honestly believe that scientific findings, which have proven so important in dispelling the prejudiced European concepts of the "barbarous savage," are somehow deleterious to their well-being? And are Native Americans truly indifferent to the fact that their unwritten cultural legacy is seriously endangered because of the activities of uncaring looters, or do they simply feel powerless to do anything about it?

These are but a few of the questions in need of careful thought by Native Americans. They are questions that should be answered not for the sake of archaeologists but, rather, for the long-term well-being of the respective cultures. The ancient cultures that are brought back to life by archaeologists through studies of their carefully excavated artifacts provide critical linkages for Native Americans to their past. Through the act of reburial, our only hard evidence of the existence of some ancient cultures will be permanently expunged from the archaeological record. Are proponents of repatriation really correct in assuming that future generations of Native Americans will approve of what is transpiring today? Again, these are important questions that are best considered outside the sphere of emotional debate, and without pressing external influences.

The large-scale attrition of archaeological sites by looters on the one hand, in conjunction with the repatriation of our only scientifically derived collections from major museums and universities on the other, should certainly provide archaeologists with food for thought in contemplating the future of archaeological research and site preservation. Clearly archaeologists have not performed well in critical areas of public education and public involvement—and our past tendency to ignore living Native American peoples has come full circle. The pantheon of errors created by archaeologists, Native Americans, artifact collectors, journalists, and the public during the debate over repatriation has generally served as a recipe for chaos rather than enlightenment. But we can and should learn from the experience.

It should be patently obvious to archaeologists by now that the public cannot be expected to benefit educationally from archaeological research when the end products of such research are long, mind-numbing technical reports. The inability of much of the public—including many Native Americans and journalists—to differentiate at this late date between professional archaeologists and artifact collectors is alarming and graphically points out the urgent need for archaeologists to critically evaluate their philosophy and goals.

If archaeological research culminates in products that are only comprehensible to other archaeologists, how can we hope to generate anything beyond a superficial, arrowhead stereotype in the public at large? If the public has no conception of what we mean by the term "scientific potential," how can we expect a positive reaction to our requests for public participation in site preservation? After a century of scientific archaeological research in the New World, our library shelves should be teeming with highly readable texts for children and adults alike—but they are not, and prospects appear dim for the immediate future. We should cater to the average person's innate curiosity about the past through clearly written, informative, and well-conceived educational and preservation-oriented publications. Since it is the romanticism of the past that invites public interest in the first place, archaeologists should become more adept at writing popular narratives that encourage, rather than discourage, emotional linkages to the past. If carefully conceived, these writings can be achieved without loss of archaeological and historical accuracy.

Even more importantly, archaeologists must seriously enter the realm of telecommunications to carry their message to the public. While this only can be achieved through cooperative ventures with people specializing in the preparation of audiovisual materials, archaeologists can help to provide raw material both for archival and educational use by filming aspects of their survey, excavation, and laboratory projects. Communications specialists need to be added to—and must become integral parts of—our archaeological staffs. Perhaps the single greatest challenge facing archaeological preservationists is the need to become involved with prime time, as well as educational, television. The exorbitant costs of placing public service announcements on prime time television are intimidating, but ways must be found to pursue this goal if we are to reach the majority of the public. In addition, archaeologists must stay abreast of and exploit developments in computer-related communications, which undoubtedly will set the pace for the future. Archaeologists and other preservationists cannot hope to stem the tide of site looting by themselves, but they must be willing to provide a focus for the efforts of all concerned. The active participation of landowners, teachers, Native American and other ethnic groups, avocational archaeologists, and various other segments of our population are critical to success. We should expand existing programs, such as avocational stewardship networks and planning groups, that directly involve the public in archaeological research and preservation. Whenever possible, open-door educational tours for the public at active scientific excavations should be pursued to bring the public into direct contact with professional and avocational archaeologists. An open-door educational approach should definitely be extended to appropriate cultural resource management projects that use tax money. Since we must have the public's help and its funding in order to save our resource base, we must learn to give as much back to the public as we can—it is, after all, a two-way street.

Hard-core looters and commercial artifact dealers, of course, pose a special problem for archaeologists and preservationists, since they typically are oblivious to preservation efforts. On those rare occasions when looters initiate contact with professional archaeologists concerning a significant discovery, we should make an effort to work with them in the interest of the resource base, and we should do so in a very forthright manner. Our educational focus, however, should be centered on those segments of the population that are receptive to our message—particularly children, teachers, landowners, artifact hobbyists, and others. Although terribly destructive, hard-core looters make up a relatively small proportion of the artifact-collecting public, and they can best be dealt with through landowner education and legal avenues. Our potentially most effective weapons in the battle with looters are Native Americans and other victimized ethnic groups, who through activism and emotional appeal could accomplish a great deal more than archaeologists.

I hope that the beginning of this century can be spent wisely in search of new and innovative ways of reaching out to the public and in expanding existing programs that have been tested and proven effective. It should also be a time for healing of wounds between two natural allies—the archaeological and Native American communities. Change cannot necessarily be directed or controlled, and the twenty-first century will undoubtedly see significant changes in archaeology. Importantly, as noted by J. Frank Dobie in *Voice of the Coyote,* "it takes more power of thought to meet change than to make it" (1950:31)

References

Dobie, J. Frank. 1950. *The Voice of the Coyote.* Boston: Little, Brown and Co.

Ray, Cyrus N. 1932. "Archeological Research in Central West Texas." *Bulletin of the Texas Archeological and Paleontological Society* 4: 63–70.

Smith, Victor J. 1931. "Archeological Notes of the Big Bend Region." *Bulletin of the Texas Archeological and Paleontological Society* 3: 60–69.

4

Patricia M. Landau and D. Gentry Steele

Why Anthropologists Study Human Remains

> Let me ask you this question. Why do you study them for? What do you
> get out of it? What's the purpose?–Roger Byrd, Lakota Sioux, 41st
> Plains Conference, Rapid City, Iowa, November 4, 1983

One of the most controversial kinds of studies anthropologists undertake is
that of the biological remains of Native Americans. The motivations of
physical anthropologists to study human remains often seem unfathomable
to some members of Native American communities, and our methods seem
also to be misunderstood. We recognize the differences between the values
and spiritual beliefs of Native Americans and those of other Americans, and
we respect the right of all people to maintain their personal belief and ethical systems. We want to explain the reasons why some physical anthropologists value the study of human biology and history, and why we place so
much importance on the study of human remains. We also want to explain
what kinds of information can be gained from such studies, the methods
used in them, and the impact of these on the remains being studied.

The Native American Graves Protection and Repatriation Act (NAGPRA,
P.L. 101-601) calls for the repatriation of Native American remains whose
cultural affiliation can be determined by a preponderance of evidence. Physical anthropologists are willing to comply with NAGPRA's terms, but the need
remains for long-term study of some skeletal collections before repatriation.

Why Do Physical Anthropologists Study the
Biological Remains of the Deceased?

An innate need to know is universally characteristic of humans, even
though the subjects of our inquiry may vary from culture to culture. Physical anthropologists have an interest in learning just who humans are—their

origins and their heritage. Although no simple statement can explain all the reasons why some physical anthropologists study human remains, one very fundamental reason is that human remains offer direct, tangible evidence of our history, how we have become biologically suited to the many environments in which we live, and how we behave.

Other people have similar interests in origins and heritage, but the means used to answer these questions vary widely. How we come to know ourselves varies from individual to individual as well as from society to society. Some societies rely on personal revelation, on the advice of spiritual leaders, or on oral traditions. Physical anthropologists, like other scientists, adhere to methods that have their roots in the ancient societies of the Mediterranean and North Atlantic. Explanations or hypotheses are proposed to explain relationships between facts or conditions of the physical world. These explanations are then tested by observation of additional measurable facts or physical conditions; if an explanation is supported by these additional observations, it can be accepted as valid or true. The results of the tests of hypotheses or explanations must be repeatable: if an explanation is tested a second or third time the results must be the same as the results of the first test, and if the explanation is tested using the same method on other material, the results of that test must also be the same or very similar. Further, observers should be interchangeable; any trained individual performing the test must get the same or very similar results. If any of these conditions are not met, the explanation is speculative at best or must be rejected.

This method of acquiring knowledge and understanding is based on a belief system that relies on empirical data gathered from the observation of the material world. Knowledge, for those who share this belief system, is gained through the accumulation of many interrelated insights about the issue being studied.

In examining our heritage, physical anthropologists seek to understand the biological history and origins of all humans in all geographical areas. Our focus is on all humankind. While each human society has its own history, all human societies can be linked by migration and intermarriage through time to be categorized as a single species, *Homo sapiens,* humankind. Each society's biological history is an integral part of the complete and continuing story of all humankind.

Why Is the Information We Get from Skeletal Remains Unique, and Why Can't It Be Acquired from Living Peoples?

There are three ways in which data is gathered about past populations: (1) by the study of the artifacts left behind, (2) by the study of the living, and (3) by the study of biological remains. Each of these ways of studying our past has advantages and disadvantages, but the study of the remains themselves has the unique advantage of providing direct information about our ancestors.

Consider questions regarding the health of our ancestors. Did they suffer from the same diseases as we do? Did their particular lifeways or habits subject them to specific diseases and hardships? Were they subjected to new diseases or biological disorders when their lifestyles changed or they came into contact with new peoples migrating into their area? A study of the plant and animal debris discarded in prehistoric living areas gives some evidence of what they ate, and certainly this provides valuable indirect evidence of their health. The study of coprolites, preserved human feces, may reveal more directly what they ate. Further, this line of evidence can give unique information about some of the parasites that may have affected their health. Even the examination of artifacts, such as figurines depicting people who lived in the community, or tools such as lice scratchers or bloodletters, can provide evidence of the health of past peoples. However, each of these lines of evidence is indirect.

A clear example of a health study that documents the singular contribution of studies of human remains is the question of the origin of treponemal disease. Treponemae, a type of spirochetal organism, causes syphilis, pinta, and yaws. Although these diseases are all caused by treponemae, their distribution and mode of transmission are different. Yaws thrives in hot, humid tropical environments worldwide, while pinta is found in the tropical New World. Endemic syphilis is found in subtropical North Africa and the Near East and temperate zones of Asia (Ortner and Putschar 1981). None of these conditions requires sexual contact for transmission. In contrast, venereal syphilis has a worldwide distribution and is spread through sexual contact. It is unclear whether these diseases are all caused by different treponemal organisms. One hypothesis is that all treponemal organisms are descended from an early Old World organism that was not exclusively sexually transmitted (Cockburn 1961); another view suggests that yaws, pinta, endemic syphilis, and venereal syphilis are caused by the same organism and that the physical expression of the disease depends on climatic and social factors like urbanization, sanitation, and population density (Hudson 1963, 1965).

Studies of living populations in which the disease is present and of historical records of the spread of the disease could not determine its origin or how it reacted when encountering new populations. In Europe, a particularly virulent epidemic seemed to spread shortly after the discovery of the Americas. In the New World, syphilis spread rapidly and tragically among Native American populations as they came into contact with Europeans. The examination of prehistoric skeletal remains in the New World, however, has documented the presence of the disease in the Americas before the arrival of Columbus (Bullen 1972; Elting and Sterna 1984; Powell 1988; Reichs 1986). Ample evidence also exists for the presence of syphilis or other treponemal diseases in Europe prior to Columbus' return to the New World (Brothwell 1961; Madrid 1986; Steinbock 1976; Stewart and Spoehr 1967). Knowing this, it has become evident that the disease, probably in the form of a new and virulent strain, reinfected historic Native American populations with tragic results (Baker and Armelagos 1988). The study of syphilis, with the use of prehistoric human remains as evidence, has provided humankind with one of the best documented records of the complex origin, spread, and reinfestation of a population by a contagious and deadly disease. Our understanding of our relationship to all contagious diseases has been dramatically improved by our unraveling of the history of treponemal diseases.

A brief examination of the history of cranial modification in the Americas provides another example of how the study of the biological remains of past peoples furnishes unique and valuable evidence. The basic shape of the human head is roughly globular, but this shape can be modified by placing uneven pressures on the head of a growing child. This uneven pressure can be brought about unintentionally by placing a baby in the same resting position time after time, such as in a cradle board or crib. Intentional alteration of cranial shape also has been practiced on a worldwide basis. Although intentional cranial modification is usually not practiced in North America today, many early Native American groups deliberately altered skull shapes by compressing the heads of infants with bands or flat surfaces. Ninety-two percent of all individuals in a prehistoric Adena population displayed evidence of the intentional modification of cranial shape (Webb and Snow 1945), and an early study of an Ohio population revealed that 77 percent of all crania exhibited evidence of intentional modification (Hooten 1920). By historic times, however, these societies had changed and cranial shape alteration became much less widely practiced. Without the information provided by the study of biological prehistoric remains, the widespread nature of this practice in the Mississippi valley would not be known.

A recent study of the biological remains of a Mimbres population in the American Southwest by Holliday (1993) has added an interesting twist to the story of cranial shape modification in the Americas. Her work has documented that, not uncommonly, infections developed in the bone at the point of contact at which pressure was applied. In some cases this infection was serious enough to endanger the life of the child by directly exposing the underlying brain to infection. Again, the analysis of human remains has provided singular evidence of common health threats in past populations.

Many aspects of prehistoric life would be unknown without the analysis of human remains, and these aspects are not restricted to health, daily activities, and other behaviors. Crow Creek Village, a large fourteenth-century settlement encompassing nearly eighteen acres, was the home to at least 800 people. The analysis of skeletal remains excavated from this site reveals that a minimum of 486 men, women, and children were killed in a massive siege of the village. Roughly 90 percent of the dead showed evidence of scalping, and indications of decapitation were seen in about 25 percent of the victims. Equally important, the presence of healed and healing wounds suggestive of scalping in some individuals indicates that this form of violence was not a unique happening (Willey 1990). The occurrence of this prehistoric massacre would not have been known without the recovery of data from human remains.

The study of human remains also provides useful corroboration of ethnographic accounts of historical events. The analysis of skeletal material from the King site, a Georgia site occupied between A.D. 1535 and 1570, may support accounts of atrocities perpetrated by the Spanish during the early years after European contact (Blakely and Mathews 1990). This study indicates that King site residents enjoyed uncharacteristically good health with relatively low levels of nutritional and environmental stress. Paradoxically, an unusually high death rate was documented. More than 20 percent of the individuals who died displayed cuts and punctures on their bones. The form, angle, and position of the wounds indicated the victims were struck from above with a metal blade at least 60 cm long while facing their assailants. A significant number of these individuals were interred in common graves rather than the single interments seen in the majority of the burials at this site, a burial pattern characteristic of mass disasters in small communities. The victims were predominantly young adult females and people of both genders over forty. Ethnographic and historical data indicate that Native American groups in this time period and area customarily killed young adult males while taking females captive. Thus, if these people were victims of a conflict with another Native American group, we would expect to find mostly young adult males in the common graves and very few females. Therefore, because young adult males appear to have been selectively excluded from the conflict, it appears that these individuals do not represent victims of conflict between Native American groups. Historical and ethnographic sources record that the de Soto expedition sometimes captured older individuals and young females for slave labor and forced prostitution (Hudson et al. 1988). The type of wounds, the demographic identities of the wounded, and ethnographic and historical data indicate that these individuals represent casualties of a Native American–Spanish conflict, most probably an attack by the Spanish on a carefully selected portion of a Native American community, perhaps as part of an attempt to capture slaves.

One of the most amazing aspects of humanity's biological heritage that has been elucidated by the study of human biological remains is cannibalism. Ethnographic and archaeological evidence supporting the rare occurrence of cannibalism in modern humans and our ancestral species of *Homo* is a matter of some debate (Arens 1979; Binford 1981), but direct evidence from the study of human remains clearly indicates that cannibalism, a practice recorded in many other parts of the world (Bowden 1984; Forsyth 1985; Villa et al. 1986), occurred under rare circumstances in the American Southwest as well (Turner 1989, 1983; Turner and Turner 1992; White 1992).

These examples illustrate that information gathered during the analysis of human remains is unique because it provides direct data that can come from no other source. Other anthropological disciplines and ethnographic data can supplement, but not replace, information gathered during the study of human remains. The information gathered from the study of human remains is valuable to physical anthropologists and other scientists because it provides unique direct data and because it allows us to answer questions about prehistoric human life in great depth from many different perspectives.

What Can We Learn about Our Ancestral Origins from the Study of Human Remains?

The colonization of the Americas is one of the largest and most recent events in the spread of humanity throughout the world, which is why it is of such enormous interest to physical anthropologists. Many lines of evidence have been presented to explain the peopling of the Americas, including the study of human biological remains. Christy G. Turner, relying on the study of teeth, has substantiated the other lines of evidence that have indicated that the ancestors of Native Americans came from northern Asia near the end of the Pleistocene. Using the evidence gathered from examination of early Native American teeth, Turner has proposed that the peopling of the Americas occurred in three migrations. The first, representing the ancestors of most Native Americans, arrived near the end of the Pleistocene, passing through an ice-free corridor in Canada, and rapidly spreading throughout North and South America. Peoples of the second migration were the Na-Dene, ancestors of the Athabascan-speaking peoples, most of whom settled along the Northwest Coast of North America. Some of these peoples, however, penetrated into the American Southwest within the last few thousand years. The final migration Turner proposes was the spread of the Eskimo-Aleut peoples, a population that came to inhabit the northern fringes of North America.

While Turner's explanation for the peopling of the Americas is well-documented, there are other studies that provide modifications of his explanation. Brace and Tracer (1993) have proposed that, instead of a single migration before that of the Athabascan-speaking peoples, there were at least two populations present in the Americas prior to the Athabascans. Steele and Powell (1992, 1993, 1994) have provided information that early North American populations differed in appearance from living Native Americans and northern Asians by having a relatively longer and narrower braincase and a narrower face. These studies, and those of Brace and Tracer, suggest that the earliest northern Asian peoples in the New World arrived before the broader features of living northern Asians and Native Americans had developed.

What Information about the Behavior of Past Peoples Can Be Acquired from the Study of Human Remains?

The examination of human remains also yields information about an area that is frequently difficult or impossible to explore, the mundane daily activities of peoples of the past. A proven relationship exists between the shape of an individual's body and the activities in which the individual engaged; habitual or prolonged activities often cause skeletal and dental tissues to assume unusual shapes and forms (Kennedy 1989). Therefore, we often can infer some activities of past populations from irregularities in altered skeletal and dental morphology. Many indications of activity patterns are related to the consumption of particularly abrasive foods or grinding the teeth in an abnormal pattern, as evidenced by the abnormal anterior tooth loss seen in some prehistoric Sadlermiut females who softened skins with their teeth (Merbs 1983). Evidence of the use of teeth as a tool also is seen in unusual grooves related to cordage production on the anterior dentition of Native Americans at the Stone Lake site in California (Schulz 1977).

Other signature indications of daily activities found on human skeletal material include enlarged, roughened attachment sites for massive muscles and signs of stress in the related joints. An example of this is seen in the overdeveloped attachment site of the muscle in the lower arm and arthritis in the elbow joint that is related to spear throwing (Angel 1966) and slinging and pitching (Kennedy 1989). Further examples of indications of daily activities are seen in the changes in articular surfaces of bones of the leg and ankle (Barnett 1954; Das 1959; Kostick 1963; Singh 1959; Ubelaker 1979) detected in people who spend a good deal of time in squatting positions. Some habitual activities may cause stress fractures like those seen in the vertebrae of individuals who carry heavy loads on the tops of their heads (Scher 1978); other types of more generalized stress may be indicated by bone degeneration and bone spurs in the lower portion of the vertebral column associated with generalized stress and lateral bending and flexion (Kelley 1982).

Although daily activities like these might be inferred to occur in past populations, skeletal and dental markers offer direct, empirical proof of their common occurrence. These reconstructions of mundane daily behaviors of past peoples are important because they provide indications of everyday activities that were important, and in some cases necessary, in the lives of our ancestors.

How Do Anthropologists Gather Information from Human Remains?

Physical anthropologists have used many methods to gather information from human remains. Early anthropologists relied on observation of anatomical characteristics, and this remains a mainstay of physical anthropology. Observation of macroscopic anatomical characteristics, or traits large enough to be seen without magnification or any other type of technological assistance, is suitable for the study of traits that vary in their form, some observations pertinent to health and nutrition, and most methods of age and sex determination. One of the chief advantages of macroscopic examination of bones is that it requires little or no permanent alteration of the remains, and most commonly no preparation of the remains besides gentle cleaning. Another advantage is that it requires little or no special equipment other than good light; this means that these methods can be used almost anywhere. However, an important disadvantage of reliance on macroscopic characteristics is that the material must be complete or almost complete, and in a relatively good state of preservation.

Microscopic techniques, on the other hand, may require alteration of the material that is sometimes permanent and perhaps destructive, although the amount of material needed for these techniques is usually very small, often less than a thimbleful. These methods allow us to extract information from even fragmentary and poorly preserved material. Significant drawbacks to microscopic analyses are that they require specialized tools and equipment that usually are costly and not easily transported to the field, and they may result in the destruction of some of the material.

Osteometric analysis relies on measurement of remains with standardized tools that include tape measures, calipers, and different types of calibrated boards. Osteometric analysis is useful in answering questions such as ancestral/descendant relationships, health and nutrition, sexual dimorphism, estimated stature, and sex assessment. This type of analysis has many of the same benefits and drawbacks as the observation of macroscopic characteristics. Although it is noninvasive and nondestructive and requires little preparation of the remains, it usually requires relatively complete remains in a relatively good state of preservation. However, unlike macroscopic observations, osteometric studies require specialized tools that often are expensive, although the equipment is usually small and easily carried to the field.

Chemical analysis of remains is similar to microscopic analysis in some ways: it can extract valuable, detailed information from fragmentary and poorly preserved remains, but it requires sensitive and specialized equipment that is not easily transported. Moreover, chemical analysis techniques are invasive, require preparation of material, and usually require the destruction of small amounts of bone. The value of chemical analyses lies not only in their ability to obtain data that can be gotten in no other way, but also in their utility as a vehicle for testing, revision, and confirmation of hypotheses formulated using data gathered from other sources. Chemical analyses are particularly useful in reconstructing diets (Keegan 1989), establishing genetic affinities, assessing metabolic abnormalities and other questions of health, making behavioral correlations, and establishing dates (Aufderhiede 1989).

Why Do We Restudy Human Remains?

The foundation for scientific research methods is that explanations, or hypotheses, are formulated, tested, and refined before they can be accepted. Each explanation in turn generates new ideas, new interpretations, and new questions. Physical anthropology, like all sciences, is accretionary; each new discovery is the foundation for subsequent research that addresses fresh topics or deals with earlier topics from a different perspective. This testing, retesting, and expanding of interpretations is dependent on the restudy of the biological remains recovered from sites.

Science, like life, is not static. Technology, like methods, hypotheses, and perspectives, changes through time. A survey of articles published between 1950 and 1980 describing results of studies of skeletal remains indicates that 26 percent of the studies used techniques unavailable at the time the material was recovered (Buikstra and Gordon 1981). Stable isotope analysis, chemical analysis, and the extraction of DNA from prehistoric bone are only some of the relatively recent innovations. Methodological advances are only part of the story. Equipment is improved or made more affordable. Computer use originally was restricted to the very well-funded because of the cost of the equipment; it has been made affordable for individuals only relatively recently. Similar statements can be made about photographic equipment, x-ray imaging, and even four-wheel drive transportation.

This perspective from which we address topics also changes over time, and often is changed by technological advances like those mentioned above. Questions of biological affinity, for example, have long been prominent research topics. The development of computer technology has given impetus to large-scale studies of many traits considered simultaneously, which in turn has spurred the development of new areas of investigation.

Technological advances, the development of new methods that include more sophisticated research design, and accompanying shifts in perspective are reasons for the restudy of remains (Ubelaker and Grant 1989). Each of these also influences the development of new areas of interest. An examination of physical anthropology research published in a fifty-year span is illustration of this principle (Lovejoy et al. 1982). Studies of human remains published between 1930 and 1950 reveal that works of the 1930s were overwhelmingly descriptive in character, with studies of single metric and discrete traits being the major means of data analysis through the 1940s and 1950s. Descriptive reports of the incidence of metric and nonmetric traits also dominated the 1940s, but a slight rise in methods of identification of age, sex, and race also was evident. The 1950s saw continued emphasis on descriptive reports. This era is also notable for an increase in studies of growth, development, maturation, and aging. The 1960s brought a shift away from purely descriptive studies to analytical approaches that used multivariate statistical techniques. Paleodemography, growth, stature, and health status also became important research topics during the 1960s, with organized symposia on paleodemography, paleopathology, and skeletal population studies fueling research. The 1970s saw an amplification of the trend toward the use of multivariate statistical techniques; researchers found fresh applications for these techniques in age and sex determination. As technology was developed and new interests were followed, previously studied skeletal assemblages were the basis of new studies as well.

Within the framework of global and national research trends, regional shifts also can be identified. In anthropological studies in south Texas,

Steele and Olive (1988) identified a drift away from studies attempting to identify biological affinity toward studies concerned with prehistoric health status. These local inclinations reflected an increased national interest in prehistoric human adaptation and paleoecology. Such theoretical shifts are to be expected in any science. In fact, they are desirable and even necessary because they provide a framework for new research questions. It easily is seen, however, that it is impossible to design a single study that will anticipate all future research trends.

These reasons explain the need for the restudy of human remains, but the significance of reevaluation of old hypotheses cannot be overemphasized. Reexamination of previous studies is critical for physical anthropology, as it is for any science, because it allows us to discard erroneous conclusions and outdated ideas and to identify ineffective methods and practices. Buikstra and Gordon (1981) found that close to 74 percent of studies applying new techniques to previously explored questions reached new conclusions. We restudy remains to re-evaluate conclusions as well as to test new hypotheses and methods, to move forward in our understanding of past Native American populations and, by extension, all humans past and present.

Why Do We Study So Many Individuals?

The study of the remains of a single person can provide information that allows us to characterize that individual. In contrast, the study of the remains of many individuals from a population provides data that can be used to generalize about other people of the society in which they lived. Skeletal analyses may embrace all of the individuals whose remains were recovered from a site, as in Patrick's (1988) osteometric and demographic analysis of remains from the NAN Ranch Ruin site; target a particular group within the population, as in Marek's (1990) study of growth patterns in children whose remains were recovered from the same site; or use an individual study to address specific questions with implications for a community, as in the study of an individual from the NAN Ranch site presented by Shafer et al. (1989).

Additional studies use pooled samples comprised of remains from several sites. Workers may choose to combine samples from a restricted geographic area, as seen in Gregg and Gregg's (1987) evaluation of South Dakotan remains dating from 3800 B.P. until historic times, addressing questions about health status, trauma, and mortality. Researchers also may combine samples from a wide geographic range, as illustrated by Newman's (1953) evaluation of the effects of nutrition and the environment on body size in aboriginal peoples of the New World. Questions about particular groups during a specific time period may require the examination of samples from a geographically restricted area. These examples constitute only a few of the many ways in which data gathered from several discrete samples may be pooled to address research questions.

Physical anthropologists can reach conclusions by examining relatively small samples, but to ensure that their conclusions are valid they require large samples. Without the examination of many individuals, physical anthropologists cannot be sure that data gathered during skeletal analysis are representative of the society and not idiosyncratic of the few individuals studied. If a condition is identified in one individual, its subsequent identification in other individuals is corroboration that its presence in the community might be noteworthy.

Physical anthropologists also need to examine remains from large numbers of individuals to determine the range of variation within a population. Averaging the occurrence of traits tells us one thing, but the range of variability within a population tells us another. Large sample sizes are necessary to provide evidence of rare skeletal variations in a population. These traits are noteworthy because their presence may be used to identify ancestor-descendant relationships among prehistoric groups and between historic and prehistoric groups. As an example, Ossenberg (1974) concluded that Illinois Hopewell groups and later Plains tribes that included Dakota, Assiniboin, Blackfoot, and Cheyenne populations were not closely related after an examination of the remains of 942 individuals for the incidence of 26 skeletal traits of the cranium. Most of these traits occurred in less than 20 percent of the individuals. Similarly, most of the discrete traits upon which dental studies are based occur in less than 10 percent to 20 percent of the individuals examined.

Given the value of large samples, other questions present themselves. How large must the sample be? How many individual remains are enough? There is no clear answer to these questions. In cases where rare cranial, dental, and other traits are being studied, many individuals must be examined before important traits even can be identified, and the same traits must be observed in many individuals before their significance can be assessed. The same can be said of the analysis of skeletal indications of habitual activities. Such traits may be interpreted as indications of idiosyncratic behavior when seen in one individual, but the same trait takes on new significance when seen in a relatively small but significant segment of the population. We cannot be sure that any anomaly we observe is unimportant unless we can determine with certainty that it does not occur with a significant frequency in a single population or across several separate populations; in other words, its absence in an individual is as important in some ways as its presence. Therefore, all individuals are important; the examination of each is critical. This is a simple but important reason why many physical anthropologists advocate the detailed examination of many human remains.

Why Do Analyses Take Such a Long Time?

A skeletal analysis is more than just looking at bones. The study of human remains is an analysis, in the true sense of the word, requiring the meticulous examination and assessment of human remains in all their component parts from many perspectives. Analyses may include the evaluation of ancestral/descendant relationships, health, nutrition, human adaptation, growth, and development. Each topic is integrated into a synthetic interpretation of the lives of past peoples. A skeletal analysis is a demanding and time-consuming undertaking; it must be done thoroughly.

As a practical matter, collections of skeletal material can never be analyzed completely because of time and financial constraints. In spite of this, physical anthropologists strive to achieve as complete an analysis as possible, because they know that it is not possible to attain reliable, valid conclusions from a partial analysis; a hurried analysis can result in overlooking critical details that may be of importance at some point later in the study, or that may be crucial in subsequent studies.

Basic information about the minimum number of individuals represented by the material, including age and gender, are determined during the initial analysis. Identification of skeletal indicators of trauma, disease, or other disorders, nutritional status, gross morphological characteristics, and other concerns are more complex undertakings, as are the application of chemical analysis, dating techniques, and microscopic evaluation. Gathering osteometric data, which sometimes requires the reconstruction of broken or fragmentary elements, and compiling data on the incidence of nonmetric traits are quite exacting and time-consuming. As lengthy as they are, these processes do not consume the bulk of time spent on analysis.

Early studies of human remains from archaeological contexts were chiefly descriptive, but current trends in studies of prehistoric skeletal biology are problem-oriented and directed at answering specific questions. Problem-oriented studies often require the formulation of new techniques, and workers require time to design and refine new methods. Even the smallest sample requires a great time investment for planning the data gathering and contemplating and statistically processing the data. Large amounts of time also are spent in library research on related archaeological sites from the same area or time period. Often unusual characteristics of the skeletal material require comparison with other skeletal collections, and this restudy requires longer periods of access to skeletal remains. Suitable comparative samples may not be readily available, or may be housed at distant facilities. Similarly, if other physical anthropologists need to be consulted, they may not be immediately available. While some consultations may occur via telephone, most often the material itself must be examined for a definitive opinion, so travel time is also a consideration.

Early studies of human remains were primarily grounded in anthropological theory. The current trend in research, though, rests on multidisciplinary studies, those that employ workers and techniques from other scientific disciplines. Their utility for the resolution of specific problems is inestimable because such studies address the unique characteristics of each sample from more than one theoretical framework and technological approach. Interdisciplinary research allows the amassing of data that could not be collected by anthropological techniques alone. However, the time spent in the planning stages of problem-oriented research represents a significant portion of the total time spent on the analysis, and this is particularly true for multidisciplinary research. These studies require more time because they require the participation of teams of scholars rather than a single analyst. It is often difficult to assemble a team that can labor on one study or issue simultaneously in the face of all other commitments of the participants. This is especially true for scientists outside the anthropological disciplines, for whom anthropological studies may represent a tangential study away from the majority of their work. Because most scholars are working on several projects simultaneously, the need for coordination with other workers represents a logistical problem that is usually not quickly or easily resolved. Added to this is the dilemma of the limited number of specialists in some areas.

Among the additional factors that contribute to the need for long-term study of remains is the reality of North American physical anthropology: Many researchers work as staff, students, or faculty in universities where research is only one facet. An additional factor is the overwhelming abundance of important questions about past populations that need to be addressed: Most physical anthropologists work on several projects at once.

Another important issue warranting the long-term study of human remains is that the rarity of some samples may make it difficult to acquire an adequate sample to represent the population. The small sample of Paleoindian remains is the classic example of this problem. The earliest Native Americans, like later hunter-gatherer groups, appear to have existed in small nomadic bands that seldom stayed in one place long enough to create large cemeteries. This situation is compounded by the poor preservation and fragmentary nature of ancient remains. The paucity of remains of Paleoindians and later hunter-gatherer groups presents a profound impediment to meaningful research. This problem can be addressed by pooling several small samples to obtain a larger sample. The remains of a scant twenty-one individuals from sixteen sites can be securely dated at 8500 B.P. or older (Steele and Powell 1992); while the remains of each of these individuals are scientifically important when considered separately, their collective significance when pooled into one group is increased (Steele and Powell 1992).

How Does the Study of Human Remains, Particularly the Study of Native American Remains, Benefit Living People?

The study of treponemal disease in past populations and its ancient distribution has provided valuable information on how epidemics spread among populations. Other studies of medical disorders affecting past populations have had measurable impact on modern health and treatment of disease as well.

The study of rheumatoid diseases like arthritis is such an example. Human remains offer unique opportunities for the study of rheumatoid diseases because an entire bony joint can be examined three-dimensionally, an option not available in the study of living individuals. This is important because diagnosis by visual assessment of bony changes has proven to be much more sensitive than assessment by x-ray of the impaired joint. In a recent study, rheumatoid anomalies were readily detected by visual examination in sixteen of twenty-four skeletal specimens, while the analysis of x-rays of the same material revealed abnormalities in only two of the same twenty-four individuals (Rogers et al. 1990). It is possible to gather detailed information about changes in bony joints during the early stages of rheumatoid disorders using visual inspection that might escape detection (Rogers and Dieppe 1990). Therefore, the study of prehistoric and historic skeletal samples has aided in our understanding of the patterns of early development of this disorder, and this knowledge in turn may be used eventually in the early diagnosis and treatment of living peoples suffering from rheumatoid arthritis.

Information gathered from the reconstruction of ancient diets, accomplished in part through the chemical analysis of human remains, is helpful in tackling modern health problems. The causes of chronic kidney failure, or end-stage renal disease, in children are not fully understood, but information gathered from the study of the diets of past populations is giving new insight into its causes and, most importantly, its treatment. Data indicates that prolonged hyperfiltration, excessive filtering of liquid in the kidneys, plays an important role in the development of this condition. Hyperfiltration occurs in healthy kidneys as a response to a sudden rise in the amount of urea, a substance produced during protein digestion, and other waste products that must be flushed from the body. Ethnographic evidence indicates hunter-gatherer populations had an intermittent, feast-or-famine dietary pattern that may have resulted in the evolution of many physiological mechanisms to accommodate fluctuations in nutrient intake. Analyses of human skeletal remains can provide corroborative evidence for feast-or-famine patterns among early peoples through the identification of indications of periodic episodes of dietary stress. Because feast-or-famine patterns were characteristic of early human groups, hyperfiltration may have developed as an appropriate response to the sudden rise of digestive waste products, especially those from protein digestion. As humans began to consume relatively less animal protein, this physiological response became less critical for survival but lingered on in our genetic makeup (Kallen 1991). The traditional medical approach to chronic kidney disease associated with hyperfiltration included an elevated protein intake. Recent studies, though, suggest that dietary protein restrictions are beneficial (Acchiardo et al. 1986; Ihle et al. 1989; White 1989; Zeller et al. 1991).

Studies of human remains also corroborate ethnographic accounts of our history. Ethnographic accounts are important evidence, especially when they offer information about the early days of European contact and colonization of North America. Ethnographic accounts do not necessarily require corroboration by other data, but they are strengthened when they are confirmed by physical evidence. As an example, physical evidence of European atrocities committed during the exploration and colonization of the New World may be provided by study of remains from sites like the King Site in Georgia (Blakely and Mathews 1990).

And how can knowledge of the prehistoric Crow Creek massacre or the practice of scalping be viewed as helpful to people of today? The answer can only be that our total history is who we are. The good and the violent. The noble and the ignoble. That is all of our history. Certainly, violence and scalping (Iscan and Kennedy 1989; Reece 1940; Ortner and Putchar 1981) were not behaviors found only in the New World. They are part of human history in the Old World as well. We can only hope that by acknowledging that history can we keep it from being a part of our future.

In this presentation, we have explained why we want to study the past, why we want to study human skeletal remains, and why these studies are important. Many of these views have been expressed by other physical anthropologists (Buikstra 1983; Owsley 1986; Ubelaker and Grant 1989). We recognize that our beliefs may not be appreciated or accepted by all, but we believe our views are as valuable and supportable as are alternative, Native American views. Just as Native Americans experience a heartfelt sense of responsibility toward the skeletal remains of ancestral peoples, physical anthropologists feel an equally profound, personal sense of responsibility toward the remains of peoples of the past. Like Native Americans, we believe that ancestry is not always limited to the closest of kin; in a broad sense, all ancient peoples are the ancestors of modern peoples. We revere all ancestors by preserving their memories and by unraveling mysteries, mundane and extraordinary, about their lives. We wish to recover lost information about ancient peoples; to accomplish this, we gather tiny threads of information from whatever source we can, constantly revising our picture of the past.

Balancing these beliefs against other spiritual and emotional needs is a difficult task, but it is a goal worth pursuing, and effective communication of ideas will help us to attain it.

Note

The authors wish to acknowledge all those who contributed to this work. We extend our special thanks to Dr. Glen Doran, Dr. Jerome Rose, Dr. D. H. Ubelaker, and Dr. Larry Zimmerman for their generous assistance in the very early stages of preparation of this manuscript. The thoughtful comments of B. Baker, P. Clabaugh, G. Colby, H. Dockall, C. Judkins, and S. McCormick were also especially appreciated. We also thank Dr. Harry Shafer and Dr. David Carlson, whose insightful comments were extremely helpful.

References

Angel, J. L. 1966. "Early skeletons from Tranquility, California." *Smithsonian Contributions to Anthropology* 2(1).

Arcchiardo, S. R., L. W. Moore, and S. Cockrell. 1986. "Does low protein diet halt the progression of renal insufficiency?" *Clinical Nephrology* 25: 289–94.

Arens, W. 1979. *The Man-eating Myth: Anthropology and Anthropophagy.* Oxford: Oxford University Press.

Aufderheide, A. C. 1989. "Chemical analysis of skeletal remains." In M. Y. Iscan and K. A. R. Kennedy (eds.), *Reconstruction of Life from the Skeleton.* New York: Alan R. Liss.

Baker, B. J., and G. J. Armelagos. 1988. "The origin and antiquity of syphilis: A paleopathological diagnosis and interpretation." *Current Anthropology* 29: 702–20.

Barnett, C. H. 1954. "Squatting facets on the European talus." *Journal of Anatomy* 88: 509–13.

Binford, L. R. 1981. *Ancient Men and Modern Myths.* New York: Academic.

Blakely, R. L., and D. S. Mathews. 1990. "Bioarchaeological evidence for a Spanish–Native American conflict in the sixteenth-century southeast." *American Antiquity* 55(4): 718–44.

Bowden, R. 1984. "Maori cannibalism: An interpretation." *Oceania* 55(2): 81–99.

Brace, C. L., and D. P. Tracer. 1992. "Craniofacial continuity and change: A comparison of late Pleistocene and recent Europe and Asia." In T. Akazawa, K. Aoki, and T. Kimura (eds.), *Evolution and Dispersal of Modern Humans in Asia.* Tokyo: Hokusen-Sha.

Brothwell, D. A. 1961. "Paleopathology of early British man: An essay on the problems of diagnosis and analysis." *Journal of the Royal Anthropological Institute* 91: 318–44.

Buikstra, J. E. 1983. "Reburial: How we all lose." *Society for California Newsletter* 17(1): 2–5.

Buikstra, J. E., and C. C. Gordon. 1981. "The study and restudy of human skeletal series: The importance of long-term curation." In A. Cantwell, J. B. Griffin, and N. A. Rothschild (eds.), *The Research Potential of Anthropological Museum Collections.* Annals of the New York Academy of Sciences 376: 449–65.

Bullen, A. K. 1972. "Paleoepidemiology and distribution of prehistoric treponemiasis (syphilis) in Florida." *Florida Anthropologist* 25: 133–74.

Cockburn, T. A. 1961. "The origin of the Treponematoses." *Bulletin of the World Health Organization* 24: 221–28.

Das, A. C. 1959. "Squatting facets on the talus in U.P. (Uttar Pradesh) subjects." *Journal of the Anatomical Society of India* 8(2): 90–92.

Elting, J. S., and W. J. Sterna. 1984. "A possible case of pre-Columbian treponematosis from New York State." *American Journal of Physical Anthropology* 65: 267–73.

Forsyth, D. W. 1985. "Three cheers for Hns. Staden: The case for Brazilian cannibalism." *Ethnohistory* 32(1): 17–36.

Gregg, J. B., and P. S. Gregg. 1987. *Dry Bones: Dakota Territory Reflected. An Illustrated Descriptive Analysis of the Health and Well-Being of Previous People and Cultures as Is Mirrored in Their Remnants.* Sioux Falls SD: Sioux Printing.

Holliday, D. H. Y. 1993. "Occipital lesions: A possible cost of cradleboarding." *American Journal of Physical Anthropology* 90: 283–90.

Hooten, E. A. 1920. *Indian village site and cemetery near Madisonville, Ohio.* Peabody Museum Papers 8(1). Cambridge MA: Peabody Museum.

Hudson, C., C. DePratter, and M. T. Smith. 1988. "The victims of the King Site Massacre: A historical detectives' report." In R. L. Blakely (ed.), *The King Site: Continuity and Contact in Sixteenth-Century Georgia.* Athens: University of Georgia Press.

Hudson, E. H. 1965. "Trepanematosis and man's social evolution." *American Anthropologist* 67: 885–901.

———. 1963. "Trepanematosis and anthropology." *Annals of Internal Medicine* 58: 1037–49.

Ihle, B. U., G. I. Becker, J. A. Whitworth, R. A. Charlwood, and P. S. Kincaid-Smith. 1989. "The effect of protein restriction on the progression of renal insufficiency." *New England Journal of Medicine* 321: 1773–77.

Iscan, M. Y., and K. A. R. Kennedy (eds.). 1989. *Reconstruction of Life from the Skeleton.* New York: Alan R. Liss.

Kallen, R. J. 1991. "Paleonephrology and reflux nephropathy: From the 'big bang' to end-stage renal disease." *American Journal of the Diseases of Childhood* 145: 860–64.

Keegan, W. F. 1989. "Stable isotope analysis of prehistoric diet." In M. Y. Iscan and K. A. R. Kennedy (eds.), *Reconstruction of Life from the Skeleton.* New York: Alan R. Liss.

Kelley, M. A. 1982. "Intervertebral osteochondrosis in ancient and modern populations." *American Journal of Physical Anthropology* 59(3): 271–79.

Kennedy, K. A. R. 1989. "Skeletal markers of occupational stress." In M. Y. Iscan and K. A. R. Kennedy (eds.), *Reconstruction of Life from the Skeleton.* New York: Alan R. Liss.

Kostick, E. L. 1963. "Facets and imprints on the upper and lower extremities of femora from a western Nigerian population." *Journal of Anatomy* 97: 393–402.

Lovejoy, C. O., R. P. Mensforth, and G. J. Armelagos. 1982. "Five decades of skeletal biology as reflected in the *American Journal of Physical Anthropology.*" In F. Spencer (ed.), *A History of American Physical Anthropology 1930–1980.* New York: Academic.

Madrid, A. 1986. "Work in historical osteology at the National Museum of Antiquities in Sweden." *Museum* 38(3): 155–57.

Marek, M. 1990. "Long Bone Growth of Mimbres subadults from the NAN Ranch (LA 15049), New Mexico." M.A. Thesis, Texas A&M University.

Merbs, C. F. 1983. "Patterns of activity-induced pathology in a Canadian Inuit population." National Museum of Man Mercury Series, Archaeological Survey of Canada no. 119. Ottawa: National Museum.

Newman, M. T. 1953. "Ecological rules and racial anthropology." *American Anthropologist* 55: 311–27.

Ortner, D. J., and W. G. J. Putschar. 1981. "Identification of pathological conditions in human skeletal remains." Smithsonian Contributions to Anthropology no. 28. Washington DC: Smithsonian Institution.

Ossenberg, N. S. 1974. "Origins and relationships of Woodland peoples: The evidence of cranial morphology." In E. Johnson (ed.), *Aspects of Upper Great Lakes Anthropology: Papers in Honor of Lloyd A. Wilford.* St. Paul: Minnesota Historical Society.

Owsely, D. W. 1986. "Human bones from archaeological contexts." *Museum Anthropology* 8: 2–8.

Patrick, S. S. 1988. "A Description and Demographic Analysis of a Mimbres

Mogollon Population from LA 15049 (NAN Ruin)." M.A. Thesis, Texas A&M University.

Powell, M. L. 1988. *Status and Health in Prehistory: A Case Study of the Moundville Chiefdom.* Washington DC: Smithsonian Institution Press.

Reese, H. H. 1940. "The history of scalping and its clinical aspects." *Yearbook of Neurological Psychiatric Endocrinology* 8: 3–19.

Reichs, K. J. 1986. "Trepanematosis: A possible case from the late prehistoric of North Carolina." *American Journal of Physical Anthropology* 79: 289–303.

Rogers, J., and P. Dieppe. 1990. "Skeletal paleopathology and the rheumatic diseases: Where are we now?" *Annals of the Rheumatic Diseases* 49: 887–88.

Rogers, J., I. Watt, and P. Dieppe. 1990. "Comparison of visual and radiographic changes at the knee joint." *British Medical Journal* 300: 367–68.

Scher A. T. 1978. "Injuries to the cervical spine sustained while carrying loads on the head." *Paraplegia* 16: 94–101.

Schultz, P. D. 1977. "Task activity and anterior tooth grooving in prehistoric California Indians." *American Journal of Physical Anthropology* 46(1): 87–92.

Shafer, H. F., M. Marek, and K. J. Reinhard. 1989. "A Mimbres burial with associated colon remains from the NAN Ranch Ruin, New Mexico." *Journal of Field Archaeology* 16(1): 17–30.

Singh, I. 1959. "Squatting facets on the tibia and talus in Indians." *Journal of Anatomy* 93: 540–50.

Steele, D. G., and B. W. Olive. 1988. "Bioarchaeological research in central and southern Texas: Documentation of the value of curated collections of prehistoric human skeletal remains." Paper presented at the Annual Meeting of the Society of American Archaeologists, April 29.

Steele, D. G., and J. F. Powell. 1994. "Paleobiological evidence of the peopleing of the Americas: A morphometric view." In R. Bonnichsen and D. G. Steele (eds.), *Method and Theory for Investigating the Peopling of the Americas.* Corvalis OR: People of the Americas Publications, Center for the Student of the First Americans, Department of Anthropology, Oregon State University.

——. 1993. "Paleobiology of the First Americans." *Evolutionary Anthropology* 2(4): 138–46.

——. 1992. "Peopling of the Americas: Paleobiological evidence." *Human Biology* 64(3): 303–36.

Steinbock, R. T. 1976. *Paleopathological Diagnosis and Interpretation.* Springfield IL: Thomas.

Stewart, T. D., and A. S. Spoehr. 1967. "Evidence on the paleopathology of yaws." In D. Brothwell and A. T. Sandison (eds.), *Diseases in Antiquity.* Springfield IL: Thomas.

Turner, C. G., II. 1989. "Teeth and prehistory in Asia." *Scientific American* Feb: 88–96.

——. 1983. "Taphonomic reconstructions of human violence and cannibalism based on mass burials in the American Southwest." In G. M. LeMoine and A. S.

MacEachern (eds.), *A Question of Bone Technology.* Calgary: University of Calgary Archaeological Association.

Turner, C. G., II, and J. A. Turner. 1992. "The first claim for cannibalism in the Southwest: Walter Hough's 1901 discovery at Canyon Butte Ruin #3 in northeast Arizona." *American Antiquity* 57: 661–82.

Ubelaker, D. H. 1979. "Skeletal evidence for kneeling in Prehistoric Ecuador." *American Journal of Physical Anthropology* 51: 679–85.

Ubelaker, D. H., and L. G. Grant. 1989. "Human skeletal remains: Preservation or reburial?" *Yearbook of Physical Anthropology* 32: 249–87.

Villa, P., C. Bouville, J. Courtin, D. Hjelmer, E. Dmahieu, P. Shipman, G. Belluomini, and M. Branca, 1986. "Cannibalism in the Neolithic." *Science* 233: 431–36.

Webb, W. S., and C. E. Snow. 1945. *The Adena People.* Reports in Anthropology and Archaeology 6. Lexington: University of Kentucky.

White, R. H. R. 1989. "Vesicouretieric reflux and renal scarring." *Archives of the Diseases of Childhood* 64: 407–12.

White, T. D. 1992. *Prehistoric cannibalism at Mancos 5 MTUMR-2346.* Princeton NJ: Princeton University Press.

Willey, P. 1990. *Prehistoric Warfare on the Great Plains: Skeletal Analysis of the Crow Creek Massacre Victims.* New York: Garland Publishing.

Zeller, K., E. Whittaker, L. Sullivan, P. Raskin, and H. Jacobson. 1991. "Effect of restricting dietary protein on the progression of renal failure in patients with insulin-dependant diabetes mellitus." *New England Journal of Medicine* 324: 78–84.

5

Devon A. Mihesuah

American Indians, Anthropologists, Pothunters, and Repatriation

Ethical, Religious, and Political Differences

Among the many problems American Indians have to contend with today is the removal of their ancestors' remains along with sacred tribal items from burial grounds for the purpose of scientific study and museum display, or for sale through the underground market and at auctions. The argument between Indians who want Indian skeletal remains and funerary objects repatriated (or "matriated," as one Indian puts it) and anthropologists who do not is a volatile one, taking on emotional, spiritual, intellectual, and monetary elements. For black-market grave robbers, the issue appears to be purely monetary.

Throughout the years, I have heard or read the same statements at committee meetings, conferences, and in the scholarly literature:

"Indians are too ignorant to know what's good for them."

"The only good Indian is a dead, unreburied one."

"How would you like it if your grandparents were dug up?"

"I wouldn't mind if my ancestors were studied since only the spirit goes to heaven, not the entire body."

"Archaeologists and anthropologists are the only ones who benefit from studying Indian remains."

"How has the study of Indian skeletal remains helped to alleviate the problems Indians face today?"

"Since we all emerged from the same place—Africa—then why should anyone mind if remains are studied; my past is your past."

The comments go on, of course, but this short list does illustrate the complexity of the problem.

The desecration debate appears to be everywhere. Since becoming in-volved in the repatriation issue about fifteen years ago, I have learned that not all peoples possess the same religious, moral, or philosophical values when it comes to disinterment of the deceased and funerary items. While a graduate student at Texas Christian University in Fort Worth, I was a member of the Texas Indian Commission's and the Texas Historical Commission's Committee for the Protection and Preservation of Skeletal Remains and Cultural Objects—a committee comprising anthropologists, museologists, tribal leaders, Indian activists, educators, lawyers, and concerned citizens, both Indian and non-Indian.[1] All members learned a great deal through the activities and dialogues of this very active committee.

I had the opportunity to visit many museums and to view Indian bones displayed in almost every one, the strangest presentation being hand bones on the windowsill of the ladies' room in a small east Texas museum. I walked through archives of universities that held thousands of Indian skeletal remains in dust-covered boxes and watched as customers haggled over the price of skulls and medicine bundles at Texas gun shows. I read newspaper articles that chronicled the adventures of would-be Texas Indiana Joneses (i.e., "amateur archaeologists") and saw burial sites that had been bulldozed and ransacked by grave robbers looking for skulls and burial items to sell. Still in my activist graduate student mode, I debated with anthropologists (such as D. Gentry Steele and Robert J. Mallouf, contributors to this volume and fellow committee members) over what I perceived to be their insensitivity to Indians' concerns, protested to hobbyists about their seemingly innocent excavations that in reality destroy sites, and argued with some staunch advocates of reburial over their desire to speak for all tribes, and indeed, their need for attention. I worked intensively on this issue for years, writing articles, speaking to reporters, and participating in conference sessions.[2]

Although I am presently a professor of applied indigenous studies, I also have taught high school biology and physics and can appreciate the theory that studying human skeletal remains can yield data that will benefit mankind. As an American Indian, however, I am all too aware of the severe physical, political, and economic problems among Indians. Where is the information anthropologists are supposed to be acquiring that can help present-day tribes? If studies of tribes in the United States are supposed to be important, how are investigations by archaeologists and physical anthropologists serving the needs of Indians today? In dialogues with social scientists, Indians plead for convincing evidence that having the remains of their ancestors scrutinized, then stored for decades in basements and vaults of universities and museums, in addition to being separated from the grave goods with which they were buried, contributes to the well-being of Indian people.

It is quite possible that at one time the study of old Indian bones did play a role in the development of medicine, proper diet, and prevention of bone disease. With the sophistication of science, however, doctors have developed the ability to perform organ transplants, limb reattachments, sex changes, and growth stimulation. It would therefore appear that further excavation and examination of Indian people is no longer necessary. Dr. Emery Johnson, former assistant surgeon general, has even commented, "I am not aware of any current medical diagnostic or treatment procedure that has been derived from research on Indian remains. Nor am I aware of any during the thirty-four years that I have been involved in American Indian health."[3]

If the Society for American Archaeology ever gives a suitable answer as to the benefits of studying Indian skeletons, some tribes might be receptive to scholars who study remains. But to date, the garnered scientific information has not been used to decrease alcoholism or suicide rates, nor has it influenced legislative bodies to return tribal lands or to recognize the sad fact that Indians are still stereotyped, ridiculed, and looked upon as novelties. Indeed, mannequins dressed as Indians stand outside tourist shops, Hollywood still portrays Indians incorrectly, and sports teams, automobiles, and clothing lines all use stereotypes of Indians to sell products. What do Indian skulls that are displayed alongside pottery in museums tell visitors? Is this a message that Indians are inferior beings, items for display, just like animals? Since other Americans are not on view like Indians are, there is without question a double standard at work: non-Indian burials are left alone and those accidentally uncovered are immediately reburied, but archaeologists and pothunters deem it good and necessary to dig up Indians and possess their remains and funerary items.[4]

This is also a monetary issue. American Indian remains, their cultural objects, in addition to their images, serve as the focal points of many anthropologists' careers. The fact that Indians exist allows these people—as well as historians—to secure jobs, tenure, promotion, merit increases, fellowships, notoriety, and scholarly identity—all without giving anything back to Indian communities.[5] Millions of dollars, hundreds of jobs, and numerous journals would be at stake if anthropologists could no longer study Indian remains and their burial items.

Indians are curious about their histories, and they do not believe that all scientific and social scientific studies are worthless. Indians are often treated as if they have no comprehension of science or are too ignorant to understand the need for continuing research. On the contrary, Indians are aware that gaps in tribal histories have been filled by the investigations of anthropologists, archaeologists, and historians. The conflict arises because many archaeologists assume that they are the caretakers and owners of the past, not respecting the fact that Indians have oral traditions. Among traditional Indians, it is the responsibility of the present generation to remember stories for future generations.[6] Despite what archaeologists think, Indians do not believe that tribal histories are created by archaeologists' findings.[7] An attractive proposition for many Indians is that Indians and archaeologists work together to help each other form a more complete picture of the past, but the problem is that most archaeologists view oral histories as "fantasy" and "embellished" and refuse to consult with Indian informants.[8] More likely, they do not want to enter into dialogue with tribes because it invites the risk of having their research project taken away from them.

Anthropologists and museum directors often offer their opinions about the intelligence of Indians; many believe that Indians will not know how to take care of items that are returned to them. In response, Raymond Apodaca, former chairman of the Human Rights Committee for the National Congress of American Indians says, "What are they talking about? These things belong to us, were created by us, and are highly respected by us." Pemina Yellow Bird, a Hidatsa/Arikara repatriation activist, agrees: "How do you think these ancient things got in their possession if Native people didn't know how to take care of them? And who are they to tell us how to take care of our own sacred objects?"[9]

To scientists, skeletal remains and funerary items are "tools of education," and any skeleton or grave more than one hundred years old is viewed as an artifact that is fair game. Scientists believe that the cradle of civilization is in Africa; therefore, because we all have common ancestors, they claim the right to study all human remains. To Indians, however, the remains represent either direct ancestors or families they consider to be their "cultural ancestors."[10] Many Indians do not believe that they crossed the Siberian land bridge to North America. They believe they emerged from sacred sites on the North American continent.

Why should ancient bones be considered "fair game" for study? Is it because archaeologists feel it is safer to assert that there is no one alive who can claim relation to the old bones? After all, archaeologists have to study something. Lynne Goldstein and Keith Kintigh tell us in their 1990 essay, "Ethics and the Reburial Controversy" (chap. 9, this vol.) that "To claim that archaeologists have no right to excavate or examine an entire class of information is to deny our background and training."[11] ("Who asked them to become archaeologists and study Indians anyway?" respond Indians and non-Indians who have discussed their essay.)

Scientists and pothunters also like to hold up the Christian belief that the body and soul separate after death, so why be concerned about physical remains if the soul is (it is hoped) on his or her way to heaven? But that is not how many Indians see it. Generally speaking, because all tribes have differences in religion, unearthing of skeletal remains and funerary objects is disruptive. Among some tribes, if the bones are uncovered, and especially if they are separated from the burial relics, the spirit may not be at peace. Hence the importance of keeping remains and funerary objects buried.[12]

Indians and some social scientists have come to some agreement over how remains should be handled and studied, if at all. Like historians, there are many more archaeologists who wish Indians would stay out of it, or even better, were all dead so they would not have to deal with the descendants of the people they study. A former member of the executive committee for the Society of American Archaeology has commented, "the only good Indian is a dead, unreburied one."[13] Indeed, I have heard numerous times from anthropologists that Indians are "uneducated" and "cannot understand what we do." Despite my four university degrees and numerous academic awards, I have been told I am "ignorant" and "cannot possibly know" what I am talking about. Because of such racism, Indians often place scientists in the same category as grave robbers. To them the only difference between an illegal ransacking of a burial ground and a scientific one is the time element, sunscreen, little whisk brooms, and the neatness of the area when finished. Indians perceive many social scientists and all pothunters as adept at exploiting them for profit and see both groups as disrespectful of the individuals resting in the ground. Indians remain perplexed by the attitude of some anthropologists who assert that their work is more important than the religious beliefs and dignity of the descendants of those Indians they study.

Because pothunters, archaeologists, physical anthropologists, and paleopathologists spend a good portion of their time in graveyards and laboratories handling human remains and sacred tribal objects, this is undoubtedly a religious issue. When addressing the repatriation issue, some Indians speak from a religious standpoint, while scholars who study remains and sacred objects speak a different scientific language. Scholars cry "academic freedom," but Indians are concerned about "religious freedom,"[14] resulting in miscommunication, conflicts, and assumptions. Indians have taken refuge in the First Amendment to protect their religious beliefs, but this strategy is rarely effective, as tribal lawyers have discovered.[15] At least anthropologists and archaeologists will speak to Indians; black-market grave robbers and pothunters rarely will. Nor will they speak to archaeologists except perhaps to argue, as Arizona grave robber Peter Hester does:

Archaeology is a dead science. Archaeology is a dead end. Business is business; there are thousands of sites, and thousands of useless pots. The information has already been gained from most sites. How many pots of the same type do you need to figure something out? The only difference between what I do and the professional archaeologist do [*sic*] is that I sell what I find.[16]

The collecting of Native American art in the form of baskets, paintings, pottery, jewelry, beadwork, and rugs has been a hobby and business among non-Indians for decades. Almost everywhere whites are seen wearing turquoise rings or squash blossoms; in their homes are Navajo rugs and Pueblo pottery. Most of these common items are obtained legally from an art gallery, pow wow, or reservation tourist shop. An old problem, and one that appears to be developing, is the illegal removal of sacred tribal items and the remains of the tribal people themselves from Indian burial grounds to be sold through underground markets, either to people ignorant of the origin of these items or to disreputable collectors fully aware of what they are buying. Despite the Texas committee's differences of opinion over academia's return of Indian skeletal remains and funerary objects to tribes, one thing the committee agreed on was that the looting of Indian burial sites must be stopped (the problem in Texas is particularly serious), and that Texas museums should not display Indian skeletal remains and sacred objects. Indians and archaeologists usually can agree that burial sites should be "protected" from pothunters and that the latter should be fully prosecuted when possible. But the term "protection" has two meanings. To many Indians it means no burial-ground disturbances whatsoever. To archaeologists and physical anthropologists it means "hands off" any newly discovered site until they arrive to conduct their research. Museum directors want protection of their "collections" even if these "tools of education" are kept in archives and never seen again.[17]

Most grave robbers appear to be of a different mind-set altogether and use any excuse that comes to mind as to why they should be able to exploit graveyards for profit. An experience in 1985 led me to believe that sensitizing grave robbers to the concerns of many American Indians and sympathetic academics would be nearly impossible. The incident occurred when I and several representatives of the American Indian Movement, American Indians Against Desecration, and the aforementioned Texas committee attended a closed-door auction at the Texas Ranger Hall of Fame in Waco, Texas. The auction hall was filled with the requisite and costly Texas paraphernalia such as saddles, blankets, and antiques, but to our dismay, there also were tables laden with jewelry, pipebags, and medicine bundles with price tags informing potential buyers that they were acquired from Indian burials.

The most shocking item for sale, at least to me, was an exquisitely carved, glass-topped coffee table with a full skeleton inside that had been christened "Ernest"—probably a Mescalero Apache. After explaining to the auction officials who we were and our concerns, we were led outside by the auction guards—replete with sidearms—to a picnic table to discuss the issue. The auctioneer promised to pull the funerary items and Ernest from sale, but to our disappointment we later found out that they were auctioned by telephone to bidders in Germany and Japan. The Corps of Engineers in Fort Worth told us that this particular auctioneer made a living from selling the contents of burials from a variety of Texas and Southwest tribes.

After graduate school I moved to Arizona where, in the midst of twenty reservations (and their countless sacred sites, shrines, and burial grounds), I encountered a whole new world of desecration. Museums and archives are packed with skeletal remains and cultural objects, and wealthy grave robbers make their livings by purchasing land they know contains burials and then unearthing the remains and artifacts to sell. When finished plundering, they then sell the land and buy more.[18] Vandalism of prehistoric sites (i.e., petroglyphs, ruins, middens, and shrines) has reached such epidemic proportions in the Southwest that cartographers are considering leaving their locales off of new maps and out of guidebooks.[19]

The issue also hits me close to home. My husband, a Comanche, has numerous relatives, including a sister, buried in the Ishiti cemetery outside of Duncan, Oklahoma. Over the past twenty years, the cemetery has been vandalized and desecrated by looters looking for funerary objects the Comanches buried with their dead, such as saddles, jewelry, and medicine bundles. In response, some of the graves have been covered with cement by concerned relatives. But the looting of these burials puts us in a quandary, for where can the next generations be interred, if not in a large city cemetery? Many other Indians also have seen the desecration of their families' burials, and no doubt they wonder the same thing.[20]

Regardless of the differences in their cultures, American Indians are becoming increasingly concerned about taking proper care of unearthed remains of their ancestors and of sacred objects in or out of the ground. Despite cultural differences and the personal enmities Indians may have for one another, they share the desire to keep their ancestors resting in peace (not in pieces) as well as the desire to reinter those remains that have been disturbed. Many scientists have indeed become more sensitive to Indians' concerns, but in the meantime, grave-robbing, high-priced auctions, gun shows, private and amateur archaeology, and seemingly innocent arrowhead-hunting continue to provide excuses for collecting. The problem is complicated but is one that needs to be addressed with more sensitivity. Until the various parties involved in unearthing the deceased and sacred objects take a long hard look at all the factors—including the human one—the problem will stay with us.

Notes

1. For information on the committee see Candace Floyd, "The Repatriation Blues: Museum Professionals and Native Americans Wrestle with Questions of Ownership and Disposition of Tribal Materials," *History News* 40 (April 1985): 6–12; Frank McLemore and David Alcoze, "Texas American Indians and Colleagues Initiate Action to Protect Skeletal Remains and Sacred Objects," *Texas Association of Museums Quarterly* (spring 1985): 20. Members of the committee included (with their then-titles): Cherokee Chief Wilma Mankiller; Raymond Apodaca, executive director of the Texas Indian Commission; Rayna Green, Museum of American History; Newton Lamar, president of Wichita and Affiliated Tribes; Robert J. Mallouf, Texas State archaeologist; Ray Ramirez, superintendent of Tigua Indian Reservation; Henry Shemayme, chairman of Caddo Tribe; Gentry Steele, physical anthropologist; Amanda Stover, executive director of Texas Association of Museums; Curtis Tunnell, executive director of the Texas Historical Commission.

2. Devon Mihesuah, "Indian Burial Sites—Texas: An Indian Viewpoint on the Subject of Desecration of Sacred Burial Sites and the Questionable Need for Scientific Study of Indian Remains," *Akwesasne Notes* (spring 1986): 11; "Indians Fight Desecration of Burial Sites," *Fort Worth Star Telegram,* May 20, 1986; "Ancestors Defended by Indians," *Fort Worth Star Telegram,* May 21, 1986; "Woman Fights Indian Burial Site Robbers," *Tyler Morning Telegraph,* July 14, 1986.

3. Susan Shown Harjo, "Indian Remains Deserve Respect," *Mercury News* [San Jose], October 10, 1989.

4. The "double standard" is addressed by Roger C. Echo Hawk and Walter C. Echo Hawk in *Battlefields and Burial Grounds: The Indians' Struggle to Protect Ancestral Graves in the United States* (Minneapolis: Lerner Publications Company, 1994).

5. At universities around the country, researchers are required to have their projects approved by institutional review boards for the protection of human subjects in research and research-related activities. At Northern Arizona University in Flagstaff, researchers may soon be required to follow more stringent guidelines when it comes to researching American Indians. One question an IRB asks is: "How will your research benefit the people you study?" If no clear answer is given, the project is not approved. See Devon A. Mihesuah, "Suggested Guidelines for Institutions with Scholars Who Conduct Research on American Indians," *American Indian Culture and Research Journal* 17 (1993): 131–40.

6. For further discussion of the importance of Indian oral tradition, see Angela Cavender Wilson's two essays, "American Indian History or Non-Indian Percep-

tions of Indian History?" and "Grandmother to Granddaughter: Generations of Oral History in a Dakota Family," in *American Indian Quarterly*'s special issue on "Writing About American Indians," vol. 20, 1996, rpt. in Devon A. Mihesuah, ed., *Natives and Academics* (Lincoln: Univ. of Nebraska Press, 1998), 23–26, 27–36.

7. In his essay "Burying American Archaeology," Clement W. Meighan writes: "In my view, archaeologists have a responsibility to the people they study. They are defining the culture of an extinct group and in presenting their research they are writing a chapter of human history that cannot be written except from Archaeological investigation." He further asserts that "Indian knowledge of the traditions of their ancestors is derived in large part from the collections and scholarship that the activists among them are now seeking to destroy." See *Archaeology* (November/December 1994): 64–68. In his essay (in the same issue) "Sharing Control of the Past," Larry Zimmerman refutes Meighan's comments: "The idea that anyone can 'save' the past is a false notion. Archaeologists construct the past, they do not reconstruct it."

In "Archaeology and the Image of the American Indian" Bruce G. Trigger chronicles how archaeologists have viewed Indians since the early nineteenth century: "static," "incapable of change," "savage," "recent arrivals to North America." He also asserts that the "New Archaeology continues to treat native peoples as objects rather than subjects of research." *American Antiquity* 45 (1980): 662–76.

8. For an overview on the debate between those who believe Indians cannot accurately recall their histories and those who believe American Indian history is not "real" history without their voices, see Devon A. Mihesuah, "Voices, Interpretations, and 'The New Indians History': Comment on the *American Indian Quarterly*'s Special Issue on Writing about American Indians," *American Indian Quarterly* 20 (1996): 91–108 rpt. as the introduction to Mihesuah, *Natives and Academics*.

9. "Repatriation Demanded across the Country," *Indian Country Today*, September 22, 1993.

10. In "Bone Courts: The Rights and Narrative Representation of Tribal Bones," Gerald Vizenor proposes that bones be properly represented in court regarding their destiny. "Bones have a right to be represented and heard in court; these rights, not the assumed rights of science, or the interests of politicians, must be the principle concern in court. Science and academic power would survive; bones without representation would continue to be chattel, servitude to science." *American Indian Quarterly* 10 (1986): 319–31.

11. See chapter 9 in this volume. Originally published as Lynne Goldstein and Keith Kintigh, "Ethics and the Reburial Controversy," *American Antiquity* 55 (1990): 585–91.

12. Richard Hill, "Reclaiming Cultural Artifacts," *Museum News* 55 (May/June 1977): 43–46; Charlotte Frisbie, "Navajo Jish or Medicine Bundles and Mu-

seums," _Council for Museum Anthropology Newsletter_ (1977): 6–23; Roger C. Echo-Hawk, "Pawnee Mortuary Traditions," _American Indian Culture and Research Journal_ 16 (1992): 77–99; Jan Hammil and Robert Cruz, "Statement of American Indians Against Desecration," in _Conflict in the Archaeology of Living Traditions,_ ed. Robert Layton (Boston: Unwin Hyman, 1989); Larry J. Zimmerman, "Human Bones as Symbols of Power: Aboriginal American Belief Systems toward Bones and 'Grave Robbing' Archaeologists," in _Conflict in the Archaeology,_ ed. Layton, 211–16; Jan Hammil and Larry Zimmerman, eds., _Reburial of Human Skeletal Remains: Perspectives from Lakota Spiritual Men and Elders_ (Indianapolis: American Indians Against Desecration, 1984).

13. Larry Zimmerman, "Desecration and Reburial as an Anthropological Issue: The Tactics of Self-Delusion," paper presented at the annual meeting of the American Anthropological Association, Washington DC, 1985.

14. Ronald L. Grimes discusses the religiosity differences between Indians and anthropologists and archaeologists in "Desecration of the Dead: An Inter-religious Controversy," _American Indian Quarterly_ 10 (fall 1986): 305–18. Also see Richard Hill, "Indians and Museums: A Plea for Cooperation," _History News_ 34 (July 1979): 181–84.

15. Robert S. Michaelson, "American Indian Religious Freedom Litigation: Promise and Perils," _Journal of Law and Religion_ 3 (1985): 47–76; Steve Talbot, "Desecration and American Indian Religious Freedom," _Journal of Ethnic Studies_ 12 (winter 1985): 118. Vine Deloria Jr. briefly traces the history of religious freedom and explores the development of "civil religion"—a joining of political and religious beliefs—and how it suppresses American Indian religious freedom in "Secularism, Civil Religion, and the Religious Freedom of American Indians," _American Indian Culture and Research Journal_ 16 (1992): 9–20 (chap. 8, this vol.). Deloria writes that secularity has important bearing on repatriation, for the religious beliefs of tribes have been forced to take a backseat to state police powers. Indeed, neither the American Indian Freedom of Religion Act nor the First Amendment to the Constitution protects religious freedom.

16. Catherine Elston, "Thieves of Time: The Pillage of American Prehistory," _Wildfire_ (winter 1990): 22.

17. During the Texas committee's 1986 visit to the University of Texas at Austin's archives, a curator showed us aisle after aisle of boxes that contained Indian remains. "Some," she said, "have been here for fifty years and still have not been studied."

18. "Tribal Objections Fail to Stall Sale of Masks," _Arizona Republic_ [Phoenix], May 21, 1991; "New York Officials Inspect Three Indian Masks," _Arizona Republic,_ May 22, 1991; "The Curse of the Taalawtumsi: How the Thieves of Time Stole the Hopis' Religion," _Arizona Republic,_ March 14, 1993; "Time Bandits: Vandals De-

stroying Archaeological Sites," *Arizona Daily Sun* [Flagstaff], November 12, 1994; Elston, "Thieves of Time."

19. "Vandals, Tourists, Wiping Indian Ruins Off Maps," *Arizona Republic,* June 19, 1994. The Park Service oversees fifty-six major ruins in the Four Corners area; twenty in Arizona. Archaeologist Roger Whittaker comments that "This is a last-ditch effort to save the rest before we love it to death."

20. One solution is cremation, although among many tribes it is not the traditional way of disposing of the deceased. In some tribes it is considered "spiritual suicide," but at least Indians will not end up as "tools of education." Larry J. Zimmerman, " 'Tell Them about the Suicide': A Review of Recent Materials on the Reburial of Prehistoric Native American Skeletons," *American Indian Quarterly* 10 (fall 1986): 333–43.

6

James Riding In

Repatriation

A Pawnee's Perspective

My opposition to scientific grave looting developed partially through the birth of the American Indian repatriation movement during the late 1960s. Like other American Indians of the time (and now), I viewed archaeology as an oppressive and sacrilegious profession that claimed ownership over many of our deceased relatives, suppressed our religious freedom, and denied our ancestors a lasting burial. My first encounter with an archaeologist occurred at a party in New Mexico in the late 1970s. After hearing him rant incessantly about the knowledge he had obtained by studying Indian remains, burial offerings, and cemeteries, I suggested that if he wanted to serve Indians he should spend his time excavating latrines and leave the graves alone. Of course, he took umbrage at the tone of my suggestion and broke off the conversation. While studying history at the University of California, Los Angeles, in the mid-1980s, I became committed to pursuing the goals of the repatriation movement, which was gaining momentum. Like other reburial proponents, I advocated the reburial of all Indian remains warehoused across the nation in museums, universities, and federal agencies. I also promoted the extension or enactment of laws to protect Indian cemeteries from grave looters, including archaeologists.

While working to elevate the consciousness of the UCLA campus about the troubled relationship between archaeologists and Indians, a few of us, including students, staff, faculty, and community members, took advantage of opportunities to engage in dialogue with the anti-repatriation forces. During these exchanges, tempers on both sides often flared. Basically, the archaeologists were functioning on metaphysical and intellectual planes that differed from ours. We saw their professional activities as sacrilege and destructive, while they professed a legal and scientific right to study Indian remains and burial goods. We wanted the university to voluntarily return the human remains in its collections to the next-of-kin for proper reburial. They desired to protect excavation, research, and curatorial practices. Asserting profound respect for Indian concerns, beliefs, and values, members of the archaeology group offered a host of patronizing excuses for refusing to endorse our calls for repatriation. In this sense, the UCLA struggle mirrored the conflict over human remains ensuing throughout much of the country. In 1989, as the UCLA battle ensued, I accepted an offer to assist the Pawnee government in its efforts as a sovereign nation to reclaim the remains of its ancestors held at the Smithsonian Institution. Being a citizen of this small and impoverished nation of Indians, I welcomed the opportunity to join other Pawnee activists in the repatriation quest. Earlier that year, Congress had enacted a repatriation bill that provided a legal mechanism for Indian governments to reclaim ancestral remains and burial offerings held at the Smithsonian.

Despite the law, obdurate Smithsonian personnel sought to frustrate Indian repatriation efforts with such tactics as stonewalling, deceit, and misinformation. Although Smithsonian personnel claimed that the true identities of six skulls classified as Pawnee could not be positively established, subsequent research on my part uncovered a preponderance of evidence confirming the authenticity of the accession records. This research also showed that, after U.S. soldiers and Kansas settlers had massacred a party of Pawnee men who had been recently discharged from the U.S. army, a Fort Harker surgeon had collected some of the victims' skulls in compliance with army policy and shipped them to the Army Medical Museum for craniometric study.[1]

Since that report, I have written articles, given presentations, and, in conjunction with others, conducted research on behalf of Pawnee repatriation initiatives at Chicago's Field Museum of Natural History. I also have written a report from information found in the Native American Graves Protection and Repatriation Act (NAGPRA) summary letters showing the location of additional Pawnee remains, sacred objects, objects of cultural patrimony, and cultural artifacts.

This essay offers some of my views concerning the reburial aspect of the repatriation struggle. It seeks to show the intellectual and spiritual foundations behind the movement as a means for understanding the complexity of the controversy. It also attempts to demonstrate how repatriation advocates managed to effect discriminatory laws and practices. Finally, it conveys a message that, although old attitudes continue to function within the archaeology and museum communities, a concerted effort brought to bear by people who espouse cooperative relations is in place to bring Indian spiritual beliefs in conformity with non-Indian secular values.

At another level, I write with the intent of creating awareness about a pressing need to disestablish racial, institutional, and societal barriers that impede this country's movement toward a place that celebrates cultural diversity as a cherished and indispensable component of its social, political, and economic fabric. Despite the tone of skepticism, caution, and pessimism found within this study, I envision a society where people can interact freely, respecting one another without regard to race, color, ethnicity, or religious creed. Before this dream becomes a reality, however, America has to find ways to dissolve its racial, gender, cultural, and class barriers.

Pawnee Beliefs, Critical Scholarship, and Oppression

The acts committed against deceased Indians have had profound, even harmful, effects on the living. Therefore, as an activist and historian, I have had to develop a conceptual framework for giving meaning and order to the conflict. The foundation of my perspective concerning repatriation is derived from a combination of cultural, personal, and academic experiences. An understanding of Pawnee religious and philosophical beliefs about death, gained through oral tradition, dreams, and research, informs my view that repatriation is a social justice movement, supported by native spirituality and sovereignty, committed to the amelioration of the twin evils of oppression and scientific racism. Yet I am neither a religious fundamentalist nor a left- or right-wing reactionary. Concerning repatriation, I simply advocate that American Indians receive what virtually every other group of Americans enjoys; that is, the right to religious freedom and a lasting burial.

My training as critical scholar provides another cornerstone of my beliefs about the nature of "imperial archaeology." My writings cast the legacy of scientific body snatching within the realm of oppression. Oppression occurs when a set or sets of individuals within the dominant population behave in ways that infringe on the beliefs, cultures, and political structures of other groups of people. Acts of stealing bodies, infringing on spirituality, and resisting repatriation efforts represent classic examples of oppression.

Although exposed to years of secular interpretations about the nature of the world and the significance of archaeology for understanding the past through formal Euroamerican education, I have continued to accept Pawnee beliefs about the afterlife. To adopt any other perspective regarding this matter would deny my cultural heritage. I cannot reconcile archaeology with tradition because of the secular orientation of the former as well as its intrusive practices. Unlike archaeologists who see Native remains as specimens for study, my people view the bodies of deceased loved ones as representing human life with sacred qualities. Death merely marks the passage of the human spirit to another state of being. In a 1988 statement, then Pawnee President Lawrence Goodfox Jr. expressed a common perspective stressing the negative consequences of grave desecration on our dead: "When our people die and go on to the spirit world, sacred rituals and ceremonies are performed. We believe that if the body is disturbed, the spirit becomes restless and cannot be at peace."[2]

Wandering spirits often beset the living with psychological and health problems. Since time immemorial, Pawnees have ceremoniously buried our dead within Mother Earth. Disinterment can occur only for a compelling religious reason. Equally critical to our perspective are cultural norms that stressed that those who tampered with the dead did so with profane, evil, or demented intentions. From this vantage point, the study of stolen remains constitutes abominable acts of sacrilege, desecration, and depravity. But racist attitudes, complete with such axioms as "The only good Indian is a dead Indian," have long conditioned white society to view Indians (as other nonwhites) as intellectually inferior subhumans who lacked a right to equal treatment under legal and moral codes. Complicating matters, value judgments about the alleged superiority of the white race became interlocked with scientific thought, leading to the development of oppressive practices and policies.

Consequently, orgies of grave looting occurred without remorse. After the Pawnees removed from Nebraska to Oklahoma during the 1870s, local settlers, followed by amateur and professional archaeologists, looted virtually every Pawnee cemetery they could find, taking remains and burial offerings. Much of the "booty" was placed in an array of institutions including the Nebraska State Historical Society (NSHS) and the Smithsonian Institution.[3]

We have a right to be angry at those who dug our dead from the ground, those who established and maintained curatorial policies, and those who denied our repatriation requests. Last year my elderly grandmother chastised white society in her typically reserved but direct fashion for its treatment of our dead. After pointing to an Oklahoma bluff where many Pawnee relatives are buried, she declared, "It is not right, that they dug up all of those bodies in Nebraska."[4] What she referred to can be labeled a spiritual holocaust. When anyone denies us our fundamental human rights, we cannot sit idly by and wait for America to reform itself. It will never happen. We have a duty not only to ourselves but also to our relatives, our unborn generations, and our ancestors to act. Concerning repatriation, we had no choice but to work for retrieval of our ancestral remains for proper reburial and for legislation that provided penalties for those who disrupted the graves of our relatives.

Yet our initiatives sought redress in a peaceful manner. In 1988 Lawrence Goodfox expressed our goals, declaring, "All we want is [the] reburial of the remains of our ancestors and to let them finally rest in peace and for all people in Nebraska to refrain from, forever, any excavation of any Native American graves or burial sites."[5] In our view, reburying the disturbed spirits within Mother Earth equalizes the imbalance between the spiritual and physical worlds caused by the desecration.

National Challenges to Imperial Archaeology and Oppression

The Pawnee reburial struggle occurred within the context of a worldwide indigenous movement. What beset my people had affected Natives everywhere. In this country, few Indian nations escaped the piercing blades of the archaeologists' shovels or the slashes of the headhunters' knives. These operations infringed on Indian beliefs, burial rights, and sovereignty. The notion that this type of research had validity was so ingrained in the psyche of many non-Indians that rarely did anyone question the morality, ethics, or legality of these practices; that is, not until the repatriation movement surfaced in the late 1960s. This movement stands on a paramount footing with the valiant struggles of African Americans for civil rights and women for equality. Taking a leading role during the early stages of the repatriation movement, organizations such as the American Indian Movement (AIM), International Indian Treaty Council, and American Indians Against Desecration (AIAD) expressed in dramatic fashion Indian concerns about the excesses of archaeology and oppression. Committed to the causes of reburying all disinterred Indians and stopping grave disruptions, these groups often employed confrontational strategies. Near Welch, Minnesota, in 1972, for example, AIM members risked arrest by disturbing a dig site. In addition to burning field notes and tools, they confiscated unearthed artifacts and exposed photographic film.[6] Throughout the 1970s and 1980s AIAD challenged the human remains collections and curatorial policies of government agencies, museums, and universities. As time progressed, many college campuses saw a dramatic increase in tensions between Indians and archaeologists. These actions catapulted the repatriation movement into the consciousness of sympathetic politicians, newspaper editors, and members of the general public. Increased knowledge of the issues subsequently spawned unprecedented levels of non-Indian backing of repatriation.

As the 1980s progressed, more conciliatory Indians, often coming from the professions of law and politics, surfaced as leading figures in the movement. Unlike the universal reburial advocates, these moderates tended to see compromise as the most expedient means available to acquire the desired legislation. They often sought a balance between scientific study of Native remains and the need for Indians to gain religious, burial, and repatriation rights under the law. Organizations such as the National Congress of American Indians and the Native American Rights Fund espoused the moderate cause. Realizing that public sentiments increasingly favored the Indians' views, some archaeologists and museum administrators endorsed compromise as a means of cutting their losses and saving face. With common ground beneath their feet, individuals and organizations waged a series of intense political battles at the state and federal levels.[7]

With moderates in control, reform transpired relatively swiftly. By 1992 more than thirty states had placed laws on the books extending protection to Indian cemeteries, including several with repatriation provisions. Congress passed two pieces of legislation, the National Museum of the American Indian Act in 1989 and NAGPRA the following year. Collectively, these national laws provided Indian nations a means to obtain human remains linked to them by a "preponderance of evidence" and associated funerary offerings held by institutions that received federal funding. NAGPRA also provides penalties for individuals convicted of trafficking in human remains.[8]

Ongoing Reburial Initiatives

With legal avenues now open for Indian governments to reclaim stolen ancestral remains and associated burial objects, some of the old repressive policies fell by the wayside. The change enabled relatives to begin the task of reclaiming stolen bodies and grave offerings for reburial. Collectively, Indian nations thus far have interred thousands of stolen remains. To date (summer 1995), the Pawnees alone have placed nearly a thousand bodies back in Mother Earth. The total number of recovered bodies will surely reach the tens of thousands within a few years.

Reinterment ceremonies, along with funeral feasts, evoke a gamut of emotional expressions ranging from sorrow to joy. When conducting reburials, people rejoice at the fact that the repatriated remains are finally being returned to Mother Earth, but, like modern funerals, an air of sadness pervades the ceremonies. In particular, reinterring the remains of young children causes grieving and weeping. Mourning is part of the healing process in that reburials seek to restore harmony between the living and dead by putting restless spirits to rest. At another level, reburials bring closure to bitterly contested struggles.

Future Concerns

Legislation emanating from the repatriation movement has changed the customary ways that archaeologists and museums operate. Most notably, Indian governments now have established a sovereign right to reclaim the bodies of their ancestors from offending museums, universities, and federal agencies. In this capacity, they have the power to grant and deny access to their dead. Additionally, the new laws make face-to-face interaction routine between museums and Indian nations in certain repatriation matters. Several observers have proclaimed that the common ground signals the dawning of a new era of cooperative relations between Indians and museums.[9] Despite changing attitudes and practices, it is too soon to assess the long-term ramifications of the reburial controversy. Six problematic areas cause me concern about the future of repatriation:

First, the laws do not provide for the reinterment of ancient, unclaimed, or unidentified remains. In other words, the fate of tens of thousands of bodies, along with associated funerary offerings, is uncertain. Will those with authority take steps to provide for a proper reburial for these bodies or will they allow the continuance of old practices and policies?

Second, the absence of legislation and aggressive enforcement of burial protection laws in some states may send a message that grave looting can resume without fear of arrest, prosecution, or punishment.

Third, NAGPRA's graves protection stipulations apply only to federal lands and entities that receive federal funding. In states without both progressive reburial legislation and a substantial Indian populace, large-scale acts of grave desecration may continue. Texas offers a case in point. The nineteenth-century white Americans who occupied Texas established a republic that implemented a policy of "ethnic cleansing," consisting of slaughtering and forcibly removing Indians elsewhere. Upon entering the Union, Texas retained control over most of its lands. Today, only three relatively small Indian nations in Texas have federal recognition, a prerequisite for issuing NAGPRA claims, and about 2 percent of the state is part of the public domain.[10] Further, institutions that function without federal funds remain free to pursue the inflammatory practices that gave rise to the repatriation conflict. Even after NAGPRA became law, Dickson Mound, a state-funded museum and tourist attraction in Illinois that displayed over a hundred Indian bodies, continued business as usual. Protests by AIM and others, however, generated so much negative publicity that the governor opted to close the site and to allow the contested remains to be reburied.

Fourth, and perhaps most significant, a pervasive attitude among elements of the archaeology and museum communities keeps repressive and archaic ideas alive. In fact, members of these groups have consistently disavowed any wrongdoing by themselves and their predecessors. Rather, some present their work to the public as neutral, impartial, and objective interpretations of distant Native American cultures. To counter claims that the digging and study is disrespectful, others assert that taking remains for study shows respect for Indian people and culture. In a twisted logic, still others insist that they are the "true spiritual descendants of the original Indians and the contemporary Indians [are] foreigners who had no right to complain about their activities."[11] Like most other repatriation advocates, I reject these pleas as condescending and duplicitous acts of misguided people and lost souls.

To comprehend the depth of the problem, we should briefly consider the rise of scientific racism. European colonization of the Americas fomented an intellectual environment conducive to the development of the values, codes of ethics, and professional responsibility that imperial archaeologists of the present century espouse. Grave disruptions grew in popularity in a milieu of Indian-white relations characterized by violent territorial expansion, virulent racism, and cultural suppression. Many nineteenth-century scholars adopted a research agenda that sought to rationalize their country's aggression. Coveting Indian skulls for racial studies that used craniometric studies, they paid civilians and military personnel to loot Native cemeteries. Craniometric research sought to validate, with the stamp of scientific certainty, the alleged barbarous, savage, and warlike characteristics of Indian life. The cause of this retarded and brutish behavior accordingly could be explained by the smallness of the Indians' brains.[12] Samuel G. Morton, called "the father of American physical anthropology," was a leader in this movement. Following suit from the 1860s to the 1890s, the U.S. army accumulated several thousand Indian skulls and skeletal parts.[13] Although intelligence studies of this nature ultimately failed to achieve their objective, cravings for Native bodies escalated dramatically. Anthropologists, believing that Indians were a vanishing people, embarked on a campaign to "preserve" material and sacred objects belonging to Indian culture. Consequently, Indian remains became so central to archaeological inquiry in universities that the granting of degrees and promotions hinged on the accessibility of Indian graves to dig and bodies to study. Emerging anthropology and archaeology departments during the late nineteenth and early twentieth centuries carved out an academic niche. By studying Indian graves and remains, archaeologists soon professed an ability to extract knowledge from Native graves to reveal information about alleged primitive cultures. As historian Robert E. Bieder notes, however, "The basic theoretical assumptions derived from earlier nineteenth-century research continued—that non-whites were biologically and intellectually inferior to whites."[14]

While masquerading as the bearers of universal truth and wisdom about Indian cultures and peoples, many twentieth-century archaeologists promoted the teachings and practices of their predecessors. Professors inculcated their students with secular values that recognized Native bodies as specimens. Many of them ignored emerging notions such as cultural relativism and human subject research ethics. In their way of thinking, science had endowed them with special rights and privileges. Secular humanist values, beliefs, and ethics also served as grounds for dismissing repatriation requests as illegal, illogical, and counterproductive. After all, Congress had promoted archaeological inquiry when it enacted the Antiquity Act of 1906. This statute, considered without Indian input, bequeathed Native bodies and burial objects found on public lands to science.

With such laws stipulating the placement of remains, burial offerings, and other unearthed objects in public institutions forever, universities, state historical societies, museums, and federal agencies became mausoleums. Throughout the nation (and world), these facilities jealously guarded their share of pillaged Indian remains, which totaled in the tens of thousands, if not millions. Committed to preserving the status quo, many of them expressed indignation toward repatriation through such colonialistic organizations as the Society of American Archaeology (SAA), American Anthropology Association, and American Committee for the Preservation of Archaeological Collections (ACPAC). In 1985 an SAA executive committee member revealed the racism and passion held by many archaeologists, stating that "The only good Indian is an unreburied one."[15] ACPAC, perhaps the most outwardly haughty and imperious of the imperialist groups, even threatened to blackball members of the profession who assisted repatriation efforts.[16]

By the 1980s imperial archaeologists had produced numerous studies and reports aimed at undermining and discrediting the repatriation movement. In a widely circulated piece of propaganda, Bruce D. Smith of the Smithsonian Institution employed the acronym URPies (Universal Repatriation Proponents) to ridicule reburial advocates. Others claimed that Indian activists had simply invented religious beliefs to gain legal standing in court proceedings involving Native remains.[17]

Saving Indians from historical and cultural ignorance surfaced as another rationalization for preserving archaeology in its traditional form. Some archaeologists, ignoring the fact that oral traditions remain intact in many Native communities, asserted brashly that science had a moral obligation to teach living Indians about the past. Their research accordingly provided

Natives, along with the rest of the world, vital information about ancient cultures, including data concerning diet, life expectancy, morbidity, health, disease, cultural development, and migration patterns. When taken literally, these universal appeals to preserve human remains collections stressed that repatriation might somehow undermine the well-being and vitality of humanity. This utilitarian posturing has been dubbed the "Dr. Frankenstein defense." In other words, any research conducted in the name of science was assumed to be legitimate, necessary, and beneficial.[18] In this sanctimonious way of thinking, the ends justified the means.

Anti-repatriation advocates echoed a common refrain. They viewed their pursuits as being under attack by narrow-minded and anti-intellectual radicals who sought to destroy archaeology. Equating repatriation with book burning, some alarmists often charged falsely that Indians would not rest until they had stripped museums and universities of their Indian collections. These strategies contain elements of self-delusion, arrogance, and racism. A tacit message found in these paternalistic defenses of imperial archaeology was that Indians must, for their own good, learn to respect the work of archaeology. Equally disturbing is the notion that Indians need archaeology. However, the exact opposite is true. Beneath the self-serving rhetoric lay a deceptive ambience of cultural imperialism that masked the stark reality of how archaeology and museums infringed on Indian religion and burial rights.[19]

Fifth, imperial archaeologists have had substantial levels of support from real and pretend Indians. The phenomena of co-optation and self-interest reverberates loudly here. Usually found working in museums, universities, and government agencies, some of these individuals claim a heritage complete with a Cherokee princess, but they embrace the secular views and values of Western science. Others belonging to this camp clearly have significant amounts of Indian blood, but they rely heavily on the goodwill of their non-Indian colleagues to promote and maintain their careers. Non-institutional advocacy surfaced from some grassroots Indians. At meetings, conferences, and confrontations, archaeologists rarely failed to produce a reservation Indian or two who spoke passionately against reburial in an effort to convince the public and policymakers that Native communities lacked unanimity on the subject. Whatever their motive, degree of Indian blood, or cultural orientation, their willingness to endorse oppressive archaeological practices marks a radical departure from traditional Indian philosophy.[20]

Collectively, "wannabes" and misguided Indians may be able to damage reburial efforts. As the movement pushed for national repatriation legislation in the late 1980s, we found them sitting on committees convened by anthropology and museum associations that issued reports condemning re-patriation. In a worst-case scenario, NAGPRA and other committees stacked with them and imperial archaeologists could conceivably frustrate or un-dermine repatriation requests.

Finally, it seems that archaeologists have launched a campaign to con-vince the public, tribal leaders, and others that skeletal investigations are necessary for a variety of reasons. According to a recent *Chronicle of Higher Education* article, "More and more of those kinds of opportunities will occur, many scholars agree, when researchers learn to persuade American Indians and others that skeletal remains and artifacts represent something other than a publication toward a faculty member's promotion and tenure."[21] In other words, we are seeing archaeologists adopt less abrasive tactics to get their hands on our dead. Succumbing to subtle pressure, aimed at convinc-ing us to accept a secular view of the dead as research objects, will erode a cherished part of our belief systems and cultures. In any event, some In-dian nations have allowed the creation of archaeology programs on their reservations.

Clearly, the repatriation movement has won some major victories, but the war is unfinished. U.S. history teaches the lesson that individuals who face the threat of losing a privileged status often will devise rationaliza-tions and strategies to resist change. Southern slave owners, for example, argued against abolitionism by making the outlandish claim that involun-tary servitude was a benevolent institution that saved millions of blacks from the savagery of Africa. Historians repeated this claim well into the twentieth century.

It is conceivable that at some point someone will challenge the constitu-tionality of NAGPRA. If this occurs, will the courts respect Indian beliefs and burial rights? America's long history concerning issues of Indian religious freedom and political rights makes the possibility of a legal suit a scary thought. The Supreme Court has occasionally protected Indian sovereignty, as well as hunting, fishing, and water rights, but it also has incorporated such imperialistic notions as the doctrine of discovery and the plenary power doctrine into U.S. law. Its decisions also have eroded the power of Indian self-government by allowing the imposition of federal jurisdiction over certain crimes committed on Indian lands.

In recent years conservative justices appointed by President Ronald Rea-gan have endangered Indian religious freedom. In *Lyng v. Northwest Indian Cemetery Protective Association* (108 S. Ct. 1319 [1988]) Justice Sandra Day O'Connor wrote the majority decision stating that the U.S. government had the right to build a road through an area on federal lands sacred to Yurok, Karok, and Tolowa Indians even if such a construction project would destroy the ability of those people to worship. In *Employment Division, Department of Human Resources of Oregon v. Smith* (110 S. Ct. 1595 [1990]) the court held that a state could abridge expressions of religious freedom if the state had a compelling reason to do so. In this case, the court paved the way for states to deprive Native American Church (NAC) members of the right to use peyote in connection with their worship.[22] Fortunately, in 1994 Congress addressed the religious crisis caused by the court by enacting a law that sanctioned peyote use for NAC services.

History demonstrates that promises made by white America to help Indians have not always materialized. The administrative branch of the federal government has entered into 371 treaties with Indian nations and systematically violated each of them. The legislative record is another cause of concern. The Indian Reorganization Act of 1934 authorized Indian nations to restructure themselves politically but only in accordance with models and terms acceptable to Department of Interior officials. During the 1970s Congress declared that Indian government could exercise more powers of self-government. Federal bureaucratic controls over Indian governments, however, actually became more stringent, if not suffocating, in this era. During that decade Congress also enacted the American Indian Religious Freedom Act of 1978 in a half-hearted effort to encourage federal agencies to accommodate customary Indian worship practices at off-reservation sites. The act provided virtually no protection because federal agencies and the Supreme Court, as we have seen, have followed a tradition that sees nothing wrong with suppressing Indian religious freedom.[23] Although Indians are pursuing a legislative remedy to resolve these problems, Congress has yet to enact a true religious freedom law for them.

Facing overwhelming odds, the repatriation movement has achieved many noteworthy successes. U.S. society, including a growing number of sympathetic archaeologists and museum curators, has finally recognized that Indians are not disappearing and that Indians are entitled to burial rights and religious freedom. Nevertheless, under the new repatriation laws, many non-Indian entities still "legally" hold thousands of Indian remains and burial offerings. With many archaeologists and museum curators committed to upholding oppressive operational principles, values, and beliefs, the fate of these bodies remains in question. Moreover, others, perhaps best described as wolves in sheeps' clothing, are seeking to gain our cooperation, a euphemism meaning the delivery of another blow to our revered philosophies about the dead.

Given the durability of imperialist archaeology and the new approaches being used to gain access to the remains of our beloved ancestors, we must remain vigilant and monitor their operations. Protecting our dead must remain a moral and spiritual obligation we cannot callously abandon, for we cannot allow further erosions of our beliefs and traditions. Thus a need still exists for maintaining the cultural traditions that inspired the repatriation movement.

Notes

1. In the spring of 1995 the Smithsonian Institution and National Museum of Health and Medicine returned these six crania to the Pawnees for reburial. See James Riding In, "Six Pawnee Crania: Historical and Contemporary Issues Associated with the Massacre and Decapitation of Pawnee Indians in 1869," *American Indian Culture and Research Journal* 16, no. 2 (1992): 101–19.

2. Quoted in Robert M. Peregoy, "Nebraska's Landmark Repatriation Law: A Study of Cross-Cultural Conflict and Resolution," *American Indian Culture and Research Journal* 16, no. 2 (1992): 140.

3. Generally see Riding In, "Without Ethics and Morality: A Historical Overview of Imperial Archaeology and American Indians," *Arizona State Law Journal* 24 (spring 1992): 12–13. See also Orlan J. Svingen, "The Pawnee of Nebraska: Twice Removed," *American Indian Culture and Research Journal* 16, no. 2 (1992): 121–37; Roger C. Echo-Hawk and Walter R. Echo-Hawk, *Battlefields and Burial Grounds: The Indian Struggle to Protect Ancestral Graves in the United States* (Minneapolis: Lerner Publications Company, 1994), 41–71.

4. Ethel Riding In, who is now eighty-eight years old, made these comments several years ago as we drove within the former boundaries of the Pawnee reservation in Oklahoma.

5. Quoted in Peregoy, "Nebraska's Landmark Repatriation Law," 140.

6. "Indians and Archeologists Battle over Bones and Burials," *Amerindian* (Chicago), 20 (July–August 1972): 6.

7. For examples of writings from the moderate perspective, generally see Jack F. Trope and Walter R. Echo-Hawk, "The Native American Graves Protection and Repatriation Act: Background and Legislative History," *Arizona State Law Journal* 24 (spring 1992): 35–77 (chap. 7, this vol.).

8. Walter R. Echo-Hawk, "Preface," *American Indian Culture and Research Journal* 16, no. 2 (1992): 3. It should be noted that states began extending burial protection laws to include Indians during the 1970s. For a discussion of NAGPRA, see Trope and Echo-Hawk, "Native American Graves Protection and Repatriation Act."

9. Martin Sullivan, "A Museum Perspective on Repatriation: Issues and Opportunities," *Arizona State Law Journal* 24 (spring 1992): 291.

10. Steve Russell, "Contesting the Domain of the Dead: The Legacy of Ethnic Cleansing in Implementation of the Native American Graves Protection and Repatriation Act," 30–43. This paper was presented at the Law and Society Conference, Phoenix, Arizona, on 16 June 1994. A copy of the manuscript is on file with the author.

11. Vine Deloria Jr., *God Is Red: A Native View of Religion* (Golden CO: Fulcrum Publishing, 1994), 14.

12. Generally see Robert E. Bieder, "Collecting of Bone for Anthropological Narratives," *American Indian Culture and Research Journal* 16, no. 2 (1992).

13. Generally see Riding In, "Six Pawnee Crania."

14. Bieder, "Collecting of Bone for Anthropological Narratives," 31.

15. Larry J. Zimmerman, "Webb on Reburial: A North American Perspective," *Antiquity* 61 (1987): 462.

16. ACPAC *Newsletter* (December 1986): 5.

17. Bruce D. Smith, "URPIE Logic: An Analysis of the Structure of the Supporting Arguments of Universal Reburial Proponents," (n.d.). A copy of this manuscript is on file with the author. H. Marcus Price III, *Disputing the Dead: U.S. Law on Aboriginal Remains and Grave Goods* (Columbia: University of Missouri Press, 1991), 11–13.

18. Nancy Oestreich Lurie et al., "Statements of the American Anthropological Association Commission on the Treatment of Human Remains," (n.d.). A copy of this report is on file with the author. Riding In, "Without Ethics and Morality," 31.

19. Zimmerman, "Archaeology, Reburial, and the Tactics of a Discipline's Self-Delusion," *American Indian Culture and Research Journal* 16, no. 2 (1992): 37–56; Nebraska State Historical Society, *Historical Newsletter* 41 (February 1989): 1–4.

20. Ibid.; Lurie et al., "Statement on the Treatment of Human Remains." Two Indian anthropologists, Jo Allyn Archambault of the Smithsonian Institution and Alfonso Ortiz of the University of New Mexico, sat on a committee that issued this report in opposition to S. 1980, a repatriation bill introduced by Senator Daniel K. Inouye.

21. Ellen K. Coughlin, "Returning Indian Remains," *Chronicle of Higher Education* 16 (March 1994): 8.

22. Deloria, "Trouble in High Places: Erosion of American Indian Rights to Religious Freedom in the United States," in *The State of Native America: Genocide, Colonization, and Resistance,* ed. M. Annette Jaimes (Boston: South End Press, 1992), 271–75.

23. Generally see Deloria, "Secularism, Civil Religion, and the Religious Freedom of American Indians," *American Indian Culture and Research Journal* 16, no. 2 (1992): 9–20 (chap. 8, this vol.); Walter R. Echo-Hawk, "Native American Religious Liberty: Five Hundred Years after Columbus, *American Indian Culture and Research Journal* 17, no. 3 (1993): 33–52. For a case study, see D. Michael Pavel, Gerald B. Miller, and Mary J. Pavel, "Too Long, Too Silent: The Threat to Cedar and the Sacred Ways of the Skokomish," *American Indian Culture and Research Journal* 17, no. 3 (1993): 53–80.

Part 3

Legal and Ethical Issues

7

Jack F. Trope and Walter R. Echo-Hawk

The Native American Graves Protection and Repatriation Act

Background and Legislative History

Introduction

On November 23, 1990, President George Bush signed into law important human rights legislation: the Native American Graves Protection and Repatriation Act ("NAGPRA").[1] This legislation culminates decades of struggle by Native American tribal governments and people to protect against grave desecration, to repatriate thousands of dead relatives or ancestors, and to retrieve stolen or improperly acquired religious and cultural property for Native owners.

In many ways, NAGPRA is historic, landmark legislation for Native Americans. It represents fundamental changes in basic social attitudes toward Native peoples by the museum and scientific communities and the public at large. NAGPRA provides nationwide repatriation standards and procedures for the return of Native remains and certain protected materials from federal agencies and federally funded institutions. Because of the massive scope of the repatriation problem, however, a lengthy implementation period can be expected for this human rights legislation.[2] This article seeks to facilitate implementation of the new national policy by providing attorneys, Indian tribes, museums, and scientists with (1) background on the repatriation issue; and (2) an informed analysis of the provisions of NAGPRA and their interaction.

The Native American repatriation topic involves a wide array of complex, and sometimes competing, social interests, including human rights, race relations, religion, science, education, ethics, and law. Much has been written on the topic from the perspective of these social interests.[3] Admittedly, the law has played a relatively minor role in considering these often conflicting interests. It is appropriate, however, that the law play a significant role because it should embody the highest values and ethics of the society that it is intended to serve.[4]

Across the nation, society has vigorously debated these issues in recent years. Museums and scientists have argued that Native human remains have scientific and educational value and, therefore, should be preserved for these important purposes. Tribes have argued that protection of the sepulchre of the dead is an important attribute in our society. This protection includes fundamental legal rights that everyone—except Natives—can take for granted. Unfortunately, the law and policy that protect the sanctity of the dead and the sensibilities of the living have failed to protect North Americans. This article suggests that American laws have indeed failed to accord equal protection. Moreover, the resulting disparate racial treatment has caused painful human rights violations in tribal communities. As the repatriation struggle became protracted and reached the federal level, it became a test for our country's commitment to the underlying values of the Bill of Rights and to our American sense of social justice.

Much of the national debate culminated in the passage of NAGPRA—though implementation of that law and its new national policy remain. NAGPRA is a primary subject of this article, which will cover four areas: (1) the historical origins, nature, and scope of the controversy from a Native American perspective; (2) a summary of legal and political rights that are at stake when Indian tribes seek to repatriate their dead relatives; (3) legal and legislative activities in this area of rapid social change; and (4) a description of the background, legislative history, and provisions of NAGPRA.

The Origins, Scope, and Nature of the Repatriation Issue

Human Remains and Funerary Objects

In all ages, humankind has protected the sanctity of the deal. Indeed, respect for the dead is a mark of humanity and is as old as religion itself. British Prime Minister William Ewart Gladstone once wrote: "Show me the manner in which a nation or a community cares for its dead, and I will measure with mathematical exactness the tender sympathies of its people, their respect for the laws of the land, and their loyalty to high ideals."[5]

Like most other nations, respect for the dead is deeply ingrained in American social fabric and jurisprudence. One legal commentator noted:

> After a lifetime of investigation of the origin of religious structure, the great Sir James G. Frazier concluded that awe toward the dead was probably the most powerful force in forming primitive systems for grappling with the supernatural.

The sepulture of the dead has, in all ages of the world been regarded as a religious rite. The place where the dead are deposited all civilized nations, and many barbarous ones, regard in some measure at least, as consecrated ground. In the old Saxon tongue the burial ground of the dead was "God's Acre."

[American cases] all agree in principle: The normal treatment of a corpse, once it is decently buried, is to let it lie. This idea is so deeply woven into our legal and cultural fabric that it is commonplace to hear it spoken of as a "right" of the dead and a charge on the quick. [No] system of jurisprudence permits exhumation for less than what are considered weighty, and sometimes compelling reasons.[6]

These basic values are strictly protected in all fifty states, and the District of Columbia, by statutes that comprehensively regulate cemeteries and protect graves from vandalism and desecration.[7] Criminal laws prohibit grave robbing and mutilation of the dead and ensure that human remains are not mistreated. Statutes in most states guarantee that all persons—including paupers, indigents, prisoners, strangers, and other unclaimed dead—are entitled to a decent burial.[8]

Disinterment of the dead is strongly disfavored under American common law except under the most compelling circumstances,[9] and then only under close judicial supervision or under carefully prescribed permit requirements, which may include judicial consent.[10] Common law goes to great lengths to protect the sanctity of the dead.[11]

Unfortunately, the above legal protections—which most citizens take for granted—have failed to protect the graves and the dead of Native people. Massive numbers of Indian dead have been dug up from their graves and carried away. National estimates are that between one hundred thousand and two million deceased Native people have been dug up from their graves for storage or display by government agencies, museums, universities, and tourist attractions.[12] The practice is so widespread that virtually every Indian tribe or Native group in the country has been affected by non-Indian grave looting.

The dark and troubling circumstances of how these Native dead were obtained has been thoroughly documented by historians. Human remains were obtained by soldiers, government agents, pothunters, private citizens, museum collecting crews, and scientists in the name of profit, entertainment, science, or development.[13]

The problem that the law seeks to remedy is one that has characterized Indian-white relations since the Pilgrims landed at Plymouth Rock in 1620. The first Pilgrim exploring party returned to the Mayflower with corn taken from Indian storage pits and items removed from a grave: "We brought sundry of the prettiest things away with us, and covered up the corpse again."[14]

Early interest in systematically collecting Indian body parts began before the Civil War. Dr. Samuel Morton, the father of American physical anthropology, collected large numbers of Indian crania in the 1840s. His goal was to scientifically prove, through skull measurements, that the American Indian was a racially inferior "savage" who was naturally doomed to extinction.[15] Morton's findings established the "Vanishing Red Man" theory, which was embraced by government policymakers as "scientific justification" for relocating Indian tribes, taking tribal land, and conducting genocide—in certain instances—against American Indians.[16]

Later, the search for Indian body parts became official federal policy with the Surgeon General's Order of 1868. The policy directed army personnel to procure Indian crania and other body parts for the Army Medical Museum.[17] In ensuing decades, over four thousand heads were taken from battlefields, burial grounds, POW camps, hospitals, fresh graves, and burial scaffolds across the country. Government headhunters decapitated Natives who had never been buried, such as slain Pawnee warriors from a western Kansas battleground,[18] Cheyenne and Arapaho victims of Colorado's Sand Creek Massacre,[19] and defeated Modoc leaders who were hanged and then shipped to the Army Medical Museum.[20] One 1892 account of rainy night grave robbing of fifteen Blackfeet Indian graves is chilling:

> I collected them in a way somewhat unusual: the burial place is in plain sight of many Indian houses and very near frequent roads. I had to visit the country at night when not even the dogs were stirring . . . after securing one [skull] I had to pass the Indian sentry at the stockade gate which I never attempted with more than one [skull], for fear of detection.
>
> . . .
>
> On one occasion I was followed by an Indian who did not comprehend my movements, and I made a circuitous route away from the place intended and threw him off his suspicions. On stormy nights—rain, snow or wind & bitter cold, I think I was never observed going or coming, by either Indians or dogs, but on pleasant nights—I was always seen but of course no one knew what I had in my coat . . . the greatest fear I had was that some Indian would miss the heads, see my tracks & ambush me, but they didn't. I regret the lower maxillae are not on each skull, I got all I could find, and they are all detached save one. There is in the box a left radius & ulna of a woman, with the identical bracelets on

that were buried with her. The bones of themselves are nothing, but the combination with the ornaments make them a little noticeable.[21]

During this period collecting crews from America's newly founded museums engaged in competitive expeditions to obtain Indian skeletons. As Franz Boas, the famous American anthropologist, observed in the 1880s, "it is most unpleasant work to steal bones from graves, but what is the use, someone has to do it."[22] Scientific means were not always used by museum collecting expeditions during this period, which can better be described, in some instances, as "fervid rip-and-run operations."[23] Some museums employed outright deception in order to obtain skeletons. New York's American Museum of Natural History, for example, literally staged a fake funeral for a deceased Eskimo to prevent his son from discovering that the museum had stolen the remains.[24] In 1990 one Sioux leader decried these museum activities in testimony before the United States Senate:

> [T]his [Bieder Report] is a very difficult report for an Indian to read. Earlier I talked about meeting with many of the traditional people. They constantly tell us that the white man won't believe you unless it's written in black and white. It's got to be written in black and white. . . . So today we have something written in black and white. It's a very sad account of the atrocities. It's a shameful account of how museums—some of the museums that were here today actually competed with each other and hired people to rob graves of Native American people.[25]

At the turn of the century Congress continued its deplorable federal policy with the passage of the Antiquities Act of 1906.[26] That act, which was intended to protect "archaeological resources" located on federal lands from looters, defined dead Indians interred on federal lands as "archaeological resources" and, contrary to long-standing common-law principles, converted these dead persons into "federal property."[27] The Antiquities Act allowed these dead persons to be dug up pursuant to a federal permit "for the permanent preservation [of the remains] in public museums."[28] Since then, thousands of Indian dead have been classified as "archaeological resources" and exhumed as "federal property."[29]

In summary, American social policy has historically treated Indian dead differently than the dead of other races. Unfortunately, it has been commonplace for public agencies to treat Native American dead as *archaeological resources, property, pathological material, data, specimens,* or *library books,* but not as *human beings.* Many contemporary examples of mistreatment of Native graves and dead bodies occurred in recent years under this rubric, which shocked the Nation's conscience as social ethics have changed and society has become more sensitive to this equal protection problem.

Sacred Objects and Cultural Patrimony

One pattern that defines Indian-white relations in the United States is the one-way transfer of Indian property to non-Indian ownership. By the 1870s, after most tribes were placed on small reservations, the government's acquisition of Indian lands had in large part been accomplished. Thereafter the pattern shifted from real estate to personalty and continued until most of the material culture of Native people had been transferred to white hands. That massive property transfer invariably included some stolen or improperly acquired Native sacred objects and cultural patrimony. Native owners who sought the return of their property, as it turned up in museums, experienced inordinate difficulty in securing its return.[30]

One historian commented on the enormous transfer of cultural property that occurred in a short, fifty-year period:

> During the half-century or so after 1875, a staggering quantity of material, both secular and sacred—from spindle whorls to soul-catchers—left the hands of their native creators and users for the private and public collections of the European world. The scramble . . . was pursued sometimes with respect, occasionally with rapacity, often with avarice. By the time it ended there was more Kwakiutal material in Milwaukee than in Mamalillikulla, more Salish pieces in Cambridge than in Comox. The City of Washington contained more Northwest Coast material than the state of Washington and New York City probably housed more British Columbia material than British Columbia itself.
>
> . . .
>
> In retrospect it is clear that the goods flowed irrevocably from Native hands to Euro-American ones until little was left in possession of the people who had invented, made, and used them.[31]

Though some of that property transfer was through legitimate trade and intercourse, a significant amount of Native property was acquired through illegitimate means. This problem was brought to the attention of Congress by the Carter Administration in 1979 following a one-year study mandated by the American Indian Religious Freedom Act,[32] as follows:

> Museum records show that some sacred objects were sold by their original Native owner or owners. In many instances, however, the chain of title does not lead to the original owners. Some religious property left the original ownership during military confrontations, was included in

the spoils of war and eventually fell to the control of museums. Also in times past, sacred objects were lost by Native owners as a result of less violent pressures exerted by federally-sponsored missionaries and Indian agents.

Most sacred objects were stolen from their original owners. In other cases, religious property was converted and sold by Native people who did not have ownership or title to the sacred object.

Today in many parts of the country, it is common for "pothunters" to enter Indian and public lands for the purpose of illegally expropriating sacred objects. Interstate trafficking in and exporting of such property flourishes, with some of these sacred objects eventually entering into the possession of museums.[33]

The adverse impacts that a refusal to return stolen or improperly acquired sacred material has upon First Amendment rights of tribal religious practitioners,[34] and upon basic property rights,[35] has been noted by scholars and commentators. This issue has increasingly become of great concern among tribes and traditional religious practitioners. NAGPRA establishes a national standard and procedure for the return of this property to Native owners.[36]

Legal Rights to Repatriate the Dead

The Failure of the Legal System to Protect Native Burial Sites

COMMON LAW

The legal system also contributed to the disparate treatment of Native American human remains and funerary objects by failing to incorporate indigenous needs and values into the common law as it developed in the United States. The jurisprudence that protects the sanctity of the dead and the sensibilities of the living is the common law, which we inherited from England. Common law is judge-made law that is supposed to safeguard considerations of justice and equity; it evolves and changes over time to meet society's changing needs.[37] Unfortunately, during its development in this country, the common law failed to take into account unique indigenous burial practices and mortuary traditions. As explained by one legal scholar:

At a sensitive point in time when American courts were developing a foundation of experience-based common law and legislators were enacting specific statutes for cemeteries and burials reflecting the American condition and requirements, the courts and law makers were deprived of the benefit of consideration of practical issues of appropriate disposition of prehistorical aboriginal remains and grave goods and the property rights of Indians to these items. Thus, when issues later surfaced in the courts, the judicial system was forced to attempt to apply an established body of statutes and experience-based common law to situations that law had not previously considered and with which it was ill suited to deal.[38]

The lack of access to courts by Native Americans during this formative period is understandable. Disputes between Native people and American citizens were usually settled on the battlefield, instead of in courtrooms. Furthermore, in light of prevailing racial views of the time, Indians had little realistic hope of a fair hearing in American courts. Just as racial oppression against African Americans was justified by United States Supreme Court decisions such as *Plessey v. Ferguson,*[39] similar decisions branded Indian Nations as ignorant and uncivilized.[40] Supreme Court decisions characterized Indians "as an inferior race of people, without privileges of citizens."[41] It was not until 1879 that a federal court ruled that an Indian was a "person" within the meaning of federal law.[42] Moreover, Indians were not granted citizenship until 1924.[43]

Hence, American legal protections for the dead did not take into account unique Native mortuary practices such as scaffold, canoe, or tree burials.[44] The law did not protect unmarked Native graves like it protected marked European graves. Nor did the law recognize that Native people maintain close religious connections with ancient dead; instead, the right to protect the dead was limited to the decedent's immediate next of kin. The law also failed to take into account relevant historical circumstances such as government removal of tribes away from their burial grounds and the need to accord legal protection for the graves and cemeteries that were involuntarily left behind.

Native people were faced with highly ethnocentric decisions in some common-law cases. For example, in *Wana the Bear v. Community Construction, Inc.,*[45] the court held that a historic Indian cemetery was not a "cemetery" within the meaning of state cemetery-protection laws.[46] In *State v. Glass,*[47] the court held that older human skeletal remains are not considered "human" for purposes of an Ohio grave-robbing statute, which leaves only aboriginal remains in an unprotected status in that state.[48] The decision in *Carter v. City of Zanesville*[49] held that a cemetery may be considered "abandoned" if no further interments are done.[50] The abandonment doctrine might make sense if applied to European communities that voluntarily abandon local cemeteries, but it becomes highly ethnocentric when applied to cemeteries of relocated Indian tribes.

STATE STATUTORY LAW

Loopholes in state statutory law, which universally supplement common-law protections, contributed to the failure to protect Native graves.[51] State grave and cemetery protection statutes typically regulated and protected marked graves but not unmarked graves. Because in many instances Indian graves are unmarked, they received no statutory protection. As such, many unmarked Indian graves were discovered, disturbed, or dug up through construction, natural causes, or pothunting—and the remains were never re-buried. For example, Illinois, despite comprehensive grave-protection laws, allowed an entire Indian cemetery containing 234 men, women, and children to be uncovered for public display at the Dickson Mounds Museum.[52]

Legal Theories Supporting Protection and Repatriation of Native Dead
Despite the failure of law and social policy to protect Native American graves in the past, a proper nondiscriminatory application of the law provides a strong legal basis for tribal grave protection and repatriation efforts. In addition to new statutory rights, five sources of law exist that can provide the underpinning for tribal grave protection efforts and repatriation claims: (1) the common law; (2) the equal protection clauses of the Fifth and Fourteenth Amendments; (3) the First Amendment; (4) the sovereign right of Indian tribal governments to govern internal domestic affairs; and (5) Indian treaties.

COMMON LAW

If applied equally, common law offers a variety of protections for Native Americans. Although the area of common law that protects the dead is voluminous and sometimes obscure, it dispels many popular myths and legal fictions that have been injurious to Native Americans. First, no "property interest" exists in a dead body in the eyes of the common law.[53] This rule makes it impossible to own the remains of a Native American; the dead of any race are simply not chattels to be bought or sold in the marketplace.

Second, the popular fiction that a landowner may own and sell the contents of Indian graves located on his land is legally erroneous. A landowner only has *technical possession* of graves located on his land and is required to hold them *in trust* for the relatives of the deceased.[54] Therefore, no institution may have title to dead Indians obtained from landowners because landowners have no title to convey.[55]

Another harmful myth that is popular among pothunters and private collectors is that objects *found* in Indian graves belong to the finder under a *finders keepers, losers weepers* rule. This myth runs afoul of the rule that personal possessions interred with the dead[56] are not abandoned property. To the contrary, whenever funerary objects are removed from graves, they belong to the person who furnished the grave or to his known descendants.[57] Thus, the title that pothunters and collectors have to objects that were removed from Indian graves may be invalid under the common law.

In summary, common-law protections should apply to Indian graves and Indian dead with the same force that the courts have applied them to the dead of other races. In fact, some courts have applied the common law to protect Indian dead.[58]

EQUAL PROTECTION

Disparate racial treatment in matters affecting Indian dead may run afoul of the equal protection clauses of the Fifth and Fourteenth Amendments.[59] An equal protection claim may arise if government agencies treat Indian graves or remains differently than the dead of other races. Laws and policies that treat Indian dead as *archaeological resources, property,* or *historic property* are suspect when compared to laws that ordinarily protect the dead of other races. Overt discrimination, such as the 1868 Surgeon General's Order, could not pass muster today under the equal protection clause.

FIRST AMENDMENT

First Amendment free exercise rights are implicated if the government withholds Indian dead from next of kin or tribes of origin. Humankind has always buried the dead with religion, and Native Americans are no different. Therefore, it is not surprising that Native religious beliefs and practices may be infringed upon when tribal dead are desecrated, disturbed, or withheld from burial by the government. In 1855 Chief Seattle told U.S. treaty negotiators, "To us the ashes of our ancestors are sacred and their resting place is hallowed ground."[60]

Indeed, Indian Tribes, Native Alaskans, and Native Hawaiians commonly believe that if the dead are disturbed or robbed, the spirit is disturbed and wanders—a spiritual trauma for the deceased that can also bring ill upon the living.[61] The adverse impacts of such interference on tribal religion were described by the Carter Administration to Congress in 1979 as follows:

> Native American religions, along with most other religions, provide standards for the care and treatment of cemeteries and human remains. Tribal customary laws generally include standards of conduct for the care and treatment of all cemeteries encountered and human remains uncovered, as well as for the burial sites and bodies of their own ancestors. Grounded in Native American religious beliefs, these laws may, for example, require the performance of certain types of rituals at the burial

site, specify who may visit the site or prescribe the proper disposition of burial offerings.

The prevalent view in the society of applicable disciplines is that Native American remains are public property and artifacts for study, display, and cultural investment. It is understandable that this view is in conflict with and repugnant to those Native people whose ancestors and near relatives are considered the property at issue. Most Native American religious beliefs dictate that burial sites once completed are not to be disturbed or displaced, except by natural occurrence.[62]

State interference with religious-based mortuary beliefs and practices has given rise to a free exercise cause of action when other citizens are concerned.[63] The continuing strength of First Amendment protection, however, must be reassessed in light of a recent United States Supreme Court decision. In *Employment Division of Oregon v. Smith,*[64] the Supreme Court seriously weakened religious liberty for all citizens.[65]

SOVEREIGN RIGHTS

Political rights of Indian Nations as sovereigns can provide another legal basis to repatriate dead tribal members and ancestors. One basic attribute of tribal sovereignty that has been repeatedly recognized by the Supreme Court is the right of Indian tribes to govern domestic internal affairs of their members.[66] In *United States v. Quiver,*[67] the court said that "the relations of the Indians among themselves—the conduct of one toward another—is to be controlled by the customs and laws of the tribe, save when Congress expressly or clearly directs otherwise."[68]

One internal domestic matter that falls squarely within this zone of tribal sovereignty is the relationship between the living and the dead. Therefore, domestic relationships involving the dead may not be interfered with by federal or state government except "when Congress expressly or clearly directs otherwise."[69] In *Mexican v. Circle Bear,*[70] the court applied these principles and granted comity to a tribal court order that provided for the disposal of the body of an Indian who had died within state jurisdiction, even though tribal and state law differed.[71] Thus Indian tribal governments, acting in their *in parens patriae* capacity, may act to repatriate tribal dead in the same way that the United States acts for its citizenry to repatriate MIAs from Southeast Asia.

TREATIES

Indian treaty rights may also provide a legal theory for tribes to repatriate members or ancestors who have been exhumed from lands ceded by treaty.[72]

A treaty is "not a grant of rights to the Indians, but a grant of rights from them—a reservation of those not granted."[73] Simply stated, if a treaty does not expressly delineate the reserved tribal powers or rights, it does not mean that they have been divested.[74] To the contrary, "when a tribe and the Government negotiate a treaty, the tribe retains all rights not expressly ceded to the Government in the treaty so long as the rights retained are consistent with the tribe's sovereign dependent status."[75]

Therefore, no treaty expressly granted the United States a right to disturb Indian graves, expropriate Indian dead from ceded lands, or divest a tribe of its preexisting power to protect those dead.[76] If burials are removed from lands ceded by treaty, a strong argument exists that the signatory tribe implicitly retained or reserved the right to repatriate and rebury the remains.

An implied treaty right becomes apparent when applicable canons of Indian treaty construction are applied to most land cession treaties. The canons require a court to interpret the treaties as understood by the Indians, given their practices and customs as of the date that the treaty was consummated.[77] Thus, even though treaties ceded tribal lands to the United States, it cannot be implied that signatory tribes also relinquished their right to protect tribal dead buried in the ceded lands. Grave robbing was abhorrent to tribal religion.[78] Therefore, the intent to allow desecration cannot fairly be imputed to the chiefs who signed the treaties.

Similarly, it cannot be presumed that the United States intended to obtain Indian lands in order to desecrate Indian graves and obtain dead bodies—at least not until the 1868 Surgeon General's Order. This type of activity was a common-law felony, and the canons of treaty construction preclude imputing an illegal intent to the United States as the fiduciary for Indian tribes.

Although a bundle of legal rights is clearly secured to Indian tribes by the Bill of Rights, treaties, common law, and Federal Indian law, the court system is too costly, time consuming, uncertain, and erratic to adequately redress massive repatriation problems. This is especially true for small, impoverished tribes faced with the problem of having to repatriate large numbers of tribal dead from many different states. Instead, remedial human rights legislation is the superior alternative.

Pre-NAGPRA Legislation

State Legislation

There are two types of relevant state legislation: (1) protection for unmarked graves; and (2) actual repatriation legislation.

PROTECTION FOR UNMARKED GRAVES

Thirty-four states have passed unmarked burial-protection laws in recent years, and there is a definite national trend toward the passage of such legislation.[79] These laws typically prohibit intentional disturbance of unmarked graves, provide guidelines to protect the graves, and mandate disposition of human remains from the graves in a way that guarantees reburial after a study period. The constitutionality of these laws has been uniformly upheld in recent cases such as *People v. Van Horn*,[80] *Thompson v. City of Red Wing*,[81] and *State of Oregon and the Burns-Paiute Tribe v. Castoe*.[82]

REPATRIATION LEGISLATION

Five states have passed repatriation statutes since 1989. Three statutes were passed in response to specific repatriation and reburial matters, and three are general repatriation laws. The five states are California, Hawaii, Kansas, Nebraska, and Arizona.

In 1989 Hawaii appropriated $5 million from its Land Banking Law to purchase a Native Hawaiian burial ground owned by a private developer who had dug up over nine hundred remains in order to build a hotel—five hundred thousand dollars of those funds were used to rebury the dead.[83]

Similarly, in 1989 Kansas passed implementing legislation concerning a reburial agreement between state officials; the owner of a tourist attraction, which displayed 165 Indians from an Indian burial ground; and three Indian tribes that provided that the dead would be reburied by the descendent tribes.[84] In addition, in 1991 the Kansas State Historical Society obtained legislation to allow it to deaccession and repatriate Pawnee Indian remains in its collection.[85] The remains had been obtained from vandalized graves.[86]

In 1989 Nebraska enacted a general repatriation statute entitled the "Unmarked Human Burial Sites and Skeletal Remains Protection Act."[87] This landmark legislation requires all state-recognized museums to repatriate "reasonably identifiable" remains and grave goods to tribes of origin on request.[88] Under Nebraska's law, the Pawnee Tribe repatriated over four hundred Pawnee dead from the Nebraska State Historical Society.[89] The Pawnee Tribe reburied the dead in 1990—despite continued resistance by the Nebraska State Historical Society.[90]

In 1990 Arizona passed a sweeping repatriation statute to repatriate human remains, funerary objects, sacred objects, and objects of tribal patrimony.[91] Under this law, culturally or religiously affiliated remains held by state agencies are repatriated to tribes of origin.[92] Moreover, remains that are not culturally affiliated with a tribe still must be reburied within one year, nearest to the place where the remains were discovered.[93]

Finally, in 1991 California passed a law that makes it the policy of the state that Native American remains and associated grave artifacts shall be repatriated.[94]

During the same period that individual states started to enact legislation designed to ensure appropriate treatment of Indian human remains and funerary objects, the federal government, at the urging of Indian tribes and national organizations, also began to seriously consider the need for uniform, national legislation addressing this issue. That process culminated in the enactment of the Native American Graves Protection and Repatriation Act in 1990.

Federal Legislation

BACKGROUND

In 1986 a number of Northern Cheyenne leaders discovered that almost 18,500 human remains were warehoused in the Smithsonian Institution.[95] This discovery served as a catalyst for a concerted national effort by Indian tribes and organizations to obtain legislation to repatriate human remains and cultural artifacts to Indian tribes and descendants of the deceased. Between 1986 and 1990 a number of bills were introduced in the 99th, 100th, and 101st Congresses to address this issue.

In the 99th and 100th Congresses, Senator John Melcher, a Democrat from Montana, introduced bills that would have provided for the creation of a Native American Museum Claims Commission.[96] The commission was intended to provide a mechanism for the resolution of disputes between museums and Native Americans regarding the repatriation of "skeletal remains, cultural artifacts, and other items of religious or cultural significance."[97] The bill's purpose was "to demonstrate basic human respect to Native Americans on these issues which are fundamentally important to them."[98] In its final form, the commission would have been empowered to mediate disputes, and, if such efforts failed, to issue orders following an evidentiary hearing.[99] The legislation was vigorously opposed by, inter alia, the Smithsonian Institution, the American Association of Museums, and the Society for American Archeology.[100] Consequently, the bill was not enacted.

In the 101st Congress, the commission approach was abandoned in favor of legislation that would directly require repatriation of human remains and cultural artifacts and protect burial sites. Senator John McCain, a Republican from Arizona; Senator Daniel Inouye, a Democrat from Hawaii; Representative Morris Udall, a Democrat from Arizona; and Representative

Charles Bennett, a Democrat from Florida, each introduced bills dealing with different aspects of the repatriation issue.[101]

Each of the bills attempted to protect against the future illegal excavation of burial sites, albeit in a different manner.[102] The McCain, Inouye, and Udall bills provided for an inventory, notice, and repatriation process for human remains and certain cultural artifacts in the possession of federal agencies[103] and also provided for a repatriation process applicable to federally funded museums.[104] The Inouye and Udall bills extended the inventory and notice requirement to federally funded museums.[105] The McCain, Udall, and Bennett bills included criminal penalties for illegal trafficking in protected remains or objects.[106] The Inouye and one of the Udall bills created a review committee to oversee implementation of the legislation.[107] These bills were each considered at the congressional hearings that preceded the enactment of NAGPRA.[108] The provisions in these bills were subsumed in or superseded by the final enacted legislation.

Two other activities that would have a critical impact upon the effort to obtain general repatriation and grave protection legislation also occurred during this period.

NATIONAL MUSEUM OF THE AMERICAN INDIAN ACT

The first event occurred on November 28, 1989, when the National Museum of the American Indian Act ("Museum Act")[109] was enacted into law.

The Museum Act created a National Museum of the American Indian within the Smithsonian Institution.[110] Of significance for this article, the legislation also addresses the issue of human remains and funerary objects in the possession of the Smithsonian.[111]

The Museum Act requires the Smithsonian, in consultation with Indian tribes and traditional Indian religious leaders, to inventory human remains and funerary objects in its possession or control.[112] The purpose of the inventory is to identify the origins of such remains based upon the best available scientific and historical documentation.[113] If the tribal origin of remains or objects is identified by a preponderance of the evidence, the Indian tribe must be promptly notified.[114] Upon request of a lineal descendant or culturally affiliated tribe, human remains and funerary objects associated with those remains are required to be expeditiously returned.[115] Associated funerary objects include both those objects found with the remains and objects "removed from a specific burial site of an individual culturally affiliated with a particular Indian tribe."[116] The Museum Act establishes a special committee to monitor and review the "inventory, identification, and return of Indian human remains and Indian funerary objects," including assistance in the resolution of disputes concerning repatriation.[117]

The repatriation provisions in the Museum Act were the result of an agreement between the Smithsonian Institution and Indian leaders.[118] The Museum Act's repatriation provisions were aimed at rectifying "some of the injustices done to Indian people over the years" and providing the promise that "one day their ancestors will finally be given the resting place that they so deserve."[119] In his statement during debate, Senator John McCain, Republican from Arizona, specifically noted that this bill "is an important first step . . . [that] sends a clear signal to those in the museum community who have dismissed repatriation as a transitory issue that they would be wise to carefully consider the bills [pertaining to museums and federal agencies other than the Smithsonian] currently before the Congress."[120]

The Museum Act set an important precedent later cited by supporters of the Native American Graves Protection and Repatriation Act during the floor debate preceding the passage of NAGPRA.[121]

PANEL FOR A NATIONAL DIALOGUE ON MUSEUM—NATIVE
AMERICAN RELATIONS

The second event involved the creation of a yearlong dialogue, which was suggested by the American Association of Museums and sponsored by the Heard Museum in Arizona. The participants in the dialogue were museums, scientists, and Native Americans. The dialogue centered around the appropriate treatment of human remains and cultural artifacts. In early 1990, the *Report of the Panel for a National Dialogue on Museum/Native American Relations* was issued.[122] As summarized in the report of the Senate Select Committee on Indian Affairs pertaining to NAGPRA, the major conclusions of the panel were as follows:

> The Panel found that the process for determining the appropriate disposition and treatment of Native American human remains, funerary objects, sacred objects, and objects of cultural patrimony should be governed by respect for Native human rights. The Panel reports states that human remains must at all times be accorded dignity and respect. The Panel report indicated the need for Federal legislation to implement the recommendations of the Panel.
>
> The Panel also recommended the development of judicially-enforceable standards for repatriation of Native American human remains and objects. The report recommended that museums consult with Indian tribes to the fullest extent possible regarding the right of possession and treatment of remains and objects prior to acquiring sensitive

materials. Additional recommendations of the Panel included requiring regular consultation and dialogue between Indian tribes and museums; providing Indian tribes with access to information regarding remains and objects in museum collections; providing that Indian tribes should have the right to determine the appropriate disposition of remains and funerary objects and that reasonable accommodations should be made to allow valid and respectful scientific use of materials when it is compatible with tribal religious and cultural practices.[123]

As the legislative history indicates, the Panel report "provided a framework" for NAGPRA.[124]

NAGPRA

On November 16, 1990, the Native American Graves Protection and Repatriation Act was signed into law.[125] NAGPRA is a complex law that sets out detailed procedures and legal standards governing the repatriation of human remains, funerary objects, sacred objects, and objects of cultural patrimony and provides for the protection and ownership of materials unearthed on federal and tribal lands.

Legislative Intent
NAGPRA is, first and foremost, human rights legislation. It is designed to address the flagrant violation of the "civil rights of America's first citizens."[126] When NAGPRA was passed by the Senate, Senator Daniel Inouye stated that:

When the Army Surgeon General ordered the collection of Indian osteological remains during the second half of the 19th Century, his demands were enthusiastically met not only by Army medical personnel, but by collectors who made money from selling Indian skulls to the Army Medical Museum. The desires of Indians to bury their dead were ignored. In fact, correspondence from individuals engaged in robbing graves often speaks of the dangers these collectors faced when Indians caught them digging up burial grounds.

When human remains are displayed in museums or historical societies, it is never the bones of white soldiers or the first European settlers that came to this continent that are lying in glass cases. It is Indian remains. The message that this sends to the rest of the world is that Indians are culturally and physically different from and inferior to non-Indians. This is racism.

In light of the important role that death and burial rites play in native

American cultures, it is all the more offensive that the civil rights of America's first citizens have been so flagrantly violated for the past century. Even today, when supposedly great strides have been made to recognize the rights of Indians to recover the skeletal remains of their ancestors and to repossess items of sacred value or cultural patrimony, the wishes of native Americans are often ignored by the scientific community. In cases where native Americans have attempted to regain items that were inappropriately alienated from the tribe, they have often met with resistance from museums. . . .

[T]he bill before us is not about the validity of museums or the value of scientific inquiry. Rather, it is about human rights. . . . For museums that have dealt honestly and in good faith with native Americans, this legislation will have little effect. For museums and institutions which have consistently ignored the requests of native Americans, this legislation will give native Americans greater ability to negotiate.[127]

Other parts of the legislative history also emphasize the "human rights" genesis of NAGPRA. The antecedents and progenitors of NAGPRA were repatriation provisions of the National Museum of the American Indian Act and the Report of the Panel for a National Dialogue on Museum/Native American Relations—both of which placed a major emphasis upon "human rights."[128]

Congress viewed NAGPRA as a part of its trust responsibility to Indian tribes and people, specifically stating that it "reflects the unique relationship between the Federal Government and Indian tribes and Native Hawaiian organizations."[129] The trust responsibility of the federal government to Indian tribes and people is a judicially created concept that requires the United States to "adhere strictly to fiduciary standards in its dealings with Indians."[130] The trust doctrine has given rise to the principle that enactments dealing with Indian affairs are to be liberally construed for the benefit of Indian people and tribes[131]—a canon of construction similar to that applicable to remedial civil rights legislation.[132]

The bill that was enacted reflected a compromise forged by representatives of the museum, scientific, and Indian communities.[133] NAGPRA was designed to create a process that would reflect both the needs of museums as repositories of the nation's cultural heritage and the rights of Indian people. Most importantly, NAGPRA was intended to "establish a process that provides the dignity and respect that our Nation's first citizens deserve."[134] Congress believed that NAGPRA would "encourage a continuing dialogue between museums and Indian tribes and Native Hawaiian organizations and . . . promote greater understanding between the groups."[135] The primary features of the Native American Graves Protection and Repatriation Act of 1990 are summarized below.

Repatriation: Human Remains and Associated Funerary Objects

NAGPRA requires federal agencies (excluding the Smithsonian Institution)[136] and museums (including state and local governments and educational institutions)[137] to return human remains and associated funerary objects upon request of a lineal descendent, Indian tribe,[138] or Native Hawaiian organization[139] where the museum or agency itself identifies the cultural affiliation of the items through the required inventory process.[140] In addition, if a museum or agency inventory does not establish the affiliation of the human remains or associated funerary objects, the Indian tribe or Native Hawaiian organization may still obtain the return of the remains or objects if it can prove, by a preponderance of the evidence, that it has a cultural affiliation with the item.[141] In seeking to prove cultural affiliation, a claimant may utilize "geographical, kinship, biological, archaeological, anthropological, linguistic, folkloric, oral traditional, historical, or other relevant information or expert opinion."[142]

Upon request, Indian tribes and Native Hawaiian organizations must be provided with available documentation by agencies and museums.[143] NAGPRA indicates that such documentation shall be made available to Indian tribes or Native Hawaiian organizations that receive or should have received notice pursuant to 25 U.S.C.A. § 3003(d)—namely, those tribes that are believed to be culturally affiliated with specific items. The legislative history recognizes that § 3003(d) is to be liberally construed to include all tribes that have "a potential cultural affiliation (regardless of whether the showing of such affiliation would be based upon museum records or nonmuseum sources)."[144] Available documentation includes "a summary of existing museum or Federal agency records, including inventories or catalogues, relevant studies, or other pertinent data."[145] This requirement, however, is not an authorization for the initiation of new scientific studies— although it does not preclude further scientific study either.[146]

"Cultural affiliation" is defined as "a relationship of shared group identity which can be reasonably traced historically or prehistorically between a present day Indian tribe or Native Hawaiian organization and an identifiable earlier group."[147] The House committee explained that this requirement "is intended to ensure that the claimant has a reasonable connection with the materials."[148] Congress recognized, however, that

[I]t may be extremely difficult, in many instances, for claimants to trace an item from modern Indian tribes to prehistoric remains without some reasonable gaps in the historic or prehistoric record. In such instances, a finding of cultural affiliation should be based upon an overall evaluation of the totality of the circumstances and evidence pertaining to the connection between the claimant and the material being claimed and should not be precluded solely because of some gaps in the record.[149]

Therefore, claimants need not establish cultural affiliation with "scientific certainty."[150]

"Associated funerary objects" includes two categories of objects. First, it includes objects "reasonably believed to have been placed with individual human remains either at the time of death or later . . . as part of the death rite or ceremony" where both the human remains or objects are presently in the possession or control of a federal agency or museum.[151] The remains and objects need not be in the possession or control of the same agency or museum—only in the possession or control of *a* museum or agency so that a connection between the objects and remains is possible.[152] Moreover, the "possession or control" language indicates congressional intent to include objects consigned to individuals or museums not covered under NAGPRA if the ultimate determination as to the disposition of those objects is reposed in a federal agency or museum covered by NAGPRA.[153]

Second, "associated funerary objects" includes objects "exclusively made for burial purposes or to contain human remains."[154]

Two exceptions exist to the requirement that human remains and associated funerary objects be "expeditiously returned" after cultural affiliation has been determined.[155] The first exception is in those circumstances where the item is "indispensable for completion of a specific scientific study, the outcome of which would be of major benefit to the United States."[156] If this exception applies, the terms must be returned within ninety days after the completion of the study.[157] There is no prohibition, however, against voluntary agreements between claimants and agencies or museums that would permit additional studies or other arrangements in regard to cultural items.[158]

The second exception applies if multiple requests for a cultural item are made and the federal agency or museum "cannot clearly determine which requesting party is the most appropriate claimant."[159] In such a case, the federal agency or museum may retain the item until the parties agree upon disposition (with the Review Committee available for a mediating role) or the dispute is resolved by a court of competent jurisdiction.[160]

As for human remains and associated funerary objects whose cultural affiliation cannot be determined, NAGPRA provides that the statutorily created Review Committee[161] compile an inventory of culturally unidentifiable human remains and recommend "specific actions for developing a process for disposition of such remains."[162] The Review Committee's recommendations are to be made "in consultation with Indian tribes and Native Hawaiian organizations and appropriate scientific and museum groups."[163] This issue was referred to the Review Committee because there was "general disagreement on the proper disposition of such unidentifiable remains. Some believe that they should be left solely to science while others contend that, since they are not identifiable, they would be of little use to science and should be buried and laid to rest."[164]

Repatriation: Unassociated Funerary Objects, Sacred Objects, and
Items of Cultural Patrimony
NAGPRA requires museums and federal agencies to repatriate unassociated funerary objects, sacred objects, and items of cultural patrimony pursuant to a four-step process.

IDENTIFICATION OF THE ITEM
First, the claimant must show that the item claimed is an unassociated funerary object, sacred object, or item of cultural patrimony.[165] "Unassociated funerary object" is defined as an object "reasonably believed to have been placed with individual human remains either at the time of death or later . . . as part of a death rite or ceremony" where the human remains are *not* presently "in the possession or control of" a federal agency or museum, but the object can be related to specific individuals, families, or known human remains, or to a specific burial site of a culturally affiliated individual.[166]

"Sacred objects" are defined as "specific ceremonial objects which are needed by traditional Native American religious leaders for the practice of traditional Native American religions by their present day adherents."[167] As the House report explains,

> [T]he definition of "sacred objects" is intended to include both objects needed for ceremonies currently practiced by traditional Native American religious practitioners and objects needed to renew ceremonies that are part of traditional religions. The operative part of the definition is that there must be "present day adherents" in either instance.[168]

In explaining its legislative "intent . . . to permit traditional Native American religious leaders to obtain such objects as are needed for the renewal of ceremonies," the House Interior Committee recognized that "the practice of some ceremonies has been interrupted because of governmental coercion, adverse societal conditions or the loss of certain objects through means beyond the control of the tribe at the time."[169] Significantly, the definition recognizes that the ultimate determination of continuing sacredness must be made by the Native American religious leaders themselves because they must determine the current ceremonial need for the object. Thus the term *sacred* is not defined explicitly in the legislative definition. Rather the definition will vary according to the traditions of the tribe or community.[170] Of course, a religious leader's "determination" of sacredness could be challenged on the basis of its "sincerity" just as a First Amendment claim might be similarly challenged.[171] Moreover, the leader cannot simply proclaim that an object is sacred—the object must meet the statutory criteria of having traditional religious significance and future use in a religious ceremony before it can be classified as a "sacred object."[172]

"Cultural patrimony" is defined as "an object having ongoing historical, traditional, or cultural importance central to the Native American group or culture itself."[173] Further, the object must have been considered inalienable by the Native American group when the object was separated from such group, rather than property that was owned and transferable by an individual Native American; thus, tribal law or custom is determinative of the legal question of alienability at the time that the item was transferred.[174] The Senate Committee report, explaining a similar cultural patrimony provision in an earlier version of the NAGPRA bill, indicated that cultural patrimony refers to items of "great importance" such as Zuni war gods or the Wampum belts of the Iroquois.[175]

CULTURAL AFFILIATION AND PRIOR OWNERSHIP OR CONTROL
Once it has been shown that an item is an unassociated funerary object, sacred object, or item of cultural patrimony, either the cultural affiliation must be determined[176] or, in the case of sacred objects and items of cultural patrimony, the requesting tribe or Native Hawaiian organization must show that the object was previously owned or controlled by the tribe, organization, or a member thereof.[177] A direct lineal descendant may also request repatriation of a sacred object owned by an ancestor.[178] If a tribe or Native Hawaiian organization is making a claim based upon prior ownership or control by a tribal member, as opposed to the tribe, the claimant must show that no identifiable lineal descendants exist or that the lineal descendants have been notified and have failed to make a claim.[179]

RIGHT OF POSSESSION: CLAIMANT'S PRIMA FACIE CASE
The third step in the process requires a claimant to present "evidence which, if standing alone before the introduction of evidence to the contrary, would support a finding that the Federal agency or museum did not have

the right of possession" of the items.[180] Because the original "transfer" of many of these objects occurred when recordkeeping of such transactions was virtually nonexistent—and because of the near impossibility of proving that a legal document does not exist—evidence, by necessity, may include oral traditional and historical evidence, as well as documentary evidence. In making its prima facie case, the claimant is entitled access to "records, catalogues, relevant studies or other pertinent data" possessed by the federal agency or museum that relate to "basic facts surrounding acquisition and accession" of the items being claimed.[181]

"Right of possession" means "possession obtained with the voluntary consent of an individual or group that had authority of alienation."[182] This term was intended "to provide a legal framework in which to determine the circumstances by which a museum or agency came into possession of these . . . objects."[183]

Right of possession is based upon the general property law principle that "an individual may only acquire the title to property that is held by the transferor."[184] Authority to alienate would be determined by the law of the governmental entity having jurisdiction over a transaction.[185] In most cases, the initial transfer of the item out of tribal control would presumably be governed by tribal law or custom.[186] The definition does not apply only in the rare instance when its application would result in a Fifth Amendment taking of private property for a public purpose without just compensation.[187] If there would be a taking within the meaning of the constitutional provision, applicable federal, state, or tribal law would apply.[188] In this rare instance, however, the party asserting a Fifth Amendment taking first would be required to obtain a ruling from the Court of Claims upholding such an assertion before federal, state, or tribal laws would be used to replace the statutory standard.[189] In summary, the definition of "right to possession" is designed to ensure that the object did not pass out of tribal or individual Native American possession without appropriate consent.[190]

RIGHT OF POSSESSION: BURDEN OF PROOF

If the claimant surmounts these three hurdles, the fourth step places a burden upon the museum or agency to prove that it has a right of possession in regard to the items in question.[191] If the museum or agency cannot prove right of possession, the unassociated funerary object, sacred object, or item of cultural patrimony must be returned—unless the scientific study or competing claims exceptions apply.[192]

NAGPRA makes clear that these provisions, as well as those pertaining to human remains and associated funerary objects, are not meant to limit the general repatriation authority of federal agencies and museums.[193] Further,

NAGPRA does not preclude agencies or museums from entering into agreements with tribes and organizations regarding any Native American objects owned or controlled by museums or agencies.[194]

Inventory: Human Remains and Associated Funerary Objects

NAGPRA requires museums and federal agencies to complete an item-by-item inventory of human remains and associated funerary objects.[195] "Inventory" is defined as a "simple itemized list that summarizes the information called for by this section."[196] As part of the inventory, the museum or agency is required to "identify the geographical and cultural affiliation of each item," to the extent possible, based upon information within its possession.[197] This provision does *not* "require museums . . . to conduct exhaustive studies and additional scientific research to conclusively determine . . . cultural affiliation."[198] In fact, NAGPRA specifically states that it "shall not be construed to be an authorization for the initiation of new scientific studies of such remains and associated funerary objects or other means of acquiring or preserving additional scientific information from such remains and objects."[199] Rather, NAGPRA's intent is merely to require a good faith effort to identify cultural affiliation based upon presently available evidence.[200]

The inventory is to be conducted in consultation with Native American governmental and traditional leaders and the Review Committee.[201] The inventory must be completed by November 16, 1995.[202] Extensions, however, may be granted by the secretary of the interior for good cause.[203] Interaction between tribes and museums is expected to occur during the inventory process. The intent of the process is to "allow for the cooperative exchange of information between Indian tribes or Native Hawaiian organizations and museums regarding objects in museum collections."[204] Moreover, the inventory process is not intended to delay any pending actions on repatriation requests.[205] Notice of culturally affiliated objects identified in the inventory is to be provided "throughout the process"—not merely after completion of the entire inventory.[206] Within six months after the completion of the inventory, final notice must be sent to all tribes that are reasonably believed to be culturally affiliated with human remains or associated funerary objects in the possession or control of the museum or agency.[207]

The notice shall include information about the circumstances surrounding the acquisition of each identified item and information about cultural affiliation.[208] NAGPRA broadly intends that all potential tribal claimants, including Native Hawaiian organizations, receive notice.[209] A tribe or Native Hawaiian organization that receives, or should have received, notice may request additional background information from the museum or agency relevant to the "geographical origin, cultural affiliation and basic

facts surrounding [the item's] acquisition and accession."[210] The requirement to perform the inventory is not made contingent upon a museum
receiving federal funds.[211]

Summary: Unassociated Funerary Objects, Sacred Objects, and
Items of Cultural Patrimony
NAGPRA requires that federal agencies and museums summarize their collections of unassociated funerary objects, sacred objects, and items of cultural
patrimony.[212] The summary is "in lieu of an object-by-object inventory" and
requires the museum or agency to "describe the scope of the collection,
kinds of objects included, reference to geographical location, means and period of acquisition and cultural affiliation, where readily ascertainable."[213]

The museum or agency has three years to compile the summary.[214] After
the summary is completed—and presumably during its compilation—a
consultation process with Native American governmental and traditional
leaders is to occur.[215] As with the inventory process, the summary process is
not meant to delay action on pending repatriation requests.[216] The House
committee expressed its hope and expectation that the summary would lead
to "open discussions" between tribes, museums, and federal agencies.[217]
Upon request, all tribes and Native Hawaiian organizations are entitled to
obtain data pertaining to geographical origin, cultural affiliation, acquisition, and accession of these objects.[218]

Tribal Ownership and Control: Imbedded Cultural Items
NAGPRA expressly provides rules that address ownership or control of cultural items[219] that are discovered in the future on federal and tribal land.[220]
In the case of human remains and associated funerary objects, any lineal
descendants have the initial right of ownership or control.[221] If lineal descendants of the human remains and associated funerary objects cannot be
ascertained or when unassociated funerary objects, sacred objects, and items
of cultural patrimony are involved, ownership or control is determined in
the following statutory order of priority:

1. The tribe or Native Hawaiian organization owns or controls the
disposition of all cultural items discovered on tribal land.[222] Tribal land
is defined to include all lands within the exterior boundaries of a reservation, all dependent Indian communities, and any lands administered for
Native Hawaiians pursuant to the Hawaiian Homes Commission Act of
1920, as amended, and the Hawaii Statehood Bill.[223]
2. In the case of federal land, the tribe or Native Hawaiian organization
with the closest cultural affiliation to the items has ownership or con-

trol.[224] If there is a dispute between tribes, NAGPRA contemplates that the statutorily-created Review Committee may serve as a mediator of the dispute, and that agreements between tribes regarding disputed items could occur.[225]

3. If cultural affiliation of the items cannot be established, but the objects are discovered on aboriginal land that has been the subject of a final judicial determination by the Indian Claims Commission or United States Court of Claims, the tribe that has obtained the judgment has the right of ownership and control over the items, unless another tribe can show a stronger cultural relationship.[226]

The secretary of the interior is authorized to promulgate regulations pertaining to the disposition of cultural items unclaimed under this section in consultation with the Review Committee, Native American groups, museums, and scientists.[227]

Whenever a party intends to intentionally excavate cultural items for any purpose, that party must obtain a permit pursuant to the Archeological Resources Protection Act of 1979.[228] If tribal lands are involved, the items may be excavated only after notice to and consent of the tribe or Native Hawaiian organization.[229] If federal lands are involved, the items may be excavated only after notice and consultation with the appropriate tribe or Native Hawaiian organization.[230] As described previously, the tribe or Native Hawaiian organization retains ownership or control over remains and objects unearthed on lands covered by this provision.[231]

If imbedded cultural items have been inadvertently discovered as part of another activity, such as construction, mining, logging, or agriculture, the person who has discovered the items must temporarily cease activity and notify the responsible federal agency in the case of federal land or the appropriate tribe or Native Hawaiian organization in the case of tribal land.[232] When notice is provided to the federal agency, that agency has the responsibility to promptly notify the appropriate tribe or Native Hawaiian organization.[233] The intent of this provision is to "provide a process whereby Indian tribes and Native Hawaiian organizations have an opportunity to intervene in development activity on Federal or tribal lands to safeguard Native American human remains, funerary objects, sacred objects or objects of cultural patrimony."[234]

If there is inadvertent discovery, Indian tribes or Native Hawaiian organizations are afforded thirty days to make a determination as to the appropriate disposition of the human remains and objects.[235] Activity may resume thirty days after the secretary of the appropriate federal department or the Indian tribe or the Native Hawaiian organization certifies that notice has been received.[236] Federal department secretaries may delegate their responsibilities under this provision to the secretary of the interior.[237] Ownership and control of items inadvertently discovered are governed by the provisions described previously.[238]

PROHIBITIONS AGAINST TRAFFICKING

NAGPRA prohibits all trafficking in Native American human remains for sale or profit except for remains that have been "excavated, exhumed or otherwise obtained with full knowledge and consent of the next of kin or the official governing body of the appropriate culturally affiliated Indian tribe or Native Hawaiian organization."[239] The prohibition is intended to prevent trafficking in human remains that were wrongfully acquired, regardless of when and where obtained, including those removed prior to the enactment of NAGPRA.[240] Violators are subject to a fine of up to $100,000 and face up to a one-year jail sentence for a first offense; subsequent violations subject the offender to a fine of up to $250,000 and a maximum of five years in jail.[241]

NAGPRA also prohibits trafficking in other cultural items obtained in violation of the act.[242] Penalties for violation of this prohibition are the same as for trafficking in human remains.[243] The antitrafficking provision, as it applies to funerary objects, sacred objects, and items of cultural patrimony, is for prospective acquisitions only.[244] The prospective limitation, however, does not prevent the application of existing state or federal law involving theft or stolen property if relevant to the possession or sale of Indian cultural items.[245]

REVIEW COMMITTEE

NAGPRA creates a Review Committee, appointed by the secretary of the interior, to monitor and review the implementation of NAGPRA.[246] The Review Committee consists of seven members—three appointed by the secretary from nominations submitted by Indian tribes, Native Hawaiian organizations, and traditional Native American religious leaders (at least two of the three must be traditional Native American religious leaders); three appointed from nominations submitted by national museum and scientific organizations; and one person chosen from a list compiled by the other six members.[247] Federal officers and employees may not serve on the Review Committee.[248]

The Review Committee composition and nomination process differs from that of the National Museum of the American Indian Act special review committee, which has been heavily criticized as being biased in favor of archaeological interests.[249] NAGPRA seeks to secure a more diverse composition.[250]

The Review Committee's function is to:

(1) monitor the inventory and identification process;[251]

(2) upon request, make findings related to the cultural affiliation and return of cultural items, and facilitate the resolution of disputes between interested parties;[252] these findings are non-binding, but are admissible in any court proceeding filed pursuant to NAGPRA;[253]

(3) compile an inventory of culturally unidentifiable human remains and make recommendations as to an appropriate process for their disposition;[254]

(4) consult with the secretary of the interior in the development of regulations to implement NAGPRA;[255]

(5) make recommendations as to the future care of repatriated cultural items;[256] and

(6) submit an annual report to Congress.[257]

ENFORCEMENT AND IMPLEMENTATION OF NAGPRA

NAGPRA provides for the secretary of the interior to assess civil penalties against museums that do not comply with NAGPRA.[258] The amount of the penalties is determined by (1) the archaeological, historical, or commercial value of the item involved; (2) economic and noneconomic damages suffered by an aggrieved party; and (3) the number of violations.[259]

The penalty provision is not meant to be an exclusive remedy for violations of NAGPRA. NAGPRA specifically provides that an aggrieved party can allege a violation of NAGPRA through a legal cause of action to enforce NAGPRA's provisions. Federal courts have authority to issue any necessary orders.[260] This action is in addition to any existing procedural or substantive legal rights secured to tribes or Native Hawaiian organizations.[261] If a museum repatriates an item in good faith, however, it is not liable for claims against it predicated upon a claim of wrongful repatriation, breach of fiduciary duty, public trust, or violations of state law.[262]

To facilitate implementation, NAGPRA authorizes the secretary of the interior to make grants to museums to undertake the inventory and the summary.[263] Tribes and Native Hawaiian organizations may also receive grants to assist them in repatriating cultural items.[264] Unfortunately, Congress failed to appropriate any funding under these provisions in 1991.[265] Because sufficient funding is critical to completely fulfill the promise of NAGPRA, funds hopefully will be made available for these purposes in future fiscal years. Finally, the secretary of the interior is authorized to issue regulations by November 16, 1991, to carry out NAGPRA's provisions.[266]

Conclusion

After centuries of discriminatory treatment, the Native American Graves Protection and Repatriation Act finally recognizes that Native American human remains and cultural items are the remnants and products of living people and that descendants have a cultural and spiritual relationship with the deceased. Human remains and cultural items can no longer be thought of as merely "scientific specimens" or "collectibles."

In interpreting NAGPRA, it is critical to remember that it must be liberally interpreted as remedial legislation to benefit the class for whom it was enacted. This article, hopefully, will aid in the interpretation of NAGPRA in a manner consistent not only with the words of the statute but also with its spirit.

This article was also written to remind people that NAGPRA is a part of a larger historical tragedy: the failure of the United States Government, and other institutions, to understand and respect the spiritual and cultural beliefs and practices of Native people. Governmental policies that threaten Native American religions are not merely historical anachronisms but continue to have a devastating impact upon contemporary Native Americans. Sites sacred to traditional Indian religious practitioners are currently threatened with destructive development. Centuries-old religious peyote use is threatened by ethnocentric court decisions. Native American prisoners are unable to practice their religions in a manner comparable to the respect accorded Judeo-Christian religious practice. Legislation to address this religious discrimination will be considered by Congress in the near future.

NAGPRA is unique legislation because it is the first time that the federal government and non-Indian institutions must consider what is *sacred* from an Indian perspective. Future legislation must be imbued with this same heightened consciousness of the nature of Indian culture and spirituality. The authors hope that the understanding, sensitivity, and moral outrage that gave rise to and is reflected in NAGPRA will likewise result in across-the-board protection and respect for traditional Native American religions—which continue to be under assault in the last decade of the twentieth century.

Notes

1. 25 U.S.C.A. §§ 3001–3013 (West Supp. 1991) (reprinted in appendix).

2. Human rights laws that seek to alleviate widespread civil rights violations

usually take a long time to implement. For example, the federal civil rights legislation of the 1960s is still being implemented today.

3. See, e.g., *American Indian Sacred Objects', Skeletal Remains', Repatriation and Reburial: A Resource Guide* (Rayna Green & Nancy Marie Mitchell eds., 1990) (providing a bibliography for the burgeoning literature on the subject, it references almost two hundred articles together with related policies, regulations, decisions, and laws).

4. General legal articles on repatriation of Native human remains are sparse. See generally H. Marcus Price III, *Disputing the Dead: U.S. Law on Aboriginal Remains and Grave Goods* (1991); Margaret Bowman, *The Reburial of Native American Skeletal Remains: Approaches to the Resolution of a Conflict,* 13 Harv. Envtl. L. Rev. 147 (1989); Walter R. Echo-Hawk, *Tribal Efforts to Protect against Mistreatment of Indian Dead: The Quest for Equal Protection of the Laws,* 14 N.A.R.F. L. Rev. 1 (1988); David J. Harris, Note, *Respect for the Living and Respect for the Dead: Return of Indian and Other Native American Burial Remains,* 39 Wash. U. J. Urb. & Contemp. L. 195 (1991).

5. Quoted in Wynne Woolley, *Caring for Old Cemetery Has Been a Lifetime Job,* Richmond News Leader, May 16, 1990, at 1.

6. R. F. Martin, Annotation, *Corpse Removal and Reinterment,* 21 A.L.R.2d 472, 475–76 (1950) (citations omitted).

7. See generally Catherine Bergin Yalung & Laurel I. Wala, Statutory Survey, *Survey of State Repatriation and Burial Protection Statutes,* 24 Ariz. St. L.J. 419 (1992).

8. See, e.g., *Hearings on S. 1021 and S. 1980 before the Senate Select Comm. on Indian Affairs,* 101st Cong., 2d Sess. (May 14, 1990) (exhibit 5 to statement of Walter R. Echo-Hawk) [hereinafter *Senate Hearing on S. 1021 & S. 1980*].

9. See, e.g., *Stastny v. Tachovsky,* 132 N.W.2d 317, 325 (Neb. 1964).

10. E.g., *Neb. Rev. Stat.* § 71-605(5), (6) (1989) (specifying that disinterment may *only* be done by a licensed funeral director under a permit from the Bureau of Vital Statistics requested by next of kin; if more than one human body is concerned, the applicant must also obtain a court order that must specify the place for reinterment).

11. See generally Percival E. Jackson, *The Law of Cadavers and of Burials and Burial Places* (2d ed. 1950).

12. No accurate national census of these dead has yet been done. Various estimates, however, are compiled in Harris, *supra* note 4, at 195 n.3, including Hass (100,000–150,000), Moore (300,000–600,000 in U.S. alone), National Congress of American Indians (more than 1.5 million), and Deloria (2 million). NAGPRA requires federal agencies and federally funded museums to inventory these dead within five years. 25 U.S.C.A. § 3003(b)(1)(B).

13. One historical study in particular was made widely available to Congress to provide a historical backdrop for NAGPRA: Robert E. Bieder, *A Brief Historical Survey of the Expropriation of American Indian Remains* (1990) [hereinafter Bieder Report], reprinted in *Senate Hearing on S. 1021 & S. 1980, supra* note 8, at 278–363; see also Robert E. Bieder, *Science Encounters the Indian 1820–1880* (1986); Douglas Cole, *Captured Heritage: the Scramble for Northwest Coast Artifacts* (1985); Stephen Jay Gould, *The Mismeasure of Man* (1981); Orlan J. Svingen, *History of the Expropriation of Pawnee Indian Graves in the Control of the Nebraska State Historical Society* (1989); James T. Riding In, *Report Verifying the Identity of Six Pawnee Scout Crania at the Smithsonian and the National Museum of Health and Medicine* (1990), reprinted in *Senate Hearing on S. 1021 & S. 1980, supra* note 8, at 211–29.

14. Dwight B. Heath, *Mourt's Relation: A Journal of the Pilgrims at Plymouth* 27–28 (1986).

15. Bieder, *supra* note 13, at 55–103.

16. *Id.;* see also Russel Thornton, *American Indian Holocaust and Survival* (1987).

17. The Surgeon General's Order is reproduced in full in Bieder Report, *supra* note 13, at 36–37.

18. Riding In, *supra* note 13, at 223.

19. See Entries in accession records for the Army Medical Museum, Anatomical Section: A.M.M. nos. 8–12 from W. H. Forwood, Assistant Surgeon, U.S. Army, Ft. Riley, Kansas, Jan. 20, 1867.

20. Bieder, *supra* note 13, at 325.

21. Bieder Report, *supra* note 13, at 45–46.

22. *Id.* at 30.

23. Cole, *supra* note 13, at 175.

24. Kenn Harper, *Give Me My Father's Body: The Life of Minik, the New York Eskimo* 89–95 (1986).

25. *Senate Hearing on S. 1021 & S. 1980, supra* note 8, at 76 (statement of Jerry Flute).

26. 16 U.S.C. §§ 431–433 (1988).

27. American common law has always held that a dead body is not "property." See, e.g., 88-73 Kan. Op. Att'y Gen. (1988); Jackson, *supra* note 11, at 129–31, 133–34; 22A Am. Jur. 2d *Dead Bodies* § 2; 25A C.J.S. *Dead Bodies* § 2; R. F. Martin, Annotation, *Corpse—Removal and Reinterment,* 21 A.L.R.2d 472, 480, 486 (1950).

28. 16 U.S.C. § 432 (1988); see also Archaeological Resources Protection Act, 16 U.S.C. § 470bb(1), 470(b)(3) (1988).

29. Preliminary figures of a few federal agencies supplied to the Native American Rights Fund in 1990 show almost 14,500 deceased Natives in their possession:

National Park Service . . . . .3,500 Dead Bodies
Tennessee Valley Authority . . . . .10,000 Dead Bodies
Bureau of Land Management . . . . .109 Dead Bodies
Fish and Wildlife Service . . . . .637 Dead Bodies
Air Force. . . . . .146 + Dead Bodies
Navy. . . . . .85 + Dead Bodies
(Survey responses in possession of the Native American Rights Fund)

30. For example, American property-law principles provide that no one may assert a claim to stolen or wrongfully acquired property; nonetheless, it took the Six Nations Confederacy seventy-five years to negotiate the return of its wampum belts, which are important communally owned patrimony of the Confederacy. See *Onondaga Nation v. Thatcher,* 61 N.Y.S. 1027, 1028, 1032 (Sup. Ct. Onondaga Co. 1899) (failed judicial attempt to repatriate belts); see also Memorandum from Thomas Sobol, Commissioner of Education, State of New York, "Proposed Return of 12 Wampum Belts to the Onondaga Nation" (undated) (on file with author).

31. Cole, *supra* note 13, at 286–310.

32. ("AIRFA"), 42 U.S.C. § 1996 (1988).

33. Secretary of the Interior Fed. Agencies Task Force, Am. Indian Religious Freedom Act Rep. 77, Aug. 1979. The report to Congress was required by § 2 of the American Indian Religious Freedom Act. 42 U.S.C. § 1996.

34. See, e.g., *The Concept of Sacred Materials and Their Place in the World* (George P. Horse Capture ed., 1989); Bowen Blair, *American Indians v. American Museums, A Matter of Religious Freedom,* 5 Am. Indian L. Rev. 13 (1979); Bruce Davis, *Indian Religious Artifacts: The Curator's Moral Dilemma,* 2 Indian L. Supp. Ctr. Rep. 1 (1980); Bowen Blair, Note, *Indian Rights: Native Americans versus American Museums—A Battle for Artifacts,* 7 Am. Indian L. Rev. 125 (1979).

35. See, e.g., Walter R. Echo-Hawk, *Museum Rights vs. Indian Rights: Guidelines for Assessing Competing Legal Interests in Native Cultural Resources,* 14 N.Y.U. Rev. L. & Soc. Change 437 (1986).

36. See *infra* text accompanying notes 165–94.

37. See, e.g., *Ney v. Yellow Cab Co.,* 117 N.E.2d 74, 79 (Ill. 1954).

38. Price, *supra* note 4, at 22.

39. 163 U.S. 537 (1896).

40. *Montoya v. United States,* 180 U.S. 261, 265 (1901).

41. *Johnson v. McIntosh,* 21 U.S. (8 Wheat.) 543, 569–70 (1823) (the "Marshall trilogy" of cases stripped Indian Nations of their sovereignty and land rights and

converted them into "domestic dependent nations" in a state of "pupilage" to the United States); see also *Worcester v. Georgia,* 21 U.S. (6 Pet.) 515 (1832); *Cherokee Nation v. Georgia,* 30 U.S. (5 Pet.) 1 (1831). Unlike *Plessy,* which was so devastating to African Americans, these Indian cases have never been overturned by the Supreme Court.

42. United States *ex rel. Standing Bear v. Crook,* 25 F. Cas. 695 (C.C.D. Neb. 1879) (No. 14,891).

43. Citizenship Act of 1924, 8 U.S.C. § 1401(b) (1988).

44. See generally H. C. Yarrow, *North American Indian Burial Customs* (1988); David Bushnell, *Burial of the Algonoquian, Siouan, and Caddoan Tribes West of the Mississippi,* 83 Bureau of Am. Ethnology Bull. (1927).

45. 180 Cal. Rptr. 423 (Ct. App. 1982).

46. *Id.* at 425–27.

47. 273 N.E.2d 893 (Ohio Ct. App. 1971).

48. *Id.* at 896–98.

49. 52 N.E. 126 (Ohio 1898).

50. *Id.* at 127.

51. See generally Yalung & Wala, *supra* note 7.

52. Hugh Dellios, "Town Fears Burial Mounds May Never Be The Same," *Chicago Tribune,* Oct. 13, 1991, at 1.

53. See *supra* note 28; see also *Charrier v. Bell,* 496 So. 2d 601, 607 (La. Ct. App.), *cert. denied,* 498 So. 2d 753 (La. 1986) (funerary objects from two-hundred-year-old Indian graves belong to descendant Indian tribe).

54. See, e.g., *Busler v. State,* 184 S.W.2d 24, 27 (Tenn. 1944).

55. See *id.*

56. These grave objects are defined as "funerary objects" in NAGPRA. 25 U.S.C.A. § 3001(3)(A), (B).

57. See, e.g., *Maddox v. State,* 121 S.E. 251 (Ga. Ct. App. 1924); *Ware v. State,* 121 S.E. 251 (Ga. Ct. App. 1924); *Ternant v. Boudreau,* 6 Rob. 488 (La. 1844); *Charrier,* 496 So. 2d at 607; *State v. Doepke,* 68 Mo. 208 (1878); *Busler v. State,* 184 S.W.2d 24 (Tenn. 1944).

58. See, e.g., *United States v. Unknown Heirs,* 152 F. Supp. 452 (W.D. Okla. 1957); *Charrier,* 496 So. 2d at 607; Matter of Indian Cemetery, Queens County, N.Y., 169 Misc. 584 (N.Y. Sup. Ct. 1938).

59. *Rice v. Sioux City Cemetery,* 349 U.S. 70, 80 (1955) (Black, J., dissenting) (a

discrimination claim by next of kin to a deceased Winnebago Indian who was refused burial in an all white cemetery was moot by the time it reached the Supreme Court).

60. Virginia Armstrong, *I Have Spoken* 78 (1971).

61. See, e.g., *Hearing on S. 187 before the Senate Select Comm. on Indian Affairs on Native American Museum Claims Commission Act,* 100th Cong., 2d Sess., 282–307 (1988) [hereinafter *Senate Hearing on S. 187*] (testimony of Roger Echo-Hawk on Pawnee Mortuary Traditions).

62. American Indian Religious Freedom Act Report 64, *supra* note 33.

63. See, e.g., *Fuller v. Marx,* 724 F.2d 717 (8th Cir. 1984).

64. 494 U.S. 872 (1990).

65. *Id.* at 883–88; see also *Intercommunity Ctr. for Justice and Peace v. I.N.S.,* 910 F.2d 42 (2d Cir. 1990); *Salaam v. Lockhart,* 905 F.2d 1168 (8th Cir. 1990); *Salvation Army v. New Jersey Dep't of Community Affairs,* 919 F.2d 183 (3rd Cir. 1990); *South Ridge Baptist Church v. Industrial Comm'n of Ohio,* 911 F.2d 1203 (6th Cir. 1990); *Cornerstone Bible Church v. City of Hastings,* 740 F. Supp. 654 (D. Mich. 1990); *Montgomery v. County of Clinton,* 743 F. Supp. 1253 (W.D. Mich. 1990); *Yang v. Sturner,* 750 F. Supp. 558 (D.R.I. 1990). A full discussion of the impact of the *Smith* decision is beyond the scope of this article.

66. See *United States v. Kagama,* 118 U.S. 375, 383–84 (1883); Ex Parte Crow Dog, 109 U.S. 556, 570 (1881). Indian Tribes have an inherent sovereign right to regulate internal social relations. See, e.g., *United States v. Antelope,* 430 U.S. 641, 645 (1977); *United States v. Mazurie,* 419 U.S. 544, 557 (1975); *McClanahan v. Arizona Tax Comm'n,* 411 U.S. 164, 173 (1973). Tribes have exercised this authority in a variety of contexts. See, e.g., *United States v. Wheeler,* 435 U.S. 313 (1978) (criminal jurisdiction to punish members for illegal activity); *Fisher v. District Court,* 424 U.S. 382 (1976) (divorce and child custody matters); *Jones v. Meehan,* 175 U.S. 1 (1899) (inheritance); *Johnson v. Chilkat Indian Village,* 457 F. Supp. 384, 388–89 (D. Alaska 1978) (regulating property rights); *Wear v. Sanger,* 2 S.W. 307 (Mo. 1886) (regulating property rights).

67. 241 U.S. 602 (1916).

68. *Id.* at 605–06.

69. *Id.*

70. 370 N.W.2d 737 (S.D. 1985).

71. *Id.* at 740–42.

72. See Echo-Hawk, *supra* note 4, at 4.

73. *United States v. Winans,* 198 U.S. 371, 381 (1905).

74. *Babbitt Ford, Inc. v. Navajo Indian Tribe,* 710 F.2d 587 (9th Cir.), *cert. denied,* 466 U.S. 926 (1983).

75. *United States v. Adair,* 723 F.2d 1394, 1413 (9th Cir. 1984); see also *Oregon Wildlife Dep't v. Klamath Tribe,* 473 U.S. 753, 764–74 (1985); *Oliphant v. Suquamish Indian Tribe,* 435 U.S. 191, 208 (1978); *United States v. Ahtanum Irrigation Dist.,* 236 F.2d 321, 326 (9th Cir. 1956), *cert. denied,* 352 U.S. 988 (1957).

76. *Felix Cohen's Handbook of Federal Indian Law* 485–608 (Rennard Strickland et al. eds., 1982) [hereinafter Cohen].

77. See, e.g., *Washington v. State Commercial Fishing Vessel Ass'n,* 443 U.S. 658, 675–76 (1979); *Choctaw Nation v. Oklahoma,* 397 U.S. 620, 631 (1970); *United States v. Winans,* 198 U.S. 371, 381 (1905); *Worcester v. Georgia,* 31 U.S. (6 Pet.) 515, 551–54 (1832); *United States v. Adair,* 723 F.2d 1934, 1412–13 (9th Cir. 1984); *United States v. Top Sky,* 547 F.2d 486, 487 (9th Cir. 1976).

78. See, e.g., *Senate Hearing on S. 187, supra* note 61.

79. These states are: Arizona, Arkansas, Montana, Kansas, Nebraska, Oklahoma, North Dakota, South Dakota, Iowa, Missouri, Minnesota, Colorado, Idaho, New Mexico, New Hampshire, North Carolina, Oregon, Washington, Florida, California, Maine, Massachusetts, West Virginia, Tennessee, Alaska, Delaware, Nevada, Connecticut, Hawaii, Wisconsin, Illinois, Indiana, Mississippi, and Virginia. These laws are summarized in Harris, *supra* note 4.

80. 267 Cal. Rptr. 804 (Ct. App. 1990).

81. 455 N.W.2d 512 (Minn. Ct. App. 1990).

82. No. 90-06-9830-E, slip op. at 5-8 (Cir. Ct. Harney County, Or., Feb. 11, 1991).

83. 1989 Haw. Sess. Laws 316, item K-16.

84. Kansas Appropriations Act of 1989 (S.B. No. 39 & S.B. No. 68).

85. 1991 Kansas Senate Bill No. 7.

86. *Id.*

87. Neb. Rev. Stat. § 12-1201 (1990); see also Robert Peregoy, *The Legal Basis, Legislative History, and Implementation of Nebraska's Landmark Reburial Legislation,* 24 Ariz. St. L.J. 329 (1992).

88. Neb. Rev. Stat. §§ 12-1209-1210 (1990).

89. Bob Reeves, "Pawnee Remains Going 'Home' After Long Wait," *Lincoln Star,* Sept. 11, 1990, at 1, 5.

90. After the repatriation law passed, the Nebraska State Historical Society ("NSHS") sued the tribe to prevent it from examining NSHS records relating to its

collection of dead Pawnee Indians. NSHS claimed that it was not a public agency subject to state open records laws. *Nebraska State Historical Soc'y v. Pawnee Tribe,* No. 448 (Lancaster, Neb. filed Jan. 23, 1990). The State of Nebraska intervened on the tribe's side, and all NSHS claims were rejected by the court (Order of May 31, 1991). (The tribe's motion for attorney's fees is pending.) In addition, even though NSHS returned almost four hundred dead to the tribe in September 1990, an arbitration award requires NSHS to repatriate additional remains and burial goods to the Pawnee Tribe. *In re* Pawnee Tribe (Arbitration Award, Mar. 12, 1991). For an in-depth treatment of this controversy, see generally Roger C. Echo-Hawk and Walter R. Echo-Hawk, "Repatriation, Reburial and Religious Rights," in *Handbook of American Indian Religious Freedom* 63–80 (Christopher Vecsey ed., 1991).

91. Ariz. Rev. Stat. Ann. §§ 41-844, -865 (1992); see also Paul Bender, *1990 Arizona Repatriation Legislation,* 24 Ariz. St. L.J. 391 (1992).

92. Ariz. Rev. Stat. Ann. § 41-844(K), (F).

93. *Id.* § 41-844(K), (G).

94. California Pub. Res. Code § 5097.99 (West 1991). In announcing passage of this law, its sponsor, Assemblyman Richard Katz, stated that: "[N]o other race has had to endure the injustice that the Native American community has had to suffer in knowing that their relatives' and ancestors' skeletal remains are lying in a box in some university or museum, when what they deserve is a proper burial by their loved ones. . . . The passage of this bill is the first step in the settlement of a long-overlooked human rights issue." Letter from Richard Katz, California Assemblyman, to Walter R. Echo-Hawk, Attorney, Native American Rights Fund (Sept. 18, 1991) (on file with author).

95. Douglas J. Preston, "Skeletons in Our Museums' Closets," *Harper's,* Feb. 1989, at 68.

96. S. 2952, 99th Cong., 2d Sess. (1986); S. 187, 100th Cong., 1st Sess. (1987).

97. *Senate Hearing on S. 187, supra* note 61, at 1 (statement of Sen. Inouye).

98. *Id.* at 92 (statement of Sen. Melcher).

99. *Id.* at 25–46 (amended text of S. 187 & statement of Sen. Inouye).

100. *Id.* at 46–72, 95–137, 376–81.

101. Senator McCain introduced S. 1021, 101st Cong., 1st Sess. (1989); Senator Inouye introduced S. 1980, 101st Cong., 1st Sess. (1989); Rep. Udall introduced H.R. 1646, 101st Cong., 1st Sess. (1989) & H.R. 5237, 101st Cong., 2d Sess. (1990); and Rep. Bennett introduced H.R. 1381, 101st Cong., 1st Sess. (1989). In addition, Rep. Bennett sought to attach a comprehensive graves protection and repatriation bill to the Fiscal Year 1991 Defense Appropriations Bill, H.R. 4739, 101st Cong., 2d Sess. (1990).

102. S. 1021, 101st Cong., 1st Sess. § 5 (1989); S. 1980, 101st Cong., 1st Sess. § 4 (1989); H.R. 1381, 101st Cong., 1st Sess. § 3 (1989); H.R. 1646, 101st Cong., 1st Sess. § 4(b), (c) (1989); H.R. 5237, 101st Cong., 2d Sess. § 3 (1990).

103. S. 1021, 101st Cong., 1st Sess. § 6 (1989); S. 1980, 101st Cong., 1st Sess. § 3 (1989); H.R. 1646, 101st Cong., 1st Sess. § 5 (1989); H.R. 5237, 101st Cong., 2d Sess. §§ 5, 6 (1990).

104. S. 1021, 101st Cong., 1st Sess. § 8 (1989); S. 1980, 101st Cong., 1st Sess. § 3 (1989); H.R. 1646, 101st Cong., 1st Sess. § 6 (1989); H.R. 5237, 101st Cong., 2d Sess. §§ 5, 6 (1990).

105. S. 1980, 101st Cong., 1st Sess. § 3 (1989); H.R. 5237, 101st Cong., 2d Sess. § 5 (1990).

106. S. 1021, 101st Cong., 1st Sess. § 4 (1989); H.R. 1381, 101st Cong., 1st Sess. § 4 (1989); H.R. 1646, 101st Cong., 1st Sess. § 4(a) (1989) (limited to skeletal remains); H.R. 5237, 101st Cong., 2d Sess. § 4 (1990).

107. S. 1980, 101st Cong., 1st Sess. § 3(d) (1989); H.R. 5237, 101st Cong., 2d Sess. § 7 (1990).

108. H.R. Rep. No. 877, 101st Cong., 2d Sess. 111-12 (1990), reprinted in 1990 U.S.C.C.A.N. 4367, 4367-4392 [hereinafter House Report 877]; S. Rep. No. 473, 101st Cong., 2d Sess. 1, 3-4 (1990) [hereinafter Senate Report 473].

109. 20 U.S.C.A. §§ 80q to 80q-15 (West 1990).

110. *Id.* § 80q-1.

111. *Id.* § 80q-9.

112. *Id.* § 80q-9(a)(1).

113. *Id.* § 80q-9(a)(2).

114. *Id.* § 80q-9(b).

115. *Id.* § 80q-9(c).

116. *Id.* § 80q-9(d).

117. *Id.* § 80q-10(a).

118. 135 *Cong. Rec.* S12388 (daily ed. Oct. 3, 1989) (statement of Sen. Inouye).

119. *Id.;* 135 *Cong. Rec.* H8448 (daily ed. Nov. 13, 1989) (statement of Rep. Rahall).

120. 135 *Cong. Rec.* S12397 (daily ed. Oct. 3, 1989) (statement of Sen. McCain).

121. 136 *Cong. Rec.* H10988–10989 (daily ed. Oct. 22, 1990) (statements of Rep. Campbell and Rep. Rhodes); 136 *Cong. Rec.* S17174–17175 (daily ed. Oct. 26, 1990) (statements of Sen. Inouye and Sen. Akaka).

122. Report of the Panel for a Nat'l Dialogue on Museum/Native American Relations (Feb. 28, 1990).

123. Senate Report 473, *supra* note 108, at 2-3. The House Report pertaining to NAGPRA noted further that the "majority [of the Panel] believed that 'Respect for Native human rights is the paramount principle that should govern resolution of the issue when a claim is made." House Report 877, *supra* note 108, at 10-11.

124. 136 *Cong. Rec.* S17173 (daily ed. Oct. 26, 1990) (statement of Sen. McCain); see also 136 *Cong. Rec..* H10989 (daily ed. Oct. 22, 1990) (statement of Rep. Rhodes) (report "helped immensely to shape the policies contained in this bill"); 136 *Cong. Rec.* S17174 (daily ed. Oct. 26, 1990) (statement of Sen. Inouye); Senate Report 473, *supra* note 108, at 6 ("The Committee agrees with the findings and recommendations of the Panel for a National Dialogue on Museum/Native American Relations").

125. 25 U.S.C.A. §§ 3001–3013.

126. 136 *Cong. Rec.* S17174 (daily ed. Oct. 26, 1990) (statement of Sen. Inouye).

127. *Id.* at S17174–17175.

128. See *supra* text accompanying notes 117–22.

129. 25 U.S.C.A. § 3010. For this reason, Congress stated in this section that NAGPRA should not be interpreted "to establish a precedent with respect to any other individual, organization or foreign government." *Id.*

130. Cohen, *supra* note 76, at 207.

131. *Id.* at 223–24.

132. See, e.g., *Green v. Dumke,* 480 F.2d 624, 628 n.7 (9th Cir. 1973); *Schorle v. City of Greenhills,* 524 F. Supp. 821, 825 (S.D. Ohio 1981).

133. 136 *Cong. Rec.* S17173 (daily ed. Oct. 26, 1990) (statement of Sen. McCain); see also Daniel Monroe & Walter Echo-Hawk, "Deft Deliberations," *Museum News,* July/Aug. 1991, at 55–58. In fact, a broad spectrum of national museum, scientific, and Native American organizations jointly sent a letter to President Bush urging him to sign this legislation. Letter from American Anthropological Association, Association of Physical Anthropologists, Archeological Institute of America, Association on American Indian Affairs, Native American Rights Fund, National Conference of State Historic Preservation Officers, National Congress of American Indians, National Trust for Historic Places, Preservation Action, Society for American Archaeology, Society for Historical Archaeology, and Society for Professional Archaeology to President Bush (Nov. 2, 1990) (on file with author).

134. 136 *Cong. Rec.* S17173 (daily ed. Oct. 26, 1990) (statement of Sen. McCain). Both Senators McCain and Inouye recognized the importance of museums in maintaining our cultural heritage, as well as the interest of Native Americans in the

return of ancestral human remains and funerary objects, sacred objects, and items of cultural patrimony. 136 *Cong. Rec.* s17173–17175 (daily ed. Oct. 26, 1990).

135. Senate Report 473, *supra* note 108, at 6.

136. 25 U.S.C.A. § 3001(8). The Smithsonian Institution is required to inventory and return culturally affiliated human remains and funerary objects pursuant to the National Museum of the American Indian Act, 20 U.S.C.A. §§ 80q to 80q-15 (West 1990). See *supra* text accompanying notes 109–21. The Museum Act does not cover sacred objects and items of cultural patrimony. See *id.* Senator Daniel K. Inouye, Democrat from Hawaii, has introduced a bill pertaining to the Smithsonian Institution in the 102d Congress that includes provisions addressing sacred objects and items of cultural patrimony. S. 235, 102d Cong., 1st Sess. (1991). The National Museum of the American Indian ("NMAI") has adopted its own repatriation policy, which provides for the repatriation of communally owned property and sacred objects pursuant to certain criteria. Most of the NMAI, however, consists at present of those Indian remains and cultural objects that were part of the Heye collection in New York prior to the absorption of the Heye collection by the Smithsonian Institution. See 20 U.S.C.A. § 80q-2. It does not cover the Smithsonian Institution itself, which possesses a large number of human remains and funerary objects.

137. "Museum" is defined as "any institution or State or local government agency (including any institution of higher learning) that receives Federal funds and has possession of, or control over, Native American cultural items." 25 U.S.C.A. § 3001(8). The term *museum* is used in this article to refer to institutions that meet this definition unless otherwise indicated.

138. "Indian tribe" is defined as a "tribe, band, nation, or other organized group or community of Indians, including any Alaska Native village . . . which is recognized as eligible for the special programs and services provided by the United States to Indians because of their status as Indians." *Id.* § 3001(7). This definition includes tribes eligible for special programs and services from any part of the United States government, not merely those receiving services from the secretary of the interior. See *id.*

139. "Native Hawaiian organization" is defined as "any organization which: (A) serves and represents the interests of Native Hawaiians, (B) has as a primary and stated purpose the provision of services to Native Hawaiians, and (C) has expertise in Native Hawaiian affairs." *Id.* § 3001(11). The Office of Hawaiian Affairs and Hui Mālama I Nā Kūpuna 'O Hawai'i Nei are specifically included in the definition. *Id.*

140. 25 U.S.C.A. § 3005(a)(1); see also *infra* text accompanying notes 147–50.

141. 25 U.S.C.A. § 3005(a)(4). Section 3005(a)(4) does not explicitly provide for a claim to be filed by a known lineal descendant. *Id.* It is unlikely that § 3005(a)(4)

was intended to exclude claims by descendants, however, because 25 U.S.C.A. § 3005(a)(1) specifically permits descendant claims for human remains and associated funerary objects if the inventory process leads to the identification of a known descendant. Moreover, 25 U.S.C.A. § 3005(a)(5)(A) permits a lineal descendant of an individual who owned a sacred object to claim that object. Indeed, NAGPRA is based, in part, upon common law pertaining to the control of human remains and funerary objects. Common law recognizes that the next of kin retains control over buried human remains and associated funerary objects. See *supra* text accompanying notes 53–57. Thus, the exclusion of descendants from § 3005(a)(4) is undoubtedly because that section establishes rules for proving cultural affiliation—a requirement not applicable to descendants. The legislative history supports this interpretation. The House report describes § 3005 as requiring "all returns to be completed in consultation with the requesting descendent, tribe or Native Hawaiian organization." House Report 877, *supra* note 108, at 19.

142. 25 U.S.C.A. § 3005(a)(4).

143. *Id.* § 3003(b)(2).

144. House Report 877, *supra* note 108, at 16.

145. 25 U.S.C.A. § 3003(b)(2).

146. *Id.*

147. *Id.* § 3001(2).

148. House Report 877, *supra* note 108, at 14.

149. *Id.*

150. Senate Report 473, *supra* note 108, at 8. The Senate Report's statement referred to the application of a stricter definition of cultural affiliation that was contained in an earlier version of NAGPRA. S. 1980, 101st Cong., 2d Sess. (1990). That version included a definition of "cultural affiliation" that would have required that "a continuity of group identity from the earlier to the present day group" be "reasonably establishe[d]." *Id.*

151. 25 U.S.C.A. § 3001(3)(A).

152. *Id.*

153. See, e.g., *id.* §§ 3001(3)(A),(B), 3001(8), 3003(a), 3004(a).

154. *Id.* § 3001(3)(A). If the human remains are no longer in the possession or control of an agency or covered museum (and the funerary objects were not specifically made for burial purposes or to contain human remains), the objects may be classified as "unassociated funerary objects." *Id.* § 3001(3)(B); see *infra* text accompanying note 165.

155. 25 U.S.C.A. § 3005(a)(1) and the portion of § 3005(a)(4) applicable to human

remains and associated funerary objects refer only to subsections (b) and (e) of 25 U.S.C.A. § 3005 as exceptions to the requirement that the remains and associated funerary objects be expeditiously returned.

156. 25 U.S.C.A. § 3005(b).

157. *Id.*

158. *Id.* § 3009(1)(B).

159. *Id.* § 3005(e).

160. *Id.* Section 3005(e) also provides that the dispute may be settled "pursuant to the provisions of the Act." *Id.* This refers to the authority of the review committee created by 25 U.S.C.A. § 3006 to "facilitat[e] the resolution of any disputes among Indian tribes, Native Hawaiian organizations, or lineal descendants and Federal agencies or museums relating to the return of such items including convening the parties to the dispute if deemed desirable." *Id.* § 3006(c)(4). Although any findings of the committee are admissible in a court proceeding, the committee has no binding authority upon any of the parties. *Id.* § 3006(d). Thus, while the committee can certainly play an important role in resolving these disputes, ultimately the disputes must be resolved by agreement or judicial determination.

161. 25 U.S.C.A. § 3006.

162. *Id.* § 3006(c)(5).

163. *Id.* § 3006(e).

164. House Report 877, *supra* note 108, at 16. The House Interior Committee indicated that it "look[ed] forward" to the review committee's recommendations. *Id.* The Report of the Panel for a National Dialogue on Museum/Native American Relations also reflected a division on this issue. *Id.* at 11.

165. See generally 25 U.S.C.A. §§ 3001(3), 3005.

166. *Id.* § 3001(3)(B).

167. *Id.* § 3001(3)(C).

168. House Report 877, *supra* note 108, at 14.

169. *Id.*

170. Senate Report 473, *supra* note 108, at 6.

171. See, e.g., *United States v. Ballard*, 322 U.S. 78 (1944); *Martinelli v. Dugger*, 817 F.2d 1499, 1503 (11th Cir. 1987); *United States v. Kuch*, 288 F. Supp. 439, 445 (D.D.C. 1968).

172. 25 U.S.C.A. § 3001(3)(C).

173. *Id.* § 3001(3)(D).

174. *Id.*; see also Echo-Hawk, *supra* note 35, at 441–44.

175. Senate Report 473, *supra* note 108, at 7–8.

176. Cultural affiliation can be determined by the summary process, 25 U.S.C.A. §§ 3004, 3005(a)(2), or, in the case of unassociated funerary objects, by the claimant making a showing by a preponderance of the evidence. *Id.* § 3005(a)(4). See *supra* text accompanying notes 140–49 for a discussion of requirements of 25 U.S.C.A. § 3005(a)(4).

177. 25 U.S.C.A. § 3005(a)(5).

178. *Id.* § 3005(a)(5)(A).

179. *Id.* § 3005(a)(5)(C).

180. *Id.* § 3005(c).

181. *Id.* § 3004(b)(2).

182. *Id.* § 3001(13).

183. Senate Report 473, *supra* note 108, at 8; see also Rennard Strickland, *Implementing the National Policy of Understanding, Preserving, and Safeguarding the Heritage of Indian Peoples and Native Hawaiians: Human Rights, Sacred Objects, and Cultural Patrimony,* 24 Ariz. St. L.J. 175 (1992).

184. 136 *Cong. Rec.* s17176 (daily ed. Oct. 26, 1990) (statement of Sen. McCain).

185. See generally 16 Am. Jur. 2d *Conflict of Laws* §§ 43, 44 (1979 & Supp. 1991).

186. See generally Echo-Hawk, *supra* note 35.

187. 25 U.S.C.A. § 3001(13).

188. *Id.;* see also House Report 877, *supra* note 108, at 15; Ralph Johnson & Sharon Haensly, *Fifth Amendment Takings Implications of the 1990 Native American Graves Protection and Repatriation Act,* 24 Ariz. St. L.J. 151 (1992).

189. 25 U.S.C.A. § 3001(13).

190. See Senate Report 473, *supra* note 108, at 8.

191. 25 U.S.C.A. § 3005(c).

192. *Id.* § 3005(b), (e). See *supra* text accompanying notes 154–59.

193. 25 U.S.C.A. § 3009(1)(A).

194. *Id.* § 3009(1)(B).

195. *Id.* § 3003(a).

196. *Id.* § 3003(e).

197. *Id.* § 3003(a).

198. Senate Report 473, *supra* note 108, at 12.

199. 25 U.S.C.A. § 3003(b)(2).

200. Senate Report 473, *supra* note 108, at 12.

201. 25 U.S.C.A. § 3003(b)(1)(A), (C).

202. *Id.* § 3003(b)(1)(B).

203. *Id.* § 3003(c).

204. Senate Report 473, *supra* note 108, at 11.

205. 25 U.S.C.A. § 3009(2).

206. Senate Report 473, *supra* note 108, at 12.

207. 25 U.S.C.A. § 3003(d)(1), (2).

208. *Id.* § 3003(d)(2).

209. See *supra* text accompanying note 144.

210. 25 U.S.C.A. § 3003(b)(2); see also *supra* text accompanying notes 143–46.

211. 25 U.S.C.A. 3008(b) permits, but does not require, the secretary of the interior to make grants to museums to conduct the inventory and summary required by the act. See *infra* text accompanying notes 263–65.

212. 25 U.S.C.A. § 3004; see also *supra* text accompanying notes 166–75 for the definitions of these items.

213. 25 U.S.C.A. § 3004(a), (b)(1)(A).

214. *Id.* § 3004(b)(1)(C).

215. *Id.* § 3004(b)(1)(B), (C).

216. *Id.* § 3009(2).

217. House Report 877, *supra* note 108, at 15.

218. 25 U.S.C.A. § 3004(b)(2).

219. NAGPRA defines cultural items to include human remains, associated and unassociated funerary objects, sacred objects, and items of cultural patrimony. See *id.* § 3001(3).

220. *Id.* § 3002.

221. *Id.* § 3002(a)(1).

222. *Id.* § 3002(a)(2)(A).

223. *Id.* § 3001(15).

224. *Id.* § 3002(a)(2)(B). NAGPRA defines "Federal lands" as nontribal land "controlled or owned by the United States, including lands selected by but not yet conveyed to Alaska Native corporations and groups pursuant to the Alaska Native Claims Settlement Act of 1971." *Id.* § 3001(5).

225. Senate Report 473, *supra* note 108, at 9.

226. 25 U.S.C.A. § 3002(a)(2)(C).

227. *Id.* § 3002(b).

228. *Id.* § 3002(c)(1); 16 U.S.C. §§ 470aa–mm (1988 & West Supp. 1991). A permit may be issued pursuant to the Archeological Resources Protection Act of 1979 ("ARPA") upon a showing that the applicant is qualified; the undertaking is designed to advance archaeological knowledge in the public interest; the resources will remain the property of the United States and be preserved in an appropriate institution (this is modified by the NAGPRA); and the activity is consistent with the applicable land management plan. 16 U.S.C. § 470cc(b) (1988). Notice must be provided to tribes which may consider a site of religious or cultural importance. *Id.* § 470cc(c). Tribal consent is required for excavations located on tribal land. *Id.* § 470cc(g)(2). NAGPRA expands upon these requirements only marginally. NAGPRA requires notice to tribes with an aboriginal claim to the land. Notice is not limited to sites that are specifically of religious or cultural importance as under ARPA. Moreover, NAGPRA specifically requires consultation with the appropriate tribes if excavation involves culturally affiliated material or if it occurs on Federal land that has been the subject of adjudicated aboriginal claims. ARPA speaks only to notice, not consultation, although the regulations allow (but do not require) "discussions" with interested tribes. Compare 25 U.S.C.A. § 3002(c)(2), (3) with 16 U.S.C. § 470cc(c) and 43 C.F.R. § 7.7 (1990).

229. See 25 U.S.C.A. § 3002(c)(2).

230. See *Id.*

231. *Id.* § 3002(c); see also text accompanying notes 222–26.

232. 25 U.S.C.A. § 3002(d)(1). In the case of Alaska Native Claims Settlement Act lands (still owned by the Federal government) selected by, but not conveyed to, the Alaska Native corporation or group, that corporation or group is the appropriate organization to be notified. *Id.*

233. See Senate Report 473, *supra* note 108, at 10.

234. *Id.;* see also 136 *Cong. Rec.* S17176 (daily ed. Oct. 26, 1990) (statement of Sen. McCain).

235. *Id.*

236. 25 U.S.C.A. § 3002(d)(1).

237. *Id.* § 3002(d)(3).

238. *Id.* § 3002(d)(2).

239. *Id.* § 3001(13); 18 U.S.C.A. § 1170(a) (West Supp. 1991).

240. Senate Report 473, *supra* note 108, at 11.

241. 18 U.S.C.A. § 1170(a).

242. *Id.* § 1170(b).

243. *Id.;* see also *supra* text accompanying note 241.

244. See *id.*

245. 25 U.S.C.A. § 3009(5).

246. *Id.* § 3006(a). NAGPRA required that the review committee be appointed by March 16, 1991. *Id.* The secretary did not meet this deadline. In fact, a notice in the Federal Register soliciting nominations to the review committee was not published until August 28, 1991. 56 Fed. Reg. 42635 (1991). The committee's initial six members were not appointed until March 3, 1992, and as of the date of this article, the seventh member had yet to be chosen. The review committee ceases existence 120 days after the secretary certifies that its work has been completed. 25 U.S.C.A. § 3006(i).

247. 25 U.S.C.A. § 3006(b)(1).

248. *Id.* § 3006(b)(2).

249. See, e.g., *Senate Hearing on S. 1021 & S. 1980, supra* note 8, at 79 (testimony of Suzan Shown Harjo, Director, Morningstar Foundation).

250. In the Museum of the American Indian Act, three of the five special review committee members are selected from nominations of Indian tribes and organizations. The members, however, are neither required to be Native American nor traditional leaders. 20 U.S.C.A. § 80q-10(b) (1990).

251. 25 U.S.C.A. § 3006(c)(2).

252. *Id.* § 3006(c)(3), (4).

253. *Id.* § 3006(d); see also Senate Report 473, *supra* note 108, at 13.

254. 25 U.S.C.A. § 3006(c)(5); see also text accompanying notes 161–64.

255. 25 U.S.C.A. § 3006(c)(7).

256. *Id.* § 3006(c)(9).

257. *Id.* § 3006(h).

258. *Id.* § 3007.

259. *Id.* § 3007(b).

260. *Id.* § 3013. The language in the NAGPRA is that "any person" may bring an action to enforce the law's provisions. The Senate Report explains this provision as meaning that "any party; including an Indian tribe, Native Hawaiian organization, museum or agency" may bring a cause of action. Senate Report 473, *supra* note 108, at 14.

261. 25 U.S.C.A. § 3009(3), (4).

262. *Id.* § 3005(f).

263. *Id.* § 3008(b).

264. *Id.* § 3008(a).

265. See H.R. 2686, 102d Cong., 1st Sess. (1991).

266. 25 U.S.C.A. § 3011. This deadline has not been met.

8

Vine Deloria Jr.

Secularism, Civil Religion, and the Religious Freedom of

American Indians

In 1978 Congress passed the American Indian Religious Freedom Resolution. At that time, most American Indians believed that the status of their right to practice their traditional religions was protected by that special legislation, even though in floor debate Congressman Morris Udall had specifically stated that no major laws were being changed and no disruption of the existing state of affairs would take place. In the decade and a half since then, Indian litigants have cited the religious freedom resolution as an indication on the part of Congress that it was federal policy, to be followed by all federal agencies, that the particular needs of traditional religious practitioners would be accommodated.

In 1988 the Supreme Court turned aside the Indians of northern California, refusing to prohibit the building of a minor logging road that would ruin the high country where they held vision quests and gathered medicines (*Lyng v. Northwest Indian Cemetery Assn.*, 485 U.S. 439 [1988]). In the spring of 1990 the Supreme Court ruled that the state of Oregon did not have to present a compelling interest in order to pass legislation that would have the effect of virtually eliminating a religion, in this instance the use of peyote for religious ritual purposes (*Employment Div., Dept. of Human Resources of Oregon v. Smith*, 108 L. Ed. 2d 876 [1990]). The consternation that has arisen among American Indians since these decisions is genuine, and many people feel betrayed by both the Congress and the Supreme Court.

The Supreme Court is decidedly anti-Indian. That much is clear. The turning point probably was *Rosebud Sioux Tribe v. Kneip*, 430 U.S. 584 (1977), which returned a devastating 9-0 against the tribe. Since then, through *Montana v. U.S.*, 450 U.S. 544 (1981), and *Sioux Nation v. U.S.*, 448 U.S. 371 (1980), it has seemed as if the Supreme Court simply weaves an argument out of thin air to deprive tribes of long-standing rights. But there is a basic question underlying the *Smith* decision that many people have not yet asked themselves: Was the case lost because it was an Indian case or because it was a religious case? Setting aside the Indian question for the moment, let us consider the religious issue.

The Historical Background of Free Exercise

Medieval Europe achieved an intellectual synthesis in which faith and reason were regarded as equally valid paths to truth. The true faith was revealed in the Bible and the teachings of the church, but it was believed possible to arrive at a similar set of propositions by reasoning from the natural laws revealed in the design of creation. With the translation of Aristotelian philosophy in the 1200s, reason was given a comprehensive framework within which all aspects of knowledge and experience could be related. Faith thereafter acted as a conscience and control device to reign in the exuberant adventures of reason. Western science, endorsed by religion—providing it discovered the laws established by the Creator—was free to experiment and investigate to its heart's content.

Martin Luther applied reason to the theological realm, posted his 95 *Theses,* and shattered the homogeneity of Christendom by maintaining that the individual could achieve salvation by faith alone, without the intercession of the church. Thereafter, among the Protestant wing of Christianity, a process of dissent and fragmentation began, as small groups chose minor aspects of the Christian revelation around which to build their version of the true faith. Reason in the natural sciences reached the conclusion, with the philosophy and psychology of René Descartes, that the world consisted of mind and matter, mind being a province in which the church still had a voice and matter being the indissoluble atoms of the physical world.

By the time Europeans began to look seriously at the New World as a place for settlement, religious conflicts had ravaged the European continent, countries were forced to choose between the Catholic and Protestant versions of Christianity, and a significant segment of European intellectuals had become secular, if not agnostic, thinkers. Expanding technology gave secular science the edge in demonstrating to the civilized world the truth of its method and results. Hence, while religious movements contained considerably more heat than light, the process of secularization was well under way by the time the Pilgrims arrived at Plymouth Rock.

A substantial number of colonizing groups arriving on the Atlantic seaboard were driven there because of religious persecutions in their homelands. Some, such as the people in Massachusetts, promptly established theocracies equally as brutal as the situations they had fled in their original homelands. It is a historical fact that during colonial times, Catholics and Quakers were executed in Massachusetts for preaching their versions of Christianity. Other groups, such as the people in Rhode Island and Pennsylvania, saw religious conflict as disruptive of the civil order and forbade persecution of individuals because of their religious beliefs.

During the writing of the Constitution, it became apparent that some provisions had to be inserted in the nation's basic organic, political document ensuring certain freedoms that had been badly abused by the king of England and by various colonial legislatures. Thus we had the adoption of the Bill of Rights, which contained two clauses dealing with religion: (1) the prohibition of the establishment of a state religion and (2) the guarantee of free exercise of religion. Ideologically, even these clauses contained the possibility of misunderstanding, since religion itself had been carelessly defined. Jefferson saw religion as a matter of belief and felt that the state could not interfere with the manner in which people chose to view the world. Madison went further and connected religious belief with religious acts, to advocate a much larger sphere in which the guarantee and prohibitions would be operable.

American society was predominantly Protestant/secular in its early years, with few Catholics and no Asian religions; the religions of the Indians, like their other customs and beliefs, were totally outside the realm of constitutional concerns. Christianity shattered on the American shore. Ethnic immigrants reconstituted their own versions of the national churches of their home countries, but American society was subjected to periodic "revivals," surges of religious energy that left in their wake new denominations with less sophisticated and more practical theologies. The rigor and personal discipline required by Lutheranism and Calvinism became translated into the quick, emotional experience of "salvation" on the American frontier. This process of fragmentation has been a major characteristic of American Christianity ever since.

Real controversy over religious freedom did not take place until American society had to deal with the Mormon movement in the 1860s. One tenet of the Mormon faith, taken directly from the pages of the Old Testament, with certain American innovations, was polygamy, and the Mormons practiced it with some vigor and notoriety. Beginning in 1862 and continuing until the Tucker Edmund Act of 1887, Congress attempted to prohibit the practice of polygamy in spite of the constitutional prohibition of this effort, justifying its attempts on the basis that Utah was a territory ruled by Congress and therefore not entitled to Bill of Rights protection until it had become a state. In *Reynolds v. U.S.*, 98 U.S. 145 (1879), the Supreme Court adopted the Jeffersonian interpretation of religion, ruling, in effect, that Mormons were free to believe in polygamy but not free to practice it.

Other than the Mormon controversy, little was done in the religious realm until the Second World War. Congress prohibited the use of federal funds in support of sectarian schools on Indian reservations, but the Supreme Court, in *Quick Bear v. Leupp*, 210 U.S. 50 (1908), found that churches could use tribal funds for their schools, since Catholic Indians needed to have religious freedom. During the First World War some cases arose but were as easily characterized as free speech cases as instances of oppression of religious practice. With the surge of patriotism in the Second World War came the flag salute cases, in which the Supreme Court first said it was permissible to require Seventh Day Adventist children to salute the flag and then reversed itself and ruled otherwise.

In the interim period between the adoption of the Bill of Rights and the advent of the Second World War, a process of rapid secularization took place. During colonial days, churches dealt with most of the social problems that government handles today. Charity for the poor was a church function, as were education, hospital care, and even some aspects of penitentiary administration. With the great fragmentation of Christendom in America, it was impossible that any one denomination could resolve societywide problems, although the Roman Catholics, from start to finish, insisted on having their own school system. Nevertheless, over the decades, churches withdrew from active involvement in domestic problems and confined their activities to gathering new members and issuing pious pronouncements endorsing the actions of government.

Only since the end of the Second World War has there been a significant amount of litigation involving either free exercise or the establishment of religion. In general, the free exercise cases have involved overly zealous members of recognized Protestant churches whose allegiance to the articles of faith, in practice, have created conflicts with civil law. Establishment cases have dealt primarily with efforts to provide financial support to Catholic school systems or with the presence of Christian symbolism in displays of public celebration, particularly on what were once religious holidays. Supreme Court justices have tiptoed with extreme caution through the thickets of the free exercise clause, hoping not to arouse a religious constituency. Thus, numerous "tests" have been devised by the court to provide guidance for lower courts in handling religious free exercise cases. Until *Smith*, the test most frequently used originated in *Sherbert v. Verner*, 374 U.S. 398 (1963), which involved a three-step process for determining when the state could constitutionally impinge on religious activities, the most important step being a demonstration that the state had a compelling interest in controlling specific kinds of behavior.

With *Smith,* the *Sherbert* test was discarded. In its place was substituted the strange and nonhistoric proposition that the right of free exercise of religion had to be linked to some other freedom guaranteed in the Bill of Rights: Free exercise could not stand alone. It is important to note that the Court did not say anything about Indians, although it had the opportunity to do so with the Indian position fully briefed and the presence of a federal regulation specifically exempting the Native American Church from the enforcement of drug laws because of its religious ritual use of the cactus.

American Indian Religious Freedom

Government treatment of traditional Indian religions has been inconsistent, fluctuating with the perceptions of Congress and the Bureau of Indian Affairs. Early treaties sought only to obtain the permission of the tribes for missionaries to visit them; later treaties gave some denominations grants of land in exchange for providing educational or health services. During the Grant administration, churches were allowed to appoint Indian agents for most reservations, and suppression of tribal religions was seen as a positive step in preparing Indians for American citizenship. This program failed dismally when many of the church-appointed agents proved incompetent and others embezzled tribal and government funds during their tenure as representatives of civilization. In the 1890s an Indian agent named "Pussyfoot" Johnson prowled the Oklahoma Indian settlements, attempting to quash the use of peyote, while in Washington DC the commissioner of Indian affairs denied that such activity was taking place.

At the close of the First World War, hearings were held to consider a prohibition against the use of peyote, but social scientists, defending this practice as cultural, turned back the efforts of major missionary churches to ban use of the substance. With the New Deal religious freedom for traditional religious activities was encouraged; and since 1934 more and more Indians have felt free to bring suppressed ceremonies into the open. Throughout this period Indians traveled to off-reservation sites to conduct ceremonies in sacred places, as they had for thousands of years. Congress even provided legislative authority for the people of Taos Pueblo to use the sacred Blue Lake area, which had been confiscated and placed in a national forest preserve. There was not much conflict between federal agencies and Indians until the 1960s, when it became apparent that tribes wanted to reclaim certain sacred areas from the government.

Taos Pueblo, in pursuing its land claim in the Indian Claims Commission, informed the government that it did not want financial compensation for its Blue Lake area—it wanted the land returned. By severing this region from its claim and seeking congressional legislation, Taos was able to get Blue Lake restored. Passage of that law was quickly followed by the return of a portion of Mount Adams to the Yakima for religious purposes. Fearful that these precedents would enable Indians to reclaim more lands, the Forest Service and the National Park Service tightened up the regulations allowing the traditional Indians to perform ceremonies at sacred places.

During the seventies tensions increased. New conservation and ecological laws meant the writing of new administrative regulations, and with each effort by the federal government to protect and administer its lands, traditional Indian practitioners were increasingly restricted in their ability to conduct ceremonial activities. Sporadic conflict over eagle feathers and other animal parts needed for ceremonial costumes and medicine bags meant further oppression. As an illustration of the inconsistencies of the situation, an Indian could have eagle feathers only for religious ceremonial purposes, while senators and congressmen could have eagle-feather war bonnets for decorative purposes.

In 1978 Congress adopted the American Indian Religious Freedom Resolution, which directed federal agencies to survey their rules and regulations and try to accommodate the practice of Indian religions. Congressman Morris Udall assured the House of Representatives that the resolution had no practical effect; later, when this resolution was cited by Indians in court, judges and justices quoted Udall and turned them aside. The resolution was, therefore, simply a cosmetic attempt to speak to an extremely complicated subject without any knowledge of the subject at all. Litigation based on this resolution increased substantially after its passage, and courts attempted to find a test by which they could determine the probable validity of the Indian claims. But determining a central belief or practice for religions that regarded the physical world as a living entity proved almost impossible.

Religious Freedom Today

A major phenomenon of this century has been the erosion of the power and influence of organized religion in American society. The trend has been one of secularization, in which churches, in order to receive the blessings of the government, have increasingly characterized their religious activities as basically secular in nature. Secular science, which routed religion in the courtroom in the 1925 *Scopes* trial in Tennessee, has gradually become entrenched as the final authority on the natural world, so that during the

1980s, when fundamentalist churches sought to include "creation science" in state curricula, the churches were turned away. The religious message increasingly has become one of simple belief, and religious hucksters now imply that the purpose of Christianity is to enable people to make money and live affluent lives. Only with the rise of the abortion question has organized religion made a move toward involvement in secular affairs, and on this question there is no united religious front.

As secularization has progressed, there has been a strange melding of political and religious beliefs, which has been characterized by Robert Bellah as the new "civil religion." In medieval Europe, after the crowning of Charlemagne by the Pope, political power was believed to be validated by the church. Civil religion—a blending of theological concepts, a generalized religion that endorses and affirms the state—moves society back toward that condition. But whereas the pope could energize Europe by calling for a Crusade, today the churches wait for the president to announce state policy so they can endorse it. The beliefs of the civil religion blend vaguely with mythical American history, so that America somehow gets a Judeo-Christian heritage sanctified by the blood of its pioneers and enthusiastic about current military adventures. The recent orgy of parades after the Persian Gulf bombing was an example of the fervor of civil religion.

Indian tribes encounter civil religion when dealing with the various federal agencies charged with administering public land and federal projects. Here the bureaucrats act in a priestly role, presiding over their forests, national monuments, and irrigation projects with the care and paranoia that formerly characterized village priests and New England ministers. But their perspective is wholly secular, determined in large part by the spate of environmental legislation passed over the last three decades. In the National Environmental Protection Act, the Wild Rivers Act, the Wilderness Act, the Clean Air Act, and many other recent federal statutes we find an articulation of the relationship between humans and nature as defined and understood by inadequately educated federal employees.

Although the hard sciences—physics, chemistry, and so on—define modern scientific methodology, the social sciences, which purport to deal with human beings, follow the general perspectives of the scientific community, which understands birds, plants, animals, and all living things, including human beings, as merely phenomena that can be subjected to scientific inquiry. No other values are recognized or admissible. It is hardly a surprise, then, to understand that one of the issues of real conflict is that of the treatment of human skeletal remains. American Indians are the chief victims of the perceived scientific need to investigate; and since the founding of the United States it has been the practice of scientists, whether their theories are well founded or not, to use Indian human remains for scientific work, teaching materials, and public displays.

The attitude of the federal agencies toward Indian remains, an attitude supported and applauded by museum directors and archaeologists, has been that they are resources, comparable in most respects to timber, oil, and water, belonging to the federal agency on whose land they were found. The Native American Rights Fund, led by Walter Echo-Hawk, challenged this conception and, in a series of negotiations, secured restoration of many human remains and saw enacted several state and federal statutes placing Indian human remains on a near-equal standing with non-Indian skeletons. Make no mistake about the power of secularity in this struggle, however, since the attitude of federal employees and social scientists was that there is no evidence that we have any relationship to the departed, once bodily functions cease. Consequently, in their view, any belief *or experience* relating to the dead or to spirits of the dead is wholly superstition. Civil religion thus denies the possibility or importance of the afterlife and limits human responsibilities to tangible things that we can touch.

A further aspect of civil religion is that the practice of religion must be within the boundaries of municipal law and civil order. Thus state police powers are believed to be the final arbiter of values in human society. Beliefs and practices must conform to city ordinances, state laws, and federal regulations; and insofar as they conflict, they must surrender themselves to civil authority. In *Lyng,* the Forest Service was determined to build a road, apparently merely in the interests of symmetry, since the evidence revealed no practical or economic reason for construction; and the practice of Indian religions had to step back.

The power of civil religion and the inability of organized religion to articulate a set of values superior to those of the state combine to define the present situation in the following manner: Religious behavior must be justified on secular grounds in order to be protected. The possible examples of this proposition are frightening. A rock-concert promoter could get permission to use a natural amphitheater, but a traditional Indian could not get permission to use the same location if he wished to perform a ceremony. A person could wear long hair as a symbol of freedom of speech but could not do the same thing if his motive were religious belief. A municipality can display a manger scene at Christmas only if it is interpreted as a generally accepted cultural tradition and not if it is for the purpose of religious devotion. That explains, perhaps, the inclusion of Rudolph, the Ninja Turtles, and some Disney characters in Christmas displays.

Since *Smith,* lower courts have discarded the old balancing test and are now placing churches under municipal ordinances, denying requests for dietary exemptions, authorizing autopsies when they are against the practices of religious groups, and generally allowing civil laws, particularly criminal laws, to be the definitive statement of what is acceptable religious behavior. The chief victims of *Smith* are mainline churches and their members, insofar as those members take their religious duties seriously.

The Quest for Religious Experience

The psychological subconscious of American society and its constituent members is a tempestuous sewer. Americans crave some form of religious experience, and they are unable to obtain it from any of the old, mainline Christian denominations. This condition became obvious in the sixties, when people began to take drugs to help them deal with the pressures of modern society. Two responses were forthcoming. The right-wing fundamentalists diluted their message even more, making Christianity a talk show phenomenon and asking only for uncritical obedience to a set of slogans articulated by reactionary politicians and huckster preachers. Fundamentalist Christianity, which loves the unborn and hates the living, has become a powerful political force in this country primarily because it has aligned itself with reactionary economic oligarchies and parroted their concerns about the status quo. The evidence is there to see: Ronald Reagan, a divorced man whose second wife was pregnant when he married her and who neglected his children, overwhelmingly was preferred by the electorate to Jimmy Carter, a Baptist who believed that beliefs should result in behavior.

Mainline Protestant churches, such as the Episcopalians, Presbyterians, Lutherans, Disciples of Christ, and United Church of Christ, responded to the public's desire for religious experience by transforming Christian doctrines into permissive declarations that endorsed secular values. Whatever problem seemed to be bothering the unchurched, these denominations found a way to endorse the most blatant secular version of the problem. In their attempt to be relevant to modern society, they became its greatest expositors. It is now impossible to find any sinful behavior that would not be endorsed or advocated by these churches. In the middle ages there were seven deadly sins and a whole host of minor or venial sins. In the past three decades the fundamentalist Christians have taken one of the deadly sins— GREED—and made it the primary Christian virtue. The mainline churches then promptly made the multitude of venial sins respectable.

The response of serious Americans has been to look elsewhere. Asian religions—including various aspects of martial arts—old European religions such as witchcraft and devil worship, astrology, reincarnation, and a bewildering variety of self-help techniques have offered a religious experience buffet to a hungry American society. A sizable number of people have come to American Indians, seeking to join tribal religious practices or take from the tribal traditions those things they find most attractive. Thus the proliferation of "medicine wheels" and "pipe carriers" in the non-Indian population has become astronomical. Even the simplest kind of religious experience in an Indian setting or with an Indian theme is held as a cherished memory by non-Indians.

Traditional people in every tribe have made astounding progress in reviving the old ceremonies. Dances and ceremonies that had not been held for generations are now common once again in the isolated parts of the reservations. Traditional religion and customs are widely believed to be the real solution to many of the pressing social problems plaguing Indian communities today. Within a decade it will be necessary to be a traditional religious leader to be elected to office in many tribes. If the rest of American society is not solving its basic quest for religious experience, Indians are doing so.

Most people miss the critical distinction between New Age "religious" life and tribal ceremonies. American society, particularly its organized religions and its political institutions, is built on the idea of the solitary individual as the foundation of everything else. A gathering of individuals becomes a congregation, a corporation, a legislature, or a club. In a mass society, rules must apply equally to everyone, since everyone is regarded as interchangeable, and that is the ideology underlying our institutions today. New Age movements, lacking an institutional base, are not hierarchical organizations designed for manipulation of the masses but are networks of people—strings of people who are linked together by similar philosophies, experiences, or desires.

Indian tribes violate this basic reality of mass society in that they are communities, as are the major Christian groups that have run afoul of the free exercise clauses—primarily Amish and Jehovah's Witnesses (held together by rigid discipline but easily identifiable). It is impossible for the institutions of mass society to reach within the tribal community and manipulate individuals, since the community is held together by blood and common sets of experiences. Hence, Indian tribes will always be askew in comparison with everything else in America, and particularly with political institutions.

Traditional religions are under attack not because they are Indian but because they are fundamentally religious and are perhaps the only consistent religious groups in American society over the long term. If kidnapping children for boarding schools, prohibiting religious ceremonies, destroying the family through allotments, and bestowing American citizenship did not destroy the basic community of Indian people, what could possibly do so? The attack today on traditional religion is the secular attack on any group that advocates and practices devotion to a value higher than the state. That is why the balancing test has been discarded and laws and ordinances are allowed primacy over religious obligations. Under the auspices of civil religion, there can be no higher value than the state. Communism was the civil religion of the Soviet Union, and it failed; chauvinistic patriotism is the civil religion of the United States right now, and it will soon break into bickering pressure groups and oppression and suppression of all dissenting views. But the quest for religious experience by human beings cannot be suppressed permanently. Consequently, we will find a solution, although we might thereby create an exceedingly unpleasant condition.

The movement to secure religious freedom in all its aspects by the Indian coalition is now getting under way. It should receive support from all serious American citizens who wish to preserve the right to have their own philosophy and their own religious experiences. This act will be the first step in rolling back the intrusions by the institutions of mass society that have changed our lives into a gray uniformity of acts and opinions. Indians can always retreat to the isolated places on the reservations, so the impact of the *Smith* decision really affects only those Indians who wish to practice their religion outside the reservations. But unless this group is protected within the constitutional framework, what chance have other groups, even Christian groups, of following their consciences or religious dictates? For the first time in American history, then, Indians have a common cause with other Americans.

9

Lynne Goldstein and Keith Kintigh

Ethics and the Reburial Controversy

"What's the big deal? Give them back the bones—we never have all the data anyway—we're used to dealing with data loss and inadequacy."

"If we give them back the bones, maybe they won't come back for the artifacts."

"What is the value of research on human bone? Surely it can't compare with the suffering that these Indians have had to bear."

"This has been done in the name of science, and I don't see why I even have to talk with these people—they aren't related to the skeletons we have."

"These people don't really care about these bones—this is just a convenient political issue."

"Only urban Indians are pushing for reburial—this issue is not a real one to most Indians in the United States."

In discussions or debates about the reburial issue, the above statements are uttered every day by archaeologists on one or another side of the issue. There is something very wrong with each of the above statements, and this essay examines the ethical issues associated with the reburial debate, in the hopes of clearing some of the murkiness and moving the discussion more squarely to what we consider the main issues. Our focus is on collections currently held by institutions, primarily because this is where most of the current controversy is centered. This essay is not written for the general public or even a specific public—it is written by archaeologists for archaeologists. We assume a basic knowledge of both anthropology and archaeology. This controversy has divided the discipline deeply, some think beyond recovery. We are optimistic that there is common ground and offer these thoughts in the spirit of reasoned discussion and thoughtful consideration.

Cultural Conflict

What are ethics? In general terms, ethics can be seen as a coherent system of values that specify a code of conduct. This definition implies that there can be more than one system of ethics. A discussion of ethics is, by definition, a discussion of moral principles, with an underlying definition of Right and Wrong. Such definitions are cultural, and all anthropologists know this. There are many examples that demonstrate this point: the death sentence passed upon Salman Rushdie for his blasphemous novel *The Satanic Verses,* the differing perspectives on abortion, and witch trials in colonial America. All of these instances represent a conflict between two (or more) systems of ethics. The important point we wish to raise here is that no particular system of ethics can be said to be absolutely right or wrong. Ethics are a cultural construction.

In the case we address here, the ethics hinge on the veneration of the dead. As anthropologists, we are well aware that treatment of the dead is highly variable and culturally determined. There is not one particular or correct way to treat the dead—at different times and different places in different cultures a variety of treatments have been used, ranging from perfunctory treatment of the deceased to elaborate funerary rights with booby traps for anyone who disturbs the grave site at a later time. One need not search the world for such diversity and variability—many examples are found within what is now the United States. Treatment of the dead is a cultural entity and the "proper" treatment at any given place and time is culturally defined. That, of course, is why the treatment of the dead is an important and relevant topic for archaeological study.

From the perspective of science, law, and anthropology, the excavation and curation of human skeletal remains is both appropriate and necessary. Science can be viewed as a culture as much as any other organized way of thinking. As such, it has a system of ethics. Although anthropologists are concerned about the cultural beliefs of the people they study, they also want to pursue the "truth."

From the perspective of Native Americans who advocate reburial, the issue often is phrased as a human-rights concern—these are ancestors and must be treated according to modern Native American wishes—human remains cannot be treated as property. Even if the remains belong to an extinct culture, the dead never gave permission to be studied and would prefer to be cared for by contemporary Native Americans who are at least their spiritual relatives.

You don't vote on ethics and you don't change ethics unless you change your culture or organized way of thinking. One of the reasons that the reburial controversy is so difficult is that we are grappling with ethical issues or moral principles that cross cultures. In a very real sense, this issue represents what we can call the ethics of cultural conflict. While cultural conflicts appear as conflicts of ethics, the main issue is the nature of the resolution of the conflict, not the ethics per se.

Politics, Tolerance, and Resolution

We have presented the reburial controversy as a case study in conflicting ethics and cultures. How are such conflicts resolved? Ethics are of little help since ethical systems are by their nature ethnocentric. Can a system of ethics based on pan-cultural values be developed to handle this matter? Such systems have been tried, with limited success; examples include international laws, treaties, covenants, the League of Nations, and so on. Such agreements and institutions, of course, are products of political processes. Political systems are in fact systems for dealing with conflicts.

Historically, political systems deal with the application of power to situations of conflict. Political resolutions of conflict are often based on the principle of "Might makes Right," regularly disguised and cloaked in more palatable terms as "majority rule," "traditional values," "will of the people," "manifest destiny," and "right of conquest." Political systems work to resolve conflict both between and within nations.

The United States political system is founded on the notion of the rule of law, and since we live in the United States, its political and cultural systems, for our purposes, prevail. Modern American ideology espouses tolerance and respect in dealing with its cultural diversity. Thus there are basically two approaches for dealing with conflict: (1) dominance: exercise of political power, which may include confrontation, threats, and violence, with the intent of suppressing an alternative point of view, either by intimidation or by enacting laws that force one group's perspective down the throats of the other; or (2) tolerance: acceptance of peaceful coexistence, with respect, conciliation, cooperation, and above all, compromise. Such compromise, of course, also may be embodied in law.

How do we choose between the two alternatives? The Constitution and laws of the United States provide mechanisms for us to deal with cultural conflicts, both in terms of an ethics of tolerance and an ethics of resolution. The ethics of tolerance is embedded in the Constitution, which dictates tolerance of the beliefs, rituals, and practices of others. Clearly, to the extent that beliefs do not infringe on the actions of others, they are to be tolerated. But while beliefs, rituals, and practices must be tolerated, they are not absolute rights if they infringe on the rights of others. This assessment is nothing more than a restatement of several well-known Supreme Court decisions, including several on the freedom of religion and the fact that freedom of speech does not give one the right to cry "Fire!" in a crowded theater. You may believe what you wish, but you cannot indiscriminately act on those beliefs.

Given that there are limitations on our rights in terms of what each of us can actually do, how do we resolve conflicts outside a specific culture or group but within our larger political system? We have an ethics of resolution, or political processes that can lead the views of one group to legally prevail. In this very real sense, one avenue to settle such disputes is strictly political—if you can get a law passed, you can win the battle. Likewise, if you lose, you can work to change what has been passed. Being political is not wrong or bad—it is often very successful. It does not, however, always go well with the ethics of tolerance.

Ethics and Negotiations

If the reburial issue did not involve physical remains, there would be no argument; no one is questioning anyone's right to believe. Material objects and human remains are the center of attention. What is it about such remains that they can generate such conflict? On one level, the power of objects is simple: they can be possessed and they cannot be in more than one place at one time. In the United States it is difficult to usurp the idea and right of possession, and the argument for classifying human remains and artifacts as a special kind of property is clearly a cultural argument. This reflects another kind of ethics, the ethics of property rights, which are both cultural and political.

It should be clear at this point that the issue of whether human remains should be reburied (and whether the artifacts should be included) cannot be solved strictly as a matter of ethics. That question is itself one manifestation of the broader question of how we resolve issues of cultural (ethical) conflict.

We can, however, speak to the narrower question of archaeological ethics—what is an ethical archaeologist? In examining this issue, we think we can shed some light on how to resolve this particular cultural conflict.

To claim that archaeologists have no right to excavate or examine an entire class of information is to deny our background and training. We know that there is much to be learned from the study of human bone and mortuary practices, and this knowledge may well prove useful and important to present and future generations. Eliminating sites or portions of sites from excavation or analysis because of the kind of items they contain is not an ethical stance for an archaeologist. We have a mandate to preserve and protect the past for the future—an obligation to past cultures to tell their story and to future generations to preserve the past for their benefit. If you, as archaeologists, do not know the value of mortuary sites to the study of the past, it is your obligation to learn. As archaeologists, you must know why the data we collect is relevant and important. You cannot dismiss a class of information out of ignorance; just because you do not happen to study a particular kind of site or class of data you cannot simply dismiss it as insignificant.

From a perspective of tolerance, how do we balance our ethical concerns as archaeologists for knowledge and for the archaeological record with our professional ethic of cultural relativism—the belief that our values are not the only values or ethics but only one legitimate belief system? The answer is that we attempt to achieve this balance through compromise and mutual respect.

Under what circumstances can parties with conflicting ethical systems agree to try to compromise? First, obviously, both parties must accept, at the outset, a willingness to compromise. However, even with this willingness, both parties will have a legitimate concern for the legal structure in which the negotiation occurs; that is, what happens if no compromise is reached?

Each party must at some level accept the legitimacy of the others. This is where cultural relativism can become problematic. To take an extreme example, on the basis of Shirley MacLaine's belief (which seems to be strongly held) that she is a reincarnated Inca princess, should we have to negotiate with her about a claim she might make for Inca gold that is held by museums? Despite our espousement of cultural relativism, we might well decline to negotiate, relying instead on the legal system to reject such a claim. Some might argue that this is a poor example because we have confused individual beliefs and cultural values. It is not our intent to be disrespectful or confusing but only to state the extreme case in order to outline the need for limits on the legitimacy of claims. Further, a number of institutions have had claims made on their collections by individuals, and it is sometimes difficult to sort out such claims and evaluate their legitimacy.

How about pan-Indian claims for the reburial of all Native American skeletons on the grounds that they are Indian? Or how about claims of a specific tribe for remains where the archaeological and historical evidence clearly indicates that there is no relationship between the remains in question and the group? These are knotty issues involving sincerely held beliefs of substantial numbers of people, deriving from cultural traditions of varying antiquity.

Archaeologists need to sharpen their ethical instincts to deal with these situations. How do we justify the hierarchy of legitimacy based on degree of relationship with this respect for alternative belief systems?

We started this section asking under what situations compromise could be contemplated seriously. We believe that compromise often can be achieved when there is trust and mutual respect between the parties doing the negotiating. This trust obviously is enhanced through good-faith interactions, but it also is enhanced by the overall perception by all parties of a need to have a "level playing field." A level playing field is more than mutual respect—it requires that all parties have access to the same information to support their cases. It is important that the notion of a level playing field be utilized in the decision-making structure—be it a museum policy or a state or federal law. Within a framework of case-by-case negotiations, which we strongly support, our statements suggest that we also should support changes in the decision-making structure that will allow Native concerns to be equitably considered. However, despite cultural relativism, in our view these changes will need to put some limits on *legitimacy* of claims. We should strive for agreement on general principles, some of which are enumerated below. We concur with the Society for American Archaeology's position that the basis of legitimacy in the Native case is "relationship" and the basis of legitimacy for the scientific case is scientific value. To the extent that we can achieve agreement, in the abstract here, we believe that we can and should compromise. On the other hand, to the extent that some Native Americans or some archaeologists wish to have their belief systems dominate, we must strive to prevent it.

Red Herrings, Education, and Racism

Many of the typical concerns that are raised when reburial is discussed are simply red herrings. We all know that archaeologists do not just dig up Indians, but that the past of the United States is weighted heavily toward Indian cultures. Likewise, we know that we can learn much more from the study of skeletons than the fact that someone did or did not eat corn. We also know that we cannot simply give back the skeletons in the hopes that we can keep the grave goods—we can't ethically divide collections in this way.

Archaeologists are fond of saying that if only we can educate the public and the Indian communities, people would begin to understand and everything would be fine. Education is critical in this and other instances, and there is no question that we have been remiss in informing some of our most important constituencies about our work. How many of us have made sure that our work comes out in popular form as well as in scientific journals? How many of us voluntarily and automatically have contacted Native American tribes or groups after we have completed a project to inform them of our findings? How many of us have tried to answer questions about the past that such groups may have raised? We have been remiss and we must begin to right those wrongs. Nonetheless, while education is important and critical, we should not be fooled into thinking that it will solve this problem. We often naively believe that educating someone will result in their agreeing with our perspective, but education does not mean changing someone's mind. Perhaps more knowledge and more accurate knowledge will result in a change of perspective, but it will not necessarily be the change you wanted. People, even educated people, can and do respectfully disagree.

Education also plays a part in another problem associated with the ethics of archaeology, and that is an insidious form of racism. Americans tend to divide the country's history into two parts—Indian history and European history, and Indian history is often not considered the good or interesting part of the past. How many times—when you've told someone you're an archaeologist who focuses on archaeology in the United States—have you heard (with a hint or more of disappointment): "Oh, you study Indian stuff." In somewhat different contexts, Fowler (1986), Knudson (1986), and Trigger (1986) each discuss and comment on the fact that archaeological resources in the United States lack clear legal definition of ownership in part because of the lack of genetic continuity between the dominant political community and prehistoric Americans. In recent years, as Knudson (1986: 397) has indicated, the National Environmental Policy Act has provided a mechanism that overrides the private ownership concept. "Today and into the future, America's natural, social, and cultural resources are explicitly recognized as part of the public wealth and their treatment is a matter of public issue."

While public policy and law may have changed our legal perspective on the non-European past, the public perception is still largely "us vs. them." Until the public treats all of this country's past as an integral part of the whole, racism in this and other areas will continue. If you ask the "person on the street" whether human remains should be given to Indians for reburial, he or she will likely indicate that since the bones are "theirs," the Indians should probably get them. We categorize "our past" according to ethnic identities rather than in terms of the country as a whole. Fowler (1986: 151–53) expresses his dismay over this position and outlines the positive results to be gained when such a tactic is not taken, as in the case of Mexico. Changing the ethic will be difficult, but until the history and prehistory of the United States are made the history and prehistory of all Americans, Indian prehistory and history will not be treated with equal validity.

Changing the Way We Do Business

There is no question about the treatment of Native Americans in the United States. The record is abysmal and we must do all we can to rectify that treatment. Museums and other institutions have operated from a position of dominance where even a question from a Native American could be ignored without fear of consequences. We must change the way we do business. On initial consideration, one's gut reaction might be to reverse this situation of dominance by putting Indians into the position of power and dominance. As much as that might appeal to some people's desires for retribution, we think that it is ultimately a poor decision. Reversing the relationship does not remedy it—it only perpetuates the fundamental inequality.

By arguing for equality, we *are* suggesting major changes for museums and other institutions with collections—they will have to incorporate the American Indian perspective and treat Native American claims equitably. An acceptance of the cultural conflict will need to be built into decision-making processes. This process will not be easy but will benefit *all* for the future.

What might such changes mean? Hopefully, it will mean that archaeologists will be somewhat less stupid in approaching this issue. In most cases of public outcry, the institution or an individual in that institution has acted hastily without consideration of the consequences. A set of skeletons just excavated is photographed with silly hats and sunglasses on; a request for a meeting is denied out of hand; or a request for information is ignored. At best such acts are unthinking, while at worst they are rude, condescending, and racist.

We must conduct ourselves as ethical archaeologists. Only if we treat others and other cultures with respect, sensitivity, and tolerance can we expect and demand the same in return. Here is the fundamental prescription for such conduct, and some obvious points where change is required:

1. Institutions whose mission does not require the preservation, study, and interpretation of human remains, funerary objects, and sacred objects should not collect or retain such items. Collections policies should conform to the institution's mission statement.

2. Where possible and appropriate, institutions should consult with relevant living cultural groups before undertaking projects that will result in the collection of such materials, whether or not such consulta-

tion is mandated legally. Research questions relevant to the group should be considered seriously.

3. Institutions must interpret such materials with accuracy, sensitivity, and respect, including consultation with appropriate groups to the fullest extent possible. Interpretation includes publication and dissemination of information to the general public as well as to archaeologists and those who visit museums. Such interpretation can and must change as we learn more; we also must indicate the basis for such changes.

4. Although financial considerations may be a major factor, institutions should take the initiative to compile inventories of their collections, and, in any case, communicate with relevant Native groups.

5. Institutions should promptly answer questions and requests for information. In so doing, they should share what information they have, even if it is limited.

While there are cases in which claims may be seen as human-rights issues, such a determination does not automatically mandate following the wishes of a nation or group (once again, the problem of dominance). We agree with the final two paragraphs of the "Report of the Panel for a National Dialogue on Museum/Native American Relations" that outlines the process that must be followed:

> Wherever possible, the disposition and treatment of skeletal remains and other materials should be determined consensually through cooperative and timely discussions between the institution involved and all interested Native American groups. Where issues remain after such good faith discussions, an attempt should be made to settle these issues through mutually agreed upon processes of mediation or arbitration.
>
> If unresolved issues remain, applicable legal standards should be judicially enforceable. It is important that the process for enforcing these standards be equally accessible to all tribes and museums, regardless of their wealth or resources.

A case-by-case negotiation about particular human remains, involving descendants, archaeologists, and other interested parties, can often reach a consensual resolution because such a negotiation promotes an atmosphere of good faith and obviates many contentious issues. Hence, local decision-making by bodies designed to give fair consideration to diverse points of view is essential. It implements the ethics of tolerance *and* the ethics of resolution.

There will be human remains and associated funerary and sacred objects that will be returned to appropriate Indian descendants; we do not question that some items should not be kept by museums and other institutions. Arguing for a case-by-case determination must *never* be used as a stalling tactic. We *must* change the way we do business without abrogating our responsibilities to the archaeological record or the living descendants of the people we study.

We must achieve equal consideration for all relevant parties. The process of negotiating repatriation requests must be open and fair. In terms of what we have to do in the immediate future, giving back the bones would probably be the easiest immediate solution. But what's easiest is not necessarily what's right or ethical. The task we have before us is much more difficult but much more important—we have to address our various constituencies, educate all of the publics about the past, and make certain that we don't alienate or disenfranchise past, present, or future generations.

Note

An earlier version of this paper was presented in April 1990, at the Society for American Archaeology Annual Meeting in Las Vegas, Nevada. The paper was part of a symposium entitled "Personal Morals and Disciplinary Imperatives: Ethical Archaeology and Archaeological Ethics." The authors gratefully acknowledge the encouragement of the organizers of the symposium, Douglas B. Bamforth and Kathryn V. Reese.

References

Fowler, D. D. 1986. Conserving American Archaeological Resources. In *American Archaeology Past and Future: A Celebration of the Society for American Archaeology 1935–1985*, ed. D. J. Meltzer, D. D. Fowler, and J. A. Sabloff, pp. 135–62. Smithsonian Institution Press, Washington DC.

Heard Museum. 1990. Report of the Panel for a National Dialogue on Museum/ Native American Relations. Presented to the Senate Select Committee on Indian Affairs, Washington DC.

Knudson, R. 1986. Contemporary Cultural Resource Management. In *American Archaeology Past and Future*, pp. 395–414.

Trigger, B. G. 1986. Prehistoric Archaeology and American Society. In *American Archaeology Past and Future*, pp. 187–216.

10

Clement W. Meighan

Some Scholars' Views on Reburial

[T]here is something inherently distasteful and unseemly in secreting either the fruits or seeds of scientific endeavors.—Judge Bruce S. Jenkins, quoted in *Science,* 1991

The above quotation is from a court case having nothing to do with archaeology, yet if we believe that archaeology is a scientific endeavor we must agree that this statement applies to archaeology as well as medicine, chemistry, or other fields of scholarship. The recent increased attention given to the ethics of scientists and scientific organizations, with news accounts almost weekly in such journals as *Science,* requires archaeologists to examine their basic assumptions about the nature of science and their obligations to scholarship. This is brought forward most forcefully in the debate over the past twenty years about the problems of reburial of archaeological and museum collections.

The discussion by Goldstein and Kintigh (1990; chap. 9, this vol.) is a valiant effort to unravel some of the strands of conflict inherent in the controversy over the destruction of museum collections in the name of Indian religious beliefs. They seek some sort of middle ground in which scholarly and ethnic concerns can coexist in a constructive way. However, in view of the massive losses of scientific data now legislated by the federal government and some of the states, it needs to be made clear that many archaeologists do not agree with some aspects of the philosophical position taken by Goldstein and Kintigh. In particular, their statement that "We must change the way we do business" (1990:589; this vol., 187) is not justified, particularly since their suggestions for change involve the abandonment of scholarly imperatives and the adoption of an "ethical" position that accepts the right of nonscholars to demand the destruction of archaeological evidence and the concealment of archaeological data. Of course, changes in the way archaeology is done will inevitably take place, for both internal (professional) and external (social/legal) reasons. This does not mean that the basic rules of scholarly obligations to one's data should change as well.

Goldstein and Kintigh fall into the anthropological trap of cultural relativism. In asserting that we must balance our concerns for knowledge with "our professional ethic of cultural relativism," they argue that our values are not the only values or ethics but only one legitimate belief system. The implication is that all belief systems are of equal legitimacy, therefore one cannot make a clear commitment to any particular values as a guide to action. However, most individuals do make a commitment to the values that will guide their personal action. Recognizing that other people may have other values does not mean that one must accept those values or compromise his or her own ethical standards. Indeed, the dictionary has a word for believing one way and acting another—it is "hypocrisy."

Those who affiliate with organized groups, whether the Church of the Rising Light or the Society for American Archaeology (SAA), supposedly accept the beliefs and goals of the organization as stated in their bylaws or scriptures. The SAA, as an organization dedicated to scholarly research in archaeology, is bound by the general rules of scholarship that require *honest reporting and preservation of the evidence.* If the research data are subject to censorship, how can there be honest reporting? If the evidence (collections) is not preserved, who can challenge the statements of the researcher? Who can check for misinterpretations, inaccuracies, or bias? Once the collection is destroyed, we have only an affidavit from the researcher; we can believe it or not, but there is no way that additional investigation or new laboratory techniques can be applied to the collection to gain a better understanding of the evidence. The astounding new methods for medical and genetic research on ancient populations require a piece of the bone—pictures and notes won't do. Similarly, laboratory advances in dating and determining the source of artifact materials require that the relevant objects be available for study. Since we commonly proclaim that archaeological collections are unique and irreplaceable, how can we ever justify the conscious and acquiescent destruction of our data?

The suggestion of Goldstein and Kintigh that we balance our own values with the professional ethic of cultural relativism by "compromise and mutual respect" is not realistic. Many archaeologists are not going to compromise away their most fundamental scholarly beliefs. Similarly, many Indian activists are not going to compromise away their beliefs (however unsupported by evidence) that every Indian bone of the past twelve thousand years belongs to one of their ancestors. There are some instances in which compromise and mutual respect have led to satisfactory results for both sides; there are many more instances in which these valued qualities have been insufficient to prevent or postpone destruction of important archaeological finds.

Those who want to do away with archaeology and archaeological collections are of course entitled to their beliefs, and they are also entitled to use whatever political and legal machinery they can to bring about their stated goals. Originally the goals were modest, but they have escalated every year since this discussion began more than twenty years ago, as reviewed by me in an earlier article (Meighan 1984). The present-day goals have repeatedly been made clear. For example, Christopher Quayle, an attorney for the Three Affiliated Tribes, stated in *Harper's* (Preston 1989:68–69): "It's conceivable that some time in the not-so-distant future there won't be a single Indian skeleton in any museum in the country. We're going to put them out of business." The "them" refers in this statement to physical anthropologists, but it is also extended to archaeologists. For example, the recent agreement between state officials in West Virginia and a committee representing Indian viewpoints (a committee which, incidentally, includes non-Indians) states that everything in an ongoing study of a two-thousand-year-old Adena mound must be given up for reburial within a year—"everything" includes not only the bones of the mythical "ancestors" of the claimants but also all the artifacts, the chipping waste, the food refuse, the pollen samples, the soil samples, and whatever else may be removed for purposes of scientific study (West Virginia Department of Transportation [WVDOT] 1991). While the taxpayers are expected to pay for a 1.8-million-dollar excavation on the grounds that it is in the public interest for archaeological data to be preserved, *nothing* of the tangible archaeological evidence is to be preserved. Meanwhile, Indian activists are paid to "monitor" the excavation, and they were given the right to censor the final report and prevent any objectionable photographs or data from appearing (WVDOT 1991; see also Neiburger 1990).

If there is any doubt about the goals of the anti-archaeology contingent, consider the case of Dr. David Van Horn, charged with a felony in California for conducting an environmental impact study required by law and being honest enough to report what he found in the site, including some small bits of cremated bone, which required hours of study by physical anthropologists to identify as human (Riverside County Superior Court 1990). Is the reporting of a legally mandated salvage excavation a felony? It can be in California, and there are many who would like to make archaeology a crime throughout the United States. Archaeologists who accept these situations or treat them as merely local concerns (apparently the position of most scholarly organizations, including the SAA), have not just compromised, they have abandoned scholarly ethics in favor of being "respectful and sensitive" to nonscholars and anti-intellectuals. When the current round of controversy is over, this loss of scientific integrity will be heavily condemned.

So there are some situations in which compromise is not necessarily the best approach, and this is one of them. Archaeologists may well be legislated out of business, and museums may well lose all their American Indian collections, and indeed the Indians have been far more successful than the archaeologists in the political arena. Many archaeologists believe, however, that this should not occur with the happy connivance of the scholarly profession of archaeology. Over six hundred of them are members of the American Committee for Preservation of Archaeological Collections (AC-PAC), which has argued for over ten years that archaeology is a legitimate, moral, and even useful profession and that collections that were legally made should remain in museums as an important part of the heritage of the nation. Bahn (1989:123) may have had this group in mind in his news report on the "first international congress on the reburial of human remains," in his reference to "the extremists, who unfortunately did not attend the congress to put the case for rejecting the whole notion of reburial." Who are these extremists? Neither ACPAC nor any individual known to me has stated that no reburial of any kind should take place; everyone agrees that bones of known relatives should be returned to demonstrable descendants. The disagreement is over remains to which no living person can demonstrate any relationship. Museum materials five thousand years old are claimed by people who imagine themselves to be somehow related to the collections in question, but such a belief has no basis in evidence and is mysticism. Indeed, it is not unlikely that Indians who have acquired such collections for reburial are venerating the bones of alien groups and traditional enemies rather than distant relatives.

If the present attacks on archaeological data were happening in engineering, medicine, or chemistry, they would not be accepted by the general public since destruction or concealment of the facts in those areas of scientific knowledge can lead to disastrous results for many living people. The general lack of public concern about the attack on archaeology arises from the perception that archaeological conclusions really do not matter—if someone's reconstruction of the ancient past is ridiculous or unsupported by evidence, who cares? It will not affect the daily lives of anyone now alive, no matter what we believe about what happened thousands of years ago. However, the principles of scholarship and scientific evidence are the same in all scholarly research, including archaeology and anthropology, and credibility of conclusions is an essential consideration for any field of scholarship, whether or not there are immediate practical effects of the conclusions that are reached.

In one of the polemics put forward by Indian spokesmen in the student newspaper at the University of California (Los Angeles), those of us on the archaeological faculty were accused of participating in an activity that was comparable to the "killing fields of Cambodia." Even allowing for the juvenile rhetoric characteristic of student newspapers, I was dumbfounded at such a statement. How could I harm any person who had already been dead for thousands of years? How could anything that my studies did with the bones of these ancient people harm any living person? The condemnation seems extreme for a "crime" that is merely a failure to invite mythical descendants to control my research and destroy museum collections held in the public interest. When issues of respect and sensitivity are raised, it needs to be pointed out that these work both ways.

Some Legal Issues: Constitutional Requirements

The first amendment states that Congress shall make no laws respecting an establishment of religion. Most state constitutions have similar clauses; that of California says the state will *never* pass such laws. Yet California, other states, and the federal government have numerous laws on the books that are specifically written to favor aboriginal tribal religious beliefs and compel others to act in accordance with them. Religious infringement also occurs when archaeologists are excluded from evaluating claims regarding repatriation because they do not hold particular religious beliefs. Until these statutes are challenged and overturned, they remain an opening for other groups to seek similar legislation making their religious beliefs enforceable by law. Creationists, for example, have been trying for over sixty years to outlaw the teaching of evolution because it is in conflict with their religious tenets.

That there is a science vs. religion aspect is clear in the religious justification for the claiming of bones and "sacred" artifacts, as well as the proclamation of many activists that archaeologists and museums are committing sacrilege in obtaining, storing, and studying archaeological remains. I discuss bone worship elsewhere (Meighan 1990). Tonetti (1990) provides a case study of the situation in Ohio, documenting the religious roots of the anti-archaeology movement. He also reports a survey of Ohio legislators that reveals a frightening ignorance of science in general and archaeology in particular: "As Zimmerman so dramatically stated in his op ed piece in the Columbus Dispatch, he does not want the General Assembly making law dealing with science issues when over 75% do not know what his 5 year old son has known for years—that dinosaurs and humans did not coexist" (Zimmerman [1989], as quoted in Tonetti [1990:22]; recent news reports state that some Indians are now claiming dinosaur bones recovered by paleontologists).

Some Legal Issues: Cultural-Resource Laws

There is a serious conflict between the laws mandating return and destruction of archaeological material (not just bones but also artifacts and anything deemed "ceremonial" by the claimants) and those laws mandating cultural-resource management and the study and conservation of archaeological sites and remains. The Van Horn case previously mentioned put Van Horn in the position of doing an environmental impact report required by law, only to find himself spending thousands of dollars defending himself against a felony charge for violating laws based on Indian religious beliefs about cremated bones. The judge agreed with defense witnesses that there was no basis for a trial, but the state made its point that archaeologists will be heavily punished if "Indians" request it, regardless of the validity of their complaint.

The legal dichotomy between science and religion as it pertains to archaeology may be related, as Goldstein and Kintigh (1990; this vol., 186–87) point out, to the fact that public perception does not include Indian history as part of the history of the United States, even though they recognize that public policy and law include the non-European past as an integral part of the history of the nation. That part of American history that is Indian history is largely the contribution of archaeology; *all* of it prior to 1492 is the contribution of archaeology. This has been recognized and supported by the government since the Antiquities Act of 1906, and it is the basis for all the environmental impact laws dealing with archaeological remains.

Many opponents of archaeological-resource laws believe that since archaeology has no effect on public health or safety, it ought to be excluded from environmental impact laws. They are given considerable ammunition by laws that state that it is in the public interest to spend a lot of money to get archaeological materials and then state that such materials are not worth preservation but are to be reburied as soon as possible after they are dug up, in some cases within a few days or weeks of the fieldwork. Further, the belief that archaeology belongs to Indians removes it from the heritage of all of the citizens and makes it less likely that the public will be interested in supporting activities not seen to be in the broad public interest.

In these times of stringent budgets, it is hard enough to convince the taxpayers that they should finance archeological excavations without having to convince them that they should also finance the reburial of the items recovered.

There are major negative results for archaeology in the present situation where not only the federal government but states, counties, cities, and a plethora of political agencies believe that they should pass regulations controlling archaeological research. These laws and regulations conflict with one another and vary from jurisdiction to jurisdiction. In some states the conduct of archaeological research is a risky business. The smart archaeologist in California does not find certain things. If they are found, they are either thrown away or not mentioned in his or her reports. Field classes are also careful not to expose students or teachers to criminal charges, meaning that students in those classes will never expose a burial or deal with any "controversial" finds. Chipping waste is still a safe area for study.

This chilling effect on research is creating an underground archaeology of ill-trained students, dishonest researchers, and intimidated teachers who are afraid to show a picture of a burial to their classes, let alone an actual human bone. Students, who are often more perceptive than their professors, rapidly catch on and change their major or move their archaeological interests to parts of the world where they will be allowed to practice their scholarly profession. There is an increasing loss to American archaeology and of course to the Indians whose history is dependent on it.

Some Museum Issues

A negative effect of the ongoing shift to tribalism and the right of anyone to claim anything in museums is already happening. In the past most of the support for museums came from private donors, who contributed not only money but collections. Donors of collections had the tacit (and sometimes written) agreement that their materials would be preserved in the public interest. Who would contribute anything to a museum if they thought the museum was going to give their material away for reburial or destruction? When even Stanford University and other respected repositories of scientific collections decide that their first obligation is to whatever Indian claimant comes along, the donor who wants his or her material *preserved* will seek a repository in a state or country that is dedicated to that aim. It is a paradox that the National Park Service is busily developing new standards of curation for government collections at the same time the new National Museum of the American Indian is declaring that it will not keep anything that Indian claimants declare that they want.

Reviewers of this article believe that only a very small part of archaeological collections will be taken away from museums and archaeologists. This is a pious hope in view of the escalation of claims previously noted, reaching the apex in the West Virginia case in which *everything* recovered by archaeologists is to be given up for reburial. There are numerous cases in which archaeologists or museum employees have given up entire collections rather than negotiate with Indian claimants; for example, one prominent California case (the Encino excavation) included reburial of a number of dog skeletons, not required by any statute. It is true that the Smithsonian and some other museums now have committees to evaluate claims against their collections; perhaps these will protect scholarly and public interests, but it remains to be seen whether they can withstand the political pressures brought to bear. While I am sure that not all collections will entirely disappear, under current legislation all physical remains, all mortuary associations, and all items claimed to have religious or ceremonial significance are at risk—these are the major sources of information in many archaeological studies. When claimants can get museum specimens merely by using the word "sacred," it should be apparent that anything can be claimed by someone. It does happen, it has happened, and scholars can only hope that it will not happen in the future.

When scholarly classes in United States archaeology and ethnology are no longer taught in academic departments (they are diminishing rapidly), when the existing collections have been selectively destroyed or concealed, and when all new field archaeology in the United States is a political exercise rather than a scientific investigation, will the world be a better place? Certainly the leadership in archaeological research, which has been characteristic of the last fifty years of American archaeology, will be lost, and it will be left to other nations to make future advances in archaeological methods, techniques, and scholarly investigations into the ancient past.

One reviewer of this paper commented that I am engaged in a "futile attempt to resurrect a bankrupt status quo." In this view, not only can nothing be done to improve the present situation but nothing *should* be done, and we should all meekly accept the regulations, limitations, and restrictions of academic freedom that are brought forward by politicians and pressure groups. For the last twenty years those who have attempted to change these restrictions in favor of scholarly ethics and the preservation of collections have been dismissed as a small group of outmoded discontents who cannot adapt to a changing world. This is a mistake; I may represent a minority view, but it is not confined to a small number and is growing rapidly as archaeologists see more and more of their basic data destroyed through reburial. ACPAC's six hundred members (in forty-four states) include a sizeable fraction of the leading archaeologists in the United States as well as physical anthropologists, museum workers, and yes, Indians.

I am, however, triggered by the accusation that my comments lead to nothing but intransigence to offer a few suggestions for action other than "compromise," which so far has mostly meant giving in to political demands. My suggestions:

(1) Archaeologists negotiating with Indians or other groups should make an effort to be sure that *all* factions of the affected group are heard, not merely the group of activists who are first in the door. Many archaeologists have been doing this for years, and nearly all of us can report that we had little difficulty in finding Indians who would work with us in a mutually agreeable and often rewarding relationship that respected Indian interests but at the same time preserved the archaeological collections. Unfortunately, numerous instances can be cited of savage personal attacks or those Indians who agreed to share the archaeologists' task, with attempts to force the archaeologist to use other consultants and claims that the one chosen was not a real Indian (see an example in Tonetti [1990:21]). When money is involved, this is probably inevitable. However, there is no reason for archaeologists to be controlled by enemies of their discipline when they can work with friends. The existence of Indian physical anthropologists, archaeologists, and museum workers, as well as the increasing number of Indian-owned museums with scientific objectives and high standards of curation, should offer opportunities for real collaboration that do not require the destruction of evidence nor the censorship of scientific reporting.

(2) Professional organizations should work to amend the legislation dealing with archaeology to get a time cutoff inserted: Remains older than a certain age should not be subject to reburial. The present laws, which ignore time and assume that everything, regardless of age, is directly related to living people, are not scientifically valid, and the scientific organizations are in a position to make this clear, if necessary in court. The recent reburial of an Idaho skeleton dated at 10,600 years ago should never have happened, but as reported by the State Historical Preservation Office of that state, Idaho law requires *no* demonstration of any relationship between Indians and archaeological remains.

(3) Professional organizations should point out the disagreements between "preservation" laws and "religion" laws and should try to strengthen the former and eliminate the conflicts. If they are unable to resolve the issue by negotiation, they should support court cases that address the matter.

(4) If scholarly organizations are unwilling or unable to make a clear statement of their position with respect to the giving up of archaeological

collections and data, it is left to the individual archaeologist to decide his or her own professional ethics in this matter. A clear review of the moral issues is given by Del Bene (1990). This should be considered, particularly by young archaeologists entering the profession, so that they are consciously aware of the decisions they are making and the consequences for their professional future.

References

Bahn, P. G. 1989. Burying the Hatchet. *Nature* 342:123.

Del Bene, T. A. 1990. Take the Moral Ground: An Essay on the "Reburial" Issue. *West Virginia Archaeologist* 42(2):11–19.

Goldstein, L., and K. Kintigh. 1990. Ethics and the Reburial Controversy. *American Antiquity* 55:585–91 (chap. 9, this vol.).

Meighan, C. W. 1984. Archaeology: Science or Sacrilege? In *Ethics and Values in Archaeology,* ed. E. L. Green, pp. 208–33. Free Press, New York.

——. 1990. Bone Worship. *West Virginia Archeologist* 42(2):40–43.

Neiburger, E. J. 1990. Profiting from Reburial. *Nature* 344:297.

Palca, J. 1991. News and Comment. *Science* 253:844.

Preston, D. J. 1989. Skeletons in Our Museums' Closets. *Harper's.* February: 66–75.

Riverside County Superior Court. 1990. *California vs. David Van Horn and Robert Scott White, hearing transcript* (available from Coyote Press, Box 3377, Salinas CA 93912; $15.07 postpaid).

Tonetti, A. C. 1990. Ghost Dancing in the Nineties: Research, Reburial and Resurrection among the Dead in Ohio. *West Virginia Archeologist* 42(2):20–22.

West Virginia Department of Transportation [WVDOT]. 1991. *Agreement: Cotiga Burial Mound, Mingo County. May 3, 1991* [A legal challenge to this agreement has been filed by the Council for West Virginia Archaeology, the United Cherokee Indian Tribe of West Virginia, and the West Virginia Archeological Society (case no. 91-MISC-430, circuit court of Kanawha County, West Virginia).]

11

Anthony L. Klesert and Shirley Powell

A Perspective on Ethics and the Reburial Controversy

By the end of the 19th century the poets had abandoned the Indian burial grounds, leaving them to the archaeologist, and the pre-eminent right of archaeologists to these remains was unquestioned.–R. McGuire, "The Sanctity of the Grave: White Concepts and American Indian Burials"

For the past century or so, professional archaeologists in the New World have excavated sites and human remains, primarily ones Native American in origin. They have taken for granted that their scientific pursuits were reason enough to assume a proprietary interest in and control over those remains, in perpetuity, for the general good of humankind. More recently, as Native Americans and other indigenous people the world over have gained clout, this presumption has been aggressively challenged. In the United States, native peoples have joined forces and insisted that such behavior is immoral and professionally unethical and have demanded materials be repatriated and, as appropriate, reburied (Klesert and Downer 1990; Layton 1989; Quick 1985). Congress has responded to this concern with the Native American Graves Protection and Repatriation Act (NAGPRA) and has amended the National Historic Preservation Act (NHPA) to (among other things) accommodate Indian tribes.

These events have touched archaeologists in a variety of ways. Archaeologists have expressed concern about the discipline's relations with Native Americans since the mid-1970s (e.g., Cynthia Irwin-Williams, quoted in Adams [1974]; Johnson 1973:129; McGimsey 1971:126; Sprague 1974:1), and an overview of what came to be called "the reburial controversy" was first published in 1980 (Rosen 1980). Despite this, excavation and analysis of human remains has been the archaeological norm, certainly prior to the passage of NAGPRA, and even to the present, and archaeologists have defended this norm in print (e.g., Buikstra 1981; Meighan 1984, 1986, 1992; Turner 1986). With few exceptions, archaeologists justify their access to human remains and grave-associated objects by appealing to culturally embedded concepts: utilitarian arguments that emphasize the costs vs. benefits of the endeavor, and an appeal to science as necessary for the discovery of "truth." Acceptance of these Eurowestern precepts provides the premises for a logical conclusion: the study of human remains and grave-associated objects yields benefits that outweigh the cultural "costs" of or objections to such study.

Buikstra (1981), Meighan (1984, 1986, 1992 [ch. 10, this vol.]), Turner (1986), White (1991), Goldstein and Kintigh (1990, ch. 9, this vol.), Kintigh (1990), and the Society for American Archaeology (SAA) itself (various issues of the SAA *Bulletin* and Quick [1985]) all have offered opinions on reburial and repatriation. These approaches accept more or less input into the archaeological decision-making process from descendant populations. But in our opinion, they retain for themselves the "final court of appeal" on the disposition of human remains. What follows is a more inclusive perspective, one espoused in other arenas by Adams (1984), Ferguson (1984), Klesert and Downer (1990), Layton (1989), Nichols et al. (1989), Powell et al. (1993), and Zimmerman (1989).

Truth and Rights

> Objectivity is often something one seems to possess in greater measure than one's opponents.—R. Layton, "Introduction: Conflict in the Archaeology of Living Traditions"

Our concerns extend to the more general issue of how archaeologists must deal with the objects of their study—and to our right of access to remains and the extent of our obligations to them once they are obtained. In approaching the repatriation/reburial issue, archaeologists as anthropologists must be willing and able to include cultural values other than their own into the ethical and methodological equation and treat them with respect. This does not require that we embrace these values (Meighan 1992 [ch. 10]), just that we understand them.

Appeals to the "truth" can be used to justify ethnocentrism. For example, focusing on the search for "truth," Meighan (1986:12; emphasis added) suggests the proper rationale for archaeological studies is that archaeologists "owe ancient people as *true* and complete a picture of their lives as we can obtain." He further states: "the *ancient* people are informants" in this process, "even though dead" (Meighan 1986:12; emphasis added). In our opinion, this sort of logic debases all nonarchaeological interpretations of the past, while simultaneously sidestepping scientific evidence that connects modern Indians with their own history, leaving archaeologists as the final arbiters of the past. Underlying this position is a resolute commitment to objectivity and truth, a commitment that its holders seem to believe transcends cultural beliefs and is not itself to be confused as one.

Archaeologists commonly defend traditional archaeological practice by appealing to the Western "perspective of science, law and anthropology, [so that] the excavation of human skeletal remains is both appropriate and necessary" (Goldstein and Kintigh 1990; this vol., 181). Our concern is that many archaeologists do not appear to understand or accept that science is just one perspective among many (Tilley 1989). They act as if it is unequivocally good and requires no particular justification (Meighan 1992 [ch. 10]).

An underlying assumption of many of those who oppose repatriation is that indigenous insistence on reburial constitutes destruction of data to which scientists have a right and reflects a desire on the Natives' part to "own" or retain "exclusive use" of the remains in question (White 1991:423). This is simply not the case; it is an interpretation based on Euro-western cultural values and misses the point. People cannot own people, even the remains of dead people, according to virtually all Native American traditions. Thus, it is inappropriate for anyone, Indian or otherwise, to possess such remains for whatever purposes (Nichols et al. 1989:37).

We think it is clear that the rights of those being studied take precedence over the rights of anthropologists who study them (see also Adams 1984; Ferguson 1984). The "rights" in question are religious vs. remunerative; they are cultural vs. vocational; they are apples and oranges; they are not comparable. It is a perilous delusion to ever believe that archaeologists have a natural "right" or overriding "mandate" to dig up anything at all (Goldstein and Kintigh 1990; this vol., 183–84; Meighan 1984:211; Turner 1986; White 1991), much less when that act interferes with or is contrary to the religious and cultural beliefs and interests of those being studied or of their descendants (Adams 1984:239).

We also disagree with those (Meighan 1986:9–12) who suggest that Native American efforts to end what they see as desecration amounts to an infringement of academic freedom. Academic freedom involves the freedom to think, to inquire, and to espouse diverse philosophies. It does not and should not include the freedom to *act* as one pleases. Actions (methods and techniques) are not covered under academic freedom, nor should they be. Excavating, analyzing, studying details of indigenous cultures, and curating human remains are actions, not thoughts, and are therefore subject to ethical constraints.

As anthropologists, we must avoid dismissing others' beliefs as somehow unimportant and contrary to "the truth." There may or may not be such a thing as "scientific truth." But, irrespective of this belief, most Native Americans (and many others) would counter that there are also deeper, more meaningful spiritual or moral values that transcend this.

Ethics and Responsibilities

The problem of Indian burials is not a clash of good and evil, ignorance and wisdom; it is a conflict between propositions that must be accorded equal moral weight at the outset.—L. Rosen, "The Excavation of American Indian Burial Sites: A Problem in Law and Professional Responsibility"

What is an ethical archaeologist? To what or whom are we most accountable? Some find the answer exclusively in the dirt: "The implied ethical obligations of the archaeologist are therefore to data first, and to other interests second" (Meighan 1984:219); and "[e]liminating sites or portions of sites from excavation or analysis . . . is not an ethical stance," and "[w]e have a mandate to preserve and protect the past for the future" (Goldstein and Kintigh 1990; this vol., 183–84). The archaeologist's obligation, they insist, is primarily with the material remains of those past cultures. We must tell their story; this is our professional obligation—perhaps even our right. Some even establish a false dichotomy between prehistoric Indians and "modern" Native Americans (Meighan 1984, 1986, 1992 [ch. 10]; see also McGuire [1989, 1992] for further discussion of this practice), so we may thereby conclude Native Americans have no "true" connection to their own past, nor a knowledge of it, while the scientific pursuit of truth transcends time and place. Thus it is to the relics alone that we are responsible and to which we owe our fealty.

But are we relic hunters, or are we anthropologists? Most of us were schooled in an anthropological tradition. Anthropologists are ethically required to act in the interests of those studied, including their cultures, descendants, and beliefs. The code of ethics of the American Anthropological Association (AAA) (1983) places an anthropologist's obligation to the cultures and peoples studied above any duty we have to data collection or preservation (we note the Society for American Archaeology [SAA] has no comparable formal ethical guidelines for us to turn to). In other words, "the rights and wishes of the people we study supersede our own research needs" (Zimmerman 1989:66), and when those individuals are dead and gone, we must turn to their closest living descendants and their worldview for guidance. To do otherwise—to cite "cultural relativism" and then insist on the primacy of modern scientific mandates—is the height of ethical inconsistency.

To date, the only explicit statement on ethics by the SAA is from three decades ago, and it also deals exclusively with data, artifacts, things found: "Willful destruction, distortion, or concealment of the data of archaeology is censured, and provides grounds for expulsion from [the SAA]" (quoted in Green 1984:28). In this day and age, such an absolute position, lacking any context for implementation, is clearly useless. But in addition to the AAA guidelines cited above, there are others we can turn to which more firmly address the issues of real and practical concern to archaeologists.

The Society of Professional Archaeologists' (SOPA) 1981 Code of Ethics includes explicit concerns for the public, going so far as to list the public as our *primary* responsibility. Archaeologists are expected by SOPA to respect the legitimate concerns of groups whose cultures we study. Native Americans are such a group, and part of the public, and so SOPA would suggest our primary obligation extends to them.

The World Archaeological Congress's (WAC) "First Code of Ethics" (1991) is stronger still in its stance. WAC's "obligations to indigenous peoples" include not interfering with or removing human remains or objects of cultural significance without the express consent of those people. WAC also recognizes an ethical obligation to train and employ indigenous peoples, as well as to recognize indigenous methods of curation, management, and protection as valid.

There is more than one way to preserve and protect archaeological data. If archaeologists were consistent even with their own conservation ethic (e.g., Lipe 1974, 1977), and if archaeologists were disturbing *only* sites that were targeted for other kinds of (even more destructive) disturbance, we feel that some of this dispute would be defused. Native Americans and archaeologists are equally distressed at the destruction caused to sites by vandalism and by large-scale development. Archaeologists must work *with* Native Americans to preserve and protect threatened locations (White 1991:425). Such interactions also serve to deobjectify ancient human remains, allowing archaeologists to see them more as actual deceased people (Deming 1993:7; Ferguson 1984:230). If human remains were encountered during such cooperative efforts, repatriation may not be required, or perhaps some study would be permitted prior to repatriation, as is the case currently on both the Zuni and Navajo reservations (see Ferguson 1984; Klesert 1992). Whether or not analyses are allowed, it takes only a modicum of faith in anthropological tenets to accept the fact that repatriation amounts to the same amount of protection as does boxing and shelving. They are, after all, placed carefully in locations that are then scrupulously avoided. This is the motivation behind repatriation, to preserve and protect both the material and spiritual (e.g., Deloria 1992).

Repatriation and reburial can also have an ameliorative effect, both culturally and politically speaking. As Ferguson (1984:230–31) points out, "reburial of human remains and associated grave goods mitigates the adverse impact [to Zunis] of archaeological excavation and makes such excavation preferable to other types of disturbance during land-modifying activities." In the case of Navajo, Zuni, and many other tribes that have restrictive ordinances, certain analyses are allowed prior to reburial. At Navajo and Zuni, a circumspect and respectful approach toward traditional values has resulted in a mutually beneficial arrangement between archaeologists and Indians (Klesert 1992; Klesert and Downer 1990).

Many archaeologists have difficulty accepting the conservation ethic, and they have considerable difficulty accepting reburial as protection of human remains—apparently because remains that have already been in the ground for hundreds or even thousands of years are put back in the ground and access to "their" data base is restricted (Meighan 1986:10). This point leads us back to a comment we made earlier, an issue on which we disagree profoundly with others in this debate: Archaeologists have no special proprietary claim on the dead, thus they have no natural right to dig up anything at all. We believe that an archaeologist's access to things archaeological (as opposed to the cultural descendants' right to get them back or keep them away from us) is what we must negotiate on a case-by-case basis. Archaeologists have no intrinsic right to survey, excavate, or manipulate the material remains of the past, and their failure to understand this constraint is, we believe, the source of the current and continued contention between archaeologists and Native Americans.

Given that archaeologists must negotiate for right of access, on what basis ought negotiations be held; what is our obligation as professional anthropologists? At what level do we accept the legitimacy of the Native American view? If we really believe in the validity of cultural relativism, then we must be willing to accept (and not just tolerate) native criteria as valid and of equal importance to our own. Conversely, we must become cognizant of the peculiar Eurocentric context of our own beliefs and actions (McGuire 1989:181; Pearson 1990; Rosen 1980:17; Wood and Powell 1993). NAGPRA has made it clear that all types of evidence must be considered—but it is one thing to have a law and quite another to see that its intent is adhered to by all parties with a stake in the outcome.

Finally, there is an obligation to educate the public about what archaeologists do and why it is important. This is seen by many as a way of resolving the current problem of perceptions shared by those who dislike archaeology. Goldstein and Kintigh (1990; this vol., 185–86) provide a reality check to this belief by pointing out that educating people as to our point of view will not make them accept it as their own. Education does, however, serve to resolve the problems accompanying ignorance (such as fear, misinformation, and intolerance) and should be pursued. It can only help, if archaeology really does provide something of value. We would add a rhetorical question: Why is this education not mutual? Are Indians the only ones who need it, or could archaeologists gain some perspective by learning, really understanding, the Indian point of view (Adams 1984; Ferguson 1984; Klesert 1992)?

An Alternative Archaeology

> We have more than 15,000 skulls, but no brains.—Attributed to Aleš Hrdlička by A. V. Kidder, in D. R. Givens, *Alfred Vincent Kidder and the Development of Americanist Archaeology*

We suggest that since archaeologists are trained as anthropologists, we act accordingly. This applies especially to the temptation to elevate our view of "truth" above that of others. Archaeologists must recognize culturally based beliefs and perspectives on all sides and treat them truly equally. Archaeologists must be rid of the notion that they have an immutable "right" to excavate and to curate in perpetuity. Archaeologists have tended to treat Native American concerns and indigenous human remains differently than they have anyone else's, a difference that has not gone unnoticed (Klesert and Downer 1990; McGuire 1989, 1992).

Given all this, what is the best and most ethical approach professional archaeologists can take? We have the following suggestions, for consideration.

1. *Treatment of all human remains should be negotiated with descendant populations, and their wishes should be given primacy.* NAGPRA provides explicit guidelines for determining who these people are.

2. *Human remains should not be disturbed in the first place unless such disturbance is unavoidable.* Scientific research interest is ordinarily an insufficient reason, in and of itself, for disturbance.

3. *Exceptions to these rules must be resolved on a case-by-case basis only in the case of extraordinary scientific value.* If the wishes of descendants are to be overridden, the burden of proof must lie with the scientists. Otherwise, we must abide by the preferences of the legally recognized descendants, who are free to allow curation and additional analyses or to veto any

disturbance at all. In either case, all efforts must be made to judge each side on its own terms, cultural and scientific.

Such proposed rules of professional behavior are not new with us (Advisory Council on Historic Preservation 1985:18–19; Ferguson 1984; Hubert 1989; also see Quick [1985:17, appendix 2], in which Tom King and Larry Zimmerman suggest a similar approach) and simply serve to make archaeologists consistent and immune from charges of unethical, ethnocentric behavior. They do not involve compromising to "special-interest" groups, since they in fact require only that we operate in a consistent manner regardless of the group in question. They do not involve an abridgement of academic freedom, since actions and methods—not theories, thoughts, or beliefs—are what are under scrutiny. They do *not* require uniform reburial or repatriation. What they do require of us is that we conduct ourselves in a way consistent with what we as anthropologists have already declared as basic ethical operating principles.

NAGPRA provides legal remedies for many potentially complex circumstances, but only if the involved parties all apply the law in good faith. The issue of conflicting claims filed by several Indian groups can be handled either by the priority system devised in Section 3 of the law or by use of the review committee established in Section 8. The disposition of unclaimed remains is clearly defined in Section 3, and this would also appear to apply by definition to "unaffiliated" remains, since the lack of a relationship seems to imply a lack of legal claim. Claimed remains should be returned to those whom the law recognizes as legal claimants. Clearly, not all human remains ever found in a museum or uncovered by an archaeologist will be repatriated or reburied, not even all those with recognized claimants under NAGPRA, since the ultimate decision lies with the claimants (who, having established the legitimacy of their claim, may choose *not* to repatriate or rebury). This is as it should be, and it establishes a clear hierarchy in which the concerns of affected claimants have primacy over those of archaeological researchers.

This, of course, brings us back once again to one obvious conclusion: We have no inherent right to dig or study human remains. Furthermore, our obligations, once we might be *permitted* to conduct such work, go well beyond the human tissue lying in our hands, to the entire living system it represents. Until we learn to accept this individually and as a profession, we are on indefensible ground. "Giving back the bones" is *not* the easiest way out of this dilemma. If it is requested of us—and it most certainly will be in many instances—it will shake the foundations of our profession and some of its most cherished assumptions. But it is the only ethical response professional archaeologists can make. Refusing to deal consistently or honestly with the issues and parties involved is neither right nor ethical, destroys our credibility, and will virtually guarantee that in the long run we will lose much more than bones.

Note

We wish to thank Jeff Reid and the several reviewers of drafts of this paper for their critique, advice, and encouragement. Larry Benallie, Al Downer, Dennis Gilpin, Henry O. Hooper and Northern Arizona University's Organized Research Committee, Tom King, Keith Kintigh, Randy McGuire, David Ortiz, Maria Pearson, Gerald Vizenor, John Wood, Larry Zimmerman, and a host of others are all gratefully acknowledged for their insights, support, and inspiration. All opinions, and any errors or excesses, are those of the authors alone.

References

Adams, E. C. 1984. Archaeology and the Native American: A Case at Hopi. In *Ethics and Values in Archaeology,* ed. E. L. Green, pp. 236–63. Free Press, New York.

Adams, R. E. W. 1974. Report of the Secretary. *American Antiquity* 39:666–68.

Advisory Council on Historic Preservation. 1985. *Guidelines for Consideration of Traditional Cultural Values in Historic Preservation Review.* Advisory Council on Historic Preservation, Washington DC.

American Anthropological Association. 1983. *Professional Ethics: Statements and Procedures of the American Anthropological Association.* American Anthropological Association, Washington DC.

Buikstra, J. 1981. A Specialist in Ancient Cemetery Studies Looks at the Reburial Issue. *Early Man* 3(3):26–27.

Deloria, V., Jr. 1992. Indians, Archaeologists, and the Future. *American Antiquity* 57:595–98.

Deming, J. 1993. Competition and Cooperation in Archaeological Consulting. *Practicing Anthropology* 15(1):6–8.

Ferguson, T. J. 1984. Archaeological Ethics and Values in a Tribal Cultural Resource Management Program at the Pueblo of Zuni. In *Ethics and Values in Archaeology,* pp. 224–35.

Givens, D. R. 1992. *Alfred Vincent Kidder and the Development of Americanist Archaeology.* University of New Mexico Press, Albuquerque.

Goldstein, L., and K. Kintigh. 1990. Ethics and the Reburial Controversy. *American Antiquity* 55:585–91 (ch. 9, this vol.).

Green, E. L., ed. 1984. *Ethics and Values in Archaeology.* Free Press, New York.

Hubert, J. 1989. A Proper Place for the Dead: A Critical Review of the "Reburial"

Issue. In *Conflict in the Archaeology of Living Traditions,* ed. R. Layton, pp. 131–66. Unwin Hyman, London.

Johnson, E. 1973. Professional Responsibilities and the American Indian. *American Antiquity* 38:129–30.

Kintigh, K. 1990. A Perspective on Reburial and Repatriation. sᴀᴀ *Bulletin* 8(2):6–7.

Klesert, A. L. 1992. A View from Navajoland on the Reconciliation of Anthropologists and Native Americans. *Human Organization* 51:17–22.

Klesert, A. L., and A. S. Downer. eds. 1990. *Preservation on the Reservation: Native Americans, Native American Lands and Archaeology.* Navajo Nation Papers in Anthropology No. 26. Window Rock, Arizona.

Layton, R. 1989. Introduction: Conflict in the Archaeology of Living Traditions. In *Conflict in the Archaeology of Living Traditions,* pp. 1–21.

Lipe, W. D. 1974. A Conservation Model for American Archaeology. *The Kiva* 39:214–45.

——. 1977. A Conservation Model for American Archaeology. In *Conservation Archaeology: A Guide for Cultural Resource Management Studies,* ed. M. B. Schiffer and G. J. Gumerman, pp. 19–42. Academic Press, New York.

McGimsey, C. R., III. 1971. Archaeology and the Law. *American Antiquity* 36:125–26.

McGuire, R. 1989. The Sanctity of the Grave: White Concepts and American Indian Burials. In *Conflict in the Archaeology of Living Traditions,* pp. 167–84.

——. 1992. Archeology and the First Americans. *American Anthropologist* 94:816–36.

Meighan, C. W. 1984. Archaeology: Science or Sacrilege? In *Ethics and Values in Archaeology,* pp. 208–23.

——. 1986. *Archaeology and Anthropological Ethics.* Wormwood Press, Calabasas, California.

——. 1992. Some Scholars' Views on Reburial. *American Antiquity* 57:704–10 (ch. 10, this vol.).

Nichols, D. L., A. L. Klesert, and R. Anyon. 1989. Ancestral Sites, Shrines and Graves: Native American Perspectives on the Ethics of Collecting Cultural Properties. In *The Ethics of Collecting Cultural Property,* ed. P. Messenger, pp. 27–38. University of New Mexico Press, Albuquerque.

Pearson, M. D. 1990. The Indian Point of View: Exhumation and Reburial. In Klesert and Downer 1990, pp. 397–408.

Powell, S., C. E. Garza, and A. Hendricks. 1993. Ethics and Ownership of the Past: The Reburial and Repatriation Controversy. In *Archaeological Method and Theory,* vol. 4, ed. M. B. Schiffer, pp. 1–42. University of Arizona Press, Tucson.

Quick, P. McW., ed. 1985. *Proceedings of the Conference on Reburial Issues.* Society for American Archaeology, Washington ᴅᴄ.

Rosen, L. 1980. The Excavation of American Indian Burial Sites: A Problem in Law and Professional Responsibility. *American Anthropologist* 82:5–27.

Society of Professional Archaeologists. 1981. Code of Ethics and Standards of Performance. *Directory of Professional Archaeologists,* pp. 3–6. Washington University, St. Louis.

Sprague, R. 1974. American Indians and American Archaeology. *American Antiquity* 39:1–2.

Tilley, C. 1989. Archaeology as Socio-Political Action in the Present. In *Critical Traditions in Contemporary Archaeology,* ed. V. Pinsky and A. Wylie, pp. 104–16. Cambridge University Press, Cambridge.

Turner, C. G. II. 1986. What Is Lost with Skeletal Reburial? I. Adaptation. *Quarterly Review of Archaeology* 7(1):1–3.

White, T. D. 1991. *Human Osteology.* Academic Press, San Diego.

Wood, J. J., and S. Powell. 1993. An Ethos for Archaeological Practice. *Human Organization,* in press.

World Archaeological Congress. 1991. First Code of Ethics. *World Archaeological Bulletin* 5:22–23.

Zimmerman, L. 1989. Made Radical by My Own. In *Conflict in the Archaeology of Living Traditions,* pp. 60–67.

12

Suzanne J. Crawford

(Re)Constructing Bodies

Semiotic Sovereignty and the Debate over Kennewick Man

On July 28, 1996, two students discovered the half-buried remains of a ninety-three-hundred-year-old skeleton while wading in the Columbia River near Kennewick, Washington. Because of its Caucasian-like features the skeleton was first thought to be that of a nineteenth-century settler, before radiocarbon dating at the University of California at Davis showed the body to be over nine thousand years old. The body was thereafter known as Kennewick Man. Acting under a provision of the Native American Graves Protection and Repatriation Act (NAGPRA), the Army Corps of Engineers, which had jurisdiction over the area, determined to return the body for reburial to five local Native American tribes (the Confederated Tribes of the Umatilla, the Yakima Indian Nation, the Nez Perce tribe, the Wanapum band, and the Colville Confederated Tribes). This decision resulted in a maelstrom of protests from anthropologists and archaeologists throughout the country, eight of whom promptly filed a lawsuit requesting that the bones first be turned over to them for study before reburial. The lawsuit was soon joined by a third party, the Asatru Folk Assembly (AFA), a religious group located outside of Nevada City, California, that works to revive pre-Christian Celtic, Nordic, and Germanic traditions. Because of Kennewick Man's Caucasian characteristics, the group believes him to be one of their ancestors who migrated to the New World over nine thousand years ago. The five-tribe coalition, however, remains adamant that the body should be reburied as soon as possible. The tribes oppose testing of the body, especially destructive techniques such as DNA analysis and radiocarbon dating, seeing them "as desecration, with devastating spiritual consequences" (*Portland Oregonian* 10/2/97, D1).

The debate has created a series of profound controversies that extend beyond simple legal issues. The furor over Kennewick Man is a moment strikingly illustrative of the manner in which narratives explicating social identity and history are inscribed on the body. At the heart of the AFA's interest in the body is a firm belief that ancient Caucasians were in fact the first settlers of America, predating the ancestors of contemporary Native American tribes. While insisting that the find is an invaluable source of information about the physical characteristics, health, and lifestyle of America's first people, of the peopling of the Americas, and of human evolution in general, scientists also speculate upon its possible ethnic background. It is these speculations upon his possible European lineage that garner Kennewick Man the most publicity, keeping him in the public eye. All the parties involved approach Kennewick Man with their own economic desires, identity needs, and religio-ethical concerns, all of which are in turn inscribed on the body. The purpose of this paper is to examine the language used to describe Kennewick Man and other early Native American remains, in order to ask several fundamental questions: how does this language reveal the ways non-Natives have constructed the image of the Native American body? And why do we approach these bodies with the questions and agendas that we do? It is my suggestion that the creation of the fictitious "Authentic Indian" of non-Native American lore effectively cuts contemporary Native Americans off from their heritage, enabling the appropriation of Native identity by non-Natives. The ultimate goal of this appropriation is to secure a sense of place, what Yi-Fu Tuan has called "geopiety" (Tuan 1977).

In recent scholarship much attention has been focused on the role of the body within political, economic, and religious institutions. What has not been explored as fully is the relationship between the body and the construction of space and place. Ideologies of identity depend strongly upon understandings of both the body and place and the interaction of the two. A discussion of repatriation and reburial of Native American remains reveals a great deal about the manner in which cultural constructions of the body contribute to the creation of space and a sense of place, especially in dominant white culture. Through the work of feminist critical theorists such as Donna Haraway, Rosemary Hennessy, Judith Butler, and Denise Riley, as well as the work of Michel Foucault, this paper discusses the recent debate over Kennewick Man. As we will see, the Kennewick Man debate demonstrates the manner in which the dominant culture's search for the "Authentic Other," the "Real Indian," facilitates the appropriation of Native identity by non-Natives, legitimating non-Native claims to place and validating non-Native identity. It is not my intent to discuss the validity of any claims made over Kennewick Man, scientific or Native, but rather to explore why the scientific community and the popular press have asked the questions they have. It is in reading the various texts that have been inscribed on this body that latent power relations are made manifest. The debate over Kennewick Man demonstrates the challenges that face the academic community within a postcolonial context and provides an opportunity to create workable solutions to those challenges.

What quickly emerges within the Kennewick Man debate are profoundly different ways of viewing death, the body, history, and cultural identity. Debra Croswell, spokesperson for the Umatillas, argues that the bones should be returned to the ground, regardless of whether the body turns out to be Native or non-Native. "Our feelings on any human remains is that [they] should be reburied. We respect human life, unlike some other cultures, who do not" (*Oregonian* 3/29/97, B2). Horace Axtell, Nez Perce, echoes Croswell's sentiments: "We have an inherent responsibility to care for those who are no longer with us. Our tradition, spiritual beliefs, practices and culture teach us that when a body goes into the ground, it is meant to stay there until the end of time. When remains are disturbed above the ground, their spirits are at unrest. To put those spirits at ease, the remains must be returned to the ground as soon as possible" (*Oregonian* 4/30/97, A14). Armand Minthorn, tribal chairperson of the Umatillas, explained the process further: "Culturally and religiously, our religion tells us that when a body goes into the ground, it is keeping a promise that was made when time began. And the body is to remain in the ground until the end of time. And because these remains have been exposed, this is very sensitive to us, because the remains aren't part of the ground like they should be" (*Oregonian* 10/14/96, A1). The body, for the tribes, serves as a reminder of the intimate tie that exists among themselves, their ancestors, and the land. As Minthorn further explained: "My tribe has ties to this individual because he was uncovered in our traditional homeland, a homeland (in which) we still retain fishing, hunting, gathering and other rights under our 1855 treaty with the U.S. government" (*Oregonian* 10/24/96, C1).[1] The location of the body on Native lands, its residence within the soil for millennia, creates an inherent relationship of reciprocity and respect between the body and the Umatillas, who feel it is their responsibility to care for the land. The body, in its decomposition, is fulfilling a relationship of reciprocity: the earth supports the body during life, and in death, the body supports the earth. Halting this process threatens both ecological and spiritual stability.

Native peoples have methods of constructing cultural identity that are quite different from the DNA analysis and radiocarbon dating of university laboratories. Identities here stem from the land base itself, as well as from a complex and honored oral tradition. Adeline Fredin, director and manager of the Colville confederated tribes' history and archaeology department, argues that the oral traditions of the communities do indeed go back ten thousand years. "It's very clear that our ancestral people were there. How can we deny our ancestry? We're living with those kinds of stories and those kinds of Indian legends that tell us about our own ancestry" (*Oregonian* 10/14/96, A1).[2] As Marla Big Boy, an attorney representing the tribes, explains: "It would be wrong to be disturbing this individual. When laid to rest, they are laid to rest. We don't need science to tell us who we are or where our people came from" (*Oregonian* 10/2/97, D7). Larry Zimmerman has argued that the very nature of time and history is perceived radically differently among traditional Native communities: "To Native Americans, the idea that discovery is the only way to know the past is absurd. For the Indian interested in traditional practice and belief, the past lives in the present. Indians know the past because it is spiritually and ritually part of their daily existence and is relevant only as it exists in the present. . . . When archaeologists say that the Native American past is gone, extinct, or lost unless archaeology can find it, they send a strong message that Native Americans themselves are extinct" (Zimmerman 1994; see also Watson et al., 1989, 5–6).

Cultural and religious sentiments aside, the Kennewick Man controversy serves as a reminder to Native peoples of a long history of atrocities perpetrated upon Native communities by archaeologists and anthropologists. For much of U.S. history, professional academics and amateur scavengers have gathered Native remains, some recently deceased, others much older, removing them from burial grounds and shipping them to museums and universities, where they often remained, unstudied, in storage for decades. As of 1996 there were approximately one million such remains still held by public and private institutions (Mihesuah, introduction, this volume). This collection was driven by the notion that the Native peoples of the Americas were doomed to extinction by the onward march of progress in the form of Western capitalism and Christianity and that specimens of Native biology and culture should be preserved for future (white) generations to admire on the shelves of museums. This collecting took little regard for the opinions or sentiments of Native peoples themselves: they were, after all, about to disappear forever.[3] During the Indian wars of the nineteenth century, for example, fallen Native warriors were "decapitated, by order of the Surgeon General of the army for an Indian Crania Study" (Mihesuah, introduction, this volume). In 1900 explorer Alex Hrdlicka dug up the burial ground of a village at Larsen Bay, Alaska, leaving with the remains of eight hundred Konaig Natives, while living villagers watched and protested. There are many such examples, up to the present day, of both academic and amateur "grave robbing" in which bones and grave materials are removed without the permission of local Native tribes (Trafzer, 1997). It is only recently, with NAGPRA, that Native communities have been able to demand the return of their ancestors' and relatives' remains. Kennewick Man, for Native communities, cannot be seen outside of this long history of abuse and disrespect on the part of Euroamerican colonizers.

For those who insist that the body should be subjected to intensive study, however, Kennewick Man is a scientific text, which must be read for the benefit of humanity. As James Chatters, the forensic anthropologist who first studied Kennewick Man, argued in August of 1996: "It's quite exciting to turn up someone who lived then, and whose body tells so many stories" (*Oregonian* 8/28/96, A1). Stephen McNallen of the AFA likewise conjured up the image of Kennewick Man as storyteller, when he told reporters: "We share a common ancestry, and we know he has a remarkable story to tell us about how this continent was populated" (*Oregonian* 8/20/97, C1). Kennewick Man's bones "have a message for us. I don't know what that message is. . . . our task is to listen" (*Oregonian* 8/28/97, C7). As controversy around the body grew, those opposed to reburial insisted more strongly on the importance of listening to the stories that the body holds, hidden within it. As Chatters told Donald Preston of the *New Yorker*: "We didn't go digging for this man. He fell out—he was actually a volunteer. I think it would be wrong to stick him back in the ground without waiting to hear the story he has to tell. We need to look at things as [human] beings, not as one race or another. The message this man brings to us is one of unification: there may be some commonality in our past that will bring us together" (Preston 1997).

Indeed, the argument most commonly expressed by those in favor of handing Kennewick Man over to a team of anthropologists and archaeologists for intensive study is a universalist and humanistic one reflective of the dominant white culture from which it comes: the body belongs not to Native American tribes but to all humanity. Archaeologists explain that their work is directed not at a certain cultural or national group but at the global human community. This sentiment is found in Landau and Steele's explanation of the necessity of the use of human remains in archaeological study: "In examining our heritage, physical anthropologists seek to understand the biological history and origins of all humans in all geographical areas. Our focus is on all humankind. . . . Each society's biological history is an integral part of the complete and continuing story of all humankind." Landau and Steele are concerned with questions that address "our ancestors," "our ancestral species," and "our understanding of past Native American peoples, and by extension, all humans past and present," because "our total history is who we are" (Landau and Steele, chap. 4, this volume).

Pushing cultural distinctions to the side, physical anthropologists claim to address cross-cultural and cross-ethnic questions of biological evolution. Anthropologist Amy Dansie has argued that bones such as those of Kennewick Man are "priceless rare treasures of humanity. The skeleton's features are virtually indistinguishable from white ancestors and Asian ancestors. We share a common ground. These skeletons are important to remind everybody that we're all one people" (*Oregonian* 12/19/96, E10). Chatters also argues for the national appeal of Kennewick Man. "This is knowledge that everyone can have, even the descendants of the tribes. We'd like to know the history of our homeland to the fullest extent. . . . The Kennewick Man is the common heritage of all Americans and should be studied for the benefit of all" (*Chronicle of Higher Education* 5/22/98, A22). And as he pointed out shortly after Kennewick Man's discovery: "This guy's old enough to be everyone's ancestor" (*Oregonian* 8/28/96, A1). Again and again, Kennewick Man and other similar human remains used for osteological study are referred to as "national treasures" and a source from which to gather invaluable information and data to reconstruct the lives and migrations of the "first Americans," for the benefit of all Americans.

This language is found throughout the press coverage of Kennewick Man, from nonacademics as well. Richard Hill, columnist for the *Oregonian*, wrote soon after the controversy surfaced: "The quest is for our past, for the elusive first Americans" (*Oregonian* 11/27/96, A18). A letter to the editor of the *Oregonian* from Lyle T. Hubbard Jr. of Ridgefield, Washington, reads: "Humans comprise a global community. We need to know about our past so we can have, in common, a vision for our future" (*Oregonian* 11/28/96, B9). Another editorial argues in a similar strain: "This discussion ought to be less about whose ancestor he is than what he can teach all of us. This is a rare discovery that rightfully belongs to all of the people of the Americas and the world." (*Oregonian* 11/1/96, D10). Thomas McClelland, an artist who, in a striking illustration of Foucault's theory of the social construction of the body, (re)constructed Kennewick Man's face from a plaster cast of his skull, told reporters: "The interesting thing about Kennewick Man is that he could be related to anyone. And I think that's part of what this whole controversy is about, too. He does have features that could be tied to any group in the world today. He's kind of like an 'Everyman' if you will" (*Oregonian* 2/28/98, B11). Slade Gorton, the Washington State senator who has attempted to pass legislation that would facilitate the study of the remains, has argued that "My amendment makes the bones available for further scientific study, keeping the interests of all Americans in mind" (*Oregonian* 7/18/97, B7). The *Oregonian* supported the move in an editorial written soon afterward: "We hope that science prevails in the end. The information from ancient Kennewick Man is simply too important to all peoples to be buried by one people" (*Oregonian* 8/1/97, B10).

Such arguments are clearly reminiscent of an ideology of global monoculture, drawing on the American mythic ideal of the melting pot. All this raises several important questions: How do sovereign Native nations fit into this notion of American monoculture? At what point does a body become common property, and who in reality is this "common humanity" to which they refer? Is it really "all Americans" that are interested in and feel they would benefit from knowing about Kennewick Man? If Kennewick Man is envisioned as a treasure trove of ancient wisdom, one must ask what this information might be, and why do those persons who argue most vehemently in favor of scientific study feel it to be so vastly important? Why the insistence upon overlooking ethnic and cultural distinctions, agendas, and definitions and the repeated argument that Kennewick Man belongs to "all of us," is "our ancestor," and is part of the history of "our homeland"?

These questions become even more important when it is noted that the use of such terms as "Everyman" and "all one people" is immediately and continually contradicted by the argument that the primary use of scientific study of the body will be to determine its racial origin. Alan Schneider, the lawyer acting on behalf of the anthropologists in the lawsuit, argued that study must be done to "determine whether the skeleton is a Native American. . . . We're arguing that we don't know who it belongs to, and that can't be determined without study" (*Oregonian* 1/2/97, A10). The eight anthropologists in the lawsuit have argued that "more science is needed to determine whether Kennewick Man is an American Indian, or related to modern tribes" (*Oregonian* 7/3/97, E11).

Such challenges raise interesting questions about the definition of "Native American." According to Francis P. McManamon of the U.S. Department of the Interior, who is also the departmental consulting archaeologist with the National Park Service, the U.S. government understands the term "Native American" to apply to "human remains relating to tribes, peoples, or cultures that lived in what is now the United States before the documented arrival of European explorers. The remains would be considered Native American regardless of when a particular group might have begun to live in this area and regardless of whether these groups were culturally affiliated or biologically related to present-day tribes" (*Oregonian* 4/14/98, B1). By such a standard, Kennewick Man, regardless of the size of his nose, is considered to be Native American and thus subject to NAGPRA. The fact, then, that so many people are demanding that his Native status be reevaluated is extremely revealing. The question of Kennewick Man's ethnicity, of whether he is in fact "Native American," would not be made unless another possibility is being implied. And it is.

For the popular press, Kennewick Man's most glamorous appeal is his "Caucasoid" characteristics. Even those scientists who insist upon a conservative reading of the shape of his skull, arguing that he is most likely part of an earlier but still very Asian migration across the Bering Strait land bridge, cannot help but speculate a little on the possibility that the first Americans were, in fact, white guys. The AFA has requested that the bones be studied to determine whether Kennewick Man is "more closely linked to modern Native Americans, Asians, or Europeans" (*Oregonian* 10/3/97, D3). Senator Slade Gorton and State Representatives Doc Hastings, Jack Metcalf, and George Netherwitt Jr., all of Washington, have argued that preliminary scientific assessments indicate that the remains could be Caucasion. An article in the *New Yorker* does its best to argue that the first Americans may very well have been ancient Europeans: "Kennewick Man's bones are part of a growing quantity of evidence that the earliest inhabitants of the New World may have been a Caucasoid people. . . . these people may have originally come from Europe" (Preston 1997, 72). Preston quotes Chatters's description of what Kennewick Man may have looked like: "On the physical characteristics alone, he could fit on the streets of Stockholm without causing any kind of notice. Or, on the streets of Jerusalem, or New Delhi for that matter. I've been looking around for someone who matches this Kennewick gentleman, looking for weeks and weeks for people on the street, thinking, 'This one's got a little bit here, that one a little bit there.' And then, one evening, I turned on the TV and there was Patrick Stewart—Captain Picard of Star Trek, and I said, 'My God, there he is! Kennewick Man!' " (Preston 1997, 73).

Robson Bonnichsen also argues that the earliest inhabitants of the Americas may not have been those people we currently think of as indigenous. "We're getting some hints from people working with genetic data that these earliest populations might have some shared genetic characteristics with latter-day European populations" (Preston 1997, 78). *U.S. News and World Report* jumped on the sensationalized media appeal of Kennewick Man, clearly demonstrating why the remains have had such a following in popular culture: "Thus continued the dramatics attending One of the Most Startling Science Stories of the Age. K-Man, it happens, is identifiably Caucasoid, and his discovery has rocked all Extant Systems of Belief as anthropologists ponder a large and quite politically incorrect question about The Peopling of North America: Is it possible that the original 'Native Americans' were, um, white guys?" (*U.S. News and World Report* 9/22/97, 10).

Even more interesting, these texts argue that these ancient Europeans in America were wiped out in a genocidal mass by the ancestors of today's contemporary Native Americans, perhaps by warfare, perhaps by the spreading of new and unfamiliar diseases, "just as European diseases wiped out a large percentage of the Native American population after the arrival of Columbus" (Preston 1997, 80). Preston concludes his argument for the prehistoric European conquest of the Americas by posing this question: "It does raise an interesting question: If the original inhabitants of the New World were Europeans who were pushed out by Indians would it change the Indians' position in the great moral landscape?" (Preston 1997, 81). If Native Americans can be accused of prehistoric genocide against early Euroamericans, can the genocide of colonization be re-envisioned as the evening of an old score? As Bruce M. Rowe of Pierce College in Los Angeles said: "If the current Native Americans' ancestors were the second population here, then their legal battles over land based on 'They were here first' might not have as much psychological force" (*Kennewick {WA} Tri-Cities Herald*, 6/1/99).

Similarly, the AFA has argued their belief that Kennewick Man is in fact an ancient European and as such shared religious and cultural traits with ancient Germanic and Nordic peoples. Michael Clinton, lawyer for the AFA, told the *Oregonian*: "It is now thought possible that European-type groups could, in fact, have also made that long walk" (*Oregonian* 10/26/96, D3). An article in the *Runestone*, the quarterly publication of the AFA, in the spring of 1997 argued that: "An entire culture of long-skulled Caucasian proportioned people may have inhabited the American west. . . . the lore of Nevada and California is full of stories about tall, red haired mummies that don't resemble Native Americans in the slightest. . . . Kennewick Man is kin. He represents a branch of our people, a limb of the family tree that grew through America's back door long before our own forebears ever dreamed of sailing the Atlantic. . . . Someday it will be acknowledged that a Caucasoid people did in fact arrive in the Americas thousands of years ago" (McNallan 1997, 7–8).

Such arguments for the presence of ancient Europeans in the New World have been a part of archaeology and anthropology since its inception in the Americas. Enormous earthen mounds in the Midwest were for a long time argued to be the work of "a civilized, white race" that had built the mounds "only to be overrun by red savages" (McGuire 1997, 69). The mound builders were long believed to have been "exterminated by the ancestors of the American Indians." The claim reflected "the widespread belief that the Indians were genocidal savages and made the archaeological record appear to be further justification for the waging of war upon them and the seizure of their land" (Trigger 1980, 665), and to prove beyond doubt that the Native Americans "were *not* the first inhabitants of the hemisphere" (Zimmerman 1997, 95; see also McGuire 1997, 821).

Such sentiments as these are important to note, I believe, because they take shape within several common stereotypes and symbolic constructions in the popular and academic mind about Native Americans and their place in the history of the United States. Further, they are also descriptive of the ways in which the body becomes constructed as a text upon which dominant cultural norms are inscribed.

The view of the body guiding modern science emerged from the empirical, rational modes of thought of Enlightenment philosophy, in which the body was approached as something to be dissected, analyzed, and eventually mastered. As textbook, the body can be read and comprehended by the rigors of science. It is a material object that follows scientific laws and can be subjected to calculations, experimentations, and evaluation. In many ways, anthropology-as-human-science has approached Native Americans in much the same way. For most of its history, anthropologists approached Native peoples as objects and labeled their Native teachers "informants." Kennewick Man is in keeping with this tradition. He is the ideal informant: He can be read through empirical processes to provide scientifically verifiable data. He cannot speak for himself but must be spoken for. And even better, he cannot mislead researchers through misinformation or poor translations, as living Native "informants" are wont to do. Like the body of the scientific tradition, Kennewick Man is reduced to what Denise Riley has called "an obstinate core of identification" (Riley 1988, 101), that is, a reliable, verifiable source of identifying information, free of cultural or subjective input. The body is thus assumed to be a foundational *real,* a place to return to that transcends and precedes discourse.[4]

But such a perception of the body is simplistic. As they have formulated their critique of the modern subject, critical theorists such as Foucault and feminist critical theorists such as Judith Butler, Gayatri Spivak, and Riley have also critiqued the modern empirical view of the body. As these scholars have demonstrated, bodies are constructed, perceivable only through discourse that is influenced by cultural, political, and economic processes. Bodies can only be experienced through discourse, and so the language, narratives, and questions that are used about that body will dictate what sort of body is ultimately perceived. Spivak explains: "If one really thinks about the body, as such, there is no possible outline of the body as such. There are thinkings of the systematicity of the body, there are value codings of the body. The body, as such, cannot be thought, and I certainly cannot approach it" (qtd. in Butler 1993, 1). The work of Foucault has been foundational in establishing this notion of the body as a culturally constructed force, which conveys knowledge and the power associated with it. This body, for Foucault, acts as a space upon which culture and power relations are clearly inscribed. It acts as the ideal ledger of power. Foucault's body is the "ultimate micro-existence . . . the fundamental materiality on which history has been inscribed . . . a volume in perpetual disintegration" (Hennessy 1993, 44).

Foucault's argument for the body as text led many feminist critical theorists to conclude that the body is only experienced through a culturally constructed discourse, which makes the body as such completely inaccessible. Riley argues that bodies "have slipped away as objects, and become instead almost trace phenomena which are produced by the wheelings about of great technologies and politics. . . . In a strong sense, the body is really constantly altering as a concept" (Riley 1988, 102, 104). Surrounded and encoded by value-laden imagery and political manipulations, the body becomes a potent tool for constructing systems of knowledges and behaviors. Through this dense veil of significations, many theorists argue, the body becomes completely occluded. And as Camilla Griggers has argued in her analysis of the construction of faciality and bodily narratives in the contemporary fashion, media, and medical industries: "The body is not outside textuality; the body is itself a field of signification, a site for the production of cultural meanings and ideological reifications" (Griggers 1997, 54).

These perceptions do not take place in a vacuum: they are the result of political and economic conditions, and it becomes clear that privileged narratives are those that speak on behalf of the privileged class, in this case, that of the colonizer. These narratives that have been constructed about the body reflect significant political and economic concerns, and those narratives that become the privileged, dominant modes of discourse in society reflect privileged political and economic status. In other words, those in power determine which narratives will become the dominant or accepted readings of the body. Scholars in particular, occupying a place of privilege as we do, need to be aware of dominant modes of thought in our own traditions that reduce Native peoples to a farcical stereotype, that would suggest that "real" Indians lived only in prehistory. To begin to reevaluate our position as scholars requires that we first deconstruct the body that we have constructed. What do the discourse and imagery that have arisen around Kennewick Man tell us about the "Indian" body that has been constructed by the dominant culture?

Looking at the brief statements made about Kennewick Man, in light of the work of such scholars as Robert Berkhofer and Fergus M. Bordewich, we see a consistent stereotype of the "noble savage" played out throughout U.S. history, a fetishized image of Native Americans, formed out of projected shadows and needs of white society, which I will call the "Authentic Indian." "Authentic Indians" are seen as being frozen in time, the embodiment of the noble savage, in tune with nature and the mysterious spiritual world that inhabited it prior to the arrival of Western civilization. "Authentic Indians" are one with the land, wear buckskin and feathers, live in tipis, dance with wolves, and hunt buffalo while riding bareback. "Authentic Indians" behave, look like, and live as Hollywood has told us they do. To not look like the stereotype is to not be really "Indian." Indeed, Kennewick Man is said to be of European origin, because, as Douglas Owsley of the Smithsonian Institution has said, he "does not look quite like what you think of when you think about a modern Indian" (*Science* 4/10/98, 190). To any Native American this statement must sound ludicrous. Native people vary vastly in appearance from community to community and generation to generation. But because he does not fit the stereotype, Kennewick Man cannot be considered an ancestor of "our Indians." Concurrent with this stereotype of the "Authentic Indian" is the belief that the "Indian" was doomed to extinction from the moment Columbus set foot in the Americas and that the "Indians," the real ones anyway, have all ceased to exist. And indeed, the "Indian" of Americana mythology no longer exists, nor did she ever. As Rayna Green has commented: "They don't believe in us. They don't believe we're alive because we've changed. They don't believe we can carry briefcases, because the Indians they play are an invention, a figment. And they want us to live up to the Indians they play and the price for that is a mythological and sometimes real death for real Indians. . . . I'm convinced that, in order for them to really successfully play Indian, we need to be dead" (qtd. in Parkhill 1997, 85).

Contemporary Native Americans do not adequately fulfill the stereotypes that American popular culture desires to see embodied: in addition to maintaining deeply held traditional religious and cultural beliefs and practices, living Native Americans also attend college, run casinos, are shrewd legal experts, speak at academic conferences, and facilitate support groups for recovering Catholics, codependency, or alcoholism. They are not the noble primitive savages that popular American culture, living in its urban, postmodern world, needs to fulfill its fantasies. The "Authentic Indian" is the embodiment of an important part of the non-Native unconscious, and failing to have that stereotype embodied in actuality leaves the non-Native person at a loss. Who will adopt the Boy Scout into his secret ceremonial society, imparting ancient mysterious wisdom that the contemporary city dweller may be feeling hungry for? Where is the Pocahontas who will rescue us from our own spiritual angst? In the absence of "Authentic Indians" Kennewick Man provides a marvelous solution: the "real Indians" are in fact white folks! Wendy Rose has written that "The Whiteshaman reader/performer aspires to 'embody the Indian' in effect 'becoming' the 'real' Indian even when actual Native people are present. Native reality is thereby subsumed and negated by imposition of a greater or 'more universal' contrivance" (Rose 1992, 405).

Kennewick Man, when seen in this light, becomes for non-Natives a crucial and almost mystical link with one's own "inner Indian." Through Kennewick Man, white popular culture can appropriate the role of the "Authentic Indian" that Native Americans have not adequately embodied. White culture can create its own claim to being part of the landscape, to being heirs of the "Indian." And the necessary mediator, who will act to restore American society to the wisdom and strength associated with the preindustrial, preurban, preliterate society of Kennewick Man, is the scientific community. The perception of the "unbridgeable gulf" between the "Indian" in tune with nature and the white, urban, post–World War II individual has grown, and with it has come the notion that there are "rare scholar-mediators who can bridge the gap" (Parkhill 1997, 82). As Randall McGuire has observed: "The notion of the vanishing American Indian allows archaeologists to glorify their object, the Indian past, and yet detach it from the descendants of that past, living Indian people. The heroes of the prehistoric tale become archaeologists that have been able to interpret this past and not the Indian people whose lives flow from it" (McGuire 1992, 827).

It is this context that at times infuses the work of archaeologists and anthropologists with such intense importance. Archaeologists write of their work as a responsibility, duty, and right. "We have a mandate to preserve and protect the past for the future, an obligation to past cultures to tell their story and to future generations to preserve the past for their benefit" (Goldstein and Kintigh, chap. 9, this volume). If the past is to be known, archaeologists must make it known. Clement Meighan writes of the ability and duty of archaeologists to be the sole voice of the vanished "Indian." "Archaeologists have a responsibility to the people they study. They are defining the culture of an extinct group and in presenting their research they are writing a chapter of human history that cannot be written except from archaeological investigation. If the archaeology is not done, the ancient people remain without a history" (Meighan, 1994, 64). Meighan's sentiment effectively cuts contemporary Native peoples away from their predecessors, making archaeologists the true heirs of the prehistoric, "Authentic Indians." Christy Turner's 1986 piece chimes in with Meighan, when Turner argues, "I explicitly assume no living culture, religious interest group, or biological population has any moral or legal right to the exclusive use or regulation of ancient human skeletons since all humans are members of the same species, and ancient skeletons are the remnants of unduplicatable evolutionary events which all living and future peoples have the right to know about and understand" (Turner 1986, 1). The vehicle through which all living and future people will gain this knowledge, it is implied, is through archaeological and osteological investigation. While scientists involved in the debate over Kennewick Man intend for their research to transcend cultural divisions, it in fact proves to reinforce hierarchies of privilege, making the anthropologist the only legitimate voice to speak for indigenous peoples and grant identity to Native peoples, even more so than they themselves. Amy Dansie of the Nevada State Museum argues the point quite well: "We're not trying to offend Native Americans, although they're hostile to us now. . . . It seems they think we're trying to steal their ancestors and their history. We're not; we just think you shouldn't deny these ancient people their identity" (*Science* 4/10/98, 193).

Trigger and others have pointed out the problems inherent in such arguments on behalf of osteological work. Universal agendas and "Everyman" talk inevitably mean that members of the predominantly white, predominantly Western scientific community take possession of the remains and determine the course of investigation.

By treating generalizations about human behavior as being the primary goal of archaeological research, archaeologists have chosen to use data concerning the native peoples of North America for ends that have no special relevance to these people. Instead, the remains are employed in a clinical manner to test hypotheses that intrigue professional anthropologists and to produce knowledge that is justified as serving the broader interests of Euroamerican society (Trigger 1980, 671).

This tendency is reinforced by the divorce of archaeology from ethnography and the oral traditions of living Native Americans, increasing the sense of an unmendable break between "Indians" of the past and Native Americans of today. As McGuire has pointed out, this belief that "Authentic Indians" had ceased to exist, and the subsequent disarticulation of living Native peoples from their past, "provided the vehicle by which whites took over Native American heritages for nationalistic and scientific purposes. Archaeologists lifted dead Indians from their graves, in part, to help create a national heritage, and the myth of the vanishing Americans. By routing the red savages, the new, civilized white American race inherited the mantle, the heritage, of the old civilization and the legitimate claims to the land" (McGuire 1992, 818, 821).

It is here, I believe, that we begin to understand the implications of the Kennewick Man debate and the reasons behind the intensely emotional determination of non-Native popular and academic culture to glean from this ancient text the wisdom and illumination that they so firmly believe it holds for them. When discussing the work of Charles Godfrey Leland, who collected folklore among Native populations of the Northeast, and Leland's certainty that the Northeast "Indian" myths that he recorded were somehow intimately connected to Norse mythology, Thomas Parkhill turned to Yi Fu Tuan's notion of geopiety, that is, "the sense of country as one's native home, the sense that one had sprung out of its soil and was nurtured by it; the belief that one's ancestors since time immemorial were born in it" (Parkhill 1997, 98). It is this longing for a sense of geopiety that Parkhill believes to be at the root of Leland's desire to see a link between a Maliseet myth and Nordic epics. Parkhill sees Leland's construction as part of "the process by which human beings construct their place by weaving themselves into their landscapes." It is this process that is "part of a larger human endeavor to make Place for themselves" (Parkhill 1997, 99). As Parkhill further explains: "Responding to these Place-driven needs, some of us turn to the timeless, tradition-respecting 'Indian' who has a deep abiding relationship to Mother Earth. Perhaps, their part of our story goes, the 'Indians' can help us to feel a sense of belonging. . . . If the 'Indian' would only teach us some of her or his timeless secrets, we too would have access to this sacred sense of Place" (Parkhill 1997, 111). What we see happening in the battle over Kennewick Man takes Parkhill's experience with Leland's work a step further. With Kennewick Man the mystical "Indian" who will impart the wisdom necessary to restore one's relationship with the land, to achieve a sense of Place, comes one step closer: "The 'Indian' is, in fact, one of us!" And in this instance, the hope that non-Natives are, in fact, the "real Indians" thrives off of a projected need and desire for the "Authentic Indian" that has fed Americana and pop culture since the beginning of U.S. history. Through cinema, advertising, literature, and the numerous image-making techniques of late capitalism, non-Native America has depended upon the power of the "Indian" image, the projection of everything urban industrial civilization is not and secretly (or not so secretly) wishes it was. As Bonnichsen has said: "Kennewick Man has become a public icon. . . . He's pushed peoples' buttons; they are enormously interested in finding out who he is. He could well change our perception of who first settled America" (*Science* 4/10/98, 190).

To the degree that Kennewick Man facilitates the appropriation of the identity of the "Authentic Indian," he gains the attention and fascination of the American public. Parkhill's discussion of the search for Place gives light to the Kennewick Man controversy. When scholars and journalists write about "our ancestor" discovered in "our homeland" who wants to tell us things about "our past," they are weaving themselves and their lives into the history of the Northwest. Thus the body becomes our link with the land. Through the body in question, contemporary Americans will gain a means of creating a sense of Place, and establishing themselves on the land. This is seen clearly in the plans of the AFA to memorialize the site where Kennewick Man was found, to honor "the memory of someone they consider to be a revered ancestor" (*Oregonian* 1/13/98, E3). Thus, cermonially, the AFA will make a claim to space, create Place, and will establish a visible and secure tie that grants them (and other Euroamericans) a legitimacy and authenticity within the land.

Curtis Hinsley Jr. has argued that early archaeologists of the eighteenth and nineteenth centuries struggled to construct a narrative that would lend a definition and sense of identity to the newly forming nation. The bodies of Native Americans became key elements of understanding and incorporating the past into themselves, of becoming part of the landscape in which they lived. "Digging in the prehistoric dirt and constructing heroic tales on what they found, these men . . . faced the challenge of replacing a heritage of heroism built on classical literature with an identity constructed of shards and bones and preliterate silence." They set to work, painstakingly constructing the nation's own identity "by absorbing and domesticating their predecessors into themselves" (Hinsley, chap. 2, this volume). Part and parcel of this process of constructing place has been constructing an "Authentic Indian" body through which Euroamericans can have access to the land. Whether that body was the compliant Indian Maiden or the bloodthirsty savage who must be removed in order for civilization to progress, stereotypes of the "Authentic Indian" have depended upon external constructions of the Native form, which facilitated the appropriation of Native identity and Native land. In an eerie way, Kennewick Man is much the same. As his face was reconstructed from a cast of his skull, Kennewick Man took on the features of a white northern European, looking remarkably like one of the most well-known British actors on television. Mass media, pop culture, and the academic community have already made it very clear. Kennewick Man is one of us. We are the truly "Authentic Indians."[5] Michael Clinton is thus not so very mistaken when he argues that "Kennewick Man is a threat to the Indians because he jeopardizes their moral authority and argument that they were the victims of Europeans which succeeded them" (*New York Times* 4/2/98, A12). That is exactly what the media's reading of Kennewick Man's body, encouraged by academics who have not considered the political implications of their words, may very well do.

It must of course be pointed out that not all archaeologists or anthropologists participate in the appropriation of Native identities or in the collection and study of human remains without the permission of affiliated tribes. Many scholars have made great strides in becoming responsive to the needs and concerns of Native communities, in working with and for Native communities rather than around them, and in respecting the individuals whom they are studying as individuals and subjects, not as objects. Many also disapprove of the racialized language that has been used surrounding Kennewick Man. Many have insisted that use of the term "Caucasoid" to begin with was an enormous mistake on Chatters's part. In speaking so, "Chatters has given a racial identification to something that may ultimately defy racial categories. As Alan Goodman, professor of anthropology at Hampshire College in Amherst, Mass., put it, 'Kennewick Man has become a textbook example of why race science is bad science' " (*New York Times* 4/2/98, A12). Jonathan Marks of the University of California at Berkeley also challenges Chatters's position.

> Chatters argues that designation of the specimen as "Caucasoid" should be divorced from its racial implications. But how can it, if the term itself is racial and directly implies the peoples of Europe and the Near East? To call the specimen an "atypical Native American" would have been more accurate and less problematic. To call it "Caucasoid" is to connote aspects of ancestry, not simply morphology; it directly suggests that America was settled by Europeans and that those now called "Native Americans" are actually less "native" than they think. This is a strongly political statement requiring an exceptional level of validation. There is an element of responsibility to be considered here; without it, the statement represents anthropology, indeed science in general, very poorly. (Marks 1998, 1)

It must also be pointed out that this desire to construct Place is not criminal or, for that matter, a sign of a culturally impoverished people. The AFA is doing a work that many Native people applaud: encouraging non-Native seekers to seek within their own cultural past before they appropriate Native traditions for their own. The AFA's agenda is neither racist nor hate-driven: they are looking to recover an earth-based faith and tradition that was lost to Christianization. It is a cross-cultural and perhaps universally present need to locate oneself in the place one lives and to feel a sense of connection to the land. It is this assurance of identity and location that many Native peoples of the Pacific Northwest have and that many non-Native peoples crave. Does it mean that non-Native peoples do not have the right to establish a sense of Place? Of course not, nor does it necessarily mean that the readings of Kennewick Man that the academic community or the AFA might make are flawed or wrong. It is not the veracity of the scientific or religious claims that I question but rather why these claims are made, why these questions are asked to begin with, and why they maintain such a grip on the public's imagination that they continue to occupy headlines nearly three years after the lawsuit over Kennewick Man began. I have argued that it is the need to establish a sense of Place and to find the embodiment of the non-Native projection of the "Authentic Indian" that provides the emotional fascination with Kennewick Man. This projection, carried to its extreme, is most perfectly embodied in a "primitive, noble savage" who is both indigenous to the Americas and of European origin. Here we find the manner in which *cultural constructions of the body contribute to the creation of a sense of place.* With this in mind, is there a resolution to the controversy? If those parties involved recognize their underlying interest in the construction of their identities onto Kennewick Man, can it facilitate a more impartial approach toward a resolution?

Where Do We Go from Here?

The resolution begins, I believe, with recognizing that it is with such histories of archaeological and popular image-making and history-writing that we approach Kennewick Man today. History has ever and always been a narrative, written and rewritten to suit the needs of the day; history is constructed, not discovered. As Thomas Biolsi and Zimmerman have argued: "Anthropology is not a universal 'science of man' [*sic*]. It is a set of questions asked and answered by an 'interested party' in a global and highly unequal encounter, the ultimate results of which are yet to be fully worked out. Anthropology is the academic discipline that makes sense of the Others the West has both created and encountered in its global expansion since 1500" (Biolsi and Zimmerman 1997, 14).

It is this global expansion that must be remembered when we hear arguments that Kennewick Man belongs to the global community. The debate over Kennewick Man itself is a clear indicator of the political and economic forces at work in the cultural construction and reading of the body. Foucault and others have argued that it is as a site and "force of production that the body is invested with relations of power and domination. . . . the body becomes a useful force only if it is both a productive and a subjected body" (Foucault 1977, 26). It is as a tool in the process of colonial capitalism that the body gains power to signify in the contemporary Western world. Kennewick Man is valued and coveted by those fighting for the right to control the reading of his body as text, because he is both a subjected body and a productive body. He is subjected to the gaze and signification of a number of interested parties, and he likewise carries strategic potential within economic hierarchies of production and exploitation of Native lands, research grants, and fellowships, or water, land, and fishing rights. As Teresa Ebert explains: "What makes a body valuable in the world is its *economic* value" (Ebert 1996, 81, 220).

With this in mind, it becomes clear that approaching corporeality from different modes of thought, with different cultural, political, economic, and spiritual contexts, will radically affect the body that is perceived. Archaeologists and anthropologists who inscribe the body with empiricist Enlightenment agendas ask questions with regard to age, dates, race, migratory patterns, chemical measurements, and radiocarbon dating. The questions are constructed from a history of colonial discourse, which seeks to understand the Other so as to better colonize them: understanding the origins of the Natives, how they fit within the Euroamerican conception of human history, and how to integrate, assimilate, or do away with them most effectively. What must be remembered is that Native peoples are simply asking different questions when approaching their history. For instance, Native peoples may not be asking questions about origins (they know where they came from already) but rather about how best to establish their cultural and semiotic sovereignty. The fact that scientific narratives gain precedence over Native narratives about their own history is indicative of the power differential inherent in colonial relationships. Scientists who would measure craniums, DNA, and radiocarbon emissions and continue to insist that their work emerges from a material body that acts as an essential bedrock of reliable information do not realize that their own processes of inquiry are the result of certain political, economic, and social privileges.[6] We must therefore remember that the global community to which claimants in the lawsuit over Kennewick Man refer is one dominated by Western capitalism and the vestiges of colonialism. We must also remember that the search for Place and the appropriation of the "Authentic Indian" identity cannot be divorced from its economic consequences. The non-Native search for legitimation of land claims has been a source of complex spiritual and emotional paradigms, but it has also been an elementally economic one.

It is in reading this text of the body that relations of power are made manifest. As Foucault has observed, knowledge and power are intimately connected. To know something is to gain power over it. As such, the attempt by the academic community to "know" the history of Native peoples (better than they themselves do), to categorize and map the migration patterns of the past, is to gain power over history. The battle over Kennewick Man becomes a battle over who is to control historical narratives and hence who is to have power over the categories of identity that dominate and control the present and the future. As Alan Schneider, attorney for the anthropologists suing for the body, has said, "It's really a battle over who is going to control knowledge about the past" (*Oregonian* 10/14/96, A1). The claim that many well-intentioned academics have made, that their work exists outside of a politicized framework, is naive at best. As Foucault has argued: "We should abandon a whole tradition that allows us to imagine that knowledge can exist only where the power relations are suspended and that knowledge can develop only outside its injunctions, its demands, and its interests. . . . power produces knowledge. . . . power and knowledge directly imply one another. . . . There is no power relation without the correlative constitution of a field of knowledge, nor any knowledge that does not presuppose and constitute at the same time power relations" (Foucault 1977, 27).

Thus systems of knowledge that are developed as "objective" or "impartial" science can never really be what they claim to be. As children of colonial-expansionist capitalist systems, the academic community that would gaze upon and "know" the passive object can all too easily act to propitiate and further the power relations, land acquisition, and identity appropriation that enabled their work in the first place.

Occupying a place of privilege as we do, scholars within the academy need to be aware of the dominant modes of thought within which our tradition came into being and with which it continues to contend. The debate over Kennewick Man presents us with this challenge to cultivate an attitude of self-reflexive awareness. As members of the economic elite and participants in a colonizing power of political hegemony, scholars can no longer defend a strategic ignorance of our own position within power structures. We must recognize that when the body as such becomes visible to us, it does so "only under some particular gaze, including that of politics" (Riley 1988, 106). Our gaze as intellectuals is never a disembodied gaze, detached from political and economic agendas. We as scholars must scrutinize our own actions and arguments. What right do we have to subject our objects of study to our gaze? What and whose interests are we serving when doing so? And how are those questions and answers informed by our positioning as scholars of privilege?

This is not to suggest that Kennewick Man should be seen as merely a text, scribbled over with the graffiti of culturally relative narratives, none of which have any truth or grounding in reality. As many postmodern critiques have begun to point out, to abandon oneself to notions of cultural relativity and the social construction of everything brings one quickly to an impasse of cultural nihilism. Donna Haraway has argued that when cultural relativity is taken to the extreme, "We end up with a kind of epistemological electric shock therapy, which, far from ushering us into the high stakes tables of the game of contesting public truths, lays us out on the table with self-induced multiple personality disorder" (Haraway 1988, 578). The goal that Haraway suggests, a goal useful to us here, is to have both a "radical contingency for all knowledge claims . . . *and* a no-nonsense commitment to faithful accounts of a 'real' world, one that can be partially shared." She goes on to argue that the alternative to relativism "is not totalization and single vision, which is always finally the unmarked category whose power depends on systemic narrowing and obscuring. The alternative to relativism is *partial, locatable,* critical knowledges sustaining the possibility of webs of connections called solidarity in politics, and shared conversations in epistemology. . . . It is exactly in the politics and epistemology of partial perspectives that the possibility of sustained, rational, objective inquiry rests" (Haraway 1988, 579, 584).

What Haraway challenges above all is not any particular view of the body but what she calls "the god-trick," that is, "seeing everything from nowhere," the objectivity that much of Western science has made claim to. No sight, Haraway argues, is ever detached and disembodied. "All eyes . . . are active perceptual systems, building on translations and specific ways of seeing. . . . There is no unmediated photograph or passive camera obscura in scientific accounts of bodies and machines; there are only highly specific visual possibilities, each with a wonderfully detailed, active, partial way of organizing worlds" (Haraway 1988, 583). Haraway argues for objectivity that is embodied, objectivity that recognizes it is seen through the eyes of a body that is situated, that sees only partially, and that is positioned within a certain time and space. As she says: "I am arguing for the view from a body, always a complex, contradictory, structuring and structured body, versus the view from above, from nowhere, from simplicity. Only the god trick is forbidden" (Haraway 1988, 589).

The ideal is therefore not to deconstruct bodies out of existence or to suggest that the biological is merely a matter of philosophy. Rather, it is to suggest that culturally distinct agendas within inquiry be given equal value within discourse. When scholars recognize that our own arguments are as much a result of processes of situated construction as those voiced by the objects of study, we will begin the process of productive discourse. It is not, therefore, scientific discourse itself that poses a challenge to political reform but the objectification, dissection, and dismembering of Native identities and the cultivated blindness to the contributions of political hegemony and economic privilege that likewise act to construct our own discourse about the body. By challenging Native notions of identity, which are expressed within their narratives of creation, oral historic traditions, and place-based mythologies, Native peoples are deconstructed as subjects and neatly removed from the political arena. What Haraway's essay calls for in the Kennewick Man debate is that the parties involved recognize their place within a multicultural system of divergent worldviews. Objectivity within the sciences of archaeology and anthropology only exists to the degree that scholars recognize that only a small fragment of the "real" can be seen, and it is necessarily viewed through very embodied, very particularly situated lenses. In the case of Kennewick Man, it means recognizing one's own fixation with projected images of "Authentic Indians," one's failure to recognize contemporary Native Americans as legitimate heirs of their history and tradition, one's own search for Place, spatial legitimacy, and geopiety, and one's attempt to appropriate Native identities for one's own.

With this recognition of one's position as an embodied subject comes the recognition of others as subjects as well. When the god-trick is abandoned, one cannot claim to see or know the whole story. Out of necessity, others are asked to speak, to provide their piece to the greater puzzle. As Haraway argues: "Rational knowledge is power-sensitive conversation . . . ruled by partial sight and limited voice, not partiality for its own sake but, rather, for the sake of the connections and unexpected openings situated knowledges make possible" (Haraway 1988, 590). Zimmerman, following Arnold Krupat's use of the term *ethnocriticism,* defines an ethnocritical archaeology: "Ethnocriticism is concerned with differences rather than oppositions; it seeks to replace oppositional with dialogical models where cultural differences are explored and where interpretations are negotiated rather than declared" (Zimmerman, chap. 16, this volume).

The very presence of a bitter and long-winded court battle indicates that these notions of ethnocriticism, of embodied, situated objectivity, are not currently in effect. It also indicates that until now academics have preferred to declare rather than negotiate interpretations. Situated knowledge grants the object of study her or his own subjectivity, the voice to speak, to provide situated vision not available to the scholar. "Situated knowledges require that the object of knowledge be pictured as an actor and agent, not as a screen or ground or a resource, never finally as slave to the master that closes off the dialectic in his unique agency and his authorship of 'objective' knowledge" (Haraway 1988, 592). This means granting both living and deceased indigenous peoples both agency and subjectivity. It means treating Kennewick Man not merely as a bundle of bone to be radiocarbon dated and DNA to be deconstructed. It means facing the remains with the respect granted to a living human being, and it means granting Native peoples the semiotic sovereignty to speak for themselves, as subjects and not objects;

to provide their own equally valued notion of history, time, space, and ancestry.

The ability to name oneself, to assume a position of subjectivity, is an indicator of power and agency, a reversal in hierarchical systems of exploitation, and Kennewick Man is a revealing illustration of this process. The power to name, describe, and construct narratives around the body has come to be seen as an indicator of authority. To allow Native narratives to have equal voice and authenticity is to place Native use of language on an equal plane with that of Western Enlightenment empiricism and rationalism. To accept Native origin stories and historical narratives as being of equal value to those of Western science is thus to grant Native peoples *semiotic sovereignty* and as such to grant them subjectivity. It is not a question of who is correct or incorrect, but a matter of respecting the different embodied world views with which people approach their history. Like Kennewick Man, Native Americans have been subjected to study, as objects, throughout the history of their encounter with Euroamericans, and it is time they be granted the semiotic sovereignty to speak for themselves.

For too long academia has not treated Native people as subjects with languages and situated rational knowledge of their own. They have instead spoken with other languages, been told to see through eyes embodied by someone else. Cecil King has argued that the language of anthropology "traps us in linguistic cages because we must explain our ways through alien hypothetical constructs and theoretical frameworks. . . . We want to be consulted and respected as not only human beings, at the very least, but as independent nations, with the right to determine what transpires within our boundaries" (King 1997, 116, 118). Vine Deloria Jr. has argued much the same: "We have been the objects of scientific investigations and publications for too long, and it is our intent to become people once again, not specimens" (Deloria 1992, 595). Kennewick Man calls for a new understanding of ourselves as scholars, of the needs that drive our work, and the inspiration and fascination that guide the questions we ask and the narratives we construct. Finding place and understanding where we are situated within the land in which we live is an important task, one with profound spiritual and psychological consequences, not to mention political, economic, and academic ones. However, what the Kennewick Man debate shows us is that these need-driven searches for place cannot be done at the cost of some very basic principles, the most prominent being respect: respect for others' semiotic sovereignty and for every individual impacted by the work we do and the conclusions we draw. Wendell Johnson of the Colorado River Indian Tribe sums it up well: "The hell with federal laws. When it comes to dealing with people, there has to be that respect. . . . I think that's what this whole reburial thing centers around, is respect" (qtd. in Watson et al 1989, 40).[7]

Notes

1. See also two chapters in this volume: Larry Zimmerman, "A New and Different Archaeology?" (chap. 16), and Kurt E. Dongoske, "NAGPRA: A New Beginning, Not the End, for Osteological Analysis—A Hopi Perspective" (chap. 15).

2. This statement offers a stark contrast to the sentiment expressed by Grover Krantz of Washington State University: "What the Indians are doing is destroying evidence of their own history" (*Portland Oregonian,* October 14, 1996, A1).

3. See for example, Theodora Kroeber, *Ishi: A Biography of the Last Wild Indian in North America* (Los Angeles: University of California Press, 1967).

4. This can be seen among other theorists as well. Jane Gallop quotes Roland Barthes describing the body as "a bedrock given, prior to any subjectivity" (Ebert 1996, 243). And for Julia Kristeva, "the material is matter that exceeds the symbolic function, both the matter of the body and the matter of the objective world" (Hennessy 1993, 50). In much work, the body has thus been imaged as a "presymbolic, corporeal space cut off from the social workings of difference" (Hennessy 1993, 50).

5. David Cournoyer of Denver wrote in response to Chatters's reconstruction: "James Chatters, the anthropologist who reconstructed the face of the 9,300 year old skull known as Kennewick Man, likens his facial structure to that of Patrick Stewart, the 'Star Trek' actor. As an American Indian, I see the cheekbones and features of an American Indian" (*New York Times,* 4/8/98, A18). It would be hard to find a clearer illustration of the way in which bodies are constructed and read according to cultural, political, and economic positioning.

6. For a summary of the history of similar research within anthropology through the nineteenth century that contributed to racist traditions of eugenics and notions of racial evolution, see Robert E. Bieder, chap. 1, this volume.

7. As of 1 July 1999 Kennewick Man's bones have been transferred to the Burke Museum at the University of Washington for preliminary study to determine "cultural affiliation" and if the bones are indeed "Native American." Study has thus far been noninvasive and nondestructive. No conclusions have as of yet been made.

References

Berkhofer, Robert. 1978. *The White Man's Indian.* New York: Random House.
Biolsi, Thomas, and Larry Zimmerman. 1997. *Indians and Anthropologists: Vine Deloria Jr. and the Critique of Anthropology.* Tucson: University of Arizona Press.

Bordewich, Fergus M. 1996. *Killing the White Man's Indian: Reinventing Native Americans at the End of the Twentieth Century*. New York: Doubleday.

Butler, Judith. 1993. *Bodies That Matter*. New York: Routledge.

Deloria, Vine, Jr. 1992. "Indians, Archaeologists, and the Future." *American Antiquity* 57 (4): 595–98.

Ebert, Teresa. 1996. *Ludic Feminism and After: Postmodernism, Desire, and Labor in Late Capitalism*. Ann Arbor MI: Michigan University Press.

Foucault, Michel. 1977. *Discipline and Punish: The Birth of the Prison*. New York: Random House.

Griggers, Camilla. 1997. *Becoming-Woman*. Minneapolis: University of Minnesota Press.

Haraway, Donna. 1988. "Situated Knowledges: The Science Question in Feminism and the Privilege of Partial Perspective." *Feminist Studies* 14 (3): 575–99.

Hennessy, Rosemary. 1993. *Materialism, Feminism, and the Politics of Discourse*. New York: Routledge.

King, Cecil. 1997. "Here Come the Anthros." In Biolsi and Zimmerman 1997.

Kroeber, Theodora. 1967. *Ishi in Two Worlds: A Biography of the Last Wild Indian in North America*. Berkeley: University of California Press.

Marks, Jonathan. 1998. "Replaying the Race Card." *Anthropology Newsletter* 39 (5): 1–4.

McGuire, Randall. 1997. "Why Have Archaeologists Thought the Real Indians Were Dead, and What Can We Do About It?" In Biolsi and Zimmerman 1997.

———. 1992. "Archaeology and the First Americans." *American Anthropologist* 94 (4): 816–36.

McNallan, Stephen A. 1997. "Ancestral Bones: More on Kennewick Man." *Runestone* (18): 7–8.

Meighan, Clement. 1994. "Burying American Archaeology." *Archaeology* 47 (6): 64–68.

Parkhill, Thomas. 1997. *Weaving Ourselves into the Land: Charles Godfrey Leland, "Indians" and the Study of Native American Religions*. Albany: SUNY Press.

Preston, Donald. 1997. "The Lost Man." *New Yorker* 73 (16): 70–81.

Riley, Denise. 1988. *"Am I That Name?" Feminism and the Category of "Women" in History*. Minneapolis: University of Minnesota Press.

Rose, Wendy. 1992. "The Great Pretenders: Further Reflections on White Shamanism." In *The State of Native America: Genocide, Colonization and Resistance*, ed. M. Annette Jaimes. Boston: South End Press. 403–21.

Trafzer, Clifford E. 1997. *Death Stalks the Yakama*. East Lansing: Michigan State University Press.

Trigger, Bruce. 1980. "Archaeology and the Image of the American Indian." *American Antiquity* 45: 662–76.

Tuan, Yi-Fu. 1977. *Space and Place: The Perspective of Experience*. Minneapolis: University of Minnesota Press.

Turner, Christy. 1986. "What Is Lost with Skeletal Reburial." *Archaeology* 7: 1

Turner, Frederick W., III. 1971. *I Have Spoken: American History through the Voices of Indians*. Athens OH: Swallow Press.

Watson, Norman, et al. 1989. "The Present Past: An Examination of Archaeological and Native American Thinking." In *Thinking across Cultures: The Third International Conference of Thinking,* ed. Donald Topping, Doris Crowell, and Victor Kobayashi. Hove NJ: Lawrence Erlbaum Associates. 33–42.

Zimmerman, Larry. 1997. "Anthropology and Responses to the Reburial Issue." In Biolsi and Zimmerman 1997.

——. 1994. "Sharing Control of the Past." *Archaeology* 47 (6): 65–68.

——. 1992. "Archaeology, Reburial, and the Tactics of a Discipline's Self Delusion." *American Indian Culture and Research Journal* 16 (2): 37–56.

Part 4

Studies in Resolution

13

T. J. Ferguson, Roger Anyon, and Edmund J. Ladd

Repatriation at the Pueblo of Zuni

Diverse Solutions to Complex Problems

The Pueblo of Zuni has been actively involved in the repatriation of cultural property and human remains since 1977, long before the passage of the Native American Graves Protection and Repatriation Act of 1990.[1] Several key elements of the Zuni position regarding repatriation were incorporated into the act. The Zuni War Gods were mentioned by name as an exemplar of cultural patrimony to be covered by the law during the Senate hearings that preceded its passage.[2] During the last eighteen years it has become clear that repatriation is not a monolithic issue, even where the cultural concerns of a single tribe are considered. While the Pueblo of Zuni has sought repatriation of some materials to resolve problems defined by tribal religious leaders, it also has declined or deferred the repatriation of other materials.

The complexity of repatriation issues at the Pueblo of Zuni is illustrated by comparing the tribe's effort to recover stolen *Ahayu:da* (Zuni War Gods) with its approach to the management of other cultural property and human remains. The rationale and the diverse approaches employed by the Pueblo of Zuni demonstrate why the Zuni Tribe seeks a case-by-case resolution of repatriation issues. Since other tribes and museums are currently grappling with many of the issues the Pueblo of Zuni already has addressed, Zuni activities can provide instructive examples of successful repatriation. The Zuni experience with repatriation should be examined by everyone interested in NAGPRA's implementation.

The Repatriation of *Ahayu:da*

Ahayu:da are twin deities with great power. They are associated with prowess and physical skill, and they also serve as protectors of the Zuni people.

Many non-Zunis refer to *Ahayu:da* as "War Gods," but their role in Zuni culture encompasses a much wider range of concerns than simply war. Images of the *Ahayu:da* are created in the form of cylindrical wood sculptures at the winter solstice and for the less frequent ceremonies held to initiate new Bow Priests or commemorate the Bow Priesthood. Members of the Deer Clan cooperate in the creation of *Uyuyewi,* the elder brother War God, while members of the Bear Clan undertake the creation of *Ma'a'sewi,* the younger brother. The term *Ahayu:da* refers to the twin gods collectively or to a single God in a generic context. After their creation, the *Ahayu:da* are entrusted to Bow Priests who install them at two of a series of shrines surrounding Zuni Pueblo determined by a ritual sequence of rotation. When the newly created *Ahayu:da* are set in the shrines they replace the previously installed deities, which are respectfully placed on an adjacent pile of "retired" War Gods. These retired *Ahayu:da* retain an important role in Zuni ritual. All *Ahayu:da* are to remain at their shrines exposed to natural elements until they disintegrate and return to the earth.

Over the last century many *Ahayu:da* have been removed from their shrines. Some were taken in the belief that they were discarded and had no further value to the Zuni people; others were knowingly stolen to sell to museums or art collectors. Once removed from their shrines, the *Ahayu:da* cannot be supplicated by Zuni religious leaders. The Zuni people believe the removal of the War Gods causes war, violence, and natural disasters.[3] By the 1970s the removal of *Ahayu:da* from Zuni lands had resulted in such severe problems that Zuni religious leaders decided action was needed to remedy the situation.

In 1978 the leaders of the Deer and Bear Clans and the Bow Priests reached a consensus on how to resolve the problems created by the wrongful removal of *Ahayu:da*—all of the War Gods removed from Zuni lands must be returned to their shrines. In quick succession the Zuni Tribe requested the return of *Ahayu:da* from the Denver Art Museum, the Smithsonian Institution's National Museum of Natural History, and an auction at Sotheby Parke-Bernet in New York City. The Zuni Tribal Council enacted Tribal Resolution No. M70-78-991 recognizing the decision-making authority of the Zuni religious leaders regarding sacred artifacts and formally committing the tribal council to provide administrative assistance in negotiating with outside institutions. Technical assistance from attorneys at the Indian Pueblo Legal Services and anthropologists at the Zuni Archaeology Program was used to define and articulate the legal and historical issues that formed the basis of the Zunis' request for repatriation of the *Ahayu:da.*[4]

Three basic principles were articulated: (1) the *Ahayu:da* are communally owned; (2) no one has the authority to remove them from their shrines, therefore any *Ahayu:da* removed from its shrine has been stolen or illegally removed; and (3) the *Ahayu:da* need to be returned to their proper place in the ongoing Zuni religion. Anthropological research showed that these principles have a long historical continuity. Their expression in modern legal terms was not simply a recent conceptualization. The effort to recover an *Ahayu:da* from auction at Sotheby Parke-Bernet in New York was based on a legal theory invoking 18 U.S.C. § 1163, a federal law that makes it a criminal act to possess stolen tribal property. Given that the *Ahayu:da* are communally owned, the Zuni Tribe maintains they are tribal property covered by 18 U.S.C. § 1163. Since this legal theory has never been tested in litigation involving the *Ahayu:da,* no legal precedent has been established in its use with respect to cultural property. In retrospect, however, it seems that a number of institutions and private collectors thought the theory was strong enough that they did not want legally to contest the Zunis in pre-NAGPRA requests for repatriation.

For cultural and political reasons the Zunis preferred to approach museums on ethical and humanitarian grounds, saving litigation as a last resort that, it turned out, was never needed. In Zuni culture a reasonable person with a grievance goes to an adversary four time to attempt a peaceable resolution of the problem. Only after this good-faith attempt at resolution is made should stronger action be taken. This cultural precept was applied to museums and other parties, and as a result the Zunis phrased their initial requests for the return of *Ahayu:da* primarily in humanistic rather than legal terms. Other factors involved in determining the fundamental approach to repatriation stemmed from the realization that many of the ongoing problems with the theft of cultural property are tied to an illicit art market. Museums can potentially play an important role in educating private collectors about the ethics of not collecting or trafficking in stolen artifacts. In addition, the Pueblo of Zuni had a long-term goal of instituting a tribal museum and cultural center and did not want to alienate the established museums that the tribe hoped eventually would provide technical assistance and loans of appropriate material.[5]

After repatriation of the *Ahayu:da* from the auction at Sotheby Parke-Bernet, several meetings were held between the Zuni Tribe and the Denver Art Museum. In 1980 the Denver Art Museum decided to return the three *Ahayu:da* in its collection, formally recognizing that the Zunis considered the *Ahayu:da* to be an animate deity crucial to the performance of their religion rather than a symbol or art object and that as communal property the *Ahayu:da* could not have been legally sold or given away. Soon thereafter

Table 1

Ahayu:da Repatriated to the Pueblo of Zuni

Year	Institution or Collection	Number
1978	private collection, Sotheby Parke-Bernet auction	1
1980	Denver Art Museum	3
1980	Wheelwright Museum	2
1980	Museum of New Mexico	4
1981	Millicent Rogers Museum	1
1981	University of Iowa Museum of Art	1
1984	private collection, Tucson, Arizona	1
1985	Tulsa Zoological Society	1
1987	Smithsonian Institution, National Museum of Natural History	2
1987	Morningstar Gallery, Santa Fe, New Mexico	2
1988	Warhol collection, Sotheby Parke-Bernet auction	1
1988	Beloit College, Logan Museum of Anthropology	3
1988	Milwaukee Public Museum	2
1989	Southwest Museum	2
1990	Redrock State Park, Gallup, New Mexico	2
1990	Winnipeg Art Gallery, Winnipeg, Canada	1
1990	American Museum of Natural History	1
1990	Museum of the American Indian, Heye Foundation	2
1990	Hudson Museum, University of Maine	1
1990	Alvin Abrams/First Philadelphia Corporation collection	1
1990	Lowie Museum of Anthropology, University of California, Berkeley	1
1990	private collection, San Francisco	1
1990	Taylor Museum, Colorado Springs Fine Arts Center	1
1990	Arizona State Museum, University of Arizona	1
1990	Pauline Kivea, private collection, Santa Fe, New Mexico	1
1990	Courtney Sale Ross and Steven J. Ross collection, New York	1
1990	University Museum, University of Pennsylvania	1
1991	Denver Museum of Natural History	6
1991	Public Museum of Grand Rapids	1
1991	Ramona Morris, private collection, Woodside, California	1
1991	Rick Dillingham, private collection, Santa Fe, New Mexico	1
1991	Nelson-Atkins Museum of Art, Kansas City, Missouri	1
1991	Brooklyn Museum	13
1991	San Diego Museum of Man	1
1991	Lois Flury collection, Seattle	2
1991	North Carolina Museum of Art, Raleigh	1
1992	anonymous private collector (sent to tribal building)	1
1992	Chicago Art Institute	1
1993	Peabody Museum of Archaeology & Ethnology, Harvard University	1
1993	Portland Art Museum	1

Table 1
Continued

Year	Institution or Collection	Number
1993	Iowa Natural History Museum	1
1994	Rex Arrowsmith, private collection, Santa Fe, New Mexico	2
1994	Tad Anderman, private collection, Corrales, New Mexico	1
1994	Will Hershey, private collection, California	1
1994	anonymous private collection	2
1995	Metropolitan Museum of Art	1
Total		80

three museums in New Mexico voluntarily returned seven *Ahayu:da,* and two institutions in Iowa and Oklahoma voluntarily returned another two *Ahayu:da.* In addition, a private collector in Arizona also voluntarily returned an *Ahayu:da* (table 1).

The Zuni Tribe's negotiation for the repatriation of two *Ahayu:da* from the Smithsonian Institution's National Museum of Natural History took nine years.[6] This negotiation entailed numerous meetings at the Smithsonian Institution and Zuni Pueblo, copious correspondence, and the preparation of extensive reports by both the museum and the tribe. The Smithsonian agreed in principle relatively early in the process that the museum did not and could not have legal title to the *Ahayu:da* and would therefore return them. The protracted nature of the negotiations was due in large measure to the Smithsonian's request to broaden the negotiation from a specific request for the *Ahayu:da* to a more comprehensive set of recommendations from Zuni that could be used to manage the entire Zuni collection.

This was a genuine and well-intentioned attempt to sustain a dialogue and deal comprehensively with an entire collection. The Smithsonian Institution funded a delegation of Zuni religious leaders who spent three days at the National Museum of Natural History in 1978 examining the Zuni collection and conferring with museum officials (figure 1). At first the idea of making comprehensive recommendations about the entire Zuni collection seemed bureaucratically efficient, but over the years a lack of consensus at Zuni about the classification and disposition of much of the cultural property made it difficult to make decisions. In addition to the two clans and the Bow Priesthood that had requested the repatriation of the *Ahayu:da,* every religious organization at Zuni had to be consulted, including six kivas, twelve medicine societies, and a number of other clans and priesthoods. In 1987 the Smithsonian Institution decided to return the *Ahayu:da* and agreed with the Pueblo of Zuni to table all further discussion

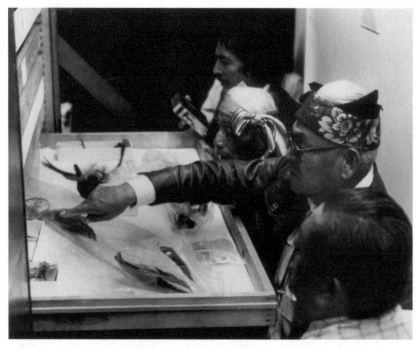

Figure 1. Edmund J. Ladd, Allen Kallestewa, Alonzo Hustito, and Chester Ma-
hooty examine the curation of Zuni cultural property at the National Museum of
Natural History, Smithsonian Institution, in 1978. Photograph by and courtesy of
T. J. Ferguson.

until such time that the Zuni Tribe reopened negotiations. NAGPRA has
now superseded that agreement and will necessitate further consideration
of the issues at Zuni Pueblo.[7]

Several things are striking in the Zuni experience with the National
Museum of Natural History. First is the great expense of the negotiation.
The administrative cost of correspondence, archiving of documents, transfer of activities between tribal council administrations, meetings, and
travel placed a serious burden on the meager resources of the tribe. This
precluded initiating negotiations with other museums. The Zuni Tribe
wanted to finish what it had begun with one museum before starting
negotiations with other institutions. Throughout the period of negotiation
with the Smithsonian Institution, the Zuni Tribe continued to respond to
other museums and private collectors who voluntarily offered to repatriate
Ahayu:da. It was not until the War Gods were returned from the National
Museum of Natural History in 1987, however, that the Zunis mounted a
comprehensive campaign to recover all *Ahayu:da* that can be found.

This campaign was initiated in 1988 after the Zunis blocked a second attempt by Sotheby Parke-Bernet to auction an *Ahayu:da,* recovering the artifact offered for sale by the Warhol Foundation.[8] The United States Department of Justice provided legal counsel for the Zuni Tribe in this endeavor. In addition, in 1988 the Logan Museum of Anthropology and the Milwaukee Public Museum voluntarily returned five *Ahayu:da.* These repatriations fueled interest at the Pueblo of Zuni in developing a coordinated effort to recover *Ahayu:da,* an effort that would avoid repeatedly having to prove and reprove the basic facts that justify repatriation.

At the beginning of this campaign the Zuni Tribal Council requested that the Institute of the North American West prepare a report that summarized the history of the tribe's repatriation of *Ahayu:da* from 1977 to 1988 and provide a list of all *Ahayu:da* known to be in museums and private collections.[9] This report was intended to provide the Tribal Council with the information needed to secure legal representation from the Department of Justice. Although the Zunis were committed to requesting that museums return *Ahayu:da* for religious and humanitarian reasons, the tribe recognized that deaccessioning museum artifacts is always a legal process. The Zuni Tribal Council thought it best to have parity in repatriation negotiations: if museums had legal counsel, so should the tribe.

In 1989, as a result of inquiries made during research for the report requested by the Zuni Tribal Council, the Southwest Museum decided to repatriate the two *Ahayu:da* remaining in its collection. Upon completion of the Institute of the NorthAmerican West's report to the Zuni Tribal Council, the Department of the Interior's Office of the Field Solicitor decided to act as the tribe's legal counsel, calling upon the Department of Justice only when its assistance was needed to recover *Ahayu:da* from private collections. At the request of the Zuni Tribe, the Institute of the NorthAmerican West continued to contribute professional assistance from 1989 to 1995, even though the Office of the Field Solicitor and the Zuni Tribe could not pay for these services.

Repatriation of *Ahayu:da* after NAGPRA

The passage of NAGPRA in 1990 added momentum to the Zunis' campaign to repatriate War Gods. Since 1990, fifty-four *Ahayu:da* have been repatriated from thirty-two museums and private collectors (table 1). In 1990 and 1991 there was a substantial increase in the number of parties returning *Ahayu:da* (figure 2). This was due in part to the fact that many museums sought to establish repatriation procedures in their institutions by negotiating the return of War Gods to the Zuni Tribe. Staff members at several museums ac-

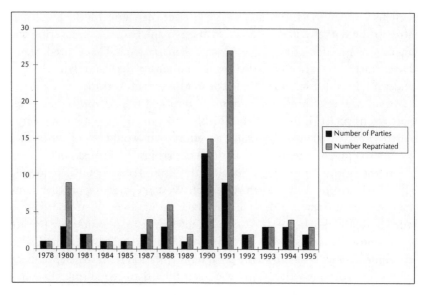

Figure 2. Number of parties returning *Ahayu:da* (filled bars) and number of re-patriated *Ahayu:da* (unfilled bars), 1978–95, by year.

knowledged that they chose to do this because the issues were well-defined, the Zunis have a reputation for being reasonable in negotiations, and the museums wanted to develop procedures in a nonconfrontational setting. The Pueblo of Zuni is well known among museum professionals as a tribe committed to resolving issues in a manner mutually satisfying to all parties. The Zuni Tribe has established this reputation at the same time it has steadfastly maintained that the repatriation of *Ahayu:da* is the only accept-able solution to the spiritual problems of concern to tribal religious leaders.

The success of the Zuni Tribe in repatriating *Ahayu:da* is due in large measure to its concentrated efforts, its quiet approach which has stressed gentle yet persuasive dialogue rather than confrontation, and its willing-ness to explain its concerns to non-Indians.[10] The Pueblo of Zuni has made substantial progress toward achieving its goal of recovering all its stolen *Ahayu:da*. Since 1978 a total of eighty *Ahayu:da* have been returned in forty-six transfers. To date, all the *Ahayu:da* the tribe knows about in the United States have either been recovered or their return currently is being negotiated. The tribe anticipates there are other *Ahayu:da* in museums and private collections in the United States and intends to pursue these re-patriations as they are discovered. In addition, one *Ahayu:da* has been returned from a foreign art museum, and the Zunis are beginning to pursue additional international repatriations.

Recovery of War Gods from Private Collectors

NAGPRA's passage clearly has helped the Zunis obtain their goals of repatriating the *Ahayu:da*. Private collectors and art dealers with *Ahayu:da* removed from Zuni prior to the passage of NAGPRA, however, are not bound by the provisions of that law. The Zunis have continued to seek the return of *Ahayu:da* from private parties using a humanitarian rationale in their initial contact with the collectors. In letters and other communication with private collectors, the Zuni Tribe has presented a persuasive case for why the *Ahayu:da* should be returned. Many collectors responded favorably on this basis alone and immediately returned the *Ahayu:da*. Since 1990 the Zunis have recovered fifteen *Ahayu:da* from twelve collectors, bringing the total number of War Gods repatriated from private collectors since 1978 to twenty.

Since 1990 only a few collectors have refused to immediately return *Ahayu:da* upon receiving a request from the Zuni Tribal Council. These collectors needed additional encouragement from the Zuni Tribe's legal counsel, who provided that impetus by beginning the preliminary procedures needed to litigate the issues if the *Ahayu:da* were not returned. When collectors seemed disinclined to voluntarily return *Ahayu:da,* the Zuni Tribal Council has urged the Office of the Field Solicitor to seek assistance from the Department of Justice in applying 18 U.S.C. § 1163 in the recovery of the War Gods. As in the period preceding NAGPRA, no private collector confronted with the Zuni's legal theory has wanted to challenge the Zuni Tribe in litigation, so the use of 18 U.S.C. § 1163 as a legal precedent remains untested. Even so, given the relatively weak penalties associated with violation of NAGPRA, 18 U.S.C. § 1163 remains a potentially useful tool for tribes seeking to recover communally owned cultural property stolen from tribal lands.

Diversity of Needs, Diversity of Approaches

Both institutions and tribes will, by necessity, develop a diversity of approaches in implementing repatriation. Institutional approaches will vary for many reasons, including the philosophical and political views of the governing bodies and staff, differing charters and bylaws, and differential access to the resources needed to support repatriation. These variables, along with diverse cultural factors, also will affect how individual tribes approach repatriation.

The diversity of approaches that can be taken with respect to repatriation are illustrated by the various ways the *Ahayu:da* have been returned to the

Figure 3. Bow Priest Perry Tsadiasi leaves the Laboratory of Anthropology, Museum of New Mexico, in Santa Fe following transfer of *Ahayu:da* repatriated by the North Carolina Museum of Art and a private collector in 1991. Edmund J. Ladd is visible in the doorway. Photograph by and courtesy of T. J. Ferguson.

Pueblo of Zuni. Some museums, like the Museum of New Mexico, the Wheelwright Museum, the Southwest Museum, and the Denver Museum of Natural History, have voluntarily returned *Ahayu:da* on the basis of what publicly was known about the Zuni Tribe's concerns. Other museums, like the Nelson-Atkins Museum of Art and the Brooklyn Museum, have requested the tribe formally answer questions about the authenticity of the artifacts as War Gods, the veracity of the Zunis' claims that the *Ahayu:da* are communally owned, the fact they were taken from Zuni shrines, and their contemporary use and context. To adequately answer these questions the Zuni Tribe found it advantageous to use an anthropologist to prepare expert reports drawing upon interviews with religious leaders and a review of published and archival documents.[11]

The actual transfer of *Ahayu:da* has run a gamut of approaches. At one end is the anonymous party who sent an *Ahayu:da* to the Zuni Tribe through the mail in 1992, causing consternation to tribal employees who opened the package since they are not ritually authorized to touch the artifact and because the *Ahayu:da* had not been ceremonially purified before arriving on tribal land. In the middle are museums that have shipped *Ahayu:da* to the Museum of New Mexico, which then held the artifacts until Zuni religious leaders could travel to Santa Fe to retrieve them (figure 3). At the other end are the repatriations involving travel of a Zuni delegation to a museum returning *Ahayu:da,* where an appropriately ceremonious transfer of the artifact is effected.

The preferred means for transferring *Ahayu:da* is for Zuni religious leaders to travel to the War Gods and hand-carry them back to Zuni, but the reality of limited travel funds sometimes precludes this. To retrieve the forty-one *Ahayu:da* returned in 1990 and 1991, the Zuni Tribe obtained grants from the Seventh Generation Fund and the Frost Foundation. Such funding is not always available to tribes, so the type of cooperative arrangement the Zuni Tribe has with the Museum of New Mexico is a community service that other museums should consider. By assisting the Zuni Tribe with interinstitutional transfers and temporary curation of artifacts, the Museum of New Mexico substantially reduces the costs of all parties involved in the physical transfer of repatriated material.

Repatriation of Sensitive Materials at the Museum of New Mexico

With respect to Zuni cultural property other than the *Ahayu:da,* the impetus for repatriation largely has come from museums rather than Zuni religious leaders. The need to respond to museum inquiries about the proper care and curation of cultural property undoubtedly will increase as the provisions of NAGPRA are implemented. The activities of the Museum of New Mexico, initiated before the passage of NAGPRA, provide a positive model of how to resolve issues raised by museums.

In 1987 the Museum of New Mexico established an ad hoc committee to consider issues relating to the identification and curation of sensitive cultural materials and human remains. In 1989 this committee was made a permanent standing committee composed of curators and administrators from the Museums of Fine Arts, History, Anthropology, and Folk Art, as well as archaeologists in the Office of Archaeological Studies.[12] Soon thereafter, the director of the Museum of New Mexico wrote to the governor of the Pueblo of Zuni informing him that the museum had artifacts and human remains whose curation was potentially a sensitive issue to the Zuni Tribe. The museum requested a consultation with the tribe concerning these items. To determine which items in the museum's collections were sensitive, the museum's curator of ethnology, Edmund J. Ladd, used a classification of Zuni cultural patrimony from a 1981 statement that the Pueblo of Zuni issued to the Smithsonian Institution regarding the proper care of museum collections.[13]

Four classes of sensitive artifacts were recognized. Class I was "highly sensitive" items communally owned by the tribe and illegally removed from Zuni lands, for example, the *Ahayu:da*. Class II included "very sensitive" items removed from Zuni lands without the consent of the religious society or priesthood responsible for their care and maintenance, for example, dance masks used by kiva leaders and some fetishes. Class III included "less sensitive" items of special concern for which specific curatorial treatment is recommended, for example, "replica" masks and prayersticks. Class IV included items that are "not sensitive," for example, dance paraphernalia, household items, and pottery. Using this classification, Ladd and his staff determined that only 123 items out of the approximately 24,000 objects in the museum's Zuni collection were potentially sensitive. The four *Ahayu:da* that the Museum of New Mexico had in its collection had been voluntarily repatriated in 1980, so the focus of the consultation was on other items of cultural patrimony.

To effect the consultation, the Museum of New Mexico invited a delegation of five Zuni religious leaders and two members of the Zuni Tribal Council to Santa Fe to survey the entire collection, including the 123 items identified as potentially sensitive. The Zuni delegation identified 23 items that concerned them and returned to Zuni Pueblo to confer with the appropriate religious leaders responsible for those objects. In 1990 a second delegation of the appropriate religious leaders visited the museum and determined that the items identified by the first delegation were indeed sensitive and should be returned to the Zuni Tribe. The entire consultation and repatriation process took two and a half years to complete and required two trips to the museum and several meetings at Zuni to make sure the proper religious leaders were consulted. When the process was completed the Zuni Tribe repatriated less than 20 percent of the items the museum had identified as sensitive.

Involvement of the Proper Zuni Authorities in the Decision-Making Process

At the Pueblo of Zuni the questions of what should be repatriated, why it should be repatriated, to whom it should be repatriated, and what should be done with it once it is repatriated are complicated issues. With six kivas, twelve medicine societies, fourteen clans, and several other religious groups and priesthoods, an enormous amount of discussion must be conducted within the tribe before any decisions can be made regarding repatriation. Zuni political leaders cannot make decisions about religious artifacts in museums, and Zuni religious leaders can only make decisions about the things for which they are personally responsible. Each societal group must find its own way of dealing with repatriation for items that are its own responsibility. They must also, if it is appropriate, identify the individual who is responsible for a certain item or set of items, and these people must then decide how to conclude the repatriation process.

Past experience at Zuni has shown that no single delegation can ever adequately represent all the Zuni religious groups. The initial delegations that inspect museum collections must return to Zuni Pueblo and meet with other religious leaders to seek their input. This was necessary in 1978 when a delegation of four Zunis inspected the Zuni collection at the National Museum of Natural History. The process took several years to complete. Similarly, in 1991 a delegation of four Zunis viewed the Zuni collection at the National Museum of the American Indian. After this trip the delegation returned to Zuni Pueblo, where the members met with twenty-five other religious leaders to discuss what they saw.[14] Additional meetings with various groups of religious leaders have been held to discuss the collection, and one or more additional visits to the museum with different religious leaders may be needed to gather the information necessary to make informed decisions about the proper care and curation of the collection.

The number of visits to museums and meetings in Zuni Pueblo needed to engage the proper Zuni authorities must be discouraging at times to non-Zunis because it seems like a redundant process. On different occasions, museums are asked to provide the same information to different Zuni political and religious leaders. Given the structure of the Zuni decision-making process, however, there is no alternative, and museums have to accept this. Repetition is an important part of the cultural repertoire of Zuni behavior, so museums should use requests for what seems like redundant consultation as an opportunity to make sure the issues are understood and presented to the proper authorities. Museums should not forget that their negotiations with the Zuni Tribe are a cross-cultural endeavor and normal museum and Zuni practices both may need to be modified.

Even though specific individuals often determine the approach to and the method of repatriation, the items in question sometimes belong to religious groups or the Zuni Tribe as a whole. This is the case with the *Ahayu:da,* and there are other special esoteric objects that also have a collective ownership. All *koko* (Kachina) dance masks, for instance, are "owned" by the individuals for whom they are made.[15] These individuals have the right to "sell" their masks to other tribal members, but they do so at the risk of shortening their lives and not being able to participate in *koko* dances in the afterworld. No Zuni has the right to alienate *koko* dance masks by selling or transferring them to people outside the tribe.

While the Zuni Tribal Council does not condone the transfer of individually owned ceremonial material to non-Indians, the Zuni Tribe has been reluctant to endorse the repatriation of individually owned religious items. At present, sensitive curatorial treatment of individually owned sacred objects is requested in lieu of repatriation. Regardless of an individual's right to dispose of his personal religious paraphernalia to other Zunis, most Zunis feel extremely sad when they see these objects curated in museum collections. Most Zunis find the curation of all ceremonial materials in museums to be repugnant. Since Zunis believe these ritual items should never be studied by non-Zunis nor placed on public exhibit, they see no reason why museums would want to retain them in their collections. Ritual objects are gifts to the spirits and should be allowed to disintegrate.

Many Zunis will offer personal opinions about the disposition of ceremonial objects in museum collections but at the same time assiduously avoid usurping the authority of the proper religious leaders to make the ultimate determination about repatriation. The lines of authority for making decisions about such objects often are blurred when it is not clear whether a museum is asking for a personal or an authoritative opinion about a particular object. The nuances in the form of the questions and the semantics of the answers often are more subtle than they first appear. Consultation about museum collections is thus an intellectually difficult process for all parties and should not be rushed. Questions sometimes need to be asked several times in several different ways to make sure the right people provide well-informed answers. It is a time-consuming process.

The cultural property of extinct religious societies is problematical since there are no living authorities to answer questions about repatriation. Some of these ceremonial objects may not even be touched by Zunis who have not been properly initiated, which means there are no living people who could physically handle the objects if they are repatriated. To date, the Zuni Tribe rarely has requested the repatriation of property belonging to extinct religious groups. The one documented exception was the 1990 Museum of New Mexico repatriation of ritual paraphernalia belonging to the *Lhewe:kwe* (Sword Swallowing Society). In this instance the Zuni religious leaders felt they had the ritual authority and obligation ceremonially to retire this material according to Zuni custom.

At Zuni Pueblo the policy of the Zuni Tribal Council recognizes the right of Zuni religious leaders to make decisions about religious issues, including the repatriation of ceremonial material.[16] The role of the Zuni Tribal Council is to provide administrative support and act as a liaison between Zuni religious leaders and museums. This division of labor provides a well-established point of contact for museums that request information from the tribe and also incorporates the traditional authority structure. Museums that deal with the Pueblo of Zuni are thus assured that they are dealing with the proper Zuni authorities.

The Issue of "Replicas" and "Models"

The Zunis' criteria of what is "real" and what is a "replica" or "model" differ from that of non-Indians. The Zuni religious leaders consider all "replicas" to be sensitive artifacts that should be repatriated. Of the twenty-three items selected as sensitive enough to repatriate from the Museum of New Mexico, eighteen were replica masks made from cardboard and clearly never used in religious ceremonies. They were nonetheless of concern to the Zuni religious leaders because of the information incorporated in their construction. The religious leaders also were concerned that these objects were made for exhibition and were thus intended to be viewed out of context.

The Zunis were first faced with the issue of replica religious paraphernalia in the 1950s when a group of Colorado Boy Scouts was discovered making full-sized models of *Shalako* masks for use in mock ceremonial dances.[17] The Zuni Tribe expressed its concerns to the Boy Scouts, which eventually led to the transfer of the masks to Zuni religious leaders and the cessation of their replication and use in Boy Scout activities. This incident was cited by Zuni leaders when the Smithsonian Institution questioned the reasoning of the Zuni governor who requested that "replica" masks be taken off display at the National Museum of Natural History in 1970.[18] Zuni leaders still have an oral history of the Boy Scout incident that is invoked whenever a museum questions Zuni concerns about items the museum does not think are "authentic."

"Replicas," whether made by Zunis specifically for museum collections or by non-Zunis for other purposes, are considered to have a "reality" not recognized by non-Indians. One of the key issues is the information inherent in the masks. The "replicas" were made either by Zuni people with access to esoteric information or by other people using masks made by Zuni priests as their model. In either event, the masks embody knowledge and power that many Zunis consider to be proprietary to Zuni religious organizations. Even the display of ersatz masks in museums should not be seen by uninitiated people, especially young Zunis. Some Zuni leaders also question why museums would want to curate "fake" items in their collections when these items should not be displayed out of context. Zunis think they have little research value.

While the Zuni religious leaders are willing to listen to and consider the justifications presented by museums for the curation of any object, they ask that the museums give them an equal chance to articulate their concerns. Zuni leaders think that only the Zuni people have the ability to decide what objects are of concern to the Zuni Tribe and why. The ways that non-Indians and Indians think often are strikingly different. The Zunis ask for parity in the different cultural systems used during museum negotiations concerning repatriation. Some "replica" masks and similar "models" of religious artifacts are sensitive enough that many Zuni religious leaders think they should be repatriated so they can be properly disposed of by Zuni religious authorities.

Proper Use and Disposition of Repatriated Artifacts

Once artifacts are repatriated to the Zuni Tribe, the Zuni religious leaders return them to the use for which they were created. In the case of some artifacts and "replicas," the objects are ritually disposed of according to Zuni precepts. Museum concepts of curatorial conservation and preservation do not always pertain to religious objects. Many artifacts like the *Ahayu:da* are intended to be placed at open shrines and eventually disintegrate into the earth. That is the natural course of things, and the Zunis do not think humans should intervene in the process. As the Zunis say, "All things will eat themselves up."

When the Zuni Tribe began to repatriate *Ahayu:da,* many museums initially said they would be willing to make permanent loans of ceremonial material to a Zuni tribal museum if and when such a facility existed. The Zuni leaders patiently explained to these museums that the ceremonial material the tribe sought to have repatriated did not belong in any museum, especially a museum in Zuni. These were religious objects whose return was requested for religious reasons. The Zunis have insisted they have the right to use or dispose of these objects according to Zuni custom, even when this conflicts with non-Indian values of preservation. The legal documents the Zunis execute when accepting repatriated artifacts clearly establish that museums give up all claims to the objects, freeing the Zunis to do whatever is culturally appropriate with the artifacts.

Tribal Responsibility for Protection of Repatriated Material

While some repatriated objects are ritually disposed of according to Zuni custom, the Zuni leaders are nonetheless concerned about security. The Denver Art Museum, the first museum to repatriate *Ahayu:da,* pointed out that they could not return the War Gods in good conscience unless the Zuni Tribe had a commitment to ensuring that they were not stolen again. The Denver Art Museum maintained that it would be a shame for these valued objects to be removed from the Zuni Indian Reservation a second time and end up in an illicit art market. With the help of the Denver Art Museum, the Zuni Tribe designed and constructed a secure facility that met Zuni cultural requirements for open exposure to the weather and elements. All repatriated *Ahayu:da* have been returned to this facility, which has provided the protection desired by both museums and the Zuni Tribe.

The protection of unsecured shrines elsewhere on the Zuni Indian Reservation is still a major law enforcement problem. In 1990 three *Ahayu:da* were stolen from an unprotected shrine.[19] The investigation of this theft by law enforcement agencies was constrained by the fact that the Zuni Tribe did not have photographs or other documentation of the stolen artifacts. To remedy this situation, the Zuni Archaeology Program obtained a grant from the Chamisa Foundation that funded the creation of an inventory of artifacts at *Ahayu:da* shrines on the reservation.[20] It is hoped that the results of this project will deter thefts and provide material assistance should thefts occur in the future.

Ultimately, however, the Zuni Tribe holds that theft of religious materials from shrines on the reservation is as much an educational problem as a law enforcement problem. While federal legislation that protects cultural property is welcomed, the Zuni Tribe argues that museums also should do more to educate non-Indians about appropriate ethics in the collection of Indian "art" and about the direct connection between the art market and thefts of cultural property. No ceremonial objects would be stolen if no one was willing to buy them. The fact that Zuni people occasionally are involved in these thefts makes them even more tragic. The Zunis involved in thefts of cultural property often are suffering from alcoholism or other social problems and are mercilessly used by non-Indians who supply the illicit art market.

The Zuni Tribe has accepted the responsibility to provide as much security as it can for repatriated artifacts and has a commitment legally to prosecute anyone involved in the theft of cultural property. The Pueblo of Zuni considers the provision of security for repatriated artifacts to be a fundamental tribal responsibility inherent in repatriation of cultural property.

Cultural Patrimony Other Than Indigenous Religious Artifacts

The interest in repatriating cultural property at Zuni Pueblo sometimes encompasses more than indigenous religious artifacts. In the late 1980s a Zuni artist painting murals in the *Nuestra Senora de Guadalupe de Zuni,* a restored seventeenth-century Catholic church in the center of Zuni Pueblo, expressed to several people his concerns about art removed from the church a century before by officials of the Smithsonian Institution. This Zuni artist wanted the art returned to Zuni Pueblo. This eventually led the Zuni Tribal Council to commission a report from the Institute of the NorthAmerican West documenting how these artifacts were removed from Zuni Pueblo.[21]

At issue were a painted hide depicting Our Lady of Guadalupe dating to about 1725 and two *bultos* (sculptures of saints) carved about 1775 by Miera y Pacheco, a famous Spanish cartographer and artist. Historical research documented that in 1879 Matilda Coxe Stevenson, a member of a Smithsonian Institution collecting expedition, removed these artifacts without the permission of Zuni authorities. After reviewing this research, the Zuni Tribal Council requested the repatriation of these artifacts. Even though they are Catholic icons, the Zuni Tribe considers them to be the cultural patrimony of the Zuni people since the artifacts were removed from a Catholic mission that had reverted to tribal ownership in the early nineteenth century.

The Smithsonian Institution agreed with the Zuni Tribal Council and in 1991 approved the repatriation of the artifacts to the Zuni Tribe.[22] Unfortunately one *bulto* had been destroyed in a fire while on exhibition at the Smithsonian Institution, so the Zuni Tribe requested that the Smithsonian's American History Museum create a facsimile that could be installed in the church.[23] The tribe also requested assistance from the Smithsonian Institution in developing the means adequately to conserve and provide security for the artifacts when they are returned. At the request of the Smithsonian Institution, the Zuni Tribal Council agreed to loan the undamaged artifacts to the Smithsonian Institution so they could be included in a 1992 exhibit. Now that these artifacts have been taken off exhibition, a new Zuni Tribal Council is negotiating the final disposition of the cultural property.

Zuni Policy Concerning Human Remains

The Pueblo of Zuni deals with its concerns about the treatment of human remains separately from issues related to the repatriation of objects of cultural patrimony. Since the Pueblo of Zuni operates a tribal program that conducts professional archaeological excavations, the tribe has a well-developed policy covering the treatment of human remains. For many years there was an unwritten policy at Zuni Pueblo that the Zuni Archaeology Program developed in consultation with the Zuni Tribal Council and Zuni religious leaders.[24] This policy dictated that human graves should not be disturbed unless they were threatened by impending development that entailed modification of the land surface. Graves threatened by development should be excavated by professional archaeologists, and the human remains and associated grave goods should be reburied as close as possible to their original locations. The Zuni Tribe allowed nondestructive osteological analysis and archaeological study of the grave goods before reburial.

In 1978 the Zuni Tribe began to deal with other issues related to the repatriation of human remains when it intervened in the sale of a prehistoric human mummy included in an auction of Indian art and artifacts in Santa Fe.[25] The Zuni Tribe was outraged that non-Indians were offering a human body for sale as if it were artifact. To prevent the sale the Zuni Tribe acted as a "friend of the deceased" to invoke the New Mexico State Dead Body and Indigent Burial Statutes. These laws clearly state that no one can have a property interest in human remains and that deceased indigent people must be buried. Although the Zuni Tribal Council did not claim the mummy as a direct ancestor, the Zuni Tribe was willing to intervene since the mummy was of Anasazi origin with a cultural affiliation to Zuni. Because the mummy was thought to have been taken from the Navajo Indian Reservation, the Zuni Tribe coordinated its actions with the Navajo Nation. After establishing that New Mexico State Statutes applied in the case, the Zuni Tribe buried the mummy in a cemetery in Gallup, New Mexico.

Approximately one year before enactment of NAGPRA, the Museum of

New Mexico asked the Zuni Tribe what should be done with the human remains in the museum's collection that had been excavated from Zuni lands. The museum asked that whatever action the tribe thought appropriate be documented with an official statement from the Zuni Tribal Council. After careful consideration of the issues, the Tribal Council responded with Tribal Council Resolution No. M70-90-L017, which applies to ancestral Zuni remains curated in all museums. This resolution states that the remains of Zuni ancestors and their associated grave goods that have been excavated and are being curated in museums and other institutions have been desecrated by removal from their ancestral homeland and that there are no adequate measures to reverse or mitigate this desecration.

Consequently, the Zuni Tribe determined that human remains in museums should not be repatriated. Instead, the museums where these human remains reside should continue respectfully to care for and curate these skeletons. The Pueblo of Zuni also requested that copies of any scientific studies of Zuni ancestral remains be provided to the Zuni Tribe. The tribe has not issued any specific instructions on what constitutes respectful care and curation of human remains. It is clear from the unwritten policies of the Zuni Tribe, however, that the proper disposition of human remains in museums precludes the display of human skeletons and destructive osteological analyses. No procedures to monitor the curation of human remains in museums have been established, so the Zuni Tribe's policy is predicated on a fundamental trust in museum practices. The Zuni Tribe recognizes that its policy may not be what other tribes choose to do with human remains. Should other tribes request the repatriation of their own ancestral human remains and grave goods, the Zuni Tribe supports their position.

In Resolution No. M70-90-L017 the Zuni Tribe also states that any ancestral Zuni burials that are excavated in the future must be reburied along with their grave goods. In 1992 this policy was elaborated with Tribal Council Resolution M70-92-L164, which includes an appended statement that explains traditional Zuni beliefs about burials, identifies the geographic and temporal range of burials culturally affiliated with the Zuni Tribe, and outlines the acceptable procedures for protecting, excavating, documenting, and reburying human remains.[26] The 1992 policy statement was in response to the development of major land-modifying projects in the Zuni aboriginal land use area outside the Zuni Indian Reservation. This statement, prepared by a Zuni Cultural Resources Advisory Team composed of tribal religious leaders, does not condone or endorse specific projects that will disturb burials. It was prepared solely to articulate acceptable means to mitigate the adverse impacts that stem from such disturbances.

As explained in the policy statement, traditional Zuni beliefs are that each person's life passes through four stages. The first stage is life as we know it. Little is known of the three other stages. It is essential that each person pass through each of the four stages of his or her life cycle before it is complete. All human burials with which the Zuni Tribe has a cultural affiliation are at some point in their journey through the latter stages of the life cycle. To disturb burials while on their life-cycle journey is not the Zuni way. The ramifications of disturbing burials cannot be determined. How disturbance affects the life-cycle journey, a journey that must be completed, is unknown, but it may well have detrimental results.

The 1992 Zuni policy makes it clear that it is best if ancestral burials are not disturbed. When burials cannot be avoided, however, the tribe's policy is that they should be excavated by professional archaeologists; that all burials must be moved out of the impact zone of projects; that only non-destructive analyses of human remains and grave goods are acceptable; that analyses of human remains and grave goods should be conducted in the field by professional archaeologists and physical anthropologists; and that human remains should be reburied in a timely manner as close as possible to their original location.

The Zuni Tribe will continue to reconsider its policies concerning the treatment and curation of human remains in the post-NAGPRA era. The Pueblo of Zuni reserves the right to elaborate or modify its policy as necessary to accommodate new issues and concerns defined by tribal religious leaders.

The Need for Repatriation on a Case-by-Case Basis

The Zuni examples discussed here demonstrate the need to resolve NAGPRA issues on a case-by-case basis. For the Pueblo of Zuni this means not just a tribally specific resolution of the issues but also a consideration of each artifact or artifact class in relation to the specific problems posed by curation in museums. It is not always possible to resolve all repatriation issues in a single interaction with a museum. The number of authorities that need to be involved at Zuni Pueblo and the complexity of the issues often makes resolution of problems a time-consuming endeavor. It is clear that issues will need to be periodically reviewed because new problems with the curation of objects and human remains may be defined by Zuni religious leaders.

A case-by-case resolution of repatriation concerns is the best means to make sure all issues are fairly and completely deliberated before action is taken. The cultural patrimony and human remains that are the subject of repatriation are powerful objects that should not be interjected back into a cultural system without careful consideration of the effect this will have on tribal members. Tribal members are the most qualified people to assess how repatriation should be conducted to ensure that the effects will be positive.

Suggestions for Successful Implementation of NAGPRA

Based on the Zuni experience we offer several suggestions for museums and other institutions involved with repatriation. The museums and tribes involved each need to make concerted and realistic efforts to understand the needs of the other party. All parties must be prepared for a long and delicate process that will require a great deal of time, effort, and funding if repatriation is to be successfully implemented. Museums and tribes should select knowledgeable representatives who realistically can be expected to have longevity in their positions so that continuity of the negotiations is assured. While we recognize that no individual can guarantee his or her longevity in any particular role or project, all parties should attempt to maintain continuity in personnel to the greatest extent possible.

At Zuni Pueblo administrative changes concurrent with Tribal Council elections occasionally have caused disruption of negotiations when new officials were not aware of what their predecessors had accomplished. The effort to familiarize new officials with what had transpired sometimes required museums to provide copies of previously submitted letters and reports. Similarly, the Pueblo of Zuni occasionally has had to provide museums with correspondence or background information that had been misplaced due to changes in museum administrative or curatorial personnel. For this reason, the whole process of repatriation negotiations should be well-documented by both parties to provide a record that can be consulted as needed. This will be especially critical for future generations of tribal members or museum personnel if issues need reconsideration.

To establish equity, understanding, and ease of communication, we recommend that museum representatives visit tribal lands and that tribal officials visit the museums with which they are negotiating. On-site visits are essential in communicating and understanding the local context that informs the values and beliefs of both parties in a repatriation negotiation. Visiting reservations helps museum officials understand tribal concerns, and visiting museums helps tribal representatives understand the roles and trust responsibilities of those institutions. Funds need to be appropriated to support these activities.

We think repatriation in any context should not be forced into the short-term constraints of legislative, regulatory, or bureaucratic needs. It is essential to have long-term strategies that provide all parties with adequate time and resources to resolve these extremely complex issues. For example, no institution should make the mistake of asking a tribe to look over an inventory list and give a "once and for all" answer to the question of what should and should not be repatriated. The results of this approach may well be catastrophic for either the institution or the tribe and may lead to confrontation and conflict. If a tribe is confronted with such a request it is likely it will either ask for everything back, which would be disastrous for the museum, or ask for nothing back, which might be detrimental to the tribe's long-term interests. As at Zuni Pueblo, the impetus for repatriation should come from the religious leaders of a tribe based on spiritual needs. Since spiritual needs may not immediately be apparent, and new concerns may become manifest in the future, tribes always should retain the right to request repatriation at any time. No tribe should ever be asked to relinquish its rights to make future claims for repatriation.

Although NAGPRA invests a property right in human remains, and other provisions of the law make repatriation an inherently political undertaking, we think that the issues warranting the return of human remains and cultural patrimony should stem from cultural concerns defined by religious rather than political leaders. Each tribe needs to determine for itself the proper role of its civil government. Much of the success that the Pueblo of Zuni has experienced with repatriation stems from the fact that it is the religious leaders who define the issues and how they are best resolved. The Zuni Tribal Council plays an integral supportive and administrative role but does not attempt to define or arbitrate cultural issues.

Tribes now face an onslaught of information provided to them by museums complying with the provisions of NAGPRA. We question how effectively tribes are able to analyze and comprehend the information contained in inventories of human remains and descriptions of cultural patrimony when these documents arrive in tribal mailrooms. Some tribes have received hundreds of these notices, straining the very capacity of the tribe to even acknowledge receipt. Even a relatively well-organized tribe like the Pueblo of Zuni is ill-prepared to manage multiple concurrent repatriation negotiations. We think that either a federal agency or a national organization (such as the American Association of Museums, the Native American Association of Museums, or the Native American Rights Fund) should organize and fund informational visits to tribal communities throughout the country to provide educational information about the data the tribes receive from museums and what rights they have under NAGPRA.

NAGPRA requires that descriptions of sacred objects be provided to appropriate tribes, but this will not always be a straightforward process. The Zuni *Ahayu:da* provide a cogent example of some of the pitfalls that occur.

In 1990 the Pueblo of Zuni wrote to the Peabody Museum of Archaeology and Ethnology at Harvard University to inquire if the museum had an *Ahayu:da* in its collection and to request its repatriation if it did. The Peabody Museum responded that it did not have a War God listed in its catalog. Two years later, however, it was determined that there was an *Ahayu:da* in the museum's collection that had been misidentified as a "carved Hopi (?) wooden post to represent a figure."[27] Photographs of the object were sent to the Pueblo of Zuni, and the Zuni religious leaders and Zuni Tribal Council made a positive identification of the object as a Zuni War God. The *Ahayu:da* was repatriated in 1993.

While it is good that this *Ahayu:da* eventually was recognized for what it is and repatriated, the fact that a relatively well-known and publicized artifact like a Zuni War God was misidentified by a major anthropological museum is not encouraging. This sort of misidentification is not an isolated occurrence, raising the issue of how museums and tribes can address problems in mislabeling, misidentification, and erroneous tribal attribution of cultural property. A substantial and long-term research effort is required of all parties to generate the accurate and detailed data needed for decision-making. Museums will have to implement procedures to ensure the confidentiality of esoteric information that tribes may make available through their research, to ensure that this information is not misused in research unrelated to the resolution of repatriation issues.

There are two conclusions that can be drawn from the analysis of Zuni repatriation activities. First, there is no monolithic way of adequately dealing with the diverse issues pertaining to the repatriation of sacred objects, cultural patrimony, and human remains even in a single tribe, much less with multiple tribes. Museums should not attempt to develop a blanket policy intended to cover all situations but should instead encourage a case-by-case resolution of the issues.

Second, the sheer volume of work anticipated as a result of NAGPRA is staggering from the perspectives of both the tribes and museums. The Pueblo of Zuni's campaign to recover all stolen *Ahayu:da* has entailed thirty-eight separate repatriations over a fifteen-year period, with individual negotiations lasting from one to nine years. The negotiations for the repatriation of a single type of artifact involved a tremendous amount of research and administrative effort on the part of both the Zuni Tribe and the museums it negotiated with. Broadening the scope of repatriation to include other types of cultural patrimony and human remains makes the issues even more complex. We believe that neither the tribes nor the museums in the United States have the funding to adequately implement

NAGPRA. For this reason we think it is essential that Congress appropriate the funding authorized in NAGPRA and provide grants to both tribes and museums to finance the work needed to justly implement the law.

Notes

1. Public Law 101-601.

2. United States Senate, Native American Grave and Burial Protection Act (Repatriation): Native American Repatriation of Cultural Patrimony Act; and Heard Museum Report. Hearing before the Select Committee on Indian Affairs, United States Senate, One Hundred First Congress, Second Session, on S. 1021 to provide for the Protection of Indian Graves and Burial Grounds, and S. 1980 to provide for the Repatriation of Native American Group or Cultural Patrimony, May 14, 1990. Pete Domenici, *Congressional Record* (October 26, 1990), 17176.

3. Charles Hustito, "Why Zuni War Gods Need to Be Returned," in *Zuni History: Victories in the 1990s,* ed. E. Richard Hart and T. J. Ferguson (Institute of the North American West, Seattle, 1991), Section II, 12; Barton Martza, "On the Trail of the Zuni War Gods," in *Zuni History,* Section II, 12; Perry Tsadiasi, "I Want our Fathers Back," in *Zuni History,* Section II, 13; T. J. Ferguson and Wilfred Eriacho, "*Ahayu:da,* Zuni War Gods, Cooperation and Repatriation," *Native Peoples* 4 (fall 1990): 6–12; and T. J. Ferguson, "The Repatriation of *Ahayu:da,* Zuni War Gods: An Interview with the Zuni Tribal Council," *Museum Anthropology* 1 (1990): 7–14.

4. Mr. Carl Bryant Rogers, then of the Indian Pueblo Legal Services, provided key legal advice and was instrumental in developing the legal theory used to structure the Zuni approach to repatriation.

5. After more than a decade of planning, the Ashiwi A:wan Museum and Heritage Center was established in 1992 as a not-for-profit corporation.

6. William L. Merrill, Edmund J. Ladd, and T. J. Ferguson, "The Return of the *Ahayu:da:* Lessons for Repatriation from Zuni Pueblo and the Smithsonian Institution," *Current Anthropology* 34 (1993): 523–67.

7. Although exempted from NAGPRA, the Smithsonian Institution has committed itself to a repatriation policy congruent with that law, as described in Timothy G. Baugh, Tamara L. Bray, and Thomas W. Killion, "Native Communities and Repatriation: The Smithsonian Institution Perspective," *Federal Archeology Report* (March 1992): 23–24.

8. E. Richard Hart, the executive director of the Institute of the NorthAmerican West, was instrumental in assisting the Zuni Tribe in their negotiation with the Warhol Foundation. The incident is reported in David Firestone, "Rescue in Manhattan: A Zuni God Goes Home," *New York Newsday* (May 27, 1988): Section II, 1–3, 6.

9. T. J. Ferguson, "*Ahayu:da:* Creation, Disposition, and Repatriation of War Gods, Preliminary Report to the Zuni Tribal Council" (ms. on file at the Pueblo of Zuni and the Institute of the NorthAmerican West, 1989).

10. Edmund J. Ladd, "An Explanation for the Return of Zuni Religious Objects Held in Museums and Private Collections," in *Exploration: Zuni and El Morro* (Annual Bulletin of the School of American Research, Santa Fe, 1983), 32; Ferguson, "The Repatriation of *Ahayu:da*"; and Ferguson and Eriacho, "*Ahayu:da,* Zuni War Gods."

11. Ferguson, "*Ahayu:da:* Creation, Disposition, and Repatriation"; Ferguson, "Report to the Zuni Tribal Council on Thirteen War Gods and Associated Shrine Offerings in the Collection of the Brooklyn Museum" (ms. on file at the Pueblo of Zuni and the Institute of the NorthAmerican West, 1990); and Ferguson, "Report to the Zuni Tribal Council Answering Questions Posed by the Nelson-Atkins Museum of Art" (ms. on file at the Pueblo of Zuni and the Institute of the NorthAmerican West, 1990).

12. Stephen Becker, Bruce Bernstein, and Edmund J. Ladd, "Repatriation, Zuni Sensitive Materials, 'Communities in Collaboration'" (ms. on file, Laboratory of Anthropology, Museum of Indian Arts and Culture, Museum of New Mexico, Santa Fe, 1991).

13. Pueblo of Zuni, "Request for the Return of Zuni Sacred Material and Recommendations for the Care and Curation of Objects of Zuni Religious Significance in the Collection of the Smithsonian Institution; Prepared by Ben Kallestewa and Edmund J. Ladd in consultation with Zuni Religious Leaders and Elders" (ms. on file at the Pueblo of Zuni, 1981); and Ladd, "Explanation for the Return," 32.

14. Edmund J. Ladd, "Preliminary Consultation and Survey of Zuni Collections at the National Museum of the American Indian" (ms. on file, Pueblo of Zuni, 1991).

15. Edmund J. Ladd, "The Zuni Ceremonial System: The Kiva," in *Kachinas in the Pueblo World,* ed. Polly Schaafsma (University of New Mexico Press, Albuquerque, 1994), 17–22.

16. Tribal Resolution No. M70-78-991.

17. Val Gendron, *Behind the Zuni Masks* (Longman, Green and Company, New York, 1958).

18. Merrill, Ladd, and Ferguson, "The Return of the *Ahayu:da,*" 528.

19. T. J. Ferguson, "Report on the Theft of Three War Gods from *Nobonni Dahna'a* Shrine on the Zuni Indian Reservation, Report submitted to the Zuni Tribal Council" (ms. on file at the Pueblo of Zuni and the Institute of the NorthAmerican West, 1990).

20. Andrew Othole, Perry Tsadiasi, and T. J. Ferguson, "Zuni War God Shrines Documentation Project, Final Report to the Chamisa Foundation" (ms. on file at the Zuni Archaeology Program, 1992).

21. E. Richard Hart, "A Brief History of Religious Objects from the Old Zuni Mission" (ms. on file at the Pueblo of Zuni and the Institute of the NorthAmerican West, 1987).

22. Letter from Robert McC. Adams, secretary of the Smithsonian Institution, to Governor Robert E. Lewis, Zuni Tribal Council, March 21, 1991.

23. Letter from Governor Robert E. Lewis, Zuni Tribal Council, to Dr. Robert McC. Adams, secretary of the Smithsonian Institution, May 28, 1991.

24. T. J. Ferguson, "Archaeological Ethics and Values in a Tribal Cultural Resources Management Program at the Pueblo of Zuni," in *Ethics and Values in Archaeology,* ed. Ernestine L. Green (Free Press, New York, 1984), 224–35.

25. T. J. Ferguson, "Application of New Mexico State Dead Body and Indigent Burial Statutes to a Prehistoric Mummified Body," in *American Indian Concerns with Historic Preservation in New Mexico,* ed. Barbara Holmes (New Mexico Archaeological Council, Albuquerque, 1982), 45–51.

26. Pueblo of Zuni, "Policy Statement Regarding the Protection and Treatment of Human Remains and Associated Funerary Objects" (ms. on file, Pueblo of Zuni, 1992).

27. Peabody Museum, "Notice of Intent to Repatriate a Cultural Item in the Possession of the Peabody Museum of Archaeology and Ethnology," enclosed with letter from David Pilbeam, director, Peabody Museum of Archaeology and Ethnology, to Head Councilman Joseph Dishta, Zuni Tribal Council, March 9, 1993.

14

Ira Jacknis

Repatriation as Social Drama

The Kwakiutl Indians of British Columbia, 1922–1980

The Kwakiutl Indians—who live at the north end of Vancouver Island and the adjacent mainland of British Columbia—are well known from the extensive collections and writings of anthropologist Franz Boas.[1] They also are the subjects of a classic and well-documented case of the repatriation of artifacts from museum collections. This essay will recount the history of this process of intercultural definition and negotiation and consider some of the more general features of Native American repatriation.

The first Westerner the Kwakiutl encountered was British trader James Strange in 1786.[2] Although they participated actively in the maritime fur trade that followed in the early nineteenth century, the Kwakiutl did not experience substantial culture change until 1849, when the Hudson's Bay Company established a post at Fort Rupert. Situated on the northeast end of Vancouver Island, Fort Rupert had not been a traditional village site, but Kwakiutl soon settled around it to take advantage of trade with the whites. By the late 1890s the village had been supplanted as the principal site of acculturation, with the growth in another new settlement, Alert Bay on nearby Cormorant Island. Established in the 1870s as a salmon saltery— soon replaced with a cannery—Alert Bay became the focal point for Kwakiutl participation in a rapidly expanding commercial economy of fishing and logging. Their success at the new ways led to a period of great prosperity (1900–1920s) and a shift to new forms of clothing, housing, and tools. The town also the site for intensive culture change through an Anglican mission and school. Governmental controls came in the form of an Indian agency and the creation of "reserves," small portions of aboriginal territory that were recognized by the federal government. At the same time, Kwakiutl population declined steadily and swiftly throughout the century, due largely to disease.

Stimulated by these developments, museum ethnologists set out frantically to collect material records of Kwakiutl culture before it disappeared altogether.[3] This collecting was embedded in a comprehensive intercultural narrative that predicted the disappearance of Native Americans physically, due to disease, and culturally, by their acceptance of Western values and customs. Although explorers, fur traders, and settlers had been casually acquiring Kwakiutl artifacts since Vancouver's time, systematic collecting did not start until the 1881–82 expedition of Johan Adrian Jacobsen, a Norwegian sailor traveling under the auspices of the Royal Ethnographic Museum of Berlin. Franz Boas made his first trip to the Kwakiutl in 1886, when he gathered a small collection for the Berlin Museum. Boas continued his Kwakiutl research, along with some minor collecting, through the 1890s, sponsored by the British Association for the Advancement of Science. Between 1895 and 1905 Boas collaborated with Kwakiutl George Hunt in amassing a major Kwakiutl collection for the American Museum of Natural History in New York.[4] Boas's chief rival as a collector of Kwakiutl artifacts was Dr. Charles F. Newcombe, a physician-turned-ethnologist, who formed a large Kwakiutl collection for Chicago's Field Columbian Museum between 1901 and 1906. Kwakiutl collections continued to be made, most notably by Samuel Barrett in 1915 for the Milwaukee Public Museum, but large-scale collecting had all but disappeared by 1920.

The Kwakiutl artifacts that are the subject of this essay were returned from several of these museum collections, but they were not gathered by anthropologists in an effort to document Native culture. Instead, they were acquired as part of legal action by the federal government of Canada. In 1885 the Canadian Parliament amended the Indian Act by outlawing Native participation in potlatches.[5] Indians of the Northwest Coast used potlatch ceremonies to mark birth, puberty, marriage, death, and other events by giving lavish feasts and distributing great quantities of property.[6] The government had adopted this moral legislation, under the pressure of missionaries, in the interests of "civilizing" the Indians and keeping them from what they believed to be "degrading" practices. Partly because of the ambiguous wording of the law, it was difficult to obtain convictions, but after a potlatch in December 1921 the local Indian agent, William Halliday, decided to try to prosecute. This potlatch, the largest ever given up to that time, had been sponsored by Daniel Cranmer, a Nimpkish chief, in order to repay his wife's family as part of the marriage settlement.[7] A fisherman and small businessman, Cranmer (1888–1959) went on to work with Franz Boas and other anthropologists after the death of George Hunt in 1933. On this occasion, Halliday was able to obtain forty-five convictions. With three on appeal, twenty individuals (including ranking chiefs and women) went to prison. However, twenty-two received suspended sentences in return for agreeing to hand over their potlatch regalia.[8] Three Kwakiutl subtribes were represented: the Nimpkish of Alert Bay (in the north), the Mamalili-kulla of Village Island (in the central area), and the Lekwiltok of Cape Mudge (in the south). A total of 750 objects were turned in, for which the government gave the Natives collectively $1,495. Many of them deny receiving any compensation, and the government never paid for the twenty copper shields handed over. From the Native point of view, these shields— abstract counters of wealth—were an even greater monetary loss than the regalia, as they represented massive amounts of property exchanged in potlatches. One Native estimate puts their worth at $35,000.[9]

As Halliday was amassing the collection, by coincidence George G. Heye, the ever-acquisitive founder of the Museum of the American Indian, happened to visit Alert Bay. Acting against instructions, Halliday sold about thirty of the finest items to Heye and shipped the rest to Ottawa. From the National Museum (then known as the Victoria Memorial Museum), part of the collection (about one hundred pieces) was transferred the next year to the Royal Ontario Museum, and eleven items were retained for his personal collection by Duncan Campbell Scott, superintendent of Indian affairs.[10]

Kwakiutl potlatching declined after 1922, although more because of the worldwide economic depression than because of governmental edict. The Kwakiutl continued to potlatch, escaping governmental view by holding them in isolated villages or disguising them as innocuous Christmas or wedding exchanges.[11]

The Kwakiutl never forgot the 1922 "confiscation," but until the anti-potlatch law was dropped in 1951 there was little they could do. That year Canadian Natives began to govern themselves under a system of local band councils; now that it was no longer illegal, potlatching increased in frequency. Throughout the 1950s the Kwakiutl created contexts for the presentation of their culture, activities that prepared the way for their cultural societies and museums of the late 1970s. One forum was a series of intercultural performances, like traditional masked dances, to benefit the local hospital (1951–57).[12] Another series of related projects was the physical transformation of Alert Bay (the principal Kwakiutl community): the restoration of the Native cemetery in 1958, the building of a library in 1959, and the construction of a large communal dance house in 1965. Finally, there were several cultural societies: the Kwakwala Arts and Crafts Society, begun in 1965, and the Coastal Indian Heritage Society at the Vancouver Museum (1971–75). In all these endeavors Natives were the prime organizers and officers. The Kwakiutl were working to present their image of their own culture, for themselves and others.

Of these cultural institutions two were particularly important in preparing the way for the founding of Native-run museums: the Alert Bay Museum-Library, opened in February 1959, and the Kwakwala Arts and Crafts Society, organized during 1964–65. Commemorative of the Provincial centennial the previous year, the museum-library was a project of the municipality of Alert Bay.[13] While support came from both Native and white communities, the Native sentiment was stronger, and largely as a result, it was constructed next to the Nimpkish cemetery, then undergoing renovation. A strong backer was Kwakiutl chief James Sewid (1913–88), a successful fisherman who had been elected the first chief councilor of the Nimpkish Band in 1950. Sewid thought it important to have a place for dance regalia: "Most of the people were just putting all their things in their basement, and people were breaking it. I put my big raven mask and the mask I wore when I was a hamatsa [cannibal dancer] in there."[14] He felt that if there had been a museum in Alert Bay earlier, perhaps Natives would not have sold their regalia.[15] House fires were another concern. While the museum exhibited pioneer heirlooms as well as Native pieces, evidently most of the display was Native, and most of these were on loan.[16]

The Kwakwala Arts and Culture Society, with James Sewid as director, was responsible for the building of the Alert Bay community house and for organizing dances for tourists. But viewed more generally, it was an association dedicated to the preservation of Kwakiutl culture. Sewid was motivated by what he felt was a loss of tradition: "Like any other nation, I would like to preserve the arts and crafts of the Indian people because I think they are beautiful. Those old people who really knew how to sing and dance and carve were dying off and I felt that something should be done to preserve those good things from the old way." As he was quick to point out, this cultural loss was not due only to Native lack of interest; the government's policy of outlawing potlatches was largely to blame.[17] As the program developed, dancing came to supplant the projected craft activity. While some items were sold to tourists in the early seasons, there was no training program. Nor was there, as hoped, an expansion of the complex with a smaller building, about twenty feet square, for the storage of paraphernalia.[18] However, the idea of a museum building was not far away.

The first recorded efforts to have the so-called Potlatch Collection returned date from 1958. At the request of Andrew Frank (a Coast Salish Indian married to a high-ranking Kwakiutl woman),[19] his local member of Parliament located the collection in storage at the National Museum in

Ottawa. One plan called for its display on permanent loan in the Native community house then being planned for nearby Courtenay. Museum officials were quoted as supporting the idea of a Native museum on the coast for the display of such material, providing there were proper facilities.[20]

When visiting the capital on business in 1963, James Sewid demanded to see the collection but was given a poor reception.[21] After finally getting to view the collection, stored in the basement, Sewid requested that the objects be returned, as they were stolen goods. When told that the government had paid fourteen hundred dollars for them, Sewid pulled out his checkbook and offered to pay for them.[22] The offer was turned down, but Sewid persisted, returning to Ottawa several times over the next few years. The encounter of 1963 marked the beginning of the period of *effective* redressive action to secure the return of the collection.

In the mid-1960s the general idea of Native museums began to gain currency. Considering plans for the celebration of the 1967 national centennial, the local paper in Alert Bay suggested "the construction of a Community House maintained as a museum." Possible support could come from the combined efforts of the local Nimpkish band, the white town, and the Department of Indian Affairs.[23] The conservator at the Provincial Museum was quite sensitive to Native desires for local control. In a comprehensive review of the "conservation of antiquities," he proposed "that the Indian material should be in their hands." Totem poles, he thought, should be re-erected on reserves, in local centers of Native population such as Alert Bay.[24]

By 1967 the federal government was moving to return the confiscated objects. That year archaeologist William Taylor became director of the newly reorganized National Museum of Man, and there was talk in both Alert Bay and Campbell River of housing the collection in their municipal museums.[25] Taylor, with support of the museum's trustees, began negotiations with a committee appointed by the Kwakiutl District Council.[26]

We can only speculate at the motivations of the federal museum for considering this action. Undoubtedly, it resulted from many conjoined factors. Issues of Native sovereignty were more salient in a period of the United States civil rights movement and the upheaval over the war in Vietnam. In Canada, the new Liberal Party government of Pierre Trudeau was advocating "participatory democracy," which it began to apply to many aspects of national life. For instance, the Department of Indian Affairs moved to transfer much of its administrative burden to the provincial level.[27] In the cultural arena, the act of repatriation may have grown out of the National Museum's policy of "democratization and decentralization," adopted in 1968 and reaffirmed in 1972. The museum attempted to make its resources more readily available to Canadians across the country, living far beyond the capital region. Under this program twenty-five institutions were declared associate museums, entitled to special funding and assistance. As part of its generally increased services to the nation's museums, the National Museum established its Museums Assistance Program, which funded half the construction costs for the Kwakiutl museums that eventually housed the Potlatch Collection.

Regionally, the talk of repatriation came at a time of intense awareness and acclaim for Northwest Coast Indian art, both historical and contemporary. Although probably a coincidence, it is interesting that the Potlatch Collection began to be exhibited at the same time that the Kwakiutl intensified their efforts. Evidently the entire collection had never been shown together, but during the 1960s a number of the pieces were displayed at several of the decade's temporary exhibitions of Northwest Coast art: the Seattle World's Fair, the Chicago Art Institute, the Lowie Museum in Berkeley, the Vancouver Art Gallery, and the Musée de l'Homme in Paris.[28]

Exhibitions such as *Arts of the Raven,* at the Vancouver Art Gallery in 1967, included work by living Northwest Coast Indian artists, among them Haidas Bill Reid and Robert Davidson, and Kwakiutls Henry Hunt (grandson of George), his son Tony Hunt, and Douglas Cranmer (son of Daniel). This period also saw the beginning of a market for the sale of contemporary Northwest Coast objects as fine art. Whether dealing in revival or continuity—the issue varied for different people and groups— these displays made the point that Native Northwest Coast cultures had not vanished as Boas and Newcombe feared they would. And if they were still alive and vibrant, perhaps their claims on the Potlatch Collection, acquired under a different set of assumptions, needed to be listened to.

With assurances of provincial support, in 1972 the Kwakiutl Council voted to build a museum for the collection at Cape Mudge. Among the reasons given for its location was its accessibility to large populations. Immediately, however, there was dissension, with people from the north maintaining that the museum should be placed in Alert Bay, citing its central location and arguing that most of the artifacts had come from the area. This cleavage was a contemporary expression of a traditional rivalry. In the rank ordering of potlatching positions that evolved in the late nineteenth century, the Nimpkish (at the mouth of the river bearing their name and later at Alert Bay) were ranked near the top, while the Lekwiltok of Cape Mudge were near the bottom. These groups led the two factions that demanded a split in the collection.[29]

A compromise was eventually struck with the formation of two cultural societies, each to run a museum housing half of the collection. In Alert Bay the U'mista Cultural Society was founded in March 1974, and in January 1975 the Nuyumbalees Society was established.[30] Both names were symbolically charged in Kwakiutl culture. *Nuyumbalees* means "stories from the beginning of the world," narratives that outline the continuity of Kwakiutl cultural patrimony from founding clan ancestors. By adopting this name the society demonstrates its mythic rights to the confiscated regalia. *U'mista* means the return home of a captive, through either payment of ransom or a retaliatory raid. According to the society, its goals were "the u'mista of our history, our language and our culture," a perfect Native gloss for repatriation.[31]

In May of 1978 the two societies met with representatives of the National Museum to work out the procedure for dividing the collection, and that November the objects left the National Museum for temporary residence at the B. C. Provincial Museum in Victoria.[32] Before they could be inspected by the families they had to be fumigated and their condition recorded. Photographs of the collection had been sent to each family to help them make identifications, allowing all but 15 percent to be attributed. The process was difficult, as the items were not identified when they were picked up and many of those originally present had since died. Early in the year the families were able to inspect the collection and the final claims made.

As the split worked out, about half the collection went to each society. On February 10, 1979, the two societies agreed to the division, and seven days later the Nuyumbalees Society agreed with the National Museum over the final terms of transfer. The U'mista Society came to an agreement some months later. The collection remained at the Provincial Museum until each museum was ready to accept its portion.

Construction of the Kwagiulth Museum, as the facility at Cape Mudge was called, began in November 1978 and was completed the following May, shortly before the opening on June 29, 1979. In Alert Bay the construction began in August of 1979, with completion about a year later.[33] After several months of installation, the U'mista Cultural Centre was dedicated on November 1, 1980.

The process of repatriation did not end with the opening of the two museums, and as might be expected, the issues were rather different for the Royal Ontario Museum (ROM) and the Museum of the American Indian. When intensive negotiations began with the ROM in late 1984, the museum felt "it had some legitimate claim to the collection," and wanted something in return for the years of curatorial care.[34] As has occurred to several museums considering repatriation, the ROM hoped that some kind of cooperative arrangement could be worked out, by which the collection could be shared or replaced with replicas. The Kwakiutl refused, on the grounds they had a legal and unconditional right to the objects. With help from the federal Department of Indian Affairs, the Kwakiutl got their way, and the ROM returned its part of the collection in 1987. On January 30, 1988, the objects were apportioned between the two Kwakiutl museums.[35]

Negotiations with the Museum of the American Indian had intensified in 1984, but there was little headway until the institution became a branch of the Smithsonian in late 1989. One of the principal problems at this institution was that many of the objects that Heye had acquired from Halliday could not be distinguished from other Kwakiutl items that Heye had collected around the same time and place. Undoubtedly, the influential factor here was the appointment of a Native American, W. Richard West Jr. (Cheyenne-Arapaho), as director in May 1990. In late 1992 the museum agreed to return what it could (nine objects), but efforts are ongoing to identify other relevant objects. Even with these transfers from the three museums in Ottawa, Toronto, and New York, there remain other objects taken from the Kwakiutl in 1922. Over the years, some of the Potlatch Collection has been deaccessioned to other repositories, such as the British Museum, so the repatriation effort will no doubt continue, although on a much reduced level.

In recent years the repatriation of Native objects has become an important fact of life for many museums, especially since the passage of the Native American Graves Protection and Repatriation Act in 1990.[36] While it is now commonplace to consider how ethnographies function as narratives,[37] a narrative approach, in general, and a dramatic model, in particular, are especially suited to an analysis of repatriation, as it encompasses ways of thinking about social action over time—with a plot, characters, and (often opposing) motivations. One may usefully speak of a poetics of repatriation.

The Kwakiutl case examined here may be profitably analyzed in terms of the "social drama," a model of conflict resolution proposed by anthropologist Victor Turner.[38] Turner defined four phases in a social drama: breach, crisis, redressive action, and reintegration. In this case, the "breach" phase corresponds to the programs of enforced acculturation impressed upon the Kwakiutl, marked by the legal prohibition against potlatches and ceremonials. The pivotal point, the moment of "crisis," was the 1922 "confiscation" of dance regalia by the Canadian government. Following this was a half century of "redressive action," in which the Natives worked with greater or lesser effect at securing the return of the "Potlatch Collection." With the return of the collection and the opening of the two museums, we have reached a period of "reintegration." For Turner, the model of a drama was a metaphoric form which both actors and analysts could use to understand fundamental social and cultural oppositions and accommodations.

For the Kwakiutl, the events of 1922 have become a central point of reference in their definition of themselves and their relation to the dominant society. They are a prime example of what Michael Harkin, following Raymond Fogelson, calls "epitomizing events."[39] These are "condensing, symbolic actions," that come to stand for larger social movements, in the way that the 1929 stock market crash ushered in the Depression. The confiscation marks a time of oppression and forced culture change, and the outcome of the drama, the return of the artifacts, symbolizes their new relationship to white society. Now the Kwakiutl have more autonomy, and there is more respect for their culture and art.

The importance of this historical narrative to the Kwakiutl is evident from the representations produced by the two cultural societies—exhibit labels, books, and films.[40] During the 1970s the societies produced accounts of the repatriation story, which they hoped would educate the world about their culture and their claims, thereby bringing about the return of the Potlatch Collection. The Cape Mudge group published *Persecution and Prosecution,* a book written by Daisy Sewid-Smith, a daughter of James Sewid. In a combination of oral history and archival documents, the volume told the story in great detail. The U'mista Cultural Society produced two films, which are frequently shown to museum visitors. *Potlatch: A Strict Law Bids Us Dance* employed an innovative collage of documentary film footage, dramatic reenactment, historical photos, and interviews. A key feature was the footage of a contemporary potlatch given by the Cranmer family, thereby making a claim for the continuity and legitimacy of the Kwakiutl potlatch in general and the Cranmer family in particular.[41] A sequel, *Box of Treasures,* dealt with the return of the collection and the opening of the Alert Bay museum. Both films included much oral testimony from elders concerning the events of 1921–22. In the book and the films, these witnesses served as physical and moral links between past and present, demonstrating the continuity of Kwakiutl culture during the enforced absence of the Potlatch Collection.[42]

The label copy at the U'mista Cultural Centre also focuses on this story. In both museums, the potlatch is taken as the organizing principle—the sequence of mask presentations at Alert Bay and family ownership at Cape Mudge. In Alert Bay, to the surprise of many white visitors, the text panels speak primarily not of the artifacts themselves nor of the potlatch ceremony but instead trace the story of the Potlatch Collection confiscation. Exhibit labels and films are different means by which the Kwakiutl are telling their version of the repatriation narrative in an otherwise static museum setting.

Almost by definition, repatriation cases invoke a sense of history, as they encompass ethnic relations in the past and in the present and the changes in these groups over time. As anthropologist Edward Bruner has pointed out, for contemporary Native Americans and anthropologists the story of intercultural encounters over the past century has a specific plot.[43] As in the Kwakiutl repatriation case, there has been a shift from a belief in culture loss and the necessity for salvage to a perception of continuity and resistance. Both sides today seem to be working within this paradigm, but we need to remember that this is a story, a way of making sense, a reading of history, and not "history" itself.

We would expect narratives to be conceived in terms of a Native style, logic, and preoccupations. As the Kwakiutl are a society founded on rank and ancestral privilege, it should not surprise us that they possess an extensive body of oral literature that narrates family histories. *Nuyem* ("myth" or "history") are largely concerned with ownership of objects, resources, and privileges. An important subgenre, the house story, focuses on continuity. As Judith Berman notes, "The importance of the chiefly crests and privileges acquired in the stories is that they *did* exist at the beginning of time, and have been handed down to the present unchanged." These themes of continuity are the substance of much of the oratory at potlatches.[44]

Significantly, repatriated objects rarely return to the original owners, but to their descendants. The facts of individual cases may differ, but questions of legitimacy and continuity inevitably arise. For the Kwakiutl, claims of cultural continuity are now central to statements about their history. As Gloria Cranmer Webster, founding director of the U'mista center, proclaims at the end of *Box of Treasures:* "We are still here and will always be." The issue has been made relevant by the very denial of their cultural autonomy and history by nineteenth-century whites—by both missionaries and anthropologists. As well, the Kwakiutl are very aware of the substantial loss of culture and discontinuity in potlatching by their Native neighbors such as the Nootka (Nuu-chah-nulth) and Haida.

The Kwakiutl also are aware of the fragility of their cultural traditions and of the struggle to hand them down to succeeding generations. As chief Harry Assu wrote, "I think that getting our potlatch goods back has done a lot to teach our youth who we really are. It will help us to hold on to our history."[45] Gloria Webster spoke in similar tones in *Box of Treasures.* It is important for the children "to know who they are." Speaking at the opening of the U'mista museum, Chief Bill Cranmer said, "It's important to know your past if you are going to fight for your future."

The Kwakiutl case was a relatively early instance of Native American repatriation, especially in Canada. Because of this, negotiations proceeded slowly, with the museums worried about setting precedents. Structurally, of course, repatriation is the inverse of collecting—as artifacts go from Western museums back to the Natives, from centralized, metropolitan repositories to localized, remote villages. Just as the original movement reflected the existing power relationships, so repatriation comes about with a readjustment in those relations. While the museums were cautious, the repatriation was undoubtedly helped along by the circumstances of the original acquisition. The question we must consider is, why was it considered appropriate to acquire the objects in 1922 and to return them in 1978? This case involved the rather unusual circumstance in which the National Museum acquired the collection as part of a legal proceeding, obtaining the objects under duress (although with some compensation) and not as part of scientific research. The legal argument that the Kwakiutl raised in negotiations was that the alienation of ceremonial objects in exchange for dropping criminal charges is contrary to principles of Anglo-American justice. Once the anti-potlatch law was dropped in 1951, the reasons for keeping the collection must have seemed less compelling to the National Museum, whatever their earlier validity. The situation might have been different if the Kwakiutl had claimed artifacts, collected by Franz Boas, for which they had been fairly paid. In that case, contemporary curators would be inclined to uphold the original motives and methods of the collector/museum.

While Natives and anthropologists may both currently accept a narrative of cultural continuity and resistance, there are likely to be significant cultural differences in the ways they cast the narrative. That the events of 1921–22 are an important story at all is due primarily to Native concerns; one sees few references to the question in Canadian writings until the Kwakiutl pressed the issue in the late 1960s.

Turner's fourth phase in his social drama model included the "recognition of schism" as well as reintegration. With the Potlatch Collection, the two sides continued to talk with one another, while recognizing basic differences. Although the Canadian government has returned the confiscated regalia, its status remains ambiguous.

These objects were essentially returned on the government's terms.[46] From the beginning of negotiations the National Museum insisted that they would not be returned until the Natives could supply a museum building with proper climate and security controls. And the government would return them not to the individuals from whom they were taken or their descendants but only to the Kwakiutl people as a whole, evidently from the concern that they could later be sold out of the country.[47]

Although the Kwakiutl and the government were able to reach an agreement, the Natives did not see the situation quite the way the officials did. The repatriation was a compromise; the Natives did get the return of their heritage, while the government was able to keep the artifacts in a museum environment (built largely with government funds). But the Native people have redefined the Western institution of an object-centered museum into a broader and more performative cultural center.[48] Secondly, they have refused to consider the artifacts as communal possessions. Sewid maintained that they "belonged to individual Chiefs, not the tribe," and other Kwakiutl regard them as a family donation to the museum.[49] In fact, at Cape Mudge they are displayed in cases devoted to specific families. The National Museum may have been able to accept both of these positions; what is of interest is the fundamentally different priorities of Native and white. As in other cases of repatriation, this is a tension which both parties have chosen not to resolve.

Narratives of repatriation are by definition intercultural. Each side has its version, often many versions, which may not coincide with those of the other(s). Like a pidgin or creole in linguistics, a shared code is developed that allows speakers of two languages to communicate, without necessarily reaching full agreement or even full comprehension.

Notes

This essay is a revised and expanded version of a paper presented at the December 1992 annual meeting of the American Historical Association. It is derived from a chapter in my book, *The Storage Box of Tradition: Museums, Anthropologists, and Kwakiutl Art, 1881–1981*, forthcoming from the Smithsonian Institution Press. Detailed acknowledgments are contained therein, but for this essay, I would like to thank Duane King and Mary Jane Lenz of the National Museum of the American Indian for unpublished information concerning their collections.

1. "Kwakiutl" is a corruption of the Kwakwala term kwagu'ł, one of about thirty autonomous subgroups, commonly called tribes, who settled in Fort Rupert after establishment of the Hudson's Bay Company post. The name was widely popularized by the writings of Franz Boas, but recently Natives have advocated the use of Kwakwaka'wakw, meaning "Kwakwala speakers." Kwakiutl is used here in the interests of historical consistency. See Helen Codere, "Kwakiutl: Traditional Culture," in *Northwest Coast,* vol. 7, ed. Wayne Suttles, *Handbook of North American Indians,* ed. William C. Sturtevant (Washington DC: Smithsonian Institution Press, 1990), 376.

2. For general reviews of Kwakiutl culture history, see Codere, "Kwakiutl: Traditional Culture," and Gloria Cranmer Webster, "Kwakiutl since 1980," in *Northwest Coast,* 387–90.

3. For a comprehensive review of the history of the collecting of Northwest Coast Indian artifacts, see Douglas Cole, *Captured Heritage: The Scramble for Northwest Coast Artifacts* (Vancouver: Douglas and McIntyre; Seattle: University of Washington Press, 1985).

4. Ira Jacknis, "George Hunt, Collector of Indian Specimens," in *Chiefly Feasts: The Enduring Kwakiutl Potlatch,* ed. Aldona Jonaitis (New York: American Museum of Natural History; Seattle: University of Washington Press, 1991), 177–224.

5. "Every Indian or other person who engages in or assists in celebrating the Indian festival known as the 'Potlatch' or in the Indian dance known as the 'Tamanawas' is guilty of a misdemenour, and shall be liable to imprisonment," Forrest E. La Violette, *The Struggle for Survival: Indian Cultures and the Protestant Ethic in British Columbia,* revised ed. (Toronto: University of Toronto Press, 1973), 43. See also Douglas Cole and Ira Chaikin, *An Iron Hand upon the People: The Law against the Potlatch on the Northwest Coast* (Vancouver: Douglas and McIntyre; Seattle: University of Washington Press, 1990).

6. For a summary of the Kwakiutl potlatch, see Jonaitis, ed., *Chiefly Feasts.*

7. Helen Codere, "Kwakiutl," in *Perspectives in American Indian Culture Change,* ed. Edward H. Spicer (Chicago: University of Chicago Press, 1961), 468–71.

8. For reviews of the confiscation, see Daisy Sewid-Smith, *Prosecution or Persecution* (Cape Mudge: Nu-yum-balees Society, 1979); Cole, *Captured Heritage,* 249–54; Harry Assu, with Joy Inglis, *Assu of Cape Mudge: Recollections of a Coastal Indian Chief* (Vancouver: University of British Columbia Press), 103–4; and Cole and Chaikin, *An Iron Hand,* 118–24.

9. For two accounts of the compensation, see Cole, *Captured Heritage,* 252–53, and U'mista Cultural Society, *U'mista Cultural Centre* (Alert Bay: U'mista Cultural Society, 1980).

10. All but two items of the Scott collection were later sold to the National Museum of Canada after his death.

11. Cole and Chaikin, *An Iron Hand,* 138–52, 161–69.

12. These led to the celebrations marking the Provincial Centennial in 1958, which, in turn, became the so-called June Sports (1959–present), combining feasting and dancing with sports.

13. Similar centennial-associated museums were established in Campbell River on Vancouver Island and in Hazelton, a town near a Tsimshian reserve.

14. James P. Spradley, ed., *Guests Never Leave Hungry: The Autobiography of James Sewid, a Kwakiutl Chief* (New Haven: Yale University Press, 1969), 204.

15. *Alert Bay Pioneer Journal,* 25 February 1959. See also the issues of 22 and 29 January 1958.

16. Alert Bay was in the vanguard of establishing local community museums in the Province. A similar project, also spawned by the centennial, was the museum-library at Hazelton.

17. Spradley, ed., *Guests Never Leave Hungry,* 236, 240.

18. Ibid., 258.

19. Frank's wife, Margaret Wilson Frank, was a granddaughter of George Hunt, the Kwakiutl assistant to Boas.

20. "Seized Indian Regalia May Be Returned to B.C.," *Native Voice* [Native Brotherhood of B.C.], March 1958, 5.

21. Although Sewid gives the year as 1963 (Sewid-Smith, *Prosecution or Persecution,* 2, cf. *Vancouver Sun,* 30 June 1979, A8), 1964 may be more accurate. Sewid remembers traveling to Ottawa with fellow Native Guy Williams for a meeting on fishing rights, which he gives as 1963 in Sewid-Smith and 1964 in his memoirs (Spradley, ed., *Guests Never Leave Hungry,* 221–24). In July 1964 the *Native Voice* (p. 1) reported Williams's examination of the part of the collection at the Royal Ontario Museum.

22. Sewid-Smith, *Prosecution or Persecution,* 2–3.

23. *Pioneer Journal,* 1 February 1963.

24. Philip Ward to Clifford Carl, 20 March 1967, Anthropological Collections Section, Royal Museum of British Columbia.

25. In 1966 a member of the Campbell River board suggested housing the collection in the new museum building (John Kyte to Dave Moon, 14 November 1966, Kwagiulth Museum file, Campbell River Museum). The following year George Moore, Provincial museums adviser, on a visit to the town discussed the possibility of expanding the Alert Bay Museum (*Port Hardy North Island Gazette,* 7 June 1967).

26. The council appointed a cultural committee of James Sewid, William Scow, and Dave Dawson to pursue the matter.

27. On participatory democracy and decentralization, see Paul Tennant, *Aboriginal Peoples and Politics: The Indian Land Question in British Columbia, 1849–1989* (Vancouver: University of British Columbia Press, 1990), 147 and 142, respectively.

28. Erna Gunther, *Northwest Coast Indian Art: An Exhibit at the Seattle World's Fair Fine Arts Pavilion, Apr. 21–Oct. 21* (Seattle: Century 21 Exposition, 1962), 77–78; Allen Wardwell, *Yakutat South: Indian Art of the Northwest Coast* (Chicago: The Art Institute of Chicago, 1990), 35; Michael J. Harner and Albert B. Elsasser, *Art of the Northwest Coast* (Berkeley: Lowie Museum, University of California, 1964), 99; Wilson Duff, Bill Holm, and Bill Reid, *Arts of the Raven: Masterworks by the Northwest Coast Indian* (Vancouver: Vancouver Art Gallery, 1967), n.p.; Wilson Duff,

"The Northwest Coast (La Côte Nord-Ouest)," in *Masterpieces of Indian and Eskimo Art from Canada* (Paris: Societé des amis du Musée de l'Homme, 1969), no. 63.

29. Sources for the decision to split the collection: Ron Rose, "The Crime of Indian-Giving," *Vancouver Sun,* 10 June 1972, 6; *North Island Gazette,* 6 and 20 July 1972. Another factor in the shift of museum activity to Cape Mudge was James Sewid's move in the early seventies to Campbell River (where he lived part of the year). In 1958 Sewid's daughter Louisa had married Don Assu, from a leading family in Cape Mudge, and Sewid soon began to work with these southern Kwakiutl.

30. In addition to the tribes of these two villages, confiscated objects had come from the people of Village Island. As Village Island had been abandoned by this time, its inhabitants, living in both of the other towns, voted for which museum they wanted their objects to go.

31. U'mista, *U'mista Cultural Centre,* n.p.

32. In 1987 the British Columbia Provincial Museum changed its name to the Royal British Columbia Museum. Sources for the final apportioning of the artifacts: *Campbell River Courier,* 6 October and 24 November 1978; *Campbell River Upper Islander,* 22 November and 29 December 1978, 28 February 1979.

33. See Assu and Inglis, *Assu of Cape Mudge,* 104–6, for an account of the founding of the Cape Mudge museum.

34. Gloria Cranmer Webster, "The 'R' Word," *Muse* [Canadian Museums Association] 6(3):43 (1988).

35. E. S. Lohse and Frances Sundt, "History of Research: Museum Collections," in *Northwest Coast,* 92.

36. For a recent summary of the rapidly burgeoning literature on repatriation, see Jeanette Greenfield, *The Return of Cultural Treasures* (Cambridge: Cambridge University Press, 1989). For a well-documented Native American case study, see William L. Merrill, Edmund J. Ladd, and T. J. Ferguson, "The Return of the *Ahayu:da:* Lessons for Repatriation from Zuni Pueblo and the Smithsonian Institution," *Current Anthropology* 34(5):523–67 (1993).

37. Edward M. Bruner, "Ethnography as Narrative," in *The Anthropology of Experience,* ed. Victor W. Turner and Edward M. Bruner (Urbana: University of Illinois Press, 1986), 139–55.

38. Victor W. Turner, *Schism and Continuity in an African Society: A Study of Ndembu Village Life* (Manchester: Manchester University Press, 1957), 91–93.

39. Michael Harkin, "History, Narrative, and Temporality: Examples from the Northwest Coast," *Ethnohistory* 35(2):101 (1988).

40. This is not the proper forum for a comprehensive analysis of the structure and functioning of the two museums; for a general overview of the Kwakiutl tribal

museums in relation to the urban museums in Victoria (Royal British Columbia Museum) and Vancouver (University of British Columbia Museum of Anthropology), see James Clifford, "Four Northwest Coast Museums: Travel Reflections," in *Exhibiting Cultures: The Poetics and Politics of Museum Display,* ed. Ivan Karp and Steven D. Lavine (Washington DC: Smithsonian Institution Press, 1991), 212–54. See also two important essays by Barbara Saunders: "Kwakwaka'wakw Museology," *Cultural Dynamics* 7(1):37–68 (1995), and "Contested Ethnie in Two Kwakwaka'wakw Museums," in *Contesting Art: Art, Politics, and Identity in the Modern World,* ed. Jeremy MacClancy (Oxford: Berg, 1997), 85–130.

41. The director of the U'mista Cultural Society and its museum from 1977 until about 1990 was Gloria Cranmer Webster, the daughter of Daniel Cranmer, who sponsored the great potlatch in question. She earned a bachelor's degree in anthropology from the University of British Columbia in 1956. Before returning to Alert Bay in the 1970s, she worked as a researcher and curator at the university's Museum of Anthropology. As the great-granddaughter of George Hunt, she has carried on his tradition of the documentation and representation of Kwakiutl culture.

42. For the books and films, see Sewid-Smith, *Prosecution or Persecution;* U'mista Cultural Society, *Potlatch: A Strict Law Bids Us Dance* [film, 55 mins., 16 mm., sound, color] (Vancouver: Pacific Cinémathêque, 1975); and *Box of Treasures* [film, 28 mins., 16 mm., sound, color] (Chicago: Chuck Olin Associates, 1983). For a relevant review of the films, see Rosalind C. Morris, *New Worlds from Fragments: Film, Ethnography, and the Representation of Northwest Coast Cultures* (Boulder CO: Westview Press), 117–38.

43. Bruner, "Ethnography as Narrative."

44. Judith Berman, "Oolachan-Woman's Robe: Fish, Blankets, Masks, and Meaning in Boas's Kwakwala Texts," in *On the Translation of Native American Literatures,* ed. Brian Swann (Washington DC: Smithsonian Institution Press, 1992), 148; see also Franz Boas, *Kwakiutl Ethnography,* ed. Helen Codere (Chicago: University of Chicago Press, 1966), 212, 216–17.

45. Assu and Inglis, *Assu of Cape Mudge,* 108.

46. Stephen Inglis, "Cultural Adjustment: A Canadian Case Study," *Gazette* [Canadian Museums Association] 12(3):29 (1979).

47. See Sewid-Smith, *Prosecution or Persecution,* 3.

48. Ira Jacknis, *The Storage Box of Tradition: Museums, Anthropologists, and Kwakiutl Art, 1881–1991* (Washington DC: Smithsonian Institution Press, forthcoming).

49. For Sewid, see Sewid-Smith, *Prosecution or Persecution,* 3; see also Rod Naknakin, Nuyumbalees board member, quoted in *Campbell River Upper Islander,* 22 November 1978.

15

Kurt E. Dongoske

NAGPRA

A New Beginning, Not the End, for Osteological Analysis—

A Hopi Perspective

Before and after passage of the Native American Graves Protection and Repatriation Act (NAGPRA) by the United States Congress in November of 1990, many archaeologists[1] and physical anthropologists[2] lamented that the act and its mandate to consult with Native Americans about the treatment and disposition of human remains recovered from archaeological sites would have dramatically negative effects on the science of archaeology and on paleodemographic, paleopathological, and paleogenetic research.

Since NAGPRA was passed, the Hopi Tribe has been involved in consultations concerning the human remains identified in four large developmental projects within the Southwest. These projects include the Transwestern Pipeline, the El Paso Gas Pipeline, the Roosevelt Dam Platform Mound Study, and the proposed Fence Lake Coal Mine and Transportation Corridor. To date, more than one thousand burials have been recovered or disturbed by these projects and the possibility of doubling that number in the near future is very real.

The tribe's involvement has caused the Hopi people to evaluate the benefits that analysis of prehistoric human remains can offer them. This has generated perspicacious dialogue between the Hopi Tribe and members of the archaeological and physical anthropological communities. This dialogue results in a research agenda beneficial for all parties.

With NAGPRA's passage the furiously debated scientific and ethical issue of repatriation and reburial became a legal mandate. Consequently, physical anthropologists and archaeologists, both in academic settings and in federal agencies, are compelled to work in an environment that is far from the ways they conducted research before NAGPRA.

Some archaeologists and physical anthropologists find the changes implemented by NAGPRA hard to swallow. They assert that the treatment of
human remains and associated funerary objects recovered from an archaeological context should revert to the conventional method of curation without consultation. Some of these arguments are based on the perceived
necessity to maintain permanent collections for future study in the advent
that new techniques of analysis are developed.[3] Others acrimoniously assert
that this is a direct violation of the separation of church and state; Native
American traditional religious fanatics and anti-archaeology activists claim
that all bones and artifacts are sacred.[4]

In this paper I contend that the reality for archaeology and physical
anthropology is not as hopeless as these malcontents would have us believe.
Moreover, this paper argues that now is the time to develop a dialogue between scientists and Native Americans that can and should result in a future
in which the concerns and interests of both parties are satisfied. The Hopi
Tribe illustrates how one Native American tribe takes very seriously the
NAGPRA consultation process and the resultant decisions concerning the
treatment and disposition of the remains of their ancestors. As a result of this
consultation process the tribe is developing a positive and mutually beneficial relationship with archaeologists and physical anthropologists alike.

The Native American Graves Protection and Repatriation Act was
signed into law in November of 1990.[5] The legislation, in part, mandates
federal agencies to consult and negotiate with Indian tribes to manage the
intentional excavation and inadvertent discovery of Native American human remains and objects on federal lands. The law requires consultation
with traditional Native American religious leaders as well as secular tribal
governments. NAGPRA protects Indian graves on federal and tribal land, and
its implementation necessitates consultation with Native American groups
claiming cultural affinity to the individuals buried in those graves. NAGPRA
also requires the repatriation of human remains and associated grave goods
found on federal lands when requested by tribes claiming cultural affinity.

Section 3 of NAGPRA defines the "ownership" of Native American human
remains and objects and sets priorities for ownership claims, based on the
degree and certainty of affiliation and land status. The first priority for
claims of ownership is given to "lineal descendants." This term is undefined
in the original language of the NAGPRA legislation. However, the Native
American Graves Protection and Repatriation Act Regulations (43 CFR
Part 10) published in the *Federal Register* define lineal descendant as:

an individual tracing his or her ancestry directly and without inter-
ruption by means of the traditional kinship system of the appropriate In-

dian tribe or Native Hawaiian organization or by the common law
system of descendance to a known Native American individual whose
remains, funerary objects, or sacred objects are being claimed under
these regulations.[6]

In most archaeological cases direct lineal descendants are not available to
issue a claim. If the remains are from an archaeological context on Indian
lands, the tribe that owns the land is considered the owner of the remains
and funerary objects and as such determines the treatment and disposition
of those remains.

If the remains or objects are discovered off reservation and on federally
owned lands, then the tribe with the "closest cultural affiliation" is the
recognized claimant. Here the law shifts from individuals as claimants
(lineal descendants) to groups (affiliated cultures).[7] "Cultural Affiliation" is
specifically defined in NAGPRA as:

> a relationship of shared group identity which can be reasonably traced
> historically or prehistorically between a present day Indian tribe or
> Native Hawaiian organization and an identifiable earlier group.

It is this form of recognized ownership under NAGPRA that the Hopi
Tribe asserts its claims throughout the greater Southwest concerning the
treatment and disposition of human remains located on federal lands that
are outside the jurisdiction of the Hopi Tribe.

The procedures for making these claims are initiated when the tribes are
notified by the federal land managing agency of an intentional excavation
and/or inadvertent discovery of human remains and associated funerary
objects. The tribe then responds by making a claim of ownership for the
remains or objects. As a part of this claim of ownership, the consulting
claimant tribe or tribes make recommendations as to how the remains will
be handled, what types of analysis will be permitted, if any, and the final
disposition of the remains, including repatriation and/or reburial.

All "unclaimed" human remains and cultural items are subject to the
NAGPRA regulations, the responsibility for which lies with the secretary of
the interior.

The ownership rights to remains found on tribal lands continue to be a
very sensitive issue for the Hopi Tribe. Under Section 10.6(a) of the final
regulations,[8] ownership rights are vested first in the lineal descendants. Second priority ownership rights in all cases, except on tribal lands, are given
to the tribe or organization with the closest affiliation with the human
remains or cultural items as determined pursuant to Section 10.14(c).

Only when the remains are found on tribal lands is the ownership vested

with the tribe that owns the land, without regard to their cultural affiliation. The Hopi Tribe's opinion is that this is inconsistent with the overall
intent and spirit of the law, which allows the cultural descendants the
option of selecting the appropriate disposition for cultural and physical
remains of their ancestors. While the Hopi Tribe recognizes the intent of
the regulations to respect individual tribal sovereignty, in doing so the
regulations fail to recognize individual tribal histories and the development
of Indian reservations.[9]

Historically, many Indians and Native Hawaiians have been relocated
several times by the federal government. Reservations are federally established political boundaries that have been imposed on Indian groups. Little
attempt was made to establish these reservations in the tribe's traditional
area. As such, contemporary tribal land ownership often reveals very little
about prereservation land use by other Native American groups. In many
instances, contemporary reservation-land ownership is not an appropriate
indicator for ascertaining the culturally appropriate treatment of prereservation human remains and cultural items.

In the past, the Hopi Tribe actively maintained its stewardship over a far
greater area than now currently composes the Hopi Reservation. As a result
of unilateral political actions by the United States government, much of the
Hopis' ancestral land claim is now contained within the jurisdiction of the
Navajo Tribe. Included in this land base are thousands of recognized ancestral archaeological sites and human remains. Unfortunately, the final
regulations give ownership rights and the determination of the final treatment and disposition of Hopi ancestral human remains and cultural items
to a culturally unrelated tribe.

NAGPRA and Hopi Consultation

Since 1991 the Hopi Tribe has been actively consulted regarding the
NAGPRA legislation as a result of the intentional archaeological excavations
and the inadvertent discoveries associated with a variety of land development projects. The projects in which the Hopi Tribe has participated in the
NAGPRA consultation process cover a geographical area extending from
southwestern Colorado in the north to southern Arizona in the south,
and from east-central New Mexico on the east to the Colorado River on
the west.

Hopi consultation on such a large geographical area in the Southwest is
based on Hopi accounts of clan migrations relating that the ancestors of the
Hopi people passed through many of these areas during their travels that
led to the gathering of clans on the Hopi mesas. During these migrations

each clan followed its own route and established its own history. The Hopi people refer to these ancestors as the Hisatsinom.[10] The Hopi people know that the area occupied by the Hisatsinom transcends the cultural areas defined by archaeologists, that is, some Hisatsinom lived in the Hohokam area of southern Arizona during the migratory period, while others resided in the Mogollon and Fremont areas as well as the Colorado Plateau.

The remains of the Hisatsinom buried in archaeological sites are also of distinct concern to the Hopi people. These ancestors are of great significance in the Hopi religion, and the Hopi people feel strongly that their physical remains need to be treated with respect. The Hopi people believe that their ancestors who were laid to rest at these archaeological sites were intended to—and continue to—maintain a spiritual guardianship over those places.[11]

It is because of these Hopi clan migration histories and the Hopi peoples' concern for the proper treatment of their ancestors that the Hopi Tribe responds to requests for consultation on such projects as the Transwestern Gas Pipeline, the El Paso Gas Pipeline, the Theodore Roosevelt Dam Modification Project, and the proposed Fence Lake Coal Mine and associated Transportation Corridor.

To date, the Hopi Tribe has responded to requests for consultation regarding the treatment and disposition of the remains of one hundred individuals in association with the Transwestern Pipeline Expansion Project, a pipeline that extends from Bloomfield, New Mexico, to Needles, California;[12] eighty to one hundred individuals from the El Paso Gas Pipeline, which also extends from Bloomfield, New Mexico, to Needles, California;[13] and approximately four hundred individuals from the Roosevelt Dam Modification Project.[14] In addition, the Hopi Tribe in association with the Pueblo of Zuni and the White Mountain Apache Tribe has recently entered into the preliminary stages of discussions with the Department of Anthropology, University of Arizona, and the Arizona State Museum concerning the repatriation and reburial of more than six hundred individuals recovered during thirty years of excavation at the Grasshopper Pueblo, in central Arizona, by the University of Arizona Archaeological Field School.

All NAGPRA consultation with the Hopi Tribe is handled through the Cultural Preservation Office. Assisting the Cultural Preservation Office in decision-making and consultation is the Cultural Resources Advisory Task Team established in 1991. This advisory team currently consists of eighteen men representing the Hopi villages and a number of prominent clans, priesthoods, and religious societies. The organization and functioning of the team is a significant accomplishment because it includes representatives from autonomous villages that decline to send representatives to the Hopi Tribal Council and do not otherwise participate in the activities of the centralized Hopi tribal government.[15]

Various issues regarding the NAGPRA consultation affect the decisions made by the Hopi Cultural Preservation Office and the Cultural Resources Advisory Task Team. One of these issues is cultural affinity and how it is defined and determined under NAGPRA. The Hopi Cultural Preservation Office realizes that it is one thing to claim cultural affinity and that it is another thing to scientifically prove affinity should a Hopi claim be challenged.

There are also different levels of cultural affinity of interest to Hopis. At a general level Hopis are concerned about all Hisatsinom remains. Hisatsinom remains often can be identified through their associated archaeological context, that is, by association with Puebloan architecture and certain types of pottery. No osteological analysis is required for this type of identification. Some Hopis are also interested in the genetic affinity between different tribes in the Southwest and what this means for prehistoric migrations. In addition to affinity, the age, sex, and pathologies of disinterred human remains are deemed to be important variables, as well as the associated funerary objects that indicate an individual held a special social status (e.g., a priest) that would warrant a specific treatment. Nondestructive osteological analyses and study of artifacts are seen as appropriate means to collect the data of interest to the Hopi Tribe.

The Hopi Cultural Preservation Office in conjunction with the Cultural Resources Advisory Task Team wants to make informed decisions during the NAGPRA consultation regarding the appropriate archaeological or scientific techniques for the study of the remains of their ancestors. For example, in consultation on the Fence Lake Mine Project, the Salt River Project facilitated a meeting with the Cultural Resources Advisory Task Team at which Dr. Charles Merbs, a physical anthropologist from Arizona State University, reviewed the state of the art of osteological analyses and what can be learned using different techniques. This allowed the Hopis to develop recommendations on the appropriate level of osteological analysis for the Fence Lake Mine Project with an understanding of what can be learned and how that knowledge can be gained. For instance, some Hopis think their interest in tribal affinity and clan migrations might be productively pursued through genetic studies that entail destructive analysis of human remains and are willing to consider this as an analytical option. Other Hopis have a more conservative view, however, and think that such analyses, while interesting, would be culturally inappropriate.

During a unique NAGPRA consultation, the Cultural Resources Advisory Task Team deliberated for more than eight hours in July of 1991 concerning a request from the Office of Contract Archaeology, University of New Mexico, to conduct more detailed, nondestructive laboratory analysis of skeletal remains from two sites associated with the Transwestern Pipeline. The skeletal assemblage consisted of the disarticulated remains of at least fourteen individuals characterized by extremely fragmented skeletal material exhibiting evidence of perimortem modification, in the form of green bone fractures, impact marks, cut marks, and burned bone.[16] Due to the extremely unusual condition of the remains and their archaeological context (i.e., scattered on the floor and bench of a Pueblo II kiva), the Hopis agreed to the requested laboratory analysis provided that the remains were reburied within four months. The Cultural Resources Advisory Task Team agreed to the time limit, because the number four is sacred and significant to the Hopi people and the premise was that if the spirits of these fragmented remains became aware of the four in the allowed time period, they would recognize the Hopi involvement and find the analysis nonthreatening.

Additionally, the Cultural Resources Advisory Task Team agreed to this laboratory analysis in order to establish whether the individuals represented by these disarticulated remains were ancestors of the Hopis or if they may have been enemies of the Hopis. The cultural affiliation of these individuals is important to the Hopis, because it would determine the necessary level and nature of any subsequent Hopi involvement in the reburial.

The important point in both of these examples is that the Hopi cultural advisers and the Cultural Preservation Office are willing to listen to archaeologists' and physical anthropologists' research designs that address specific problems of mutual interest to anthropologists and Hopis and then make their recommendations on the basis of information presented to them as tempered by their cultural values.

For the Hopis, reburial of human remains is the only acceptable mitigation measure for the disturbance of graves because of the Hopi concepts of death. Hopis believe that death initiates two distinct but inseparable journeys, that is, the physical journey of the body as it returns to a oneness with the earth and the spiritual journey of the soul to a place where it finally resides. A disruption in the physical journey by the excavation and removal of human remains interrupts and obstructs the spiritual journey. This creates an imbalance within the spiritual world and hence the natural world.[17]

The Hopis have a reburial ceremony that they conduct when ancestral human remains recovered in archaeological work are reburied. Several elders on the Cultural Resources Advisory Task Team have traveled extensively to conduct the appropriate rituals as needed on a wide range of recent projects.

NAGPRA, Reburial, and the Future

The reburial of human remains recovered from an archaeological context, subsequent to some level of data recovery, is an issue at the core of the NAGPRA controversy. As an archaeologist, the issue of reburial and the permanent loss of future research materials is of distinct concern to me. However, I cannot help but take the position that the archaeological community has created this situation through its one-hundred-plus years of insensitivity to the living descendants of the people whose villages and physical remains are the objects of our study. This insensitivity is exemplified by turn-of-the-century photographs taken by archaeologists, like Earl Morris and Jesse Walter Fewkes, documenting the bounty at the end of a field season. In these photographs the archaeologists are all standing in a row, and at their feet are the scores of whole vessels and baskets that were excavated from various sites. In front of the whole vessels and baskets are rows of human skulls.

The callous and disparate history of the handling of Native American remains by the archaeological community is unfortunately better illustrated by the excavations of a large unmarked cemetery that had been associated with an eighteenth-century and nineteenth-century Broome County poor farm in New York. The Comfort site, an eighteenth-century Indian village, and an earlier prehistoric Owasco Phase component were at the same location. Construction activities associated with the building of Interstate 81 disturbed both prehistoric and historic graves at the site. There were three episodes of grave removal: 1962–63, 1969, and 1971–72. The State of New York contracted with a local undertaker for the removal and immediate reburial of the poor-farm graves. The archaeologists in the field decided what were Indian graves and what were indigent white graves. The Department of Transportation would then call the undertaker to get the white remains. The Native American graves disinterred by the archaeologists were put in boxes and curated; they have never been studied.[18]

This example demonstrates the attitude some archaeologists have toward human and material remains of Native Americans as archaeological specimens. As data, remains require no special consideration outside of the appropriate curatorial procedures.

Given this example and others, is there little wonder that the Native American and Hawaiian communities were extremely vocal about their support of NAGPRA?

As this paper has tried to demonstrate, the past treatment of the remains of the ancestors of Native Americans and other ethnic minorities by the archaeological community has contributed to the current climate. While it is true that the reburial of skeletal remains is a loss of valuable sources of scientific data for future research, it also may mitigate the negative consequences that the excavations have for traditional cultures.

Consequently, the problem for physical anthropologists and archaeologists is the collection of data before repatriation and reburial. Often the acquisition of this data will be restricted to an in-field analysis, where the conditions can be unfavorable. As a partial solution, physical anthropologists and archaeologists alike need to develop a dialogue with Native Americans to make the various types of osteological analysis relevant to the queries Native American tribes have about their own heritages.

To illustrate this point, in February of 1991 a historic meeting was held between the Zuni, the Acoma, and the Hopi tribes to discuss the proper treatment, level of osteological analysis, and subsequent disposition of human remains recovered from archaeological excavations associated with the Fence Lake Coal Mine. At this meeting the Hopi Tribe suggested that casts be produced of all the appropriate dentition, for curation and subsequent genetic studies, as a part of the analysis of the skeletal remains. The Pueblos of Zuni and Acoma maintained a more conservative perspective, and out of respect for the Zuni and Acoma people, the Hopi Tribe agreed to their position.

Another case concerns the Peabody Western Coal Company on Black Mesa, in northeastern Arizona. Between 1967 and 1983 Peabody Western Coal Company sponsored an extensive program of archaeological survey and excavation to comply with Section 106 of the National Historic Preservation Act of 1966, as amended. This program became known as the Black Mesa Archaeological Project. Peabody initially hired Robert C. Euler of Prescott College to conduct the surface inventories, and the contract was eventually transferred to George J. Gumerman at Southern Illinois University in Carbondale.[19] By the end of the Black Mesa Archaeological Project's fieldwork in 1983, about 2,600 archaeological sites, both prehistoric and historic, had been recorded. Of these, 220 sites were mapped and partially or completely excavated during the project. Thus only 8.5 percent of all the archaeological sites identified within the coal-mine lease received some form of data recovery.

In 1989 the Hopi Tribe voiced concern over the expected destruction of the burial sites in the active mining area that had not been worked. After a long litigative process in which the Hopi Tribe used NAGPRA, the Office of Surface Mining incorporated into the mining permit for the Peabody Western Coal Company the sponsorship of a project that would identify those remaining archaeological sites that had a high potential for containing burials (e.g., middens, room blocks, and kivas).

In the spring of 1993 the Hopi Tribe commented on the proposed Reinterment Plan for Prehistoric Human Remains from Mitigated Sites with the Peabody Leasehold, Black Mesa, Arizona, submitted by the Navajo Nation Archaeology Department. The Hopi Tribe requested that proper scientific methods of data recovery be implemented and that high-quality photo documentation of the burials be saved as a part of the project. It was originally proposed that Polaroid photographs be taken and destroyed once the project was completed. The Hopi Tribe also requested the opportunity to perform a reburial ceremony at the time the remains were ready for reburial.

That summer the Navajo Nation Archaeology Department–Northern Arizona University Branch Office (NNAD-NAU) excavated all sites displaying surface indications (i.e., middens and/or kivas) within the areas to be disturbed by mining. This program integrated the suggestions of the Hopi Tribe and used black and white photographs to document the burials during excavation and color and black and white photographs to document selected skeletal remains after osteological analysis. These latter photographs documented the evidence used to determine age and sex, as well as pathological or anomalous conditions. All mortuary offerings also were photographed.[20] In July 1993 members from the Hopi Tribe performed a reburial ceremony for the thirty-one individuals recovered.

As a consequence of the Hopi Tribe's involvement in this project the human remains were more extensively documented than had originally been intended. Additionally, the Navajo Nation Archaeology Department recognized the Hopi Tribe's cultural and ancestral affiliation to the human remains by allowing the Hopi Tribe to perform a reburial ceremony on lands within the jurisdiction of the Navajo Reservation.

These examples demonstrate that as a result of NAGPRA the potential for osteological research opportunities is wider than before the legislation. Moreover, and of equal importance, the potential is greater that these analyses will be funded by federal agencies as a result of compliance with NAGPRA. The key elements are maintaining an honest dialogue with the Native American community and making the study of their ancestors' remains relevant to their understanding of their heritage. The passage of NAGPRA and its mandates for participation of Native Americans in the decision-making process about their ancestors' remains has resulted in a new beginning, not the end, for osteological analysis.

Notes

1. Clement W. Meighan, "Some Scholars' Views on Reburial," chap. 10, this volume.

2. Christy G. Turner II and Jacqueline A. Turner, "The First Claim for Cannabalism in the Southwest: Walter Hough's 1901 Discovery at Canyon Butte Ruin 3, Northeastern Arizona," *American Antiquity* 57 (Oct. 1992): 661–82.

3. Ibid., 679.

4. Clement W. Meighan, "Some Scholars' Views on Reburial," 707; this vol., 194–95.

5. "Symposium: The Native American Graves Protection and Repatriation Act of 1990 and State Repatriation-Related Legislation," *Arizona State Law Journal* 24, no. 1 (spring 1992), provides a complete, comprehensive review of the history and meaning of the passage of NAGPRA.

6. Native American Graves Protection and Repatriation Act Regulations; Final Rule, in *Federal Register* 60, no. 232 (December 4, 1995): 62159.

7. Anthony L. Klesert, "NAGPRA—THREAT, OR MENACE?" paper presented at the 90th Annual Meeting of the American Anthropological Association, Chicago, 7.

8. Native American Graves Protection and Repatriation Act Regulations; Final Rule, 62163.

9. Letter dated July 23, 1993, to Dr. Francis McManamon, Archaeological Assistance Division, National Park Service, from Mr. Vernon Masayesva, Hopi Tribal Chairman. Hopi comments concerning the NAGPRA Regulations public draft.

10. T. J. Ferguson, Kurt Dongoske, Eric Polingyouma, Mike Yeatts, and Leigh Jenkins, "Working Together: The Roles of Archaeology and Ethnohistory in Hopi Cultural Preservation," paper presented at the 58th Annual Meeting of the Society of American Archaeology, St. Louis, MO.

11. Kurt Dongoske, Leigh Jenkins, and T. J. Ferguson, "Understanding the Past through Hopi Oral History," *Native Peoples Magazine* 6 (winter 1993): 24–35.

12. Nicholas Herrmann, Marsha D. Ogilvie, Charles E. Hilton, and Kenneth L. Brown, "Human Remains and Burial Goods," in *Across the Colorado Plateau: Anthropological Studies for the Transwestern Pipeline Expansion Project,* vol. 18 (Albuquerque: Office of Contract Archaeology, University of New Mexico).

13. Alan Reed, Division of Conservation Archaeology, San Juan County Museum Association, Bloomfield, New Mexico, personal communication, 1993.

14. J. Scott Wood, forest archaeologist, Tonto National Forest, Phoenix, Arizona, personal communication, 1993.

15. T. J. Ferguson et al., "Working Together."

16. Marsha D. Ogilvie and Charles E. Hilton, "Analysis of Human Skeletal Material from Archaeological Sites 423-124 and 423-131," manuscript on file, Department of Anthropology, University of New Mexico, Albuquerque: 1–65.

17. T. J. Ferguson et al., "Working Together."

18. Randall H. McGuire, "The Sanctity of the Grave: White Concepts and American Indian Burials," in *Conflicts in the Archaeology of Living Traditions,* ed. Robert Layton (London: Unwin Hyman, 1989), 170.

19. See Shirley Powell, Peter P. Andrews, Deborah L. Nichols, and F. E. Smiley, "Fifteen Years on the Rock: Archaeological Research, Administration, and Compliance on Black Mesa, Arizona," *American Antiquity* 48 (1983): 228–52.

20. Kimberly Spurr, "NAGPRA Compliance for Peabody Western Coal Company on Black Mesa, Northeastern Arizona," Navajo Nation Archaeology Department Report No. 93-70 (October 1993).

16

Larry J. Zimmerman

A New and Different Archaeology?

With a Postscript on the Impact of the Kennewick Dispute

A dozen years ago, in the aftermath of a disastrous meeting with the Executive Committee of the Society for American Archaeology, Jan Hammil of American Indians Against Desecration and I were commiserating about how difficult it would be to convince archaeologists to change their views regarding human remains.[1] We were depressed about the prospects, and we agreed that attitudes probably would not change much within our lifetimes. Events over the past decade have proved us very wrong.

Indeed, we probably would have considered the enactment of the Native American Graves Protection and Repatriation Act to be impossible. Resistance within the anthropological community seemed so strong. Remarkably, as is well documented by the papers in this volume, dramatic change was possible, and in hindsight, some shifts of power were probably inevitable. More important than shifts of power have been the recent adjustments of attitudes by both American Indians and archaeologists. These portend more substantive changes. My task here is to try to predict what these changes might be and where the issue might be going, a difficult task given the rapidity of change. There are negatives, and I will be blunt about them, but some positive trends are apparent as archaeologists and Indians find common ground.

Syncretism

The trajectory of the reburial issue has been like that of classic syncretism—a coalescence or reconciliation of differing beliefs. In the anthropological experience this most often happens when a belief system, usually of a dominant group, imposes itself on that of a less powerful group. The result is an amalgamation, a hybrid structure in which each party can feel some comfort about sacrificing some basic principles or if not sacrificing them, at least couching them in terms acceptable to the other. The structure helps each group adjust to the other with conflicts eventually losing intensity as the syncretism expands. A similar process seems to be at work between American Indians and archaeology. (I will use *archaeology* for the remainder of this paper for the sake of simplicity, but I actually mean archaeology, physical anthropology, human osteology, museum studies, and those related fields dealing with human remains and grave goods.)

In the reburial issue the problem has been that the belief system of Western science about the past, through archaeology, had imposed itself on belief systems of indigenous peoples about their pasts and those they consider to be ancestors. After little apparent initial resistance, archaeology erroneously assumed a general indigenous acquiescence.[2] The past quarter century has demonstrated just how wrong archaeology has been.

During that time contention over human remains has ranged from acrimonious confrontation to legislative wrangling. The result has been a growing understanding that archaeologists and indigenous peoples hold a wide range of positions about the value and treatment of human remains. In effect, the parties have begun reconciling their beliefs, each incorporating some views of the other.

For North America the question of just who has been dominant in the reburial issue might be raised. At the beginning of the debates archaeology was certainly dominant, even to the point of archaeologists wondering why Indians cared at all and believing that the value placed on science would somehow hold sway in the public arena. Archaeologists, however, underestimated the intensity of Indian sentiment and overestimated their own power and the amount of support they had for their work. When the Nebraska State Historical Society came up against the Pawnee in 1989, for example, the *Omaha World Herald* conducted a scientific poll, revealing that 69 percent of Nebraskans supported the return of remains and grave goods held by the historical society.[3] At numerous times, other papers carried editorials in favor of reburial, and NBC Nightly News and CBS Sunday Morning aired segments in favor of reburial.

Public sentiment certainly favored Indian positions as soon as the debate became more widely known. Argument thus could be made that Indian views actually dominated archaeologists' views and that archaeologists were forced to become more accommodating to Indian views. Even in the Senate hearings on reburial laws, the archaeological community was rumored to have been warned by a senator that if archaeologists couldn't come to grips with the issue, Congress would solve the problem for them. By late 1989 compromise was forced, first in the National Museum of the American

Indian Act (Public Law 101-185 or NMAIA) of 1989 and then in the Native American Graves Protection and Repatriation Act (Public Law 101-601 or NAGPRA) of 1990.

With reburial and repatriation laws now in place, syncretism will be accelerated. Looking back from this perspective allows me to say that many archaeologists did understand some of the Indian concerns and perhaps even the "rightness" of many of their demands. Vested interest in the important archaeological information contained in the remains, however, compelled many archaeologists to speak forcibly against reburial. At the same time, I know that many Indians did understand the importance of archaeology to their "history." Issues of sacredness and of control over their own past were more important to them than benefits gained from archaeology that in fact might have complemented and strengthened their own versions of their past gained from oral tradition. Because of the need for control some adopted rhetorical positions that initially demanded rejection of *all* archaeology. Thus there was tension, but with an underlying realization that compromise could be mutually beneficial.

Uneasy Compromise

Transcripts of debates on the reburial issue show both the tension and the wish to compromise. For example, at the 1989 World Archaeological Congress (WAC) Inter-Congress on Archaeological Ethics and the Treatment of the Dead the debate was sometimes nasty, but in the end, passage of the Vermillion Accord showed that the parties to the issue recognized the legitimacy of each other's concerns and that those concerns were to be respected.[4]

As the syncretic process was developing, some Indian people, some archaeologists, and most media reporters seemed intent on seeing and portraying the issue as bipolar, thinking that such a portrayal would be helpful. For Indian people it kept the attention of Congress and the media; for archaeologists it helped suggest that they spoke with one voice; for the media it kept the public interest so they could "sell papers." Such perceptions and portrayals simply were and are erroneous. As people learn that these inaccurate characterizations of a vastly complex situation cause tension and conflict, the characterizations will begin to erode.

NAGPRA may actually help archaeologists come to terms with the complexity of their own circumstance. As a colleague suggested to me, being forced by law to consult and cooperate with Indians may help some archaeologists to save face. NAGPRA will allow those who were sympathetic to Indian demands but felt compelled to speak forcibly in defense of archaeology to give in honorably. Archaeologists may also benefit in that collections ignored for decades may finally be analyzed, forced by the necessity of undertaking a NAGPRA inventory. NAGPRA also may bring a feeling of control to the situation and a sense of victory in that some archaeological interests will be protected.

NAGPRA has claimed the spotlight, as perhaps it should, but both Indians and archaeologists have had doubts. Many suspected that implementation of a federal law could undercut local or regional solutions. NAGPRA was passed after many states already had reburial laws in place. Many of these had been enacted after sometimes torturous negotiations. How would it affect these laws? How, too, would NAGPRA mesh with the proposed amendments to the American Indian Religious Freedom Act? Fine-tuning, if not major amendment, will be necessary as problems inevitably develop.

Many Indian people continue to remain suspicious. Demonstration of genetic and cultural affiliation of contemporary groups to skeletal remains is largely an Indian task. Although the kinds of acceptable evidence have been broadened to include oral history and other "unscientific" sources of information, many feel this is and will be used as delaying tactics by archaeologists. For example, rumors have been floating around Indian country that the Smithsonian thinks it will have to return only about 10 percent of the remains in its collections because Indians will be unable to demonstrate affiliation. Some archaeologists already have used affiliation as a tactic, but Congress is taking notice. Several recent calls to Indians from Congressional offices indicate that Congress will not allow regulation or technicality to impede the spirit of the law.

Many archaeologists still remain angry about NAGPRA; in fact, at a session on the draft NAGPRA regulations held at the fifty-sixth Society for American Archaeology (SAA) meeting (New Orleans, 1991), some indicated extreme dissatisfaction, with one past president of the SAA saying: "We've been hoodwinked." The delays in both drafting and implementing NAGPRA and proposed amendments to the American Indian Religious Freedom Act leave many archaeologists and Indians uneasy. Many frankly believe that, in the end, making NAGPRA work will still come down to local, case-by-case solutions.[5] If NMAIA can be seen as a precedent, this trend is already well demonstrated by Smithsonian responses.[6]

As is important in syncretism, both sides are in the process of "re-mythologizing," that is, making their belief system seem as if it is not exactly what it earlier seemed to be. For example, to maintain the notion that the discipline was speaking with one voice, no views from archaeologists favoring reburial have appeared in mainstream literature until very recently, but the re-mythologizing process was nonetheless operating to make the profession *seem* more reasonable.

The best example of this is a sequence of commentaries that appeared in *American Antiquity,* the journal of the SAA. Although the controversy had raged since the early 1980s, little of significance about repatriation appeared in the journal except for the fine print appearance of the SAA's reburial policy in business meeting minutes. Finally, in 1990 *American Antiquity* published a commentary by Lynne Goldstein and Keith Kintigh on "Ethics and the Reburial Controversy" (chapter 9, this volume). The authors took a "middle-of-the-road" position, suggesting that archaeologists be more attentive to Indian concerns but noting that archaeologists must "address our various constituencies, educate all of the publics about the past, and make certain that we don't alienate or disenfranchise past, present, or future generations."

Although the authors were writing as individuals, many took this to be a softening of the SAA position, given that Goldstein had been SAA secretary and Kintigh had been head of the SAA ad hoc Committee on Reburial. Anthony L. Klesert and Shirley Powell, two archaeologists who had worked closely with Indians, submitted a critique of this commentary to the journal but were rejected. Soon thereafter the journal editor noted that he had attended the Third Southwest Symposium, where he left a plenary of Native Americans commenting on archaeology and of archaeologists astounded by "new and rather startling" realizations that Indians didn't trust archaeology or its accounts of the Indian past. In fact, the Native Americans saw those accounts as a threat. He concluded that "[a] North American prehistory irrelevant to North American Indians would seem to be in jeopardy or, minimally, in serious need of epistemological adjustment."[7] Two issues later, Reid chose to publish a very negative critique of Goldstein and Kintigh's article by Clement Meighan, among the more vocal archaeologists against reburial (chapter 10, this volume). Whether or not by intention, publication of the Meighan critique clearly put archaeologists who opposed reburial on the radical conservative fringe while at the same time bolstering Goldstein and Kintigh by making them seem very, very reasonable.[8] In mid-1993 the commentary by Klesert and Powell finally appeared, but with its criticisms of Goldstein and Kintigh dramatically toned down (chapter 11, this volume). In a related matter, the SAA also began to work on revision of its ethics code. One principle proposes that archaeologists be more aware of and responsible toward the concerns of nonarchaeologists with interests in archaeology. Supporting statements specifically mentioned Native Americans and reburial. One can predict that this re-mythologizing process will continue, probably to the point where it seems that archaeology was always in favor of reburial and really just was trying to seek clarification of issues.

The process is not as clear for Indians, but it is happening. In their recent dispute with the Nebraska State Historical Society, the Pawnees relied heavily on very traditional archaeological views of Pawnee origins to bolster their case for cultural affiliation of remains. A Pawnee tribal historian involved in that case, Roger Echo-Hawk, has recently had to defend his acceptance of this and other archaeology to a mixed-nation group of Native Americans in Colorado, where he acted as a monitor for archaeology on construction of the Denver airport.[9] Indians will probably not have to go as far in their re-mythologizing because their position is more likely to be understood by the public as "right."

Professional Ethics

While the re-mythologizing process has been going on, some groups have tried to cement relationships between indigenous peoples and archaeologists. Certainly the Society of Professional Archaeologists took into account the rumblings during the early 1970s about reburial and included in their ethics code that archaeologists be "sensitive to, and respect the legitimate concerns of, groups whose culture histories are the subject of archaeological investigations."[10] Other groups have recently been more direct, not re-mythologizing but going directly to archaeology's indigenous constituents for solutions.

Hirini Matunga, a Maori who attended the 1989 WAC Inter-Congress, almost immediately began to work with other indigenous people including American Indians who were at the meeting, and drafted a code of ethics. Matunga drew from his experience as a regional planner in Auckland dealing with heritage issues, local authorities, government agencies, and private developers. On his arrival at World Archaeological Congress II in Barquisimeto, Venezuela, in September 1990, he called a meeting of indigenous representatives on the WAC Council and Executive and invited one nonindigenous archaeologist.

At that meeting the group discussed each element of the draft code and a variety of other issues, eventually agreeing that they shared a goal: indigenous control over indigenous heritage. They also saw that some nonindigenous heritage specialists understood their obligations to others and knew that freedom to pursue academic and scientific inquiry are not sacrosanct but must be injected with humanity toward the aspirations of others.[11] They were concerned about how the archaeological community would react to the code and worried that it might be overly demanding. In this regard they solicited the comments of the nonindigenous archaeologist. After working over a number of issues, they presented the document to the

WAC Council (composed of one person from each country attending the congress) and later to the WAC Executive. Both groups, after some discussion, passed the code.

The code consists of two parts, eight "principles to abide by," and seven "rules to adhere to." They are:

PRINCIPLES TO ABIDE BY: Members agree that they have obligations to indigenous peoples and that they shall abide by the following principles:

1. To acknowledge the importance of indigenous cultural heritage, including sites, places, objects, artefacts, human remains to the survival of indigenous cultures.

2. To acknowledge the importance of protecting indigenous cultural heritage to the well-being of indigenous peoples.

3. To acknowledge the special importance of indigenous ancestral human remains, and sites containing and/or associated with such remains, to indigenous peoples.

4. To acknowledge that the important relationship between indigenous peoples and their cultural heritage exists irrespective of legal ownership.

5. To acknowledge that the indigenous cultural heritage rightfully belongs to the indigenous descendants of that heritage.

6. To acknowledge and recognise indigenous methodologies for interpreting, curating, managing and protecting indigenous cultural heritage.

7. To establish equitable partnerships and relationships between Members and indigenous peoples whose cultural heritage is being investigated.

8. To seek, whenever possible, representation of indigenous peoples in agencies funding or authorising research to be certain their view is considered as critically important in setting research standards, questions, priorities and goals.

RULES TO ADHERE TO: Members agree that they will adhere to the following rules prior to, during and after their investigations:

1. Prior to conducting any investigation and/or examination, Members shall with rigorous endeavor seek to define the indigenous peoples whose cultural heritage is the subject of investigation.

2. Members shall negotiate with and obtain the informed consent of representatives authorised by the indigenous peoples whose cultural heritage is the subject of investigation.

3. Members shall ensure that the authorised representatives of the indigenous peoples whose culture is being investigated are kept informed during all stages of the investigation.

4. Members shall ensure that the results of their work are presented with deference and respect to the identified indigenous peoples.

5. Members shall not interfere with and/or remove human remains of indigenous peoples without the express consent of those concerned.

6. Members shall not interfere with and/or remove artefacts or objects of special cultural significance, as defined by associated indigenous peoples, without their express consent.

7. Members shall recognise their obligation to employ and/or train indigenous peoples in proper techniques as part of their projects, and utilise indigenous peoples to monitor the projects.

Codes of ethics are no panacea; they should never be prescriptive. They are meant only to apprise people of key issues. The WAC code is unique, however, because it demonstrates a shift of power and, most important, because it was drafted by indigenous people in terms of how they would like archaeologists to behave rather than by archaeologists in terms of archaeologists' views of ethical obligations. The power shift is a crucial element here in that it portends an increasing transition toward what Shirley Powell, C. E. Garza, and A. Hendricks eloquently label "covenantal archaeology."[12]

Covenantal Archaeology

Among the major complaints about archaeology is that it has benefited only itself and its practitioners. But many archaeologists have worked closely with Indian people in very successful programs. The "classic," fully developed programs are those of the Navahos, Zunis, and Hopis in the Southwest, and they have been extremely successful. As many archaeologists who have worked closely with Indian people have discovered, archaeology need not come to a screeching halt if archaeology accedes to Indian demands. Many have discovered that if a relationship of trust can be built, archaeologists may gain increased access to materials and sites. At the same time, control of the archaeology shifts to Indian hands and a benefit is seen to the people being studied. The kind of work done is essentially a covenant between archaeologists and Indians; this is fundamentally what indigenous peoples have asked for in the WAC ethics code. The approach will work, and I agree with Powell, Garza, and Hendricks that it will flourish as soon as its benefits are more widely realized.

The covenants will include not only research but education. At first many archaeologists believed that if they could just educate Indians about what archaeology does, then Indians would come to appreciate it more.

Many archaeologists still do not understand, however, that supposedly beneficial educational programs such as the proposed scholarships offered by the SAA and the Plains Anthropological Society, for example, can be seen as an effort to co-opt Indian people and are viewed with suspicion. If the attitude, on the contrary, is to train Indian people in archaeology theory and method and to apply these tools to their own research questions and *not* necessarily to get them to buy into archaeological interpretations, then these programs have a good chance of success.

If covenantal archaeology works, archaeological interpretation will change to better meet Indian interpretations of the past. That will change what archaeologists teach the non-Indian public about Indians, perhaps downplaying such solid archaeological "dogma" as the Bering land bridge migration route to the Americas and the like. This grates on archaeological sensibilities because archaeology must find grounding for interpretation in the material record from the past, not in peoples' belief systems about themselves and their origins.[13]

A Very Different Archaeology

For relations between archaeologists and Indians to have a chance to improve, archaeology must change. An approach like that suggested by Arnold Krupat would be beneficial.[14] Krupat writes from the perspective of literary criticism, especially criticism of Native American literature. He is suspicious of any scientific theory or position that looks like a metaphor of social ideology or that can be construed as contributing to the alienation of any class or group, which is exactly what archaeology tends to do. In essence, compromises between archaeology and Indians still reflect the positions of the opposing sides. For archaeology this has meant simply another way of telling "our" own story, of "turning 'their' [Indians'] incoherent jabber into an eloquence of use only to ourselves."[15] As an alternative, however, archaeology could apply what Krupat calls "ethnocriticism," which suggests that scholars work at the boundaries of their usual ways of knowing. In this intellectual frontier, oppositional sets like West/rest, us/them, anthropological/biological, historical/mythical, and so on often tend to break down. On the one hand, cultural contact can indeed produce mutual rejections, the reification of differences, and defensive retreats into celebrations of what each group regards as distinctly its own. On the other hand, it may also frequently be the case that interaction leads to interchange—and transculturalization.[16] "Oppositional" views are simply useless. As they once justified imperial domination, they now serve to justify postcolonial, revisionist, "victimist history." One can acknowledge that some people have been hurt by others in the colonial context, but to what does that lead except more rhetoric? Ethnocriticism is concerned with differences rather than oppositions; it seeks to replace oppositional models with dialogical models where cultural differences are explored and where interpretations are negotiated rather than declared. Claims to accuracy, systematicity, and knowledge would reside in their capacity to take more into context, that is, to be more flexible and open to new ideas and approaches that deal with differences.

The result is a relative truth, but one that does have rules. Archaeologists still can be scientific but in ways meaningful to Indians by negotiating the methods and procedures to be followed and by indicating the empirical and logical components of reasoning. In other words, the science is clearly articulated and is placed fully into an explicit social context. This is the essence of a covenantal archaeology where research questions and methods are negotiated and support a mutually agreed upon agenda. As this approach becomes more commonplace, archaeological science will become more modest and very different from what it has been. It will be the end product of the syncretism begun with the reburial issue.

Conclusions

Some may see this change as an evil and will fight it. Indeed, some of the currently raging debate in archaeology over processual and postprocessual approaches is about exactly this kind of issue. I see these changes as doing nothing but good, and I am optimistic about the future of relationships between archaeologists and Indians (but I am not as naive as I used to be!).

Let me summarize my ideas about what is and will be happening regarding the reburial issue, American Indians, and archaeology. Both archaeologists and Indians are undergoing a process of reconciliation akin to syncretism. This process will continue, with each group "re-mythologizing" its position in relation to the other but with archaeology changing the most, making it seem more sympathetic to Indian concerns. Archaeology must change the most because it has the most to lose if it does not. Change will occur in terms of standards of ethical practice, theory and method, and power relationships with those studied. As both groups realize mutual benefit, archaeologists and Indians will develop more covenantal programs.

NAGPRA will cause problems and many battles will be fought over it. The law and its implementing regulations will be refined, but new laws probably will not be necessary. NAGPRA and any new versions or successors will speed along the process of reconciliation.

Archaeology needs to see the reburial issue as a potential rather than a threat, and it needs to start examining the bases of the real world-view differences between archaeology and American Indians. Reliance on law, historical precedent, or arguments of science versus religion are poor substitutes for real understanding. If it follows this more enlightened path, archaeology may realize the humanistic potential of which it is certainly capable. I truly believe that an ethnocritical archaeology can be of benefit to Indian people; I hope that we archaeologists can show good faith in demonstrating that benefit. I hope that Indian people will continue to be patient with us and will give us the chance to do so.

A Postscript on the Impact of the Kennewick Disupte

Since this article was initially published, the discovery of the remains of an individual who died approximately eighty-five hundred years ago along the Columbia River near Kennewick, Washington, has presented the most serious challenge to NAGPRA since its passage.[17] The challenge goes directly to the heart of NAGPRA's major problem, the matter of cultural affiliation. The central issue seems to be whether cultural or genetic affiliation with any living American Indian nation can reasonably be demonstrated for remains of such antiquity. The issues are compounded by an initial attribution of Caucasoid cranial characteristics to the Kennewick remains. The courts became involved after a small group of archaeologists and osteologists sought and received an injunction to prevent repatriation of the remains to the Umatilla nation, near whose lands the remains were found.

The suggestion that the remains had Caucasoid attributes brought substantial attention and broadened debates about the who, how, and when of human habitation of the Americas. Whether by accident or design—"playing the race card" as some have called it—the anti-NAGPRA elements in the scientific community could not have been happier with the results. Efforts by some in Congress to amend NAGPRA, and even the suggestion that it be abandoned altogether, were mostly thwarted, making it just one of those battles that continue to occur in a war that has substantially been won.

Of particular interest in all this is that the scholars initially sought to stop *immediate* repatriation and never directly sought to keep the remains from eventually being repatriated to the Umatillas. Rather, they wanted adequate time for study *before* repatriation. Had the scholarly community approached the situation a bit differently, that access might have come more readily, though it is unlikely permissions for any destructive tests would be granted. Had the Army Corps of Engineers acted a bit more reasonably and not rushed to repatriate for the sake of administrative convenience, the court case also might not have been necessary. But all this is speculation.

For all the wrangling about the remains and the hope on the part of some archaeologists that the Kennewick case might overturn NAGPRA, most archaeologists, whether they like it or not, recognize that the law is here to stay in at least some form that substantially favors repatriation. Kennewick will not be the last test of NAGPRA, nor will it stop the almost inevitable process of syncretism of Indian and archaeological views on the treatment of human remains.

Notes

This paper has benefited from discussions with many people, including Tom King, Brian Molyneaux, Roger Echo-Hawk, Tristine Smart, Elizabeth Prine, Maria Pearson, Randy McGuire, Tony Klesert, Jan Hammil, and Robert Clinton.

1. For a description of that meeting see Larry J. Zimmerman, "Made Radical by My Own: An Archaeologist Learns to Accept Reburial," in *Conflict in the Archaeology of Living Traditions,* ed. Robert Layton (London: Unwin Hyman, 1989), 60–67.

2. For a critical summary of Indian-archaeology relationships see Randall H. McGuire, "Archaeology and the First Americans," *American Anthropologist* 94, no. 4 (1992): 816–36.

3. Robert M. Peregoy, "Nebraska's Landmark Repatriation Law: A Study of Cross-Cultural Conflict Resolution," *American Indian Culture and Research Journal* 16, no. 2 (1992): 160.

4. Jane Hubert, "First World Archaeological Congress Inter-Congress, Vermillion, South Dakota, USA," *World Archaeological Bulletin* 4 (1989): 18.

5. Compare with Shirley Powell, C. E. Garza, and A. Hendricks, "Ethics and Ownership of the Past: The Reburial and Repatriation Controversy," *Archaeological Method and Theory* 5 (1993): 2.

6. For an example of problems see Richard A. Knecht and Philomena Hamlet Knecht, "The Smithsonian Response to the Larsen Bay Repatriation Request: Research, Rhetoric and Recrimination" (paper presented at Kodiak Island and the Larsen Bay Repatriation, ninety-first annual meeting of the American Anthropological Association, San Francisco, 1992).

7. J. Jefferson Reid, "Editor's Corner: Recent Findings on North American Prehistory," *American Antiquity* 57 (1992): 195.

8. Although I objected to many of the points in Goldstein and Kintigh, I must admit that after reading Meighan, they seemed thoroughly reasonable! Although

it may not have been the editorial intent, Meighan's article clearly made the SAA seem forward looking.

9. Roger C. Echo-Hawk, "Working Together: Exploring Ancient Worlds," SAA *Bulletin* 11, no. 4 (1993): 6.

10. Society of Professional Archaeologists, "Code of Ethics and Standards of Performance," *Directory of Professional Archaeologists* (St. Louis: Society of Professional Archaeologists, 1981), 3–6.

11. Hirini Matunga, "The Maori Delegation to WAC 2: Presentation and Reports," *World Archaeological Bulletin* 5 (1991): 53.

12. Powell, Garza, and Hendricks, "Ethics and Ownership of the Past," 29.

13. This is a fundamental issue akin to debates between scientists and creationists. There is a major difference, however, in that in reburial we are dealing with "archaeological colonialism." The archaeological pasts have been imposed on Indian pasts without opportunity for debate. There is, in other words, a major difference in power relationships between the two issues. They are analogues, not homologues.

14. Arnold Krupat, *Ethnocriticism: Ethnography, History, Literature* (Berkeley: University of California Press, 1992).

15. Krupat, *Ethnocriticism,* 261.

16. Krupat, *Ethnocriticism,* 15.

17. For a longer treatment of the Kennewick case and a substantial bibliography on the matter, see Larry J. Zimmerman and Robert N. Clinton, "Kennewick Man and Native American Graves Protection and Repatriation Act Woes," *International Journal of Cultural Property* 8, no. 1 (1999): 212–28.

Appendix

Native American Graves Protection and Repatriation Act

Public Law 101-601
101st Congress
An Act
To provide for the protection of Native American graves, and for other purposes.

Be it enacted by the Senate and House of Representatives of the United States of America in Congress assembled,

SECTION 1. SHORT TITLE.

This Act may be cited as the "Native American Graves Protection and Repatriation Act."

SEC. 2. DEFINITIONS.

For purposes of this Act, the term—

(1) "burial site" means any natural or prepared physical location, whether originally below, on, or above the surface of the earth, into which as a part of the death rite or ceremony of a culture, individual human remains are deposited.

(2) "cultural affiliation" means that there is a relationship of shared group identity which can be reasonably traced historically or prehistorically between a present day Indian tribe or Native Hawaiian organization and an identifiable earlier group.

(3) "cultural items" means human remains and—

(A) "associated funerary objects" which shall mean objects that, as a part of the death rite or ceremony of a culture, are reasonably believed to have been placed with individual human remains either at the time of death or later, and both the human remains and associated funerary objects are presently in the possession or control of a Federal agency or museum, except that other items exclusively made for burial purposes or to contain human remains shall be considered as associated funerary objects.

(B) "unassociated funerary objects" which shall mean objects that, as a part of the death rite or ceremony of a culture, are reasonably believed to have been placed with individual human remains either at the time of death or later, where the remains are not in the possession or control of the Federal agency or museum and the objects can be identified by a preponderance of the evidence as related to specific individuals or families or to known human remains or, by a preponderance of the evidence, as having been removed from a specific burial site of an individual culturally affiliated with a particular Indian tribe,

(C) "sacred objects" which shall mean specific ceremonial objects which are needed by traditional Native American religious leaders for the practice of traditional Native American religions by their present day adherents, and

(D) "cultural patrimony" which shall mean an object having ongoing historical, traditional, or cultural importance central to the Native American group or culture itself, rather than property owned by an individual Native American, and which, therefore, cannot be alienated, appropriated, or conveyed by any individual regardless of whether or not the individual is a member of the Indian tribe or Native Hawaiian organization and such object shall have been considered inalienable by such Native American group at the time the object was separated from such group.

(4) "Federal agency" means any department, agency, or instrumentality of the United States. Such term does not include the Smithsonian Institution.

(5) "Federal lands" means any land other than tribal lands which are controlled or owned by the United States, including lands selected by but not yet conveyed to Alaska Native Corporations and groups organized pursuant to the Alaska Native Claims Settlement Act of 1971.

(6) "Hui Malama I Na Kupuna O Hawai'i Nei" means the nonprofit, Native Hawaiian organization incorporated under the laws of the State of Hawaii by that name on April 17, 1989, for the purpose of providing guidance and expertise in decisions dealing with Native Hawaiian cultural issues, particularly burial issues.

(7) "Indian tribe" means any tribe, band, nation, or other organized group or community of Indians, including any Alaska Native village (as defined in, or established pursuant to, the Alaska Native Claims Settlement Act), which is recognized as eligible for the special programs and services provided by the United States to Indians because of their status as Indians.

(8) "museum" means any institution or State or local government agency (including any institution of higher learning) that receives Federal funds and has possession of, or control over, Native American cultural items. Such term does not include the Smithsonian Institution or any other Federal agency.

(9) "Native American" means of, or relating to, a tribe, people, or culture that is indigenous to the United States.

(10) "Native Hawaiian" means any individual who is a descendant of the aboriginal people who, prior to 1778, occupied and exercised sovereignty in the area that now constitutes the State of Hawaii.

(11) "Native Hawaiian organization" means any organization which—

(A) serves and represents the interests of Native Hawaiians,

(B) has as a primary and stated purpose the provision of services to Native Hawaiians, and

(C) has expertise in Native Hawaiian Affairs, and shall include the Office of Hawaiian Affairs and Hui Malama I Na Kupuna O Hawai'i Nei.

(12) "Office of Hawaiian Affairs" means the Office of Hawaiian Affairs established by the constitution of the State of Hawaii.

(13) "right of possession" means possession obtained with the voluntary consent of an individual or group that had authority of alienation. The original acquisition of a Native American unassociated funerary object, sacred object or object of cultural patrimony from an Indian tribe or Native Hawaiian organization with the voluntary consent of an individual or group with authority to alienate such object is deemed to give right of possession of that object, unless the phrase so defined would, as applied in section 7(c), result in a Fifth Amendment taking by the United States as determined by the United States Claims Court pursuant to 28 U.S.C. 1491 in which event the "right of possession" shall be as provided under otherwise applicable property law. The original acquisition of Native American human remains and associated funerary objects which were excavated, exhumed, or otherwise obtained with full knowledge and consent of the next of kin or the official governing body of the appropriate culturally affiliated Indian tribe or Native Hawaiian organization is deemed to give right of possession to those remains.

(14) "Secretary" means the Secretary of the Interior.

(15) "tribal land" means—

(A) all lands within the exterior boundaries of any Indian reservation;

(B) all dependent Indian communities;

(C) any lands administered for the benefit of Native Hawaiians pursuant to the Hawaiian Homes Commission Act, 1920, and section 4 of Public Law 86-3.

SEC 3. OWNERSHIP.

(a) NATIVE AMERICAN HUMAN REMAINS AND OBJECTS.—The ownership or control of Native American cultural items which are excavated or discovered on Federal or tribal lands after the date of enactment of this Act shall be (with priority given in the order listed)—

(1) in the case of Native American human remains and associated funerary objects, in the lineal descendants of the Native American; or

(2) in any case in which such lineal descendants cannot be ascertained, and in the case of unassociated funerary objects, sacred objects, and objects of cultural patrimony—

(A) in the Indian tribe or Native Hawaiian organization on whose tribal land such objects or remains were discovered;

(B) in the Indian tribe or Native Hawaiian organization which has the closest cultural affiliation with such remains or objects and which, upon notice, states a claim for such remains or objects; or

(C) if the cultural affiliation of the objects cannot be reasonably ascertained and if the objects were discovered on Federal land that is recognized by a final judgment of the Indian Claims Commission or the United States Court of Claims as the aboriginal land of some Indian tribe—

(1) in the Indian tribe that is recognized as aboriginally occupying the area in which the objects were discovered, if upon notice, such tribe states a claim for such remains or objects, or

(2) if it can be shown by a preponderance of the evidence that a different tribe has a stronger cultural relationship with the remains or objects than the tribe or organization specified in paragraph (1), in the Indian tribe that has the strongest demonstrated relationship, if upon notice, such tribe states a claim for such remains or objects.

(b) UNCLAIMED NATIVE AMERICAN HUMAN REMAINS AND OBJECTS.— Native American cultural items not claimed under subsection (a) shall be disposed of in accordance, with regulations promulgated by the Secretary— in consultation with the review committee established under section 8,— Native American groups, representatives of museums and the scientific community.

(c) INTENTIONAL EXCAVATION AND REMOVAL OF NATIVE AMERICAN HUMAN REMAINS AND OBJECTS.—The intentional removal from or excavation of Native American cultural items from Federal or tribal lands for purposes of discovery, study, or removal of such items is permitted only if—

(1) such items are excavated or removed pursuant to a permit issued under section 4 of the Archaeological Resources Protection Act of 1979 (93 Stat. 721; 16 U.S.C. 470aa et seq.) which shall be consistent with this Act;

(2) such items are excavated or removed after consultation with or, in the case of tribal lands, consent of the appropriate (if any) Indian tribe or Native Hawaiian organization;

(3) the ownership and right of control of the disposition of such items shall be as provided in subsections (a) and (b); and

(4) proof of consultation or consent under paragraph (2) is shown.

(d) INADVERTENT DISCOVERY OF NATIVE AMERICAN REMAINS AND OBJECTS.—(1) Any person who knows, or has reason to know, that such person has discovered Native American cultural items on Federal or tribal lands after the date of enactment of this Act shall notify, in writing, the Secretary of the Department, or head of any other agency or instrumentality of the United States, having primary management authority with respect to Federal lands and the appropriate Indian tribe or Native Hawaiian organization with respect to tribal lands, if known or readily ascertainable, and, in the case of lands that have been selected by an Alaska Native Corporation or group organized pursuant to the Alaska Native Claims Settlement Act of 1971, the appropriate corporation or group. If the discovery occurred in connection with an activity, including (but not limited to) construction, mining, logging, and agriculture, the person shall cease the activity in the area of the discovery, make a reasonable effort to protect the items discovered before resuming such activity, and provide notice under this subsection. Following the notification under this subsection, and upon certification by the Secretary of the department or the head of any agency or instrumentality of the United States or the appropriate Indian tribe or Native Hawaiian organization that notification has been received, the activity may resume after 30 days of such certification.

(2) The disposition of and control over any cultural items excavated or removed under this subsection shall be determined as provided for in this section.

(3) If the Secretary of the Interior consents, the responsibilities (in whole or in part) under paragraphs (1) and (2) of the Secretary of any department (other than the Department of the Interior) or the head of any other agency or instrumentality may be delegated to the Secretary with respect to any land managed by such other Secretary or agency head.

(e) RELINQUISHMENT.—Nothing in this section shall prevent the governing body of an Indian tribe or Native Hawaiian organization from expressly relinquishing control over any Native American human remains, or title to or control over any funerary object, or sacred object.

SEC. 4. ILLEGAL TRAFFICKING.

(a) ILLEGAL TRAFFICKING.—Chapter 53 of title 18, United States Code, is amended by adding at the end thereof the following new section:

"1170. Illegal Trafficking in Native American Human Remains and Cultural Items

"(a) Whoever knowingly sells, purchases, uses for profit, or transports for sale or profit, the human remains of a Native American without the right of possession to those remains as provided in the Native American Graves Protection and Repatriation Act shall be fined in accordance with this title, or imprisoned not more than 12 months, or both, and in the case of a second or subsequent violation, be fined in accordance with this title, or imprisoned not more than 5 years, or both.

"(b) Whoever knowingly sells, purchases, uses for profit, or transports for sale or profit any Native American cultural items obtained in violation of the Native American Grave Protection and Repatriation Act shall be fined in accordance with this title, imprisoned not more than one year, or both, and in the case of a second or subsequent violation, be fined in accordance with this title, imprisoned not more than 5 years, or both."

(b) TABLE OF CONTENTS.—The table of contents for chapter 53 of title 18, United States Code, is amended by adding at the end thereof the following new item:

"1170. Illegal Trafficking in Native American Human Remains and Cultural Items."

SEC. 5. INVENTORY FOR HUMAN REMAINS AND ASSOCIATED FUNERARY OBJECTS.

(a) IN GENERAL.—Each Federal agency and each museum which has possession or control over holdings or collections of Native American human remains and associated funerary objects shall compile an inventory of such items and, to the extent possible based on information possessed by such museum or Federal agency, identify the geographical and cultural affiliation of such item.

(b) REQUIREMENTS.—(1) The inventories and identifications required under subsection (a) shall be—

(A) completed in consultation with tribal government and Native Hawaiian organization officials and traditional religious leaders;

(B) completed by not later than the date that is 5 years after the date of enactment of this Act, and

(C) made available both during the time they are being conducted and afterward to a review committee established under section 8.

(2) Upon request by an Indian tribe or Native Hawaiian organization which receives or should have received notice, a museum or Federal agency shall supply additional available documentation to supplement the information required by subsection (a) of this section. The term "documentation" means a summary of existing museum or Federal agency records, including inventories or catalogues, relevant studies, or other pertinent data for the limited purpose of determining the geographical origin, cul-

tural affiliation, and basic facts surrounding acquisition and accession of Native American human remains and associated funerary objects subject to this section. Such term does not mean, and this Act shall not be construed to be an authorization for, the initiation of new scientific studies of such remains and associated funerary objects or other means of acquiring or preserving additional scientific information from such remains and objects.

(c) EXTENSION OF TIME FOR INVENTORY.—Any museum which has made a good faith effort to carry out an inventory and identification under this section, but which has been unable to complete the process, may appeal to the Secretary for an extension of the time requirements set forth in subsection (b)(1)(B). The Secretary may extend such time requirements for any such museum upon a finding of good faith effort. An indication of good faith shall include the development of a plan to carry out the inventory and identification process.

(d) NOTIFICATION—(1) If the cultural affiliation of any particular Native American human remains or associated funerary objects is determined pursuant to this section, the Federal agency or museum concerned shall, not later than 6 months after the completion of the inventory, notify the affected Indian tribes or Native Hawaiian organizations.

(2) The notice required by paragraph (1) shall include information—

(A) which identifies each Native American human remains or associated funerary objects and the circumstances surrounding its acquisition;

(B) which lists the human remains or associated funerary objects that are clearly identifiable as to tribal origin; and

(C) which lists the Native American human remains and associated funerary objects that are not clearly identifiable as being culturally affiliated with that Indian tribe or Native Hawaiian organization, but which, given the totality of circumstances surrounding acquisition of the remains or objects, are determined by a reasonable belief to be remains or objects culturally affiliated with the Indian tribe or Native Hawaiian organization.

(3) A copy of each notice provided under paragraph (1) shall be sent to the Secretary who shall publish each notice in the Federal Register.

(e) INVENTORY.—For the purposes of this section, the term "inventory" means a simple itemized list that summarizes the information called for by this section.

SEC. 6. SUMMARY FOR UNASSOCIATED FUNERARY OBJECTS, SACRED OBJECTS, AND CULTURAL PATRIMONY.

(a) IN GENERAL.—Each Federal agency or museum which has possession or control over holdings or collections of Native American unassociated funerary objects, sacred objects, or objects of cultural patrimony shall provide a written summary of such objects based upon available information held by such agency or museum. The summary shall describe the scope of the collection, kinds of objects included, reference to geographical location, means and period of acquisition and cultural affiliation, where readily ascertainable.

(b) REQUIREMENTS.—(1) The summary required under subsection (a) shall be—

(A) in lieu of an object-by-object inventory;

(B) followed by consultation with tribal government and Native Hawaiian organization officials and traditional religious leaders; and

(C) completed by not later than the date that is 3 years after the date of enactment of this Act.

(2) Upon request, Indian Tribes and Native Hawaiian organizations shall have access to records, catalogues, relevant studies or other pertinent data for the limited purposes of determining the geographic origin, cultural affiliation, and basic facts surrounding acquisition and accession of Native American objects subject to this section. Such information shall be provided in a reasonable manner to be agreed upon by all parties.

SEC. 7. REPATRIATION.

(a) REPATRIATION OF NATIVE AMERICAN HUMAN REMAINS AND OBJECTS POSSESSED OR CONTROLLED BY FEDERAL AGENCIES AND MUSEUMS.—(1) If, pursuant to section 5, the cultural affiliation of Native American human remains and associated funerary objects with a particular Indian tribe or Native Hawaiian organization is established, then the Federal agency or museum, upon the request of a known lineal descendant of the Native American or of the tribe or organization and pursuant to subsections (b) and (e) of this section, shall expeditiously return such remains and associated funerary objects.

(2) If, pursuant to section 6, the cultural affiliation with a particular Indian tribe or Native Hawaiian organization is shown with respect to unassociated funerary objects, sacred objects or objects of cultural patrimony, then the Federal agency or museum, upon the request of the Indian tribe or Native Hawaiian organization and pursuant to subsections (b), (c) and (e) of this section, shall expeditiously return such objects.

(3) The return of cultural items covered by this Act shall be in consultation with the requesting lineal descendant or tribe or organization to determine the place and manner of delivery of such items.

(4) Where cultural affiliation of Native American human remains and funerary objects has not been established in an inventory prepared pursuant to section 5, or the summary pursuant to section 6, or where Native American human remains and funerary objects are not included upon any such inventory, then, upon request and pursuant to subsections (b) and (e) and, in the

case of unassociated funerary objects, subsection (c), such Native American human remains and funerary objects shall be expeditiously returned where the requesting Indian tribe or Native Hawaiian organization can show cultural affiliation by a preponderance of the evidence based upon geographical, kinship, biological, archæological, anthropological, linguistic, folkloric, oral traditional, historical, or other relevant information or expert opinion.

(5) Upon request and pursuant to subsections (b), (c) and (e), sacred objects and objects of cultural patrimony shall be expeditiously returned where—

(A) the requesting party is the direct lineal descendant of an individual who owned the sacred object;

(B) the requesting Indian tribe or Native Hawaiian organization can show that the object was owned or controlled by the tribe or organization; or

(C) the requesting Indian tribe or Native Hawaiian organization can show that the sacred object was owned or controlled by a member thereof, provided that in the case where a sacred object was owned by a member thereof, there are no identifiable lineal descendants of said member or the lineal descendent, upon notice, have failed to make a claim for the object under this Act.

(b) SCIENTIFIC STUDY.—If the lineal descendant, Indian tribe, or Native Hawaiian organization requests the return of culturally affiliated Native American cultural items, the Federal agency or museum shall expeditiously return such items unless such items are indispensable for completion of a specific scientific study, the outcome of which would be of major benefit to the United States. Such items shall be returned by no later than 90 days after the date on which the scientific study is completed.

(c) STANDARD OF REPATRIATION.—If a known lineal descendant or an Indian tribe or Native Hawaiian organization requests the return of Native American unassociated funerary objects, sacred objects or objects of cultural patrimony pursuant to this Act and presents evidence which, if standing alone before the introduction of evidence to the contrary, would support a finding that the Federal agency or museum did not have the right of possession, then such agency or museum shall return such objects unless it can overcome such inference and prove that it has a right of possession to the objects.

(d) SHARING OF INFORMATION BY FEDERAL AGENCIES AND MUSEUMS.— Any Federal agency or museum shall share what information it does possess regarding the object in question with the known lineal descendant, Indian tribe, or Native Hawaiian organization to assist in making a claim under this section.

(e) COMPETING CLAIMS.—Where there are multiple requests for repatriation of any cultural item and, after complying with the requirements of this Act, the Federal agency or museum cannot clearly determine which requesting party is the most appropriate claimant, the agency or museum may retain such item until the requesting parties agree upon its disposition or the dispute is otherwise resolved pursuant to the provisions of this Act or by a court of competent jurisdiction.

(f) MUSEUM OBLIGATION.—Any museum which repatriates any item in good faith pursuant to this Act shall not be liable for claims by an aggrieved party or for claims of breach of fiduciary duty, public trust, or violations of state law that are inconsistent with the provisions of this Act.

SEC. 8. REVIEW COMMITTEE.

(a) ESTABLISHMENT.—Within 120 days after the date of enactment of this Act, the Secretary shall establish a committee to monitor and review the implementation of the inventory and identification process and repatriation activities required under sections 5, 6 and 7.

(b) MEMBERSHIP—(1) The Committee established under subsection (a) shall be composed of 7 members,

(A) 3 of whom shall be appointed by the Secretary from nominations submitted by Indian tribes, Native Hawaiian organizations, and traditional Native American religious leaders with at least 2 of such persons being traditional Indian religious leaders;

(B) 3 of whom shall be appointed by the Secretary from nominations submitted by national museum organizations and scientific organizations; and

(C) 1 who shall be appointed by the Secretary from a list of persons developed and consented to by all of the members appointed pursuant to subparagraphs (A) and (B).

(2) The Secretary may not appoint Federal officers or employees to the committee.

(3) In the event vacancies shall occur, such vacancies shall be filled by the Secretary in the same manner as the original appointment within 90 days of the occurrence of such vacancy.

(4) Members of the committee established under subsection (a) shall serve without pay, but shall be reimbursed at a rate equal to the daily rate for GS-18 of the General Schedule for each day (including travel time) for which the member is actually engaged in committee business. Each member shall receive travel expenses, including per diem in lieu of subsistence, in accordance with sections 5702 and 5703 of title 5, United States Code.

(c) RESPONSIBILITIES.—The committee established under subsection a) shall be responsible for—

(1) designating one of the members of the committee as chairman;

(2) monitoring the inventory and identification process conducted under sections 5 and 6 to ensure a fair, objective consideration and assessment of all available relevant information and evidence;

(3) upon the request of any affected party, reviewing and making findings related to—

(A) the identity or cultural affiliation of cultural items, or

(B) the return of such items;

(4) facilitating the resolution of any disputes among Indian tribes, Native Hawaiian organizations, or lineal descendants and Federal agencies or museums relating to the return of such items including convening the parties to the dispute if deemed desirable;

(5) compiling an inventory of culturally unidentifiable human remains that are in the possession or control of each Federal agency and museum and recommending specific actions for developing a process for disposition of such remains;

(6) consulting with Indian tribes and Native Hawaiian organizations and museums on matters within the scope of the work of the committee affecting such tribes or organizations;

(7) consulting with the Secretary in the development of regulations to carry out this Act;

(8) performing such other related functions as the Secretary may assign to the committee; and

(9) making recommendations, if appropriate, regarding future care of cultural items which are to be repatriated.

(d) Any records and findings made by the review committee pursuant to this Act relating to the identity or cultural affiliation of any cultural items and the return of such items may be admissible in any action brought under section 15 of this Act.

(e) RECOMMENDATIONS AND REPORT.—The committee shall make the recommendations under paragraph (c)(5)in consultation with Indian tribes and Native Hawaiian organizations and appropriate scientific and museum groups.

(f) ACCESS.—The Secretary shall ensure that the committee established under subsection (a) and the members of the committee have reasonable access to Native American cultural items under review and to associated scientific and historical documents.

(g) DUTIES OF SECRETARY.—The Secretary shall—

(1) establish such rules and regulations for the committee as may be necessary, and

(2) provide reasonable administrative and staff support necessary for the deliberations of the committee.

(h) ANNUAL REPORT.—The committee established under subsection (a) shall submit an annual report to the Congress on the progress made, and any barriers encountered, in implementing this section during the previous year.

(i) TERMINATION.—The committee established under subsection (a) shall terminate at the end of the 120-day period beginning on the day the Secretary certifies, in a report submitted to Congress, that the work of the committee has been completed.

SEC. 9. PENALTY.

(a) PENALTY.—Any museum that fails to comply with the requirements of this Act may be assessed a civil penalty by the Secretary of the Interior pursuant to procedures established by the Secretary through regulation. A penalty assessed under this subsection shall be determined on the record after opportunity for an agency hearing. Each violation under this subsection shall be a separate offense.

(b) AMOUNT OF PENALTY.—The amount of a penalty assessed under subsection (a) shall be determined under regulations promulgated pursuant to this Act, taking into account, in addition to other factors—

(1) the archaeological, historical, or commercial value of the item involved;

(2) the damages suffered, both economic and noneconomic, by an aggrieved party, and

(3) the number of violations that have occurred.

(c) ACTIONS TO RECOVER PENALTIES.—If any museum fails to pay courts an assessment of a civil penalty pursuant to a final order of the Secretary that has been issued under subsection (a) and not appealed or after a final judgment has been rendered on appeal of such order, the Attorney General may institute a civil action in an appropriate district court of the United States to collect the penalty. In such action, the validity and amount of such penalty shall not be subject to review.

(d) SUBPOENAS.—In hearings held pursuant to subsection (a), subpoenas may be issued for the attendance and testimony of witnesses and the production of relevant papers, books, and documents. Witnesses so summoned shall be paid the same fees and mileage that are paid to witnesses in the courts of the United States.

SEC. 10. GRANTS.

(a) INDIAN TRIBES AND NATIVE HAWAIIAN ORGANIZATIONS.—The Secretary is authorized to make grants to Indian tribes and Native Hawaiian organizations for the purpose of assisting such tribes and organizations in the repatriation of Native American cultural items.

(b) MUSEUMS.—The Secretary is authorized to make grants to museums for the purpose of assisting the museums in conducting the inventories and identification required under sections 5 and 6.

SEC. 11. SAVINGS PROVISIONS.

Nothing in this Act shall be construed to—

(1) limit the authority of any Federal agency or museum to—

(A) return or repatriate Native American cultural items to Indian tribes, Native Hawaiian organizations, or individuals, and

(B) enter into any other agreement with the consent of the culturally affiliated tribe or organization as to the disposition of, or control over, items covered by this Act;

(2) delay actions on repatriation requests that are pending on the date of enactment of this Act;

(3) deny or otherwise affect access to any court;

(4) limit any procedural or substantive right which may otherwise be secured to individuals or Indian tribes or Native Hawaiian organizations; or

(5) limit the application of any State or Federal law pertaining to theft or stolen property.

SEC. 12. SPECIAL RELATIONSHIP BETWEEN FEDERAL GOVERNMENT AND INDIAN TRIBES.

This Act reflects the unique relationship between the Federal Government and Indian tribes and Native Hawaiian organizations and should not be construed to establish a precedent with respect to any other individual, organization or foreign government.

SEC. 13. REGULATIONS.

The Secretary shall promulgate regulations to carry out this Act within 12 months of enactment.

SEC. 14. AUTHORIZATION OF APPROPRIATIONS.

There is authorized to be appropriated such sums as may be necessary to carry out this Act.

SEC. 15. ENFORCEMENT.

The United States district courts shall have jurisdiction over any action brought by any person alleging a violation of this Act and shall have the authority to issue such orders as may be necessary to enforce the provisions of this Act.

Approved November 16, 1990.

Contributors

Roger Anyon is a cofounder of Heritage Resources Management Consultants. He was the director of the Zuni Archaeology Program from 1985 through 1996. He is a member of the Smithsonian Institution Native American Repatriation Review Committee and serves on the executive board of the Society for American Archaeology. His master's degree in anthropology is from the University of New Mexico.

Robert E. Bieder is a professor in the School of Public and Environmental Affairs at Indiana University. He has also taught in Southeast Asia and held two Fulbright professorships to Germany and one to Hungary. The author of several books and articles, including *Science Encounters the Indian, 1820–1880: The Early Years of American Ethnology* (Norman: University of Oklahoma Press, 1986), he is a former Newberry Library and Smithsonian Institution Fellow.

Suzanne J. Crawford is completing a doctorate in religious studies at the University of California, Santa Barbara.

Vine Deloria Jr. is a professor of history at the University of Colorado at Boulder. He is a member of the Standing Rock Sioux tribe and the author of numerous books, such as *Behind the Trail of Broken Treaties* (Austin: University of Texas Press, 1985), *Custer Died for Your Sins* (Norman: University of Oklahoma Press, 1988), and *The Nations Within: The Past and Future of American Indian Sovereignty* (Austin: University of Texas Press, 1998).

Kurt Dongoske has twenty years of professional experience in archaeology and cultural resource management, including seven years as tribal archaeologist with the Cultural Preservation Office of the Hopi Tribe. He also has twelve years' experience in human osteological analysis. He received an M.A. degree in anthropology from the University of Arizona.

Walter R. Echo-Hawk, a member of the Pawnee tribe in Oklahoma, is a senior staff attorney at the Native American Rights Fund (NARF) in Boulder, Colorado. Specializing in religious freedom issues, he was a major contributor in the passage of the Native American Graves Protection and Repatriation Act (1990), the Smithsonian repatriation provisions of the National Museum of the American Indian Act (1989), and burial protection and reburial laws in Nebraska and Kansas. He is coauthor of *Battlefields and Burial Grounds: The Indian Struggle to Protect Ancestral Graves in the United States* (Minneapolis: Lerner, 1994).

T. J. Ferguson is a cofounder of Heritage Resources Management Consultants. He served as director of the Zuni Archaeology Program from 1977 to 1981 and as acting director in 1984–85. Since 1984 he has conducted archaeological and ethnohistorical research on the Zuni Indians as a research associate of the Zuni Archaeology Program. His Ph.D. in anthropology is from the University of New Mexico.

Lynne Goldstein is professor of anthropology and chair of the Department of Anthropology at the University of Wisconsin-Milwaukee. The majority of her research has been in the Midwestern United States, focusing on native cultures at around A.D. 1000, but she has also directed excavations of an Irish cemetery and a historic Russian-American cemetery. Goldstein is a former secretary of the Society for American Archaeology (SAA), and she also serves as chair of the SAA's Repatriation Task Force.

Curtis M. Hinsley Jr., who lives and works in Flagstaff, Arizona, is Regents Professor of History and Applied Indigenous Studies at Northern Arizona University. He is the author of *The Smithsonian and the American Indian: Making a Moral Anthropology in Victorian America* (Washington DC: Smithsonian Institution Press, 1994) and numerous articles on the history of American anthropology and archaeology. Currently he is at work with archaeologist David R. Wilcox, of the Museum of Northern Arizona, on a cultural history of the Hemenway Southwestern Archaeological Expedition (1886–89).

Ira Jacknis is associate research anthropologist, Hearst Museum of Anthropology, University of California at Berkeley. Previously, as assistant curator for research at the Brooklyn Museum, he was cocurator of "Objects of Myth and Memory," an exhibition of Stewart Culin's American Indian Collections.

Keith Kintigh, a Southwestern archaeologist, is now associate professor of anthropology at Arizona State University. As the chair of the Society for American Archaeology Task Force on Repatriation, he was involved in the legislative process leading to the passage of NAGPRA. His research focuses on organizational developments during the late prehistoric periods in the Zuni area and on the development and use of quantitative and formal methods in archaeology.

Anthony L. Klesert received his graduate education at Southern Illinois University at Carbondale, where he worked as a staff member for the Black Mesa Archaeological Project in northeastern Arizona. Upon graduation Klesert worked for a private consulting firm in southwestern Colorado, and he has been the director of the Navajo Nation Archaeology Department since 1982. His interests include CRM law on Indian lands and archaeological methods.

Edmund J. Ladd was a member of the Zuni tribe and published extensively on the archaeology of the Hawaiian Islands and the ethnography of the Zuni Indians. He was involved in repatriation issues for more than a decade and worked as a repatriation consultant for the Smithsonian Institution's Repatriation Office and the National Museum of the American Indian. He held a master's degree in anthropology from the University of New Mexico.

Patricia M. Landau is a former graduate student in the Department of Anthropology at Texas A&M University.

Robert J. Mallouf has been a professional archaeologist for twenty-seven years. He currently serves as director of the Center for Big Bend Studies, Sul Ross State University, and served as Texas state archaeologist from 1982 to 1995. Mallouf carried out his studies at Howard Payne University in Brownwood, Texas, the University of California at Berkeley, the American University of Cairo, Egypt, and the University of Texas at Austin. He has conducted archaeological research throughout Texas and in areas of Kansas, Oklahoma, and northern Mexico.

Clement W. Meighan was a professor of anthropology at the University of California, Los Angeles. He was the author of many books on the archaeology of California and was coeditor of *Chronologies in New World Archaeology* (New York: Academic Press, 1978).

Devon A. Mihesuah is professor of American Indian history and applied indigenous studies at Northern Arizona University in Flagstaff. She is a member of the Oklahoma Choctaw Nation and editor of the *American Indian Quarterly* and has been involved in the repatriation issue for fifteen years. Her works include *Cultivating the RoseBuds: The Education of Women at the Cherokee Female Seminary, 1850–1909* (Urbana: University of Illinois Press, 1993), *American Indians: Stereotypes and Realities* (Atlanta: Clarity Press, 1996), *Natives and Academics: Researching and Writing about American Indians* (Lincoln: University of Nebraska Press, 1998), and *The Roads of My Relations* (Tucson: University of Arizona Press, 2000).

Shirley Powell is an adjunct professor of anthropology at Fort Lewis College. She served as director of Northern Arizona University's Archaeology Laboratory between 1987 and 1992. Powell is the author of several books and articles about archaeology and has numerous years of experience with contract archaeology—including directing Peabody Coal Company's Black Mesa Archaeological Project in northeastern Arizona.

James Riding In is associate professor of justice studies at Arizona State University in Tempe. A member of the Pawnee Tribe of Oklahoma, he is the author of numerous articles focusing on repatriation.

D. Gentry Steele is professor of anthropology at Texas A&M University and author of *Anatomy and Biology of the Human Skeleton* (College Station: Texas A&M University Press, 1988) and of fifty articles and research reports dealing with human osteology. He has previously served as president of the Council of Texas Archaeologists. His current areas of interest include human osteology and North American anthropology with emphasis on the development of techniques for the analysis of human skeletal remains and the analysis of prehistoric populations.

Jack F. Trope is a partner in the law firm of Sant'Angelo & Trope, P.C., in Cranford, New Jersey, where his primary specialty is in the field of American Indian law. Previously he was senior staff attorney for the Association on American Indian Affairs in New York City from 1985 to 1991. In that capacity he was integrally involved in the negotiations that culminated in the enactment of NAGPRA.

Larry J. Zimmerman is department executive officer, American Indian and Native Studies Program, University of Iowa. He has authored or edited numerous books, journals, articles, and technical reports on topics related to Plains archaeology. He is currently executive secretary of the World Archaeological Congress.

Source Acknowledgments

The following essays were previously published in *American Indian Quarterly* 20:2 (spring 1996): "The Representations of Indian Bodies in Nineteenth-Century American Anthropology" by Robert E. Bieder; "Digging for Identity: Reflections on the Cultural Background of Collecting" by Curtis M. Hinsley Jr.; "An Unraveling Rope: The Looting of America's Past" by Robert J. Mallouf; "Why Anthropologists Study Human Remains" by Patricia M. Landau and D. Gentry Steele; "American Indians, Anthropologists, Pothunters, and Repatriation: Ethical, Religious, and Political Differences" by Devon A. Mihesuah; "Repatriation: A Pawnee's Perspective" by James Riding In; "Repatriation at the Pueblo of Zuni: Diverse Solutions to Complex Problems" by T. J. Ferguson, Roger Anyon, and Edmund J. Ladd; "Repatriation as Social Drama: The Kwakiutl Indians of British Columbia, 1922–1980" by Ira Jacknis; "NAGPRA: A New Beginning, Not the End, for Osteological Analysis—A Hopi Perspective" by Kurt E. Dongoske; and "A New and Different Archaeology? With a Postscript on the Impact of the Kennewick Dispute" by Larry J. Zimmerman.

"(Re)Constructing Bodies: Semiotic Sovereignty and the Debate over Kennewick Man" by Suzanne J. Crawford is reprinted by permission of the author.

"The Native American Graves Protection and Repatriation Act: Background and Legislative History" by Jack F. Trope and Walter R.Echo-Hawk was previously published in the *Arizona State Law Journal* 24:1 (spring 1992): 35–77. Reprinted by permission of the journal.

"Secularism, Civil Religion, and the Religious Freedom of American Indians" by Vine Deloria Jr. was previously published in *American Indian Culture and Research Journal* 16:2 (1992): 9–20. Reprinted by permission of the author.

The following essays were previously published in *American Antiquity*: "Ethics and the Reburial Controversy" by Lynne Goldstein and Keith Kintigh, 55:3 (1990): 585–91; "Some Scholars' Views on Reburial" by Clement W. Meighan, 57:4 (1992): 704–10; and "A Perspective on Ethics and the Reburial Controversy" by Anthony L. Klesert and Shirley Powell, 58:2 (1993): 348–54. Reproduced by permission of the Society for American Archaeology and the authors.

Index